Away for the WEEKEND™

SOUTHERN CALIFORNIA

Away for the WEEKEND™

S O U T H E R N   C A L I F O R N I A

Michele and Tom Grimm

Great Getaways Less Than
250 Miles from Los Angeles

Photographs by Michele and Tom Grimm
Maps by Richard Douglas
Third Revised and Updated Edition

Clarkson Potter/Publishers
New York

Published by Clarkson N. Potter, Inc., 201 East 50th Street, New York, New York 10022 and distributed by Crown Publishers, Inc. Member of the Crown Publishing Group. Random House, Inc. New York, Toronto, London, Sydney, Auckland

Previous editions of this book were published as *Away for the Weekend*™: *L.A.*

Away for the Weekend, CLARKSON N. POTTER, POTTER, and colophon are trademarks of Clarkson N. Potter, Inc.

Manufactured in the United States of America

Library of Congress Cataloging-in-Publication Data

Grimm, Michele.
  Away for the weekend Southern California

    Rev. ed. of: Away for the weekend, © 1984, © 1986, © 1989.
    Includes index.
    1. California, Southern—Description and travel—
Tours.   2. Automobiles—Road guides—California,
Southern.   3. Automobiles—Road guides—Los Angeles
Region.   I. Grimm, Tom.   II. Grimm, Michele. Away
for the weekend.   III. Title.
F867.G83   1989   917.94′90453   86-5031
ISBN 0-517-88062-8

10   9   8   7   6   5   4   3   2   1

Third Revised Edition

For Edee Greene—
Our Favorite Traveling Companion

Contents

Before You Go . . .

Getting away for the weekend offers a wonderful tonic for body and soul, especially in Southern California, where there are so many delightful and diversified places to go. Astonishing as it seems, after only a short drive from Los Angeles you can be picnicking beside a backcountry lake, skiing down a snowy slope, basking beneath the desert sun, or strolling along the ocean shore. In fact, within a radius of 250 miles from the city's center is an array of natural and man-made attractions that will entice you on an outing every weekend of the year.

For 15 years we were in pursuit of those pleasure-filled destinations as a vocation rather than a vacation, exploring Southern California as free-lance journalists for our "Trip of the Week" travel column in the *Los Angeles Times*. Now we are happy to gather and share our adventures and discoveries in a book that will guide you on 52 enjoyable excursions.

Reading our day-by-day itineraries, you'll see that the Southland, as the lower section of our oblong state is nicknamed, has something for everyone—nature lovers, history buffs, art connoisseurs, gourmet diners, mountain hikers, antique collectors, wine tasters, museum goers, tennis players, mission aficionados, flower fanciers, romantics, and more. Even armchair travelers will be tempted to leave home.

To make it easier for you to decide where to go, we've organized a selection of getaway weekends by their geographical location from the L.A. megalopolis: North Coastal Excursions, South Coastal Outings, Backcountry and Mountain Adventures, and High and Low Desert Destinations. You'll find the specific trips listed in the contents.

Every trip is planned as a two-day weekend—you can leave town on Friday afternoon or evening and return late Sunday. Some destinations that are more distant from Los Angeles or offer an abundance of attractions are better enjoyed on a longer, three- or four-day, holiday weekend.

Of course, you can adapt the trips to midweek travel as well, often avoiding the problems of overcrowding that can occur at popular spots on the weekends. And you can string two or three trips together to plan a complete vacation. Also, as you'll notice from our list of trips, three favorite Southern California cities—Palm Springs, Santa Barbara, and San Diego—deserve at least two, three, or four weekends for thorough exploration.

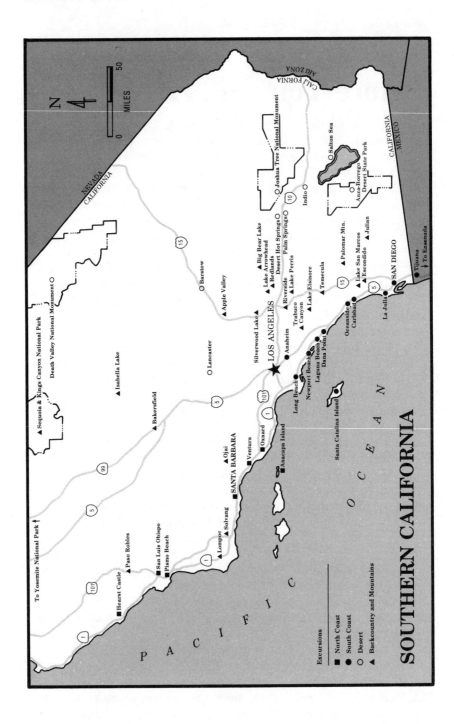

SOUTHERN CALIFORNIA

For almost every excursion we've first outlined what there is to see and do and then described each place and activity in more detail. Driving directions are included, but the essential information of any worthwhile travel guidebook—street addresses, telephone numbers, hours of operation, admission costs, and so forth—are given at the end of each weekend under "Sightseeing."

While describing a destination, we've also suggested where to spend the night and get a good meal, and the specifics of those places are given at the end of each trip under "Lodging" and "Dining." Wherever possible, we recommended only highly regarded resorts, hotels, or inns that are unique enough to make your weekend special; many are expensive, but worth it for their extra pleasures. If they are over your budget or booked up, check into one of the many hotels that can usually be found in every area. For travelers with recreational vehicles (RVs) and folks who prefer to sleep out, we've also listed some public campsites under "Camping."

As to restaurants, those we've suggested are local or personal favorites that cover a wide range of tastes. Chain restaurants usually have not been included, because most travelers already know what they're like. Besides, much of the fun of a weekend getaway is treating yourself to some different dining experiences. Regarding the cost of a meal, the restaurants we've mentioned range from the big-splurge category to unexpectedly inexpensive. No menu prices are given, because they're always changing, but you can call the restaurant and ask about the current cost of a meal before making reservations. Also, many restaurants post their menus at the door, so you can check prices before being seated at a table.

For complete lists of restaurants and lodgings, as well as brochures and additional details about the local attractions, we have indicated the destination's chamber of commerce or visitors bureau under "For More Information" at the end of each trip. It's a good idea to contact them by telephone or letter before you leave, because most often their offices are closed on weekends. Also ask about annual events at your destination that may be of special interest or extra fun for your weekend or something to avoid if you'd rather not be part of the crowd. We've mentioned most well-known Southland celebrations and their usual dates in the trip descriptions or at the end under "Events."

Two of the weekend getaways actually feature a pair of seasonal events that are major attractions in Southern California—watching the grand parade of California gray whales that cruise along the coast in wintertime and viewing the spectacular wildflowers that bloom across the desert in the springtime. For these outings, rather than describing a specific itinerary, as with the other 50 weekends, we've listed all the ports where you can board whale-watching boats and given directions to the best places to find the flowers. When you decide where to go, look up a weekend trip that's in the same area and you'll find other attractions to enjoy, as well as recommended lodgings and places to eat.

Regarding the itineraries in this book, they are intended only as guidelines, because we know everyone's interests vary. Some people will spend hours viewing the exhibits in a museum, while others would rather lounge by the pool at their hotel. For each weekend we've included both the best-known and most offbeat attractions that make a place particularly interesting and enjoyable to visit. Pick a destination, read the trip description, note the sights and activities that entice you the most, then alter the itinerary to suit yourself.

After you decide where to go, be certain to map out your route. In fact, none of the excursions should be attempted without maps in hand. Once you leave Los Angeles via the freeways, we guide you along the most scenic routes—and while most highways in Southern California are well marked, you may inadvertently miss a turn or get on the wrong road without a map to keep track of where you're going.

While the maps in this book are useful for general directions to a destination, we recommend the outstanding maps of the Southern California Automobile Club, an AAA club that's renowned for its cartography department. Unfortunately, the club's detailed freeway, city, and county road maps are available only to club members, but the membership fee is soon returned in a wide assortment of free maps and travel booklets, as well as other services to motorists, such as emergency road service and towing. The Automobile Club of Southern California has its headquarters at 2601 South Figueroa Street, Los Angeles 90007, and you'll find AAA district offices in many neighboring cities and outlying communities; look in the white pages of the telephone book for the nearest one.

Another of the Southland's major map makers is Thomas Bros. of Irvine; their detailed highway maps are sold in handy spiral bindings at many bookstores. Area maps are also available at most gas stations, while chambers of commerce and visitors bureaus usually have street maps covering their regions.

For each weekend trip we've indicated the round-trip mileage to give you an idea of the *total* amount of driving involved. The figure is not just the distance from Los Angeles to your destination and back again, but includes the driving to all attractions suggested in the weekend itinerary. Obviously, if you add or delete some sights, or choose alternate routes to the directions we've given, the mileage may be longer or shorter. By the way, our round-trip mileage measurement is made from the four-level interchange of five freeways in downtown Los Angeles, which is appropriately known as The Stack.

Also, in giving directions in this book, we usually refer to the freeways by their official route numbers rather than their common names. This is to avoid confusion for out-of-town readers, who may be misled by names such as the Pomona Freeway, which goes not only to Pomona but to Riverside as well. In addition, there may be more than one name for a freeway, or it may have one name but two different route numbers.

Also be aware that a freeway can be an Interstate, U.S., or California highway, and the sign shields with their identifying numbers are different shapes. If you are unfamiliar with the Southern California freeway system, study the map and mark your route and road numbers before starting to drive; making sudden lane changes to another freeway or an exit is dangerous, both to yourself and to other motorists.

The freeway network makes it easy to escape from Los Angeles for the weekend—unless you get caught in rush-hour traffic. If you're a stranger to the area, ask local folks the usual traffic conditions for your exit route at the time you're intending to leave town. You'll discover that Southlanders discuss auto travel in terms of time rather than miles, but only mileage is indicated in our book, because we can't predict traffic delays or know your starting time or point of departure from the city.

If you'd like to get away for the weekend without driving, public transportation by bus and train is available to some of the destinations in this book. However, since Southern California is an auto-oriented society, we haven't included details for travel on Greyhound or Amtrak. Also, once you get to a destination, local bus transportation is often inadequate or even nonexistent, and it may be impossible to walk or to take a taxi to the various attractions. Some of the coastal cities are exceptions, however, and a rail trip on Amtrak is a pleasant alternative to driving north to Santa Barbara or south to San Diego. Their train depots are located near hotels, restaurants, and some major sights, and you can easily get around by foot or local bus. For train schedules and fares you can try calling Amtrak's toll-free number, (800) 872-7245, which often is busy, or inquire at any travel agency.

For out-of-town visitors without wheels, plenty of rental cars are available in Los Angeles, and you can even rent fully equipped motor homes. Many Southern Californians like vacationing in recreational vehicles because they're more comfortable for family travel and help you cut back on the cost of accommodations and dining out. Get details and rates by contacting a major Southland RV rental dealer, Altman Winnebago, 6323 Sepulveda Boulevard, Van Nuys 91411; phone (818) 997-6622. Even if you've never driven a motor home before, Altman gives renters a personal and professional checkout, as well as a detailed operations manual that's also available in foreign languages for overseas visitors. One well-known nationwide firm you also can call about renting a motor home is Cruise America, toll-free (800) 327-7778.

Many county, state, and national parks with overnight camping sites offer RV hookups, which means you can connect up your vehicle's electricity and water, and sometimes its sewage disposal. Private campgrounds, including those belonging to nationwide chain KOA, Kampgrounds of America, often are equipped for full hookup at each site.

To camp in Southern California's most popular state parks during the summer and other holiday seasons, you must make camping reservations through MISTIX, as we've noted in the "Camping" information following certain trips. The computerized reservations agency has outlets throughout the state, and you can find the nearest location, or make reservations directly by telephone, by calling toll-free (800) 444-7275. You also can make state park camping reservations by mail; write MISTIX, P.O. Box 85705, San Diego 92138. In addition to the full camping fee for the length of your stay, you'll pay a $3.95 reservation charge. Most national park campgrounds in California are first come, first served, but reservations for Yosemite, Sequoia, and Joshua Tree should also be made through MISTIX; call toll-free (800) 365-2267 for national park campground reservations.

Fishing is a popular pastime in Southern California, and anyone 16 years or older must have a state fishing license before dropping a line in a river, a lake, or the ocean, unless you're fishing from a public pier in ocean or bay waters. For residents the annual license costs about $25, or $15 if you fish in ocean waters only. If you go on a sportfishing boat, special one-day ocean fishing licenses cost $6.25.

Before you begin reading about all the wonderful places to escape to for the weekend, here are a few final comments. If you have your heart set on staying in a specific hotel or other hostelry, make reservations well in advance of your visit. When you call or write, inquire about family plans (kids under a certain age often stay free with their parents) and discount rates for senior citizens, as well as weekend, vacation, or golf and tennis packages that are offered seasonally or year round at reduced rates. *The price quoted for the lodgings we've listed is minimum double rate at the time this book went to press.*

Of course, nothing ever stays the same, and this is true of the hotels, restaurants, and sightseeing attractions described in this guidebook. Prices and hours of operation are subject to change according to the economy and seasons. As for dining spots, their reputations and menus vary with the cooks and management. A restaurant we've suggested for French fare may since have switched to so-called California cuisine, featuring fresh locally grown ingredients presented with artistic simplicity. To avoid upsetting surprises—such as very high prices, a change in hours, or even finding that a place has gone out of business—call ahead before you go. Also, for future editions of this book, we'd appreciate hearing from you in care of the publisher regarding any corrections that should be made.

Now read on to find out about all the marvelous places in Southern California where you can get away for the weekend—or anytime. Happy travels!

Away for the WEEKEND™

SOUTHERN CALIFORNIA

North Coastal Excursions

Overleaf: Santa Barbara County Courthouse

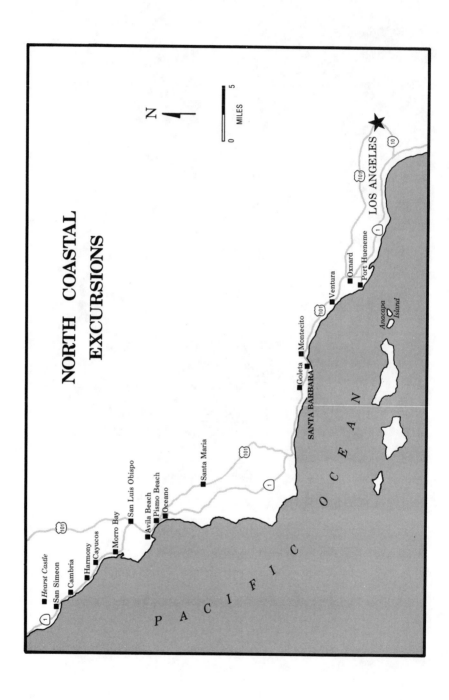

Hearst Castle and Quaint Coastal Towns

Imagine reading this "House for Sale" advertisement in the newspaper:

Hilltop Castle. Historical mansion w/38 bedrooms, 41 baths. Exquisitely furnished. On 123 acres overlooking ocean. Features baronial dining room, plush movie theater. 2 libraries, 14 sitting rooms. Indoor/outdoor swimming pools, tennis courts, space for bowling alley. Guest houses w/46 rooms. Magnificent gardens, fountains, statuary. Original cost $50,000,000. Must see to believe.

What would it cost to buy the world-renowned home that William Randolph Hearst built at San Simeon? Almost everyone agrees it's a priceless piece of real estate, one of the most imposing private residences in California and indeed the nation.

Besides, it's not for sale. However, you're welcome to visit the late publisher's palace. Once you had to be an invited guest, but Hearst's opulent hideaway was given to the state in 1958, and guided tours are now conducted daily except Thanksgiving, Christmas, and New Year's Day.

The newspaper and magazine magnate called his 115-room retreat La Casa Grande, but the public gave it another name—Hearst Castle. Visitors are awed by the mansion, which is set against the Santa Lucia Mountains on a 1,600-foot-high knoll overlooking Hearst's vast ranch and the Pacific Ocean.

Twin towers give the main building the appearance of a Spanish cathedral. The interior is like a museum, filled with furnishings and antiques that were collected all over the world and cost Hearst millions. The Persian rugs, Italian mantels, Flemish tapestries, and innumerable art treasures never fail to impress visitors at San Simeon, even those who have toured the great castles and palaces of Europe.

Outside there is more to see. Over a hundred acres are covered by gardens, terraces, pools, statuary, and a trio of palatial guesthouses. Before being deeded to the state, they were part of Hearst's mountain-to-seashore property, which exceeded a quarter of a million acres.

The Hearst San Simeon State Historical Monument will be the highlight of a weekend visit to a quartet of quaint coastal towns in

San Luis Obispo County: San Simeon, Cambria, Cayucos, and Harmony. They're located along a scenic two-lane section of California 1 between Hearst's splendid estate and Morro Bay.

Although more than a million visitors a year make their way to the publisher's hilltop retreat, you'll still find plenty of peace and quiet in this exceptionally pretty and unspoiled part of the California coast. Beachcombing and picnicking at the ocean's edge are the perfect pastimes for such a mellow and memorable weekend.

Drive north from Los Angeles on U.S. 101 to San Luis Obispo, then continue north on California 1 to the Main Street exit for Cambria (say *kam-bree-ah*). Make this charming resort and retirement community your headquarters, since there are no overnight accommodations at the historical monument. Two popular places to stay are J. Patrick House and Blue Whale Inn, both bed-and-breakfast inns. You'll also find two dozen other pleasant lodgings in the area, all convenient to Hearst Castle. Most are located near the shore along Moonstone Beach Drive, including San Simeon Pines Resort, where you can play on a nine-hole, par-three golf course. Four miles north, campers love the campsites near the ocean at San Simeon State Park.

In the morning, head a few miles north of Cambria to the place where William Randolph Hearst began construction of La Casa Grande in 1919. Even at the time of his death in 1951, at the age of 88, not everything in his elaborate building plans had been completed. Nevertheless, there is so much to view at his estate that four different daytime tours and an evening tour are offered.

Tour 1 is recommended for first-time visitors. Your group will be guided through the elaborate gardens past marble statuary, fountains, a guesthouse, and terraces to the lower level of the main building, La Casa Grande. Inside you'll be awed by the immense Assembly Room, where Hearst's many guests would gather with their host each evening before dinner. Overstuffed chairs contrast with exquisite tapestries covering the walls and Oriental rugs spanning the floors.

In the adjoining refectory, a baronial banquet hall, you can imagine dining beneath a hand-carved ceiling of saints, with silken banners and monastery stalls lining the walls. The grand walnut table, adorned by antique silver, is surprisingly set with paper napkins and bottles of catsup, mustard, and pickle relish!

Another featured room you'll see in the big house is the plush theater where the publisher played first-run movies for his guests. Today's visitors get to view some delightful home movies of Hearst and his famous friends.

Also on Tour 1 are the shimmering Neptune and Roman swimming pools, the latter one indoors and so large that two tennis courts were built on its roof. You'll be impressed by a visit to one of the three guesthouses, too.

There's much more to see, if you have time for another tour. The upper levels of La Casa Grande are displayed on Tour 2, which features Hearst's personal bedroom, two other extraordinary suites, both libraries, and the kitchen where meals for 50 or more guests were prepared.

Tour 3 shows you the guest wing of the castle and many works of art, another of the guesthouses, the gardens, and the pools. A fourth tour (offered April through October only) is for frequent visitors who want to explore even more of the fabulous estate. It focuses on the formal garden area and the largest guesthouse, including a recently discovered hidden terrace, the unfinished bowling alley, and the wine cellar.

A special evening tour is offered Fridays and Saturdays from mid-March through Memorial Day and mid-September through December. It covers the highlights of the entire estate, including the pools and gardens, which are illuminated by more than 100 historic light fixtures. To re-create the castle's 1930s heyday, docents in period clothing mill about the rooms as Hearst's guests and domestic staff, and a newsreel of the times is shown in the theater.

You must leave your car at the monument's roadside parking area at San Simeon (just off California 1 and about eight miles north of Cambria) and board a bus for a narrated five-mile ride up the hill to the castle, where the 75-minute tours begin. There is considerable walking, including 150 to 356 steps to climb, so wear comfortable shoes.

To reserve a place and avoid a long wait (sometimes overnight), get tour tickets in advance through MISTIX, toll-free (800) 444-7275, reserving the specific tour, day, and departure time. Each day's remaining tour space is sold on a first-come, first-served basis at the monument's visitors center beginning at 8 A.M.; no telephone reservations. Besides computerized ticket booths, the impressive visitors center has fast-food facilities, a gift shop, and exhibit areas where you can watch art works from the castle being restored.

If you arrive early, or after your tour, drive a half mile from the monument's parking area to the oceanside hamlet of San Simeon. In the 1920s it was a busy port, receiving and warehousing the supplies and elaborate furnishings for Hearst's mansion. Drop into Sebastian's, a rustic general store built in 1852. In summertime it serves breakfast and lunch, or you can buy food and picnic in the shade of the surrounding eucalyptus trees. Nearby the store you'll find a public fishing pier; bait and tackle are available, and no license is required. You also can depart on half-day or day-long deep-sea fishing trips from the San Simeon pier.

Besides visiting Hearst Castle, you'll enjoy exploring Cambria, a former timber and dairy center that sent shiploads of lumber and butter and cheese to San Francisco. Originally called Slabtown, because most buildings were constructed of rough-hewn boards, it was officially given the Roman name for ancient Wales in 1969. A fire destroyed the original business section of Cambria 20 years later, but the town was rebuilt near Santa Rosa Creek and has since expanded along Main Street all the way to the coast highway. More recently, sea-view homes have been built on the slopes of its pine-covered hills.

On Main Street in the newer section of town you'll find a few reminders of Cambria's past, including a century-old jail and the Santa Rosa schoolhouse, now home for an art gallery. You'll enjoy browsing in art galleries, antique shops, and gift stores, including one that features thousands of tin soldiers. Most are located along the lengthy, boomerang-shaped Main Street and Burton Drive. When you're hungry in the evening, join other visitors and towns-folk who fill up on the delicious fare at Ian's, the Brambles, Sow's Ear, Robin's, and Rigdon Hill restaurants.

After exploring the town, cross the coast highway at the north end of Main Street and take the scenic ride along Moonstone Beach Drive, which parallels the shoreline. There's a turnout where you can beachcomb amid the ocean-worn and sun-bleached trunks of pine trees to collect colorful pebbles polished by the sea. Be on the lookout for the beach's namesake, milky white moonstone. Keep your eyes open for otters frolicking in the surf and brown pelicans dive-bombing into the sea for their supper. Have a meal yourself in a nearby restaurant, the Hamlet at Moonstone Gardens, next to a garden filled with 400 varieties of cacti and succulents. Follow the paths for a close look at the plants.

Moonstone Beach Drive loops back to California 1, which you can continue to follow south toward Cayucos, another historic coastal town. Five miles down the highway, turn left for a brief stop at tiny Harmony, population 18. The old buildings that once were used by a dairy cooperative now house an art gallery, a pottery studio, a glassblower, and the town post office. Enjoy refreshments or time your visit for champagne brunch on Sunday or dinner in the Old Harmony Pasta Factory.

About eight miles farther south on California 1, exit toward the ocean to Cayucos, an active seaport in the late 1800s. Sailing ships tied up at a long wharf to take on hides, beef, and cheeses brought from inland ranches. Today the town pier is occupied mostly by fishermen, while swimmers and surfers have fun at the adjacent public beach.

Look for the weather-beaten Cass House on Ocean Avenue, built by the town's founder in 1857. Antiques and gifts will be found in shops around the town, as well as in the Way Station, a travelers' rest stop from the past century where you can still get a meal.

Cayucos has several motels, in case you can't get accommodations closer to Hearst Castle.

Continue on Ocean Avenue to rejoin California 1 to San Luis Obispo, then pick up U.S. 101 south for the journey back to Los Angeles.

Round trip is about 508 miles.

San Simeon/Cambria Area Code: 805

SIGHTSEEING _Hearst San Simeon State Historical Monument,_ off California 1 at 750 Hearst Castle Road, San Simeon 93452. Choice of four 2-hour tours given daily 8 A.M. to 5:30 P.M. in summer, 8:20 A.M. to 3:30 P.M. in winter. Departures every 10 to 30 minutes, depending on season. Each tour costs $14 adults, $8 children 6 to 12 years, ages 5 and under free if held on adult's lap aboard the tour bus; evening tour $25 adults, $13 children. Reservations from MISTIX are available up to 56 days in advance; call (800) 444-7275. Flash photographs, tripods, and baby strollers not permitted. Wheelchairs accommodated on Tour 1 with 10 days' advance notice; call 927-2020.

LODGING _Cambria Pines Lodge,_ 2905 Burton Drive, Cambria 93428, 927-4200 or toll-free (800) 445-6868; $60. Cabins, lodge rooms, and suites on 23 tree-shaded acres, indoor swimming pool and sauna. Also restaurant. • _J. Patrick House,_ 2900 Burton Drive, Cambria 93428, 927-3812; $100. 8-room B&B in Early American–style log home; all rooms with fireplaces. • _Blue Whale Inn,_ 6736 Moonstone Beach Drive, Cambria 93428, 927-4647; $115. Nice B&B. 6 minisuites with fireplaces, canopy beds, and full breakfast. • _San Simeon Pines Resort,_ Moonstone Beach Drive, San Simeon 93452, 927-4648; $70. Near beach amid cypress trees. Free par-3 golf. • _Moonstone Inn,_ 5860 Moonstone Beach Drive, Cambria 93428, 927-4815; $90. 9-room 4-star country inn across from beach. • _Blue Dolphin Inn,_ 6470 Moonstone Beach Drive, Cambria 93428, 927-3300; $75. 18 rooms with European countryside decor. Fireplaces, refrigerators, and continental breakfast. • _Sand Pebbles Inn,_ 6252 Moonstone Beach Drive, Cambria 93428, 927-5600; $75. Another nice European-style inn. Gas fireplaces and continental breakfast. • _Fog Catcher Inn,_ 6400 Moonstone Beach Drive, Cambria 93428, 927-1400 or toll-free (800) 445-6868; $80. Modern 53-room inn opened in 1992.

CAMPING *San Simeon State Park,* 3 miles north of Cambria off California 1, 927-2035. 139 sites along beach, $10 per night; reserve through MISTIX. No hookups.

DINING *The Brambles,* 4005 Burton Drive, Cambria, 927-4716. Delightful dinner house in century-old cottage with more recent Victorian-decorated additions to accommodate nightly crowds. Prime rib and fresh salmon are favorites. Sunday brunch. Reservations necessary in summer. • *Robin's,* 4095 Burton Drive, Cambria, 927-5007. Another popular restaurant in a family home, with dining on the terrace in summer. Vegetarian dishes. • *Ian's,* 2150 Center Street (off Burton Drive), Cambria, 927-8649. Local and out-of-towners' favorite for early-bird dinners and long-weekend lunches. • *Sow's Ear,* 2248 Main Street, Cambria, 927-4865. Seafood is featured at this informal dinner house; opens at 5:30 P.M. (closed Mondays). • *Rigdon Hall,* 4022 Burton Drive, Cambria, 927-5125. Also a home refurbished as a dinner house; fish and steak specialties. • *Linn's Fruit Bin,* Santa Rosa Creek Road, Cambria, 927-1499. Fun farm store on rural road a few miles from town. Gourmet foods, including preserves, and gift items; try a slice of freshly baked olallieberry pie. Renee and John Linn also have a family restaurant in town, *Linn's Main Bin,* 2277 Main Street, Cambria. • *The Hamlet at Moonstone Gardens,* 1½ miles north of Cambria off California 1, 927-3535. Pleasant restaurant convenient to Hearst Castle, offering lunch and dinner. Guests can tour adjacent cactus garden. • *Old Harmony Pasta Factory,* 5 miles south of Cambria off California 1, in Harmony, 927-5882. Lunch and dinner in rear of renovated dairy creamery; also Sunday brunch.

FOR MORE INFORMATION Contact the San Simeon Chamber of Commerce, 9190 Castillo Drive (P.O. Box 1), San Simeon 93452, 927-3500. Also the Cambria Chamber of Commerce, 767 Main Street, Cambria 93428, 927-3624.

Clamming and Jamming at Pismo Beach

If you enjoy the coast, you'll love a getaway to two quiet beachfront towns that big development and large crowds continue to pass by. Pismo Beach and Avila Beach in San Luis Obispo County offer a wonderful assortment of surprises, in addition to an array of activities found at more bustling beach retreats: tennis, golf, horseback riding, fishing, and surfing.

First, there's the fun of digging your own clams or at least savoring clam chowder, like the kind that put Pismo Beach on the map. It's also the only place in the state where you can go for a Sunday drive on the beach itself. More adventurous motorists can even ride over the windswept sands in a four-wheel all-terrain vehicle (ATV). A few miles north at Avila Beach is a fascinating deep-sea fishing port, where you can sip cocktails and dine on fresh seafood while the sun splashes color across the ocean at day's end. And in the tree-covered hills nearby, bubbling hot springs invite you to soak your cares away any time of the night or day.

Actually, it was a clam festival that brought fame to Pismo Beach and the area. Beginning with a New Year's Day clambake in 1945, Pismo's annual clam fest became the major event along the central California coast. Because of voracious sea otters and an abundance of human clammers, the famous Pismo clams have become rather scarce—but the annual Clam Festival still draws a big crowd every October.

Even more popular is Pismo's midwinter bash, the Mardi Gras Jazz Festival featuring Dixieland jazz bands. Since visitors now are more likely to dig music than clams, it's no wonder that one local wag calls it a jam festival! Even if you don't make the Mardi Gras party in February, Pismo Beach is an enjoyable weekend destination any time of the year.

Although Pismo has several attractive ocean-view motels, make lodging reservations at the area's premier resort, The Cliffs at Shell Beach. Some of the oceanfront suites in this fancy five-story clifftop hotel feature a marble whirlpool spa. There's a full-service health and fitness center in the hotel, or get some exercise by following the walkways that wander down the 50-foot-high bluff to the beach below.

Get to The Cliffs at Shell Beach from Los Angeles by driving north on U.S. 101 almost to San Luis Obispo. Exit at Spyglass Drive exit at Shell Beach, go under the freeway to the stop sign, and turn right on Shell Beach Road. You'll enjoy dinner in the hotel's Sea Cliffs restaurant.

In the morning, follow Shell Beach Road north along the freeway to join Avila Beach Drive, which leads to Avila Beach on San Luis Obispo Bay. Turn on Front Street to the sandy Avila Beach strand, where you can sunbathe, barbecue, and picnic. It's marked by a 1,570-foot fishing pier, originally called Avila Wharf and built in 1887. Facing the beach are an assortment of places to eat and drink, including the popular Old Custom House Cafe. Photographs inside show the building when it was dedicated in 1926 as a customs office for coastal vessels.

During the 1920s many visitors arrived unannounced at night. They were Prohibition rumrunners, and the secluded central coast was a perfect port of entry. Today there's still plenty going on along Avila's waterfront—in the daylight. Pirates Cove, a favorite landing sport for the clandestine booze boats, now is a popular beach for sunbathing sans suits. Most boat activity is around the third pier in the bay at Port San Luis, a protected harbor where deep-sea fishing vessels and pleasure craft bob at anchor. You'll see dozens of salmon trollers, gill netters, and albacore vessels, plus hundreds of sailboats and yachts awaiting weekend sailors. Year round you can catch rock cod and other ocean fish from Paradise Sportfishing boats that leave from the pier every morning.

Get there by following Avila Drive along the shoreline and drive out to the end of the pier, where you'll also find a fish market and the Olde Port Inn restaurant. Enjoy a takeout seafood cocktail from the market, or walk upstairs to the restaurant bar for a bowl of clam chowder.

Later, by driving back east on Avila Drive toward U.S. 101, you'll be tempted by two hot springs. The first is Sycamore Mineral Springs, which has been a spa and resort on and off since 1897. You can soak privately in outdoor redwood tubs constructed here and there on the woodsy hillside. Sycamore Mineral Springs is open 24 hours every day, but call in advance for reservations. Lodgings with hot tubs are also available at this relaxing spa, and there is a restaurant, too.

Down the road just before you reach U.S. 101 is Avila Hot Springs, discovered in 1907 while a well was being drilled for oil. At one time it was a regular stop for the Hollywood celebrities en route to San Simeon as guests of William Randolph Hearst. Now combined with an RV park, Avila Hot Springs has private tile tubs with adjustable temperature controls and an outdoor community tub maintained at 105 degrees. There's a freshwater swimming pool as well.

On Sunday, head south on U.S. 101 to Pismo Beach and exit on Hinds Avenue to reach the beach and public pier. Stroll out on the long wooden structure to watch surfers ride the waves alongside the pier's pilings. If you'd like to try your luck fishing from the pier, rods and bait are available there at Sheldon's Clam Stand. No license is required.

From the pier you'll also get a panorama of the Pismo coastline. To the north the rugged coast has coves and tide pools, while to the south stretch miles of flat and firm sandy shore where visitors are welcome to drive motor vehicles and ride horses. (There's a rental stable not far away in Oceano.) In fact, it's the only beach in California where you're allowed to drive your car. Go at low tide and keep to the 15 mph speed limit. This section of the coast is part of Pismo State Beach and also includes more than six miles of sand dunes that you can explore with a rented four-wheel ATV.

To drive on the beach and see the sand dunes, turn right off Hinds Avenue onto Cypress Street, which joins California 1 going south. If it's wintertime, pause to park on the road shoulder just past the Grover City city limits sign for a glimpse of the orange-and-black monarch butterflies resting on leaves of the eucalyptus trees. Usually they're in the area from December into March, during the insects' remarkable migration to escape the colder climes. Then continue south and turn right on Grand Avenue to the beach access auto ramp. Drive south on Pismo State Beach for a short ride on the sand and exit on the auto ramp at Pier Avenue in Oceano. Or drive farther on the beach to the sand dunes designated as a playground for off-road vehicles.

Digging for the famed Pismo clams is another favorite activity up and down the state beach park, which stretches for 12 miles from the city of Pismo Beach to the Santa Barbara County line. Determined clam diggers may be rewarded with some mouth-watering mollusks if you ask the local people where to search in the sand. (Clams must measure at least 4½ inches in diameter to be taken; limit is ten.) At area sports and liquor stores you can rent clam forks for digging, get free tide charts, and also buy the required California fishing license.

The unique Pismo cannot be caught commercially, but it's still possible to order some delicious chowder in the local restaurants— made with clams from the East Coast. Try Pismo Fish & Chips, Inc., on Cypress Street, where there's often a line of seafood fanciers waiting to get in. Other popular places to go for clam chowder and fish are Trader Nick's, Brad's, Splash Cafe, Chele's, and the restaurant at Spyglass Inn at Shell Beach.

For some old-fashioned fun on one night of your visit, reserve seats at the Great American Melodrama and Vaudeville Theater on Pacific Coast Highway (California 1) in Oceano. You'll be taken back to the Gay '90s era of stage entertainment when everyone in the audience boos the villain and cheers the hero of the old-time dramas. There are comedy and musical acts, too.

When it's time for your return to Los Angeles, rejoin U.S. 101 and head south.

Round trip is about 420 miles.

Pismo Beach/Avila Beach Area Code: 805

SIGHTSEEING   *San Luis Bay Resort Golf Course,* San Luis Bay Drive (or P.O. Box 2140), Avila Beach 93424, 595-2307. 18-hole, par-71 superscenic course in an oak-lined canyon. Weekend greens fees $25 per person plus $22 for golf cart. ● *Paradise Sportfishing,* Hartford Pier, Avila Beach 93424, 595-7200. All-day rock cod

fishing trips depart at 7 A.M. daily. Adults $28 weekends. •
Sycamore Mineral Springs, 1215 Avila Beach Drive, San Luis
Obispo 93405, 595-7302 or toll-free (800) 234-5831. Nature lovers
delight in the 23 redwood hot tubs tucked among the trees; $10 per
person per hour. Massages available. Open 24 hours. Also, overnight
lodgings (see below). • *Avila Hot Springs,* 250 Avila Beach Drive,
San Luis Obispo 93401, 595-2359. Open 8 A.M. to 10 P.M. daily.
Private mineral bath, $9 per hour; massages by appointment. Heated
outdoor swimming pool, $7.50 all day, children $5. • *Livery
Stables,* 1207 Silver Spur Place, Oceano 93445, 489-8100. Open
daily with rental horses for beach rides; $15 per hour. • *Sand
Center,* 307 Pier Avenue, Oceano 93445, 489-6014. Licensed
drivers can rent 4-wheel ATVs for beach and sand dune rides; $25
per hour. • *Great American Melodrama and Vaudeville Theater,*
1863 Pacific Coast Highway (California 1), Oceano 93445, 489-
2499. Evening shows Wednesday through Sunday; two shows on
Saturday at 5 and 9 P.M. Tickets: $9.50–$12.50.

EVENTS *Mardi Gras Jazz Festival,* annual 3-day weekend festival in late February featuring Dixieland jazz bands. Band names
and tickets ($40 for all performances) available from Pismo Beach
Convention and Visitors Bureau (see below). Also ask about the
Clam Festival and Dixieland Jubilee-by-the-Sea in October.

LODGING *The Cliffs at Shell Beach,* 2757 Shell Beach Road,
Shell Beach 93449, 773-5000; $109. Impressive 5-story cliff-top
hotel. 27 oceanfront suites feature whirlpool spa. Popular restaurant
with entertainment (see below). • *Sycamore Mineral Springs* (see
above). 27 rooms with private mineral spas on the balcony. Also
restaurant. Massages available.

CAMPING *Pismo Beach State Park,* along California 1, 489-
2684. Two camping areas available: Oceano, 82 sites (42 with
hookups) south of Pismo Beach, and North Beach, 103 sites (no
hookups) south of Grover City. Sites $16 per night, $20 with
hookups. Popular on weekends and in summer; call MISTIX for
reservations, toll-free (800) 444-7275. Also over 1,200 more campsites at private RV parks in the Pismo area.

DINING *Olde Port Inn,* Pier 3, Avila Beach 93424, 595-2515.
Fresh seafood, with a view of the fishing boats that bring it in. •
Sinfully Delicious, 1739 Shell Beach Road, Shell Beach, 773-1210.

Fine cuisine in a Victorian setting. Everything from grilled lamb chops to pasta. Open Wednesday through Sunday. • *Giuseppe's,* 891 Price Street, Pismo Beach, 773-2870. Seafood, veal, chicken, and more. Homemade desserts. Open daily at 4:30 P.M. for dinner. • *Jonathan's,* 575 Price Street, Pismo Beach, 773-6000. Bistro-style dining for lunch and dinner daily except Mondays. • *Chele's Food & Spirits,* 198 Pomeroy, Pismo Beach, 773-1020. Indoor/outdoor service by the pier for all meals. • *Splash Cafe,* 197 Pomeroy, Pismo Beach, 773-4653. Clam chowder, fish and chips, sandwiches by the pier; also takeout. • *Brad's,* 209 Pomeroy, Pismo Beach, 773-6165. Try the clam chowder and oak-pit barbecue. Open for lunch and dinner. • *SeaVenture* (see above), 773-3463. Dining nightly on top of beachfront hotel; also Sunday brunch. Enjoy drinks and appetizers on outdoor porch. • *Spyglass Inn Restaurant* (see above), 773-1222. Longtime favorite for ocean-view dining and Sunday champagne brunch. Also piano bar. • *Sea Cliffs* in The Cliffs at Shell Beach (see above), 773-3555. Open daily for all meals. Big-band music accompanies Sunday brunch. • *F. McLintock's Saloon and Dining House,* 750 Mattie Road, Shell Beach 93449, 773-1892. Informal Western-theme dinner restaurant featuring oak-pit barbecued steaks and ribs. Also ranch-style buffet on Sundays.

FOR MORE INFORMATION   Contact the Pismo Beach Convention and Visitors Bureau, 581 Dolliver Street, Pismo Beach 93449, 773-4382 or toll-free (800) 443-7778. Also, the San Luis Obispo County Visitors and Conference Bureau, 1041 Chorro Street, Suite E, San Luis Obispo 93401, 541-8000.

San Luis Obispo and the Gibraltar of the Pacific

Motorists on the busy U.S. 101 freeway often slip into San Luis Obispo for gas, grub, or a good night's sleep because it's midway on the run between Los Angeles and San Francisco. But travelers who linger awhile will discover that this attractive college town is much more than a convenient rest stop. San Luis Obispo is a wonderful weekend retreat, a friendly place where you can turn back the clock to California's early eras.

Nestled among verdant rolling hills at the foot of the Santa Lucia Mountains, this city is a real charmer. Its spick-and-span appearance reflects the pride of its residents, who want visitors to enjoy San Luis Obispo's many historical attractions, including an impressive Spanish mission, Victorian homes, and vintage businesses like the Ah Louis Store, which opened in 1874 and is still run by the founder's family.

Not far away, Mother Nature provides a spectacular attraction that also will be part of your SLO getaway, an immense volcanic outcropping that's called the Gibraltar of the Pacific. It's Morro Rock at picturesque Morro Bay, a busy fishing port and bustling summertime vacation spot.

Another area landmark, the outlandish Madonna Inn, is the place for you to sleep in San Luis Obispo. You can't miss this sprawling hillside hostelry, which is painted Pepto Bismol pink and white, and has become a must-see-it-to-believe-it tourist attraction. Some two million travelers pull in there every year, and you need to make reservations weeks in advance in order to spend the night. Each of the inn's 110 rooms has been designed and decorated at the whim of owner Alex Madonna, and guests agree that his tastes are definitely flamboyant, if not a bit bizarre.

Check into the Safari room, for instance, and you'll be surrounded by zebra stripes and leopard spots that cover everything from the wallpaper to the bedspreads. If a night in the jungle doesn't fit your fantasy, the Caveman room has an interior of rocks. Or select more restful quarters, such as the Old Mill room, which features a waterwheel that turns on and off with the flick of a switch. For folks with claustrophobia, there's the enormous Austrian suite, which stretches 76 feet and has two balconies. Unless you reserve a room by name, guests take potluck on their quarters (depending on price range and beds requested), but it doesn't matter much because all the accommodations are far from ordinary.

Begin your getaway by driving north from Los Angeles on U.S. 101 and exiting on Madonna Road to the inn on the southern side of San Luis Obispo. After checking in, have dinner in the Madonna Inn's dining room, which is extraordinarily decorated in festive seasonal motifs. With a menu featuring Australian lobster tail and French filet mignon, the food is superior to standard motel coffee shop fare, but don't be surprised when you're served pink sugar.

On Saturday, see the sights of San Luis Obispo, guided by a map in the chamber of commerce Visitor's Guide that outlines a two-mile tour called the Path of History. Plan two hours to circle the route on foot (or 20 minutes by car), plus extra time to stop at any of the 19 points of interest along the way. You also will have a delightful time seeing San Luis Obispo's vintage homes.

Begin your tour from the Madonna Inn by rejoining U.S. 101

north and taking the first exit, Marsh Street, to San Luis Obispo's downtown area. Turn left on Chorro Street to Mission Plaza, a delightful pedestrians-only area along San Luis Creek that's a lush and quiet oasis in the heart of town. It's the city's historical focal point, too.

As you'll soon observe, San Luis Obispo is a very peaceful place. However, a couple of hundred years ago it was quite a different story. When a Spanish expedition headed north from San Diego in search of Monterey Bay in 1769, they encountered numerous bears near the present town site. A hunting party cleared the way and brought back bear meat for the hungry soldiers, settlers, and local Indians.

Three years later the Spanish missionary Junipero Serra chose the scene of the hunt as the spot to erect Mission San Luis Obispo de Tolosa, fifth in his chain of Franciscan stations in California. It was named for a thirteenth-century French saint, the Bishop of Toulouse. Chumash Indians were recruited to build the adobe and thatched-roof mission, but their hostile brothers attacked it with flaming arrows on several occasions. As a result, the San Luis Obispo padres developed the fireproof tiles that became standard roofing material for all the Spanish missions in California.

Today the restored mission is the center of attention on Mission Plaza and serves as a parish church. Visit the original padres' residence, now a museum that portrays life in the state's early days. Also on Mission Plaza you'll find more Californiana—including Indian artifacts, glassware, papers, and pictures—in the San Luis Obispo County Historical Museum, once the city's Carnegie Library.

Another highlight is the Dallidet Adobe, built by a French vintner in 1853 after he arrived in the area to raise grapes. Its interior can be viewed on Sundays in summer only. Another old residence is the Murray Adobe on Mission Plaza, which was the early home of Englishman Walter Murray, a distinguished judge and journalist. For a brief return to contemporary times, enjoy the ongoing exhibits by local and visiting artists in the San Luis Obispo Art Center, across from the county museum at the edge of Mission Plaza.

Don't miss the Ah Louis Store, still operated by the same family that established it over a century ago to serve the 2,000 Chinese building railroad tunnels through the mountains nearby. Besides buying herbs and general merchandise, these itinerant laborers used the store as a bank and post office. Today it's a gift shop and state historical landmark. Also on the Path of History route is the 1874 Sinsheimer Bros. store, noted for its iron-front facade.

Some of the town's other vintage buildings have been converted to pleasing shopping and dining spots. Built in 1906, the Golden State Creamery is just called the Creamery nowadays and houses a mini-mall of shops and restaurants. Nearby on Higuera Street, a 1900s department store has become an arcade of shops and is known as the Network. As home for 22,000 students at Cal Poly State University and Cuesta Community College, San Luis Obispo is host to a great variety of lively restaurants. At Brubeck's, where Pioneer cigars were made at the turn of the century, you can enjoy dinner and live jazz. Other favorite downtown places for food and fun include Chocolate Soup and McLintocks Saloon.

Spend Sunday not far away in Morro Bay, where vacationers flock to picnic, swim, boat, fish, beachcomb, bird-watch, and play golf. Marked by the eons-old Morro Rock, the town has many other natural attractions that have been preserved for public enjoyment as state parks and beaches.

Head first to the 1,500-acre Morro Bay State Park at the south edge of that coastal town. Follow California 1 northwest from San Luis Obispo about 12 miles to the Los Oso/Baywood Park exit and the park entrance. There the highway joins park roads that lead down to the bay and a small boat harbor where boats and bicycles can be rented for leisurely explorations. There also are nature trails to walk for close-up views of the park's extensive birdlife, which includes 250 species. Go to White Point and look north for a great blue heron rookery high in the eucalyptus trees. (The big birds nest near the Inn at Morro Bay, an attractive alternative for your weekend lodgings.) Also stop at the park's Museum of Natural History to see its excellent displays about the area's birds and animals, as well as Morro Bay's earliest inhabitants, the Chumash Indians. If you have time, watch the films about local geology and oceanography.

Golfers can challenge the park's 18-hole public course, where you'll also find a driving range, pro shop, and clubhouse. Get a panoramic view of the bay and its landmark Morro Rock by following the park road that cuts through the golf course to an overlook on Black Mountain, the second of nine 50-million-year-old volcanic peaks that dot the landscape from the ocean's edge inland to San Luis Obispo.

From the observation point you'll also see the protective five-mile-long sand spit that separates Morro Bay from the Pacific. This isolated peninsula is part of the state park and the place to go for beachcombing. You can reach it by renting a small boat in the park harbor to cross the bay or by taking the Sand Spit Shuttle.

Spend some time strolling along the Embarcadero, the colorful harbor area where commercial and sportfishing boats tie up. Get there by taking Main Street into town from the park's northwest exit, then turn left on Pacific Street and go down to the waterfront. To try your luck catching rock cod, halibut, and other ocean fish, join a party-boat outing from Bob's or Virg's sportfishing, both on the Embarcadero.

For other nautical fun, cruise aboard Tiger's Folly, a pseudo-paddle wheeler that makes relaxing harbor excursions from the Harbor Hut dock, including Sunday brunch cruises. Central Coast Cruises also offers waterborne tours from the Embarcadero.

Fourteen restaurants line the waterfront as well, and all offer a feast of fresh seafood, including once-plentiful abalone, now an expensive treat. Try Rose's Landing, popular for value-priced early-bird specials and all-inclusive dinners.

Be sure to drive north on Embarcadero and cross the causeway to the dome-shaped sentinel, Morro Rock. The 576-foot-high outcropping was first noted by Portuguese explorer Juan Cabrillo when he sailed along the California coast in 1542. Long a navigational marker, it's now a state historic landmark and also serves as a preserve for the endangered peregrine falcons that nest on top. You're forbidden to climb the rock, but visitors can walk around part of its perimeter; on the north side, watch out for high waves, which are unpredictable and dangerous.

Drive past a newer landmark, the PG & E power plant with its towering trio of candlestick smokestacks, and go about a mile north to Atascadero State Beach, where beachcombing, swimming, surf fishing, and skin diving are big attractions. Another section of sandy shoreline, Morro Strand State Beach, is two miles north and makes a pleasant place to picnic.

Or head 11 miles south of Morro Bay to explore rugged Montana de Oro State Park, a 10,000-acre wildlife preserve that once was part of a vast ranch. It lives up to its name as a ''mountain of gold'' every spring, when the wildflowers are in brilliant bloom. Get a guide map at park headquarters, which was the former landowner's turn-of-the-century home.

For your return trip to Los Angeles, follow California 1 back to San Luis Obispo and rejoin U.S. 101 south.

Round trip is about 442 miles.

San Luis Obispo/Morro Bay Area Code: 805

SIGHTSEEING   *Mission San Luis Obispo de Tolosa*, on Mission Plaza at Chorro and Monterey streets, San Luis Obispo 93401, 543-6850. Museum and gardens open daily 9 A.M. to 4 P.M., to 5 P.M. in summer. Donations welcome. ● *San Luis Obispo County Historical Museum*, end of Mission Plaza, San Luis Obispo, 543-0638. Hours: 10 A.M. to noon and 1 to 4 P.M. Wednesday through Sunday. Free. ● *San Luis Obispo Art Center*, opposite historical museum at end of Mission Plaza. Hours: noon to 5 P.M. daily except Mondays. Free. ● *Dallidet Adobe*, 1185 Pacific Street, San Luis Obispo 93401.

130-year-old home, a state historical landmark, open 1 to 4 P.M. Sundays in summer. ● *Ah Louis Store,* 800 Palm Street, San Luis Obispo 93401. Open 2 to 5:15 P.M. daily except Sundays. ● *Museum of Natural History,* Morro Bay State Park, Morro Bay 93442, 772-2694. Hours: 10 A.M. to 5 P.M. daily. Adults $2, children over 6 years $1. ● *Morro Bay Golf Course,* Morro Bay State Park, Morro Bay 93442, 772-4341. 18 holes, par 71. Greens fees $15 weekends, $12.50 weekdays. ● *Tiger's Folly,* Harbor Hut, 1205 Embarcadero, Morro Bay 93442, 772-2257. 1-hour narrated cruises of the bay daily in summer season; weekends only from October through May. Adults $6, children 5 to 12 years $3; Sunday brunch cruise $16 adults, kids $8. ● *Central Coast Cruises,* 501 Embarcadero, Morro Bay 93442, 541-1435 or toll-free (800) 773-2628. 2-hour cruises along the coast. Adults $20, children 8 to 12 years $15. ● *Morro Bay Aquarium,* 595 Embarcadero, Morro Bay 93442, 772-7647. Open from 9 A.M. to 6 P.M. weekdays; weekends to 5:30 P.M. Adults $1, children $.50.

EVENTS　*Farmer's Market* is year-round fun every Thursday evening along 4 blocks of Higuera Street in downtown San Luis Obispo. There, local farmers sell their produce, restaurants barbecue food, and people dance in the streets; stores also stay open until 9 P.M. ● *Mozart Festival,* San Luis Obispo's annual August musical celebration honoring the Austrian composer's birthday with recitals and orchestra concerts. Program and tickets available from Mozart Festival Association, P.O. Box 311, San Luis Obispo 93406. ● *Harbor Festival,* Morro Bay's fall fling for families the first weekend in October, features small-boat races, seafood fair, arts and crafts, games, and a dinner dance.

LODGING　*Madonna Inn,* 100 Madonna Road, San Luis Obispo 93401, 543-3000. Rates from $82 to $170. Reservations a must. Also dining room and coffee shop (see below). No credit cards. ● Alternate accommodations can be found at nearly 30 other motels in San Luis Obispo, including Victorian-motif *Apple Farm Inn,* 2015 Monterey Street, San Luis Obispo 93401, 544-2040 or toll-free (800) 225-2040; $70–$120. 101 rooms in a homey complex along San Luis Creek. Also popular restaurant with traditional American fare (see below). ● *Embassy Suites,* 333 Madonna Road, San Luis Obispo 93405, 549-0800 or toll-free (800) 362-2779; $99–$109, including full breakfast. The area's largest luxury lodging with 195 suites. ● Or try *Garden Street Inn,* 1212 Garden Street, San Luis

Obispo 93401, 545-9802; $80–$160, including bountiful breakfast. 13-room bed-and-breakfast in a restored 1887 downtown home. • *Adobe Inn*, 1473 Monterey Street, San Luis Obispo 93401, 549-0321; $50–$85, including breakfast buffet. A motel reborn as a bed-and-breakfast inn with Southwestern decor. • *Heritage Inn*, 978 Olive Street, San Luis Obispo 93401, 544-7440, a bed-and-breakfast with 9 antique-filled rooms in the heart of town; $76. • *Morro Bay* (zip code 93442) also has over two dozen other lodgings. *The Breakers*, 780 Market Street, Morro Bay, 772-7317; $70. 25 rooms a block from the Embarcadero overlooking the ocean. Adjacent restaurant (see below). • *Inn at Morro Bay*, 19 Country Club Road, 772-5651; $85. Morro Bay's largest lodging, with 98 rooms. Scenic location at state park entrance across from the seaside golf course. • Other choices: *Blue Snail Inn* and *Embarcadero Inn*.

CAMPING *Morro Bay State Park*, off California 1, south edge of Morro Bay, 772-2560. For reservations, call MISTIX, toll-free (800) 444-7275. 135 tent and RV sites: $16 per night, $20 with hookups. • *Atascadero State Beach Park*, off California 1, 3 miles north of Morro Bay, 772-8812. 104 beachfront sites, $16 per night. • *Montana de Oro State Park*, via Pecho Road, 11 miles south of Morro Bay, 528-0513. 50 rustic sites, $9 per night.

DINING *Madonna Inn* (see above). Surprisingly good food for high volume of tourist traffic from U.S. 101. Baked goods and desserts are fresh from the motel's own bakery. Have breakfast or lunch sitting on ice cream chairs at copper-top tables in the coffee shop, but reserve a booth for dinner in the gilded and pink Gold Rush dining room. Dinner served from 5:30 to 11 P.M. Ballroom dancing except Mondays. Also Wine-cellar cocktail lounge; don't miss seeing the surprising men's room that's adjacent. • *Brubeck's*, 726 Higuera Street, San Luis Obispo, 541-8688. Dinner, including fresh fish, from 5:30 P.M. Live jazz Thursday through Saturday. • *Chocolate Soup*, 980 Morro Street, San Luis Obispo, 543-7229. Order the chocolate soup dessert. Vegetarian dishes, along with crepes, soups, salads, and specialty sandwiches. Lunch and dinner daily except Sundays. • *F. McLintock's Saloon*, 686 Higuera Street, San Luis Obispo, 541-0686. Old-time saloon with hearty Western dishes like beef stew and chili. Also sandwiches. Open daily. • *Apple Farm*, 2015 Monterey Street, San Luis Obispo, 544-6100. Home-style meals served daily. Try the old-fashioned pot roast and hot apple dumplings for dessert. Also lodgings (see above). •

1865, 1865 Monterey Street (in Somerset Manor motel), San Luis Obispo, 544-1865. Loft dining amid hanging-garden decor, with prime ribs the specialty. Open for dinner except Sundays. • *Inn at Morro Bay* (see above). Outstanding cuisine in the dining room. Open for all meals, including Sunday brunch. • *Rose's Landing,* 725 Embarcadero, Morro Bay, 772-4441. Make reservations for lunch on weekends and holidays, and dinner daily. Seafood is super. • Other busy Embarcadero eateries with treats from the sea: *The Galley Restaurant,* at No. 899, 772-2806 (with a wonderful wine list); *Great American Fish Co.,* No. 1185, 772-4407; and *Harbor Hut,* No. 1205, 772-2255. • *Dorn's Original Breakers Cafe,* 801 Market Street, Morro Bay, 772-4415. Local favorite for breakfast, lunch, or dinner. Fresh seafood. • *Brannigans Reef,* 781 Market Street, Morro Bay, 772-7321. Better-than-average restaurant chain with oyster bar and piano entertainment.

FOR MORE INFORMATION Contact the San Luis Obispo Chamber of Commerce, 1039 Chorro Street, San Luis Obispo 93401, 781-2777. Open every day. Visitor's Guide $2 at office, $2.50 by mail. Also open daily except Sundays is the Morro Bay Chamber of Commerce, 895 Napa Avenue (or P.O. Box 876), Morro Bay 93442, 772-4467. Also contact the San Luis Obispo Visitors and Conference Bureau, 1041 Chorro Street, Suite E, San Luis Obispo 93401, 541-8000 or toll-free (800) 634-1414.

Santa Barbara
Part 1: On the Waterfront

Santa Barbara is one of Southern California's most visited cities, and it's no wonder. Few places have such a cornucopia of attractions. Beauty, history, and activity are the main drawing cards, and you'll need at least three weekends to see the foremost sights and sample the city's other pleasures. Our trio of trips take you to Santa Barbara's wonderful waterfront, the historic downtown area, and the city's enchanting environs.

Santa Barbara celebrated its bicentennial in 1982, and even remnants of its first construction, a Spanish military outpost, have been preserved. It's a mission town, too, and when a devastating earthquake flattened the city's center in 1925, townsfolk began·

reconstruction with Spanish-Moorish–style stucco and red tile roofs, which have come to symbolize Santa Barbara's lovely architecture. Extensive planting and constant care of the trees and flowers also have made the city a veritable garden. Add its picturesque location, sloping down from the Santa Ynez Mountains to palm-fringed beaches, as well as the agreeable Mediterraneanlike weather, and you'll understand why visitors often say Santa Barbara is their favorite Southern California city.

One of the most stunning sections of coastline in the state also is one of the liveliest. You'll find activities for every age and interest along Santa Barbara's beautiful waterfront. A weekend there offers this seashore sampler: bicycling, visiting a zoo, roller skating, playing volleyball, fishing, enjoying an arts-and-crafts show, bird watching, sailboating, jogging, taking a shoreline cruise, and picnicking under lofty palm trees.

If you prefer less energetic alternatives, do some coastal sightseeing in your car or on foot, and pause to feast on fresh seafood at an ocean-view restaurant along the way. Santa Barbara's natural harbor enticed Spanish explorers to settle there two centuries ago, and you'll soon discover why the city's waterfront continues to captivate residents and visitors alike.

Begin your coastal weekend by driving north from Los Angeles on U.S. 101 to the exclusive residential community of Montecito at the eastern edge of Santa Barbara. Exit south on Olive Mill Road, follow it down to Channel Drive on the ocean, and check into the splendid Four Seasons Biltmore. Surrounded by acres of lush landscaping, this rambling 1920s hostelry of 236 rooms and cottage suites gives guests a sense of well-being that today's travelers rarely experience away from home. It's a dignified yet friendly place— staying there makes you feel like a weekend guest at a country estate. As one of California's few elegant oceanfront resorts, the Biltmore is the place to stay (providing your budget can afford room rates that begin at $285).

If there's no room at the Biltmore, a number of other lodgings also face the waterfront, along Cabrillo Boulevard. One is the Sheraton Santa Barbara Hotel, once headquarters for the White House staff and Washington press corps during former President Ronald Reagan's visits to his ranch nearby. Just down the street is the somewhat smaller Santa Barbara Inn, location of the Citronelle restaurant, a favorite for French cuisine. Also on Cabrillo Boulevard across from the beach is Santa Barbara's largest lodging, the sprawling Fess Parker's Red Lion Resort with 360 rooms and suites.

If you're staying at the Biltmore, relax at the hotel's secluded pool or private beach club before beginning your exploration along the waterfront in the morning. Head west on Channel Drive and follow the road inland around a cemetery to join Cabrillo Boulevard

(California 225), then bear right into a parking area for the Andree Clark Bird Refuge, a winter home for flocks of migratory birds. Resident ducks always loiter around the shoreline of its peaceful lagoon, hoping for a handout, so bring some bread from breakfast. You can have a treat, too, by dining later at Michael's Waterside Inn, an elegant French restaurant in the Victorian-style house that's near the big pond and its assortment of fine-feathered friends.

If you brought a bicycle or roller skates, the bird refuge is the place to embark on the four-mile bikeway that parallels Santa Barbara's scenic beachfront. You also can rent bikes or skates farther along West Cabrillo Boulevard at Beach Rentals. Or go around the corner on State Street to Cycles 4 Rent.

Adjacent to the bird sanctuary you'll enjoy the fauna and flora at the Santa Barbara Zoological Gardens. Turn right at the zoo entrance sign at Ninos Drive on Cabrillo Boulevard. About 500 animals are on view, everything from giraffes to gibbons and llamas to sea lions. Kids especially like the farmyard area, where they can pet and feed sheep, goats, and other tame creatures. A miniature train ride is another favorite of the small fry. You'll find playground and picnic areas, too.

Returning to the coastal boulevard and continuing west, you pass along one of Santa Barbara's prettiest and most popular gathering spots, Chase Palm Park. Come back here on Sunday, when it's the site of the city's year-round arts-and-crafts show. From 10 A.M. until dusk, local artists display and sell their paintings, drawings, graphics, sculpture, photographs, and crafts. On any day you can spread a picnic under the regal palm trees or enjoy refreshments at East Beach Grill, which overlooks the sand. Take off your shoes and stroll along adjacent Cabrillo Beach, where there are volleyball games to watch or join.

For outstanding ocean views and a panorama of the mountains that serve as the city's backdrop, head out to the end of a Santa Barbara landmark, Stearns Wharf. The owner of a local lumberyard, John P. Stearns, built the original wharf in 1872—then the longest deep-water pier between Los Angeles and San Francisco. It offered easy ocean access to the Santa Barbara area and helped that coastal city prosper. After serving passenger steamers, freighters, and fishing vessels in its early days, Stearns Wharf remained a focal point for the city's residents and visitors. Jutting 1,500 feet into the city's scenic harbor, the wooden pier was reopened to the public after $5 million worth of restoration work and now is home for a dozen shops and several eateries.

As in the past, visitors are welcome to walk or drive their cars on the wharf, a three-block extension of State Street, the city's main thoroughfare. You'll find parking spots, as well as optional valet parking for the Harbor Restaurant. Featuring fresh seafood and homemade pasta, this restaurant has long been the wharf's keystone for cuisine. Its harbor views are outstanding, too, especially from the indoor/outdoor bar upstairs.

More seafood specialties are on the menu at the Moby Dick Restaurant, while Char West serves English-style fish and chips and American mainstays like hamburgers and hot dogs. Or head to the end of the wharf and the Santa Barbara Shellfish Company to see and buy some of the local catch, including lobster, crab, and abalone in season. This fresh fish market serves seafood lunches, too. If you want to try your own luck fishing from the pier (no license required), stop next door at Mike's Bait and Tackle to rent a rod.

Be certain to visit the Sea Center, a branch of the Museum of Natural History, pet a shark, and see displays of the diverse marine life that inhabits the Santa Barbara Channel. Some are live specimens in saltwater tanks.

Nautical types will like browsing in the Old Wharf Trading Company, which has the flavor of an 1800s ship chandlery. Its seafaring gifts include marine instruments, lamps, decorator items, clothing, and books. Look for more beach- and ocean-oriented items in a shop called The Devil and the Deep Blue Sea. At Nature's Own you'll find shells, rocks, fossils, and semiprecious stones for sale.

To see the varied works of many area artists and craftspersons, visit Galeria del Mar. Topside has sportswear and items with Santa Barbara slogans. Also on the pier, at Stearns Wharf Vintners, you can sample Santa Barbara County, California, and French wines. And there's the chance to learn about your future from palmist Madame Rosinka. Matriarch of a local gypsy family, the popular palm reader and her daughters have been telling the fortunes of pier visitors for many years.

Continue west along Cabrillo Boulevard to another colorful area of the waterfront, Santa Barbara's yacht harbor, home port for more than 1,000 pleasure craft and commercial fishing boats. From the parking lot, walk out on the paved breakwater to see all the nautical activity. You can join in by renting a sailboat, powerboat, or rowboat from the Sailing Center of Santa Barbara at the breakwater. Another choice is to let someone else be captain and join Captain Don's Harbour Cruises for a tour of the waterfront. For more excitement, board one of the Sea Landing's vessels in the harbor for a coastal fishing trip, or a whale-watching cruise in winter.

Then climb the stairs to the Brophy Brothers restaurant on the breakwater to relax with a drink and a seafood cocktail and watch the sun set over the colorful harbor. On Cabrillo Boulevard you'll find some more restaurants that offer ocean views, including the longtime favorite of locals and out-of-towners, the Lobster House.

For your return to Los Angeles, rejoin U.S. 101 and head south. Round trip is about 210 miles.

Santa Barbara Area Code: 805

SIGHTSEEING *Santa Barbara Zoological Garden,* entrance from Ninos Drive at 1300 East Cabrillo Boulevard, Santa Barbara 93103, 962-6310 (recording) or 962-5339. Hours: 10 A.M. to 5 P.M. daily, summer 9 A.M. to 6 P.M. Adults $4, children and senior citizens $2. • *Stearns Wharf,* foot of State Street at the Santa Barbara Harbor, 564-5518. Shops and restaurants open daily. • *Sea Center,* on Stearns Wharf, Santa Barbara 93101, 963-1067. Minimuseum of marine life in Santa Barbara Channel, including touch tide pool and live specimens. Also gray-whale skeleton and life-size replica of mother and calf. Open daily. Adults $1.50, children 3 to 17 years $1. • *Captain Don's Harbour Cruises,* on Stearns Wharf next to the Sea Center, Santa Barbara (or P.O. Box 2234, Summerland 93607), 969-5217. Narrated harbor and coastline cruises on the hour from 11 A.M. to 6 P.M. every day June through October, all holidays, and weekends only the rest of the year. Adults $8, children 2 to 12 years $6. • *Sea Landing Sportfishing,* on the Breakwater, Santa Barbara Harbor, 963-3564. Half- to all-day ocean fishing trips; also twilight fishing excursions. • *Sailing Center of Santa Barbara,* on the Breakwater, Santa Barbara Harbor, 962-2826. Open daily for power- and sailboat rentals.

LODGING *Four Seasons Biltmore,* 1260 Channel Drive, Montecito 93108, 969-2261; $285. Acclaimed oceanfront resort with beautiful grounds, including putting green. Splurge with a suite in a garden cottage. Excellent restaurants (see below) and special Sunday brunch. • *Sheraton Santa Barbara Hotel,* 1111 East Cabrillo Boulevard, Santa Barbara 93103, 963-0744; $89. Health spa facilities. • *Santa Barbara Inn,* 901 Cabrillo Boulevard (at Milpas Street), Santa Barbara 93103, 966-2285; $110. Across street from the beach. *Citronelle* restaurant (see below) with Pacific panorama. • *Fess Parker's Red Lion Resort,* 633 East Cabrillo Boulevard, Santa Barbara 93103, 564-4333; $185. Spanish-style buildings across from the beach have 360 rooms and suites, 2 restaurants and lounges. Also tennis courts, exercise room with sauna, bicycle rentals. Santa Barbara's largest resort.

DINING *La Marina Dining Room,* in Four Seasons Biltmore (see above). Gourmet cuisine served with continental flair; jackets required at dinner. Have lunch indoors or outside at *The Patio.* Elegant and expensive Sunday brunch is worth the price. • *Michael's*

Waterside Inn, 50 Los Patos Way (at the Andree Clark Bird Refuge), Santa Barbara, 969-0307. Dress up for a special evening of French cuisine in an 1872 home. Dinner nightly; also Sunday brunch. • *Harbor Restaurant,* Stearns Wharf (at the foot of State Street), Santa Barbara, 963-3311. Lunch and dinners of fresh seafood with home-made pasta. Or snack on steamed clams and shrimp in a bucket, with one of their premium wines. • *Castagnola's Lobster House,* 15 East Cabrillo Boulevard, Santa Barbara, 965-1174. Lunch and dinner daily. All seafood is on display for your selection; great clam chow-der. • *Brophy Brothers,* on the Breakwater at the Santa Barbara Harbor, 966-4418. Casual second-story restaurant with best view of the boats. Super spot for a relaxing drink. • *Citronelle,* in the Santa Barbara Inn (see above). Fine French cuisine and dazzling ocean view for lunch and dinner. Also Sunday champagne brunch with traditional and Polynesian dishes. • *Andria's Harborside Cafe,* 336 West Ca-brillo Boulevard, Santa Barbara, 962-8159. Fresh fish with choice of cooking styles. Popular with families for breakfast, lunch, and dinner.

FOR MORE INFORMATION When in town, visit the Santa Barbara Chamber of Commerce's Visitors Information Center, 1 Santa Barbara Street at Cabrillo Boulevard (two blocks east of Stearns Wharf), Santa Barbara 93101, 965-3021. Open every day. In advance of your visit, call or write the Santa Barbara Conference and Visitors Bureau, 510 State Street, Santa Barbara 93101, toll-free (800) 927-4688. Open weekdays.

Santa Barbara Part 2: Red Tile Tour to the Past

Making a tour of a courthouse sounds like pretty dull stuff—unless you're touring the Santa Barbara County Courthouse. It's been called America's most beautiful public building. Santa Barbarans (or Barbarenos, as some folks say) taxed themselves $1.5 million to build the classic Spanish-Moorish structure in the 1920s. Today their courthouse is considered priceless.

It's just one of the joys of spending a weekend in downtown Santa Barbara exploring a host of historic sites, museums, antique shops, and art galleries. From ancient adobes to sidewalk cafes, a stroll around town presents a panorama of the city's past two centuries and its present unhurried life-style. Add to the mellow mood of your visit by staying in one of Santa Barbara's homey bed-and-breakfast inns. A half dozen B&Bs are convenient to the downtown area, which you can reach by foot, on bicycles borrowed from your innkeeper, or in just a few minutes' drive by car.

Reach Santa Barbara from Los Angeles by driving north on U.S. 101, and check into your bed-and-breakfast for the weekend. Guests often are greeted with a welcoming glass of wine.

The next morning, after a leisurely breakfast at your home away from home, head to the downtown area, where it's easy to find your way around the historic heart of the city by following the Red Tile Walking Tour. Get a map from the Visitors Information Center at the corner of Cabrillo Boulevard and Santa Barbara Street, then set your own pace for this mile-long self-guided excursion, which circles 12 blocks. Ask directions to El Paseo, an enchanting Spanish-style arcade off State Street, where you can begin your walking tour. El Paseo is adjacent to Casa de la Guerra, the original 1827 adobe home of the army commander in charge of the Spanish outpost at Santa Barbara. The commandant's impressive hacienda was once the social center for this part of California. You'll have fun browsing in the quaint cluster of shops and galleries that now surrounds the casa's Spanish-style courtyard. El Paseo also is a pleasant place to enjoy an alfresco lunch at the Wine Cask, or go across Anacapa Street to the Presidio Cafe.

Also across the street from El Paseo is the Plaza de la Guerra, which becomes a colorful outdoor marketplace during the city's annual Old Spanish Days Fiesta. California's earliest European residents always liked a good party, and the tradition is carried on in Santa Barbara every August. The five-day wingding features parades, rodeos and horse shows, street dances, a carnival, stage and musical shows, cookouts, and walking tours of historic sites.

Walk northeast along De la Guerra Street and cross Anacapa Street to tiny Presidio Avenue, the city's oldest street. There you'll find an 1840 adobe and Presidio Gardens, formerly parade grounds for the Spanish soldiers. Opposite, at the corner of De la Guerra and Santa Barbara streets, visit the treasure-filled Santa Barbara Historical Society Museum to see mementos of the city's Indian, Spanish, Mexican, and American heritage. Then follow Santa Barbara Street a block north and turn left on Canon Perdido Street to El Presidio de Santa Barbara State Historic Park. Here you can view excavations of the city's birthplace, the Spanish Presidio built in 1782, as well as El Cuartel, the original soldiers' barracks that once were part of that army fort, and the recently restored Padres' Quarters with its thick walls, dirt floor, and rawhide bed.

On the corner of Canon Perdido and Anacapa streets is the Lobero

Theater, survivor of the 1925 earthquake that demolished much of the town center. It's still used for stage performances, and traditional Spanish and flamenco dancing is featured there during the annual fiesta.

Continue on the Red Tile Walking Tour by going two blocks northwest along Anacapa Street to the striking Santa Barbara County Courthouse. Occupying an entire city block, the building and its lush gardens look more like a country castle than a government edifice. Turrets and towers rise above the red tile roof that crowns the building's bright white stucco exterior. There are curved staircases, graceful archways, and windows enhanced by balconies and iron grillwork.

Inside, the county's business goes on—in superior court rooms, judges' chambers, law library, county clerk's office, and hall of records—but many county offices have been moved to newer buildings nearby. The courthouse is a Southern California showplace, and visitors are welcome every day. Enter by the main archway beneath the clock tower on Anacapa Street. Take a free guided tour or pick up the self-guiding tour leaflet that describes the building's unusual architecture, elaborate public rooms, and historical displays. The courthouse also offers Santa Barbara's best bird's-eye view of the city, ocean, and mountains from atop an 85-foot observation tower. There's an elevator to this spectacular lookout, from which you can survey the other attractions of the historic city.

Taking Anapamu Street to State Street brings you to the imposing former post office that became the city's Museum of Art in 1941. Over the years it's been expanded to accommodate collections of Greek, Roman, and Egyptian antiquities, Oriental art and musical instruments, American and European paintings, and vintage dolls. Santa Barbara boasts dozens of art galleries, and several are clustered nearby in the attractive Spanish-tiled La Arcada, entered at 1114 State Street. If you feel like refreshments or some Mexican fare, take a table in the arcade's fountain patio, which is part of the Acapulco Restaurant and Cantina.

Detouring from the Red Tile Tour, walk a block north on State Street toward Victoria Street and the spire that marks the grand Arlington Theater, a classic 1930s movie house that is now used for the performing arts and first-run movies.

Back on the Red Tile Tour route, you'll see that the pedestrian is king in downtown Santa Barbara, especially along a seven-block section of the main thoroughfare, State Street. It was redesigned and landscaped with greenery, fountains, and benches to encourage promenading. After detouring on Carrillo Street to see a fully restored adobe built in 1826, continue south on State Street back to your tour starting point at El Paseo. Ardent shoppers who still have the energy should explore Paseo Nuevo, a distinctive two-block-square cluster of 60 shops and restaurants located between State and Chapela streets. It includes the upscale Nordstrom department store.

Downtown Santa Barbara is deserted on Sunday mornings, so it's a good time to relax at your bed-and-breakfast inn. Many restaurants, shops, and public attractions are open by noon, but save the afternoon between two and four to see two more historic homes and the types of transportation travelers used in Southern California before fast cars and freeways became part of the scene.

From downtown, drive southwest a few blocks to Castillo Street, turn left, and go under the freeway to Pershing Park and the Old Spanish Days Carriage Museum, where horse-drawn carts, carriages, and other vintage vehicles used by the area's early families and businesses have been restored and displayed. Every August they return to the streets in the fiesta parade; the rest of the year you can see them only at the museum on Sunday afternoons.

Inside this modern building are more than 40 shiny vehicles that seem to be waiting to be hitched to horses and loaded with passengers or cargo. Several are handsome black buggies, surreys, and hansom cabs. You'll also see an 1882 steam pumper fire engine that served in Los Angeles, as well as a mid-1800s funeral wagon complete with coffins. Look for the pioneer Conestoga wagons, early army wagons, and U.S. mail stages. There's an 1880s police paddy wagon, too. And don't miss the display of old and elegant saddles, worth $2 million.

Two blocks away you can visit two homes from the horse-and-buggy era, the Trussell-Winchester Adobe (1854) and the Fernald House (1878). Restored and maintained by the Santa Barbara Historical Society, both are open for escorted tours only on Sunday afternoons. From the carriage museum, walk or drive northwest on Castillo Street and turn left on West Montecito Street to the old adobe. Timbers in the house were salvaged from a side-wheeler, the *Winfield Scott,* wrecked off Anacapa Island in 1853.

The adobe was built by Captain Horatio Trussell, who came from Maine to California on the first steamboat to arrive in Santa Barbara. The cork oak tree in the front yard is an offshoot from acorns he brought with him. Later the house and property were bought by a local schoolteacher, Sara Winchester. Today the adobe is furnished with articles of the past century, including paintings, books, and china that belonged to the Trussell and Winchester families.

Walk behind the adobe to the Fernald House, a multigabled Victorian beauty that was moved here from its original site on Santa Barbara Street. On a tour of the 14-room mansion, you'll admire the carved staircase, doors, and wainscoting that was the exquisite work of a local cabinetmaker. The house was continuously occupied by Judge Fernald and his family for 80 years and has many original furnishings. The stained-glass window in the vestibule was given by the judge to his wife on their first wedding anniversary, in 1864.

Antique enthusiasts also will want to visit Brinkerhoff Avenue, a block of charming Victorian homes that now houses a wonderful assortment of antique shops. Head back on Castillo Street to Haley Street, then go right 2½ blocks to the residential avenue that was named for one of Santa Barbara's first physicians, Dr. S. B. Brinkerhoff. On both sides of the street you'll find antique items ranging from music boxes to teacups, and quilts to carousel animals. At the top of the block on the West Cota cross street is one of the most beautiful homes, now Redwood Antiques, with toys, fine crystal, and oak items.

If you feel like ending your weekend with a meal before heading home, head to 536 State Street for a very informal finale at a Santa Barbara food-and-drink institution, Joe's Cafe.

When you're ready for the drive back to Los Angeles, rejoin the U.S. 101 freeway south.

Round trip is about 215 miles.

Santa Barbara Area Code: 805

SIGHTSEEING *Santa Barbara County Courthouse,* 1100 Anacapa Street, Santa Barbara 93101, 962-6464. Open weekends and holidays 9 A.M. to 4:45 P.M.; weekdays 8:30 A.M. to 4:45 P.M. Free. Also, free guided tours Wednesdays and Fridays at 10:30 A.M., Tuesday through Saturday at 2 P.M. • *El Presidio de Santa Barbara State Historic Park,* 123 East Canon Perdido Street, Santa Barbara 93101, 966-9719. El Presidio archaeological site. The chapel, Padres' Quarters, and El Cuartel (the barracks) interiors are open daily 10:30 A.M. to 4:30 P.M. Free. • *Santa Barbara Historical Society Museum,* 136 East De la Guerra Street, Santa Barbara 93101, 966-1601. Open Tuesday through Saturday 10 A.M. to 5 P.M.; Sundays noon to 5 P.M. Free. Guided tours Wednesdays and weekends at 1:30 P.M.; $3 donation. • *Santa Barbara Museum of Art,* 1130 State Street, Santa Barbara 93101, 963-4364. Open Tuesday through Saturday 11 A.M. to 5 P.M., with Thursdays' hours extended to 9 P.M.; Sundays noon to 5 P.M. Adults $3, 6 to 16 years $1.50; free admission on Thursdays and the first Sunday of each month. • *Old Spanish Days Carriage Museum,* 129 Castillo Street (at Pershing Park), Santa Barbara 93101, 962-2353. Open 2 to 4 P.M. Sundays only. Free. • *Trussell-Winchester Adobe* and *Fernald House,* 414 West Montecito Street, Santa Barbara 93101, 966-1601. Open 2 to 4 P.M. Sundays only. Free admission to both houses, but donations appreciated. • *El Paseo,* can be entered from State, De la Guerra, and Anacapa streets, Santa Barbara, 965-0093. Stores open 10 A.M. to 5 P.M. Monday through Saturday; a few on Sunday. Also restaurant (see below). • *Brinkerhoff Avenue,* between Cota and Haley streets, Santa Barbara. The city's Antique Row, with most shops open every day except Mondays from 11 A.M. to 5 P.M. • *Pasea Nuevo,* State Street at De la Guerra, Santa Barbara 93101, 963-2202. Attractive downtown shopping complex. Open weekdays 10 A.M. to 9 P.M., Saturdays to 7 P.M., Sundays 11 A.M. to 6 P.M. Restaurants, too.

EVENTS   *Old Spanish Days Fiesta,* 962-8101, annual 5-day summer celebration of Santa Barbara's past starting first Wednesday in August. Historical and children's parades, variety shows, Spanish-style marketplace, and rodeo and horse show are highlights.

LODGING   Santa Barbara has a great variety of accommodations, including bed-and-breakfast inns that first appeared in 1980. Make reservations well in advance, because the number of B&B rooms is limited. Also ask the "house rules," which may include a 2-night stay on weekends, full prepayment, restricted smoking, and age limitations on younger guests. • *Old Yacht Club Inn,* 431 Corona del Mar, Santa Barbara 93103, 962-1277; $65–$135. Santa Barbara's first B&B, occupying a 1912 home that once served as a yacht club; 5 rooms, shared baths, full breakfast. Bicycles for guest use. Delicious Saturday night dinners cooked by innkeeper with advance notice. Also adjacent annex, *Hitchcock House,* with 4 more rooms. • *Glenborough Inn,* 1327 Bath Street, Santa Barbara 93101, 966-0589; $60–$155. B&B in 1906 home; 4 rooms, shared baths, breakfast served in bedrooms. Outdoor hot tub. Also 5 rooms and suites in 1880s cottage across the street. • *Bath Street Inn,* 1720 Bath Street, Santa Barbara 93101, 682-9680; $75–$125. 3-story B&B, built in 1895; 7 rooms with private bath. • *Bayberry Inn,* 111 West Valerio Street, Santa Barbara 93101, 682-3199; $85–$135. B&B, former 1904 boarding school for girls and later a sorority house; 8 rooms, 4 with fireplaces. • *Olive House,* 1604 Olive Street, Santa Barbara 93101, 962-4902; $80–$125. B&B in 1904 California Craftsman-style house; 6 rooms with private bath, full breakfast. Also, 3-room cottage with own kitchen and garden. • *The Parsonage,* 1600 Olive Street, Santa Barbara 93101, 962-9336; $85–$150. 1892 Victorian B&B, a former parsonage; 5 rooms and honeymoon suite. Full breakfast. • *Hotel Upham,* 1404 De la Vina, Santa Barbara 93101, 962-0058; $95–$165; suite to $295. Renovated old-fashioned hotel that's been welcoming guests since 1871; 49 rooms, continental breakfast included. Also popular restaurant (see below). • *Villa Rosa,* 15

Chapala Street, Santa Barbara 93101, 966-0851; $80–$190. Classy European-style inn with 18 rooms, all with private bath. Also pool and Jacuzzi in garden courtyard. ● *Cheshire Cat,* 36 West Valerio, Santa Barbara 93101, 569-1610; $109–$179. Two beautifully restored Victorian homes with 12 rooms.

DINING   *Wine Cask,* 813 Anacapa Street, Santa Barbara, 966-9463. Indoor or patio dining for lunch and dinner in El Paseo; extensive wine list. ● *Presidio Cafe,* 812 Anacapa Street, Santa Barbara, 966-2428. Opposite El Paseo in courtyard of historic El Presidio. Open daily for breakfast, lunch, and dinner (closed for dinner on Sundays and Mondays). ● *Acapulco Mexican Restaurant,* 1114 State Street (in La Arcada), Santa Barbara, 963-3469. Part of Acapulco dining chain but fountain patio gives a special touch. Margaritas and Mexican fare available daily from 11 A.M. to 10 P.M. ● *Louie's Restaurant* at the historic Hotel Upham (see above), 963-7003. Locally popular for lunch weekdays and dinner nightly. International menu. ● *Downey's,* 1305 State Street, Santa Barbara, 966-5006. Pricey, intimate downtown restaurant serving fine fare for lunch and dinner; closed Mondays. Menu changes daily. Reservations advised. ● *Joe's Cafe,* 536 State Street, Santa Barbara, 966-4638. Landmark eatery with big bar business too; known for steak, Italian food, and generous drinks.

FOR MORE INFORMATION   Contact the Santa Barbara Chamber of Commerce's Visitors Information Center, 1 Santa Barbara Street at Cabrillo Boulevard (two blocks east of Stearns Wharf), Santa Barbara 93103, 965-3021. Open every day. The chamber's Accommodations Directory includes listings of bed-and-breakfast inns.

Santa Barbara
Part 3: All Around the Town

While enjoying Santa Barbara's exciting waterfront and enchanting downtown, you'll undoubtedly discover that the city's pleasures extend to its beautiful environs, too. So plan a separate weekend for a scenic excursion in the Santa Ynez foothills and the Goleta and

Carpinteria valleys, which add special appeal to the Santa Barbara area.

There's plenty to see and do as you meander over the back roads that skirt the boundary of Los Padres National Forest and look out on the Pacific Ocean. Along the way are all sorts of treats: Santa Barbara's queenly mission, a botanical garden with native California flora, high-spirited polo matches, greenhouses bursting with orchids, and much more.

A one-of-a-kind resort, San Ysidro Ranch, is a rural retreat in neighboring Montecito that's just right for your holiday headquarters. Located on 525 hill-slope acres nudging the national forest, it seems more a private estate than a public guest ranch. Peace and quiet are bywords at San Ysidro, where overnight guests have been welcomed since 1893. You'll be accommodated in one of the 23 white cottages, named after the trees, shrubs, and flowers that isolate each lodging from the others. Over the years a number of famous folks have found tranquillity here, including writers such as Somerset Maugham, Sinclair Lewis, John Steinbeck, and even Winston Churchill, who often worked on his book manuscripts on the open porch of Magnolia House. Actor Ronald Colman was co-owner of the ranch from 1935 to 1958, and it became a haunt of film stars like Katharine Hepburn, Rex Harrison, and David Niven. This was also the spot Jackie and Jack Kennedy chose for their honeymoon. Children are welcome at the ranch, and family pets can come along too. Many guests explore the foothills on horses rented from San Ysidro's stables. You'll find tennis courts and a heated swimming pool as well.

Begin your weekend by driving north from Los Angeles on U.S. 101 to Montecito, the wealthy Santa Barbara suburb of impressive estates. Then take the San Ysidro Road exit toward the mountains and follow the discreet signs to the guest ranch. Excellent meals are served in its restaurant, which was a packing house in the early days when San Ysidro was a citrus ranch.

In the morning when you're ready for a picturesque excursion, go back to a foothill crossroad, California 192, and turn west toward Santa Barbara. It's called East Valley Road, but the name changes several times as you follow the twists and turns of this state route to Mission Canyon Road, part of Santa Barbara's official Scenic Drive. Turn north toward the mountains to reach the Santa Barbara Botanic Garden, a horticulturist's haven devoted to California plant life. Amble along the easy-to-walk nature trails that lead you through various botanical areas, such as the meadows that are set ablaze with wildflowers in springtime. One blossom you'll easily recognize is the brilliant Golden Poppy, the state flower. Another section, bordering the creek that flows through Mission Canyon, features California's famed redwoods.

Artists, photographers, and others in search of botanic beauty are drawn to the 76-acre garden throughout the year, but many time their visits for specific blooming seasons. For instance, from February through April you'll see California lilacs in every shade of blue, while cacti, yuccas, and other desert plants show off their flowers best in early summer.

More of Mother Nature's handiwork is on display back down Mission Canyon Road at the Santa Barbara Museum of Natural History, almost hidden in the oak trees; turn left on Las Encinas Road to Puesta del Sol Road. Housed in handsome 1920s Spanish-style buildings with red tile roofs are absorbing exhibits that range from marine life and minerals to bird life and botany. Especially fascinating is the preserved specimen of the endangered California condor that's suspended from the ceiling with its giant wings outstretched. There's a complete skeleton of a huge gray whale, too. Don't miss the California Indian Hall, with displays about the local Chumash tribes that greeted the first European explorers to the area. Watch one of the museum's planetarium shows if you have time, and take a peek at the seismograph to see how much the Santa Barbara area has been shaking lately.

An earthquake was responsible for the next attraction on your scenic itinerary: Mission Santa Barbara, an architectural beauty that's rightly called the Queen of the Missions. Founded in 1786 by Franciscan padres as the tenth in the chain of 21 California missions, its landmark twin towers and imposing stone facade were built after destructive temblors hit the area in 1812. Go down Mission Canyon Road and turn right on Laguna Street to this imposing mission, the fourth and final version erected on a magnificent site overlooking the city and the sea. The history and reconstructions of the mission, which still serves as a parish church, comes to life in the exhibits and old photos you'll see on a self-guided tour. Also on view are an early-day padre's bedroom and a kitchen complete with vintage furniture and utensils. Mission crafts and tools used by the Indian neophytes are among the displays in other museum rooms.

Be sure to see the sanctuary, the garden patio, and the walled cemetery with graves of Santa Barbara's pioneer families. In front of the mission stands a pretty fountain that overflowed into a stone trough where Indian women did laundry. Cross the road to a pleasant park, where you'll find remains of the innovative aqueduct that brought an abundance of water down the canyon to the mission.

Close by the mission you're certain to enjoy a leisurely lunch in El Encanto Hotel, with wonderful views of Santa Barbara below. Or return for dinner when the city's lights are aglow. By the way, this delightful hotel, with its cottages in a lush garden setting, is the place to stay if you prefer town to the more remote San Ysidro Ranch. Follow the city's Scenic Drive along Alameda Padre Serra and go left on Lasuen Road to El Encanto. Where Lasuen Road rejoins the Scenic Drive, you'll come to one of the three campuses of the Brooks Institute of Photography, home to a collection of photographic memorabilia from the early nineteenth century and changing exhibits of photographs.

Continue east on the Scenic Drive back to Montecito and Olive Mill Road, turning south to Coast Village Road which parallels U.S. 101. A right turn will take you to the popular Montecito Cafe for dinner. It's in the Montecito Inn, a historic hostelry that has been renovated and is another alternative for your weekend lodging.

On Sunday, plan to survey beautiful orchids, homes, and horses in the neighboring Goleta and Carpinteria valleys. Goleta is west of Santa Barbara, and you can arrive there most quickly by following U.S. 101 through the city. A more leisurely idea is to join the Scenic Drive at Olive Mill Road and follow it west along Santa Barbara's pleasurable waterfront. A block after Stearns Wharf, be sure to turn inland on Chapala Street to reach Montecito Street and an unbelievable Moreton Bay fig tree, one of the largest in the nation. Planted as a seedling by a pioneer family in 1877, the tree now has a trunk circumference of 35 feet and branches that spread so far, someone figured they could shade more than 10,000 people!

Continue west on Montecito Street, which becomes Cliff Drive and rejoins the Scenic Drive, eventually leading past resplendent homes in the rolling, wooded hills of the Hope Ranch residential area. The towering palms that line its main boulevard, Las Palmas Drive, were planted at the turn of the century.

Just beyond that luxurious community, leave the Scenic Drive route to take U.S. 101 west to Goleta. Exit south on Patterson Avenue and continue on Shoreline Drive, then go right on Orchid Drive. Turn left into the Santa Barbara Orchid Estate, where you'll encounter an amazing variety of orchids. Owner Anne Gripp caters to hobbyists seeking award-winning and exhibition-type plants. Since 1957 she and her staff have been breeding, propagating, and growing orchids of all types; their cymbidiums alone number over 950 varieties. A specialty is outdoor orchids that can live in coastal California. You're welcome to stroll on your own around this extensive nursery. Members of the staff will give you directions, or ask them for a brief tour. As a pretty remembrance of your visit, purchase a potted plant or just the orchid flowers.

If you adore old homes, return to U.S. 101 and continue west past the town of Goleta to the Los Carneros exit. Then go right to the fire station that marks the entrance road to the handsome and historic Stow House. To build this huge house back in 1872, lumber was unloaded from ships into the surf, then floated ashore and hauled a few miles inland to La Patera Ranch. That's where San Franciscan W. W. Stow had purchased over 1,000 acres of grazing land to create a showcase farm. Walnut and lemon trees eventually surrounded the impressive Stow House, which served as the family's home and farm headquarters for 95 years. Today it and the grounds have been preserved as a reminder of life in the area's early agricultural days.

You're welcome to tour the fully furnished home, a nearby blacksmith shop, and a century-old storehouse that's now a museum of farm and household implements and carriages. An addition to the property is Goleta's turn-of-the-century train depot, which was moved to the site and refurbished as a museum of railroad memorabilia.

If you fancy fine horses or want to feast your eyes on more orchids, head back east on U.S. 101 through Santa Barbara and Montecito to the Carpinteria Valley. Exit past Summerland at Santa Claus Lane, go under the freeway, then turn left on Via Real to Nidever Road and the polo field. As home for the prestigious Santa Barbara Polo and Racquet Club, it's the site of many local matches and international tournaments of this thrilling sport on horseback.

Some of the players who come from around the world bring their ponies with them. You'll marvel at the superb horsemanship as the players signal their mounts to race across the field, make quick turns, and stop abruptly as they maneuver the ball to the goal. Games are played most weekends during a six-month season, and you can watch from your car or the sidelines grandstand.

This sheltered coastal area also is ideal for growing cut flowers and ornamental potted plants, so you'll see acre upon acre of flower fields and nursery greenhouses. Just north of the polo field visitors are welcome at a major orchid grower, Stewart Orchids. One look at the breathtaking array of delicate plants and you'll be eager to buy some. Prices range from $15 up to $1,000 for very rare varieties.

Before heading home, it's fun to have dinner at the Big Yellow House in Summerland. Follow Via Real west to this family-style restaurant in a nineteenth-century Victorian mansion, a familiar landmark for travelers along U.S. 101.

Return to Los Angeles by taking U.S. 101 south.

Round trip is about 240 miles.

Santa Barbara Area Code: 805

SIGHTSEEING *Santa Barbara Botanic Garden,* 1212 Mission Canyon Road, Santa Barbara 93105, 682-4726. Open daily 8 A.M. to sunset. Free admission Tuesdays and Wednesdays; on other days, adults $3, ages 13 to 17 and seniors $2, children 5 to 12 years

$1. Guided tour daily at 10:30 A.M. and 2 P.M. Thursdays and weekends. • *Santa Barbara Museum of Natural History,* 2559 Puesta del Sol Road (off Mission Canyon Road), Santa Barbara 93105, 682-4711. Open daily 9 A.M. to 5 P.M., except Sundays and holidays from 10 A.M. Adults $3, ages 13 to 17 and senior citizens $2, children 12 years and under $1. Planetarium shows weekends only. • *Santa Barbara Mission,* upper end of Laguna Street, Santa Barbara 93105, 682-4713. Open daily 9 A.M. to 5 P.M. Adults $2, children under 12 years free. Self-guided tours of museum, garden, chapel, and cemetery. • *Brooks Institute of Photography* (Jefferson Campus), 1321 Alameda Padre Serra, Santa Barbara 93103, 966-3888. Open 8 A.M. to 5 P.M. weekdays. Photographic displays along building hallways. • *Santa Barbara Orchid Estate,* 1250 Orchid Drive, Goleta 93111, 967-1284. Open daily 8 A.M. to 5:30 P.M., except Sundays 10 A.M. to 4 P.M. Free. • *Stow House,* 304 Los Carneros Road, Goleta 93017, 964-4407. Open 2 to 4 P.M. weekends. Admission $1. Goleta railroad depot open 1 to 4 P.M. Wednesday through Sunday; free. • *Santa Barbara Polo and Racquet Club,* 3375 Foothill Road (or P.O. Box 1200), Carpinteria 93013, 684-8667 (for recorded information about upcoming matches) or 684-6683. Trophy matches played Sundays at 1 and 3 P.M. from April through October, weather permitting. Admission $6. Practice games Wednesdays, Fridays, and Saturdays are free. • *Stewart Orchids,* 3376 Foothill Road (or P.O. Box 385), Carpinteria 93013, 684-5448. Hours: daily 8 A.M. to 4 P.M., except Saturdays from 10 A.M. and Sundays from noon. Free.

EVENTS   *Santa Barbara International Orchid Show,* Earl Warren Showgrounds, U.S. 101 and Los Positas Road, Santa Barbara, 967-6331. Spectacular weekend event for orchid lovers every March. • *Santa Barbara National Horse Show,* Earl Warren Showgrounds, Santa Barbara, 687-0766. Annually in mid-July, one of the top five national horse shows.

LODGING   *San Ysidro Ranch,* 900 San Ysidro Lane, Montecito 93108, 969-5046. Double rooms from $195; cottage suites from $275 to $550 (with private Jacuzzi). Outdoor activities include guided trail rides on horseback; $50 weekends, $35 midweek. Also popular restaurant (see below). • *El Encanto Hotel and Garden Villas,* 1900 Lasuen Road, Santa Barbara 93103, 687-5000; $120 (to $280 for villas). Classy French-style country inn overlooking city. Also favorite cocktail and dining spot (see below). • *Montecito Inn,*

1295 Coast Village Road, Santa Barbara 93108, 969-7854; $105. Handsome 1920s hostelry restored and reopened in 1982.

DINING *The Stonehouse,* at San Ysidro Ranch (see above). Candlelight dining in rustic ranch setting. Fine American regional food. Also midday Sunday brunch, breakfast, and lunch daily. • *El Encanto,* in El Encanto Hotel and Garden Villas (see above). Savor French and American cuisine outdoors on the terrace or in the hotel's exquisite dining room. Excellent and expensive menu; jackets suggested at dinner. At least have a cocktail on the terrace to enjoy the spectacular view or in the romantic lounge by the fireplace. • *Montecito Cafe,* at the Montecito Inn (see above), 969-3392. A casually elegant cafe serving California cuisine for lunch and dinner. Open daily except Mondays; breakfast also available. • *The Big Yellow House,* 108 Pierpont Avenue, Summerland 93067, 969-4140. A family favorite for breakfast, lunch, and dinner. • *Ristorante Piatti,* 516 San Ysidro Road (at East Valley Road), Montecito, 969-7520. Open daily for pizza, pasta, seafood, veal. Indoor/outdoor dining.

FOR MORE INFORMATION Contact the Santa Barbara Chamber of Commerce's Visitors Information Center, 1 Santa Barbara Street at Cabrillo Boulevard (two blocks east of Stearns Wharf), Santa Barbara 93103, 965-3021. Open every day.

Adventuring in Ventura and Anacapa Island

Scores of travelers rush through Ventura on the U.S. 101 freeway without realizing that the city is an ideal destination for a weekend escape. Hugging a peaceful crescent of the Pacific coast just 60 miles northwest of Los Angeles, it has marvelous beaches and a busy pleasure-boat harbor. From there you can embark on a boating adventure to the Channel Islands, America's unique offshore national park.

A wonderful insight to early California history also is in store for visitors to Ventura, where the city's namesake—Mission San Buenaventura—celebrated its bicentennial in 1982. You even can view 3,500 years of history in one city block—an archaeological dig next to the mission has uncovered an aboriginal campsite that existed at the time the pharaohs were ruling Egypt.

To enjoy the beach, boating, and going back in time, drive north from Los Angeles on U.S. 101 to Ventura and exit toward the ocean on California Street, which takes you to the high-rise Holiday Inn on the beach. Ride the elevator to the hotel's twelfth-floor lounge to watch the sun slip into the ocean, and perhaps have dinner that night in the rooftop revolving restaurant. Not too far from the beach are alternative headquarters for your weekend—Harbortown Marina Resort, Pierpont Inn, Doubletree Hotel, or the Country Inn.

In the morning, walk along the oceanfront on Ventura's wide pedestrian Promenade, a modern "boardwalk" that leads to Surfer's Point, where you can watch acrobatic surfers ride the waves. Then stroll in the opposite direction to the Ventura Pier, one of the longest on the West Coast. Jutting into Pierpont Bay, the 1,700-foot pier was originally used by the railroad to transfer cargo to ships. After reconstruction in 1992–93 to repair winter storm damage, the pier is destined to become a favorite hangout for fishermen and a great place to walk for a view of the Pacific. You also can enjoy the ocean vista while feasting on a seafood lunch at the Pier Fish House. Plan to join the sunbathers, swimmers, and picnickers on San Buenaventura State Beach, which flanks the pier and runs several miles south to Ventura Harbor.

Devote part of the day to exploring Ventura's pleasant downtown and viewing its historical sites. From the beach, walk or drive two blocks north on California Street and go left on Main Street to the archaeological dig that's just beyond the mission. The area was being razed for new buildings in 1973 when local archaeologists got the city to halt the bulldozers so they could excavate. Among their surprising discoveries were the original mission church foundations, which had been abandoned, foundations of the adobe quarters for the mission's Indian neophytes, a 2,300-year-old earth oven, and a fire hearth dating to 1600 B.C. You'll get an overview of the excavated site from an elevated platform at the north end of the dig. Continue up the steps to a water-filtration structure at the end of a seven-mile aqueduct that the Indians built in the 1790s to bring water to the mission. Later the tiny building served as Ventura's first city jail.

Artifacts recovered from the dig are displayed in the Albinger Archaeological Museum on the site. You'll see animal bones from the earth ovens, some of the 44,500 Indian trading beads that were found, Mexican ceramics, Chinese opium pipes, and early American glassware. Don't miss the audiovisual program in the museum's theater, which spotlights some of the prize finds and puts three and a half millennia in perspective.

Cross the street to another treasure trove of yesteryear's relics, the handsome Ventura County Historical Museum. You'll learn more about the Indian, mission, and rancho periods, as well as the area's agricultural and oil-drilling activities. The excellent displays range from marine fossils to pioneer firearms and lifelike figures crafted by George S. Stuart of famous people through the ages.

Afterward, stroll a block down the street to Mission San Buenaventura. Ninth in California's chain of 21 Spanish missions, it was the last one founded by Father Junipero Serra before his death. You're welcome to explore the mission grounds and the church, where regular parish services are still held. Look for an ancient olive press in the courtyard garden.

A neighboring building on Main Street is the mission gift shop, which gives access to the mission, as well as to a small museum with more early-day articles. The collection features vestments of the Spanish padres, their European books, Chumash Indian baskets, a primitive confessional, and very rare wooden bells that once rang at the mission.

Outside, fountains bubble in Figueroa Plaza, a pedestrian mall that extends a block from the mission past the site of the city's former Chinatown to Santa Clara Street. There you'll find a renovated Victorian home, now the Seafood & Beverage Co., which is open for lunch and dinner. Opposite is the Clocktower Inn, a fire station that's been renovated as an impressive hotel and also has a window-view sidewalk museum with old-time apparatus and photos of Ventura's fire departments.

Continue walking eastward on Main Street to share more of Ventura's history. A number of the city's vintage buildings have become antique shops and are filled with furniture and other collectibles. Some serve as restaurants, such as an airy remodeled brick structure called Franky's Place. At California Street, turn left and head straight up the block to a Ventura landmark, the city hall, on Poli Street. It's a classic beaux arts building that was erected in 1912 as the Ventura County Court House. Weekday visitors can go inside to admire its Italian marble staircase, wood paneling, and stained-glass domes. In front is a statue of Father Serra.

Just west on Poli Street you'll spot the foreign flags that mark Ventura's best-known B&B, La Mer, a European-type inn with five bedrooms decorated in the styles of different nations. It's a delightful alternative for weekend lodgings, or go south from the city hall on California Street to stay in the 19-room Bella Maggiore Inn, a wonderfully remodeled 1926 hotel.

One of the area's oldest buildings you can visit is the Olivas Adobe southeast of downtown Ventura. Reach it by joining U.S. 101 and driving south to the Seaward Avenue exit. Continue south on Harbor Boulevard, skirting Ventura Harbor, then turn left on Olivas Park Drive and go past the golf course to the historic home.

One of the largest and finest adobes anywhere, its sun-baked mud and straw-brick walls are two feet thick. It was built by Don Raimundo Olivas, a wealthy rancher who needed plenty of room to raise his 22 children. Much of the money for construction of the splendid hacienda, which includes a chapel, came from the cattle Olivas drove north during the gold rush to feed hungry miners. The adobe has been completely restored and is furnished with antiques donated by the area's pioneer families.

Built beside the Santa Clara River, the Olivas home has a pleasant garden and walled patio and was frequently the site of festive weddings. An exhibit building has photos and artifacts depicting more of the rancho's history.

On your way back downtown, dine at Alexander's in the Harbortown Marina Resort off Harbor Boulevard, or at the Pierpont Inn off U.S. 101. Then get a good night's sleep, because you'll need to wake early for an adventurous day sailing the open seas and exploring Anacapa or one of the other Channel Islands.

Anacapa, Santa Cruz, Santa Rosa, San Miguel, and Santa Barbara islands make up the nation's fortieth national park. These five of the eight islands in the Channel Islands chain off the Southern California coast were designated the Channel Islands National Park by Congress in March 1980. (Not included in the park are well-known Santa Catalina and two islands controlled by the U.S. Navy, San Clemente and San Nicolas.) For decades the rugged islands have been havens for a host of animals, seabirds, plants, and marine life, and they'll continue as nature sanctuaries with limited recreational use. Anacapa and Santa Cruz are the most accessible of this quintet of islands, which can be visited by public boat transportation, charter excursions, or private vessels. (A trip by airplane can be made to Santa Rosa Island; see details in the ''Sightseeing'' section.)

The public boat trips begin at Ventura Harbor, headquarters for the Channel Islands National Park and the boat excursion company, Island Packers. Take Harbor Boulevard south and follow the signs that lead to Spinnaker Drive and the park's modern visitors center. From its observation tower you can glimpse the offshore islands and enjoy a panorama of the beautiful coast and harbor. In the main exhibit hall you'll see dioramas and maps of the islands, as well as illustrations and photographs of their animal and plant life. Well worth watching is a movie shown in the auditorium about the island chain. Kids especially enjoy the man-made tide pool with marine specimens.

Next door is the Anacapa boat departure dock, where you can board a modern diesel-powered vessel to cruise to either Anacapa or Santa Cruz Island. The Island Packers Company captain and crew double as naturalists, describing the marine life and evolution of the Channel Islands as you sail. En route you'll cross the busy Santa

Barbara shipping lane and catch glimpses of ocean oil well platforms. Watch for porpoises racing alongside your boat as well.

Most popular to visit is Anacapa, the island nearest to the mainland, just 11 miles south of Ventura. The crossing takes about 90 minutes, and then you'll be ferried to shore in order to explore the island on foot. Actually composed of three islets that stretch almost five miles, Anacapa is distinguished at its eastern end by Arch Rock, an outcropping with an opening cut through it by the ocean waves.

The most popular West Coast nesting spot for the once-endangered brown pelicans, Anacapa also is a favorite rookery of Western gulls. Bring binoculars to study all the birdlife, including cormorants, black oyster catchers, and scoter ducks.

While aboard the boat and ashore on the island, be on the lookout for sea lions, harbor seals, and sharks. In wintertime Anacapa is an outstanding place to observe California gray whales during their annual migration between the Bering Sea and the lagoons of Baja California.

Most times the boat anchors in a cove on East Anacapa and then you climb 154 stairs to the rolling plateau of the cliff-rimmed island. You may be greeted by a park ranger, the island's sole resident. There's a small visitors center, but the best way to become acquainted with Anacapa is by picking up the descriptive booklet that guides you along a 1½-mile nature trail. You'll see a churchlike building that camouflages redwood tanks holding the island's freshwater supply, which had been targets for lawless boaters with high-powered rifles. Most important of the man-made structures on Anacapa is an automated lighthouse that includes a piercing foghorn.

After time to stroll around the island top and enjoy a picnic lunch, visitors reboard the boat to cruise around the island for another look at its marine life. Also, in late summer the water is usually warm and clear enough for passengers to go swimming and snorkeling before recrossing the channel.

By late afternoon you'll arrive back in Ventura Harbor, tired but happy. Then it's time to rejoin U.S. 101 south for the return trip to Los Angeles.

Round trip is about 144 miles.

Ventura Area Code: 805

SIGHTSEEING *Albinger Archaeological Museum,* 113 East Main Street, Ventura 93001, 648-5823. Visitors center and dig open 10 A.M. to 4 P.M. daily except Mondays. Free. ● *Ventura County Historical Society Museum,* 100 East Main Street, Ventura 93001,

653-0323. Open daily from 10 A.M. to 5 P.M. except Mondays. Admission $2. ● *Mission San Buenaventura,* 211 East Main Street, Ventura 93001, 643-4318. Visitors welcome daily from 7 A.M. to 5 P.M. Enter mission museum through gift shop, 225 East Main Street. Daily hours 10 A.M. to 5 P.M., except Sundays to 4 P.M. Donation requested. ● *Olivas Adobe,* 4200 Olivas Park Drive, Ventura 93001, 644-4346. Grounds, gardens, and exhibits open daily 10 A.M. to 4 P.M., guided adobe tours weekends only, self-guided adobe tours any day except Mondays. Free. ● *Channel Islands National Park,* 1901 Spinnaker Drive, Ventura 93001, 644-8262. Visitors center open daily 8 A.M. to 5 P.M. Free. ● *Island Packers Cruises,* 1867 Spinnaker Drive (or P.O. Box 993), Ventura 93001, 642-1393 or 642-3370. All-day powerboat excursions depart year round to Anacapa Island on weekends and Mondays, Wednesdays, and Fridays at 8 or 9 A.M. Also Tuesday and Thursday trips in summer. Adult fare $37, children under 12 years $20. All-day excursions to Santa Cruz Island (Scorpion Ranch) depart year round on weekends. Also Wednesdays and Fridays in summer. Adults $49, children $32. ● *Channel Islands Aviation,* 305 Durley Avenue, Camarillo 93010, 987-1301. Offers 6-hour-long weekend trips via airplane to Santa Rosa Island for ranger-led vehicle tours and trail hikes. Departures at 9 and 10·30 A.M. from Camarillo Airport. Cost: $85, children 2 to 12 years $60; bring your own picnic lunch.

LODGING   *Holiday Inn,* 450 East Harbor Boulevard, Ventura 93001, 648-7731; $88. 225 rooms and suites at the beach; also revolving rooftop restaurant (see below). ● *Pierpont Inn,* 550 Sanjon Road, Ventura 93001, 643-6144; $68. Cottages available with fireplaces. Guests have tennis and racquetball privileges at nearby health club. Also, popular dining room (see below). ● *Clocktower Inn,* 181 E. Santa Clara Street, Ventura 93001, 652-0141; $70, continental breakfast included. Modern accommodations in former fire station. ● *Bella Maggiore Inn,* 67 S. California Street, Ventura 93001, 652-0277; $70. A 1926 downtown hotel reborn as an antique-filled 28-room B&B. ● *La Mer European Bed and Breakfast,* 411 Poli Street, Ventura 93001, 643-3600; $105. 1890s Cape Cod–style Victorian with 5 rooms featuring French, Norwegian, Austrian, English, or German decor. All with private bath. Big Bavarian breakfast included. ● *Harbortown Marina Resort,* 1050 Schooner Drive, Ventura 93001, 658-1212; $79. Modern resort with 160 rooms at Ventura Harbor; also waterfront dining (see below). ● *Doubletree Hotel,* 2055 Harbor Boulevard, Ventura 93001, 643-6000; $99. A block away from San Buenaventura State Beach. ●

Country Inn, 298 Chestnut Street, Ventura 93001, 653-1434 or toll-free (800) 447-3529; $89, full breakfast included. All mini-suites, some with fireplaces. Footbridge across freeway to beach.

DINING   *Top O'The Harbor* atop Holiday Inn (see above). Revolving 12th-floor restaurant open weekends for dinner from 5 P.M. Brunch on Sundays. ● *The Pier Fish House,* on Ventura Pier at 688 East Harbor Boulevard, Ventura, 643-4825. Open daily for ocean-view meals from 11 A.M. to 9 P.M. ● *Franky's Place,* 456 East Main Street, Ventura, 648-6282. Downtown spot for breakfast, lunch, and Sunday brunch. ● *Pierpont Inn,* dining room in the Pierpont Inn (see above). Three meals daily; continental menu with seafood and prime rib featured. Brunch on Sundays from 8 A.M. to 3 P.M. Dancing Thursday through Saturday, entertainment Monday through Wednesday. ● *Seafood & Beverage Co.,* 211 East Santa Clara Street, Ventura, 643-3264. Fresh seafood for dinner daily and lunch weekdays in restored Victorian home. ● *Alexander's* at Harbortown Marina Resort (see above). Seafood specialties, Sunday brunch, and piano bar, all with marina views.

FOR MORE INFORMATION   Contact the Ventura Visitor and Convention Bureau, 89-C South California Street, Ventura 93001, 648-2075. Visitors center open daily from 8:30 A.M. to 5 P.M. (from 10 A.M. weekends).

Seafaring Fun in Oxnard's Harbor and Port Hueneme

A New England fishing village may seem an apparition in agricultural Oxnard, but it's real enough. Wood saltbox buildings, a lighthouse, and fishing boats tied up to the pier are part of the nautical scenery you'll enjoy during a visit to Oxnard's pretty Channel Islands Harbor. This, one of the Southland's most pleasant harbors, offers boating, fishing, and shopping. You also find sandy beaches for sunbathing, a protected lagoon for swimming, green parks for picnicking, and plenty of ocean-fresh air. And it's home for a wonderful variety of restaurants, as well as deluxe accommodations on the waterfront. Make your weekend home at the Mandalay Beach Resort on the oceanfront, or the Casa Sirena

Marina Resort in the heart of the harbor, and settle down for a relaxing time at the water's edge amid the boats and the seabirds. You also can visit neighboring Port Hueneme with its own harbor, which hosts U.S. Navy ships and huge cargo vessels, and go inland to the historical sites of Oxnard.

Farming dominated the landscape at the turn of the century when four brothers by the name of Oxnard established a sugar beet business that put the city on the map. Soon after, Hollywood discovered the adjacent seashore, and movie idol Rudolph Valentino roamed across its sands in his 1921 classic *The Sheik*. Now Oxnard's official city boundaries extend to the ocean and include a pleasure-boat harbor that was dredged and dedicated in 1965.

A scenic way to reach Channel Islands Harbor in Ventura County is to drive west from Los Angeles on Interstate 10 to Santa Monica and pick up the Pacific Coast Highway, California 1. Follow it north along the shoreline past several state beaches and parks. The highway cuts inland beyond Point Mugu through some of the rich farmland that still surrounds Oxnard. Exit California 1 at Channel Islands Boulevard and follow it west through the ever-growing city to the harbor. Just past Fisherman's Wharf Village turn left on Peninsula Road to the Casa Sirena Marina Resort. Many of its balconied rooms overlook the harbor's boat slips, which are filled with 2,500 pleasure craft of all descriptions. For sunset cocktails, head to the hotel's popular rendezvous spot, the Guadalajara Lounge, then linger for a seafood feast or other dinner specialties at the Lobster Trap Restaurant. End the evening enjoying the music and entertainment in the lounge, where you're also welcome to dance.

If you decide to stay at Mandalay Beach Resort, Oxnard's only seaside lodging, continue west on Channel Islands Boulevard, bear right on Harbor Boulevard, and then turn left on Costa de Oro. You'll spot the Spanish-Colonial–style bell tower and huge stone fountain that marks the resort entrance. Lush garden courtyards surround low-profile stucco buildings with red tile roofs and all-suite accommodations. Guests enjoy a bedroom and separate parlor, two full baths, two TVs and telephones, a minirefrigerator, and a microwave oven. You can dine in style at the resort's Opus One restaurant, and top off the evening with musical entertainment in the Cabana Lounge.

Your coastal weekend can be as leisurely or as active as you wish. Both resorts have their own tennis courts, swimming pool, and Jacuzzis. You can rent a boat from Channel Islands Landing to go sailing for an hour or two or hop aboard a sportfishing vessel operated by CISCO (Channel Islands Sportfishing Center—Oxnard) for a day with rod and reel on the open sea. To enjoy the harbor's unhurried pace, ride around on the Harbor Hopper Ferry, an on-call water taxi. Then take a stroll along the boat docks and look for the old sailing-ship masts and lighthouse that mark Fisherman's Wharf at Channel Island Boulevard and Victoria Avenue. That's where you'll find the Ventura County Maritime Museum with models, artworks, and displays of new and old ships. In the shops of this mock New England village are shells, clothing, and all kinds of gifts.

You'll be tempted by seafood here too. The Oxnard Fisherman's Wharf Seafood Company is a fish market, and a restaurant that serves lunch and dinner. Or you can dine and observe the dockside scene from well-known Reuben's, a popular spot for Sunday brunch. Behind the seafood market you can watch the sea's bounty being unloaded from the fishing vessels, including spiny sea urchins with tasty eggs that are shipped to Japan. The wharf's lighthouse is really a storage house for ice, which is pumped underground through pneumatic hoses to the fishing boats that pull up to the pier.

Around the harbor are even more places to eat and drink while viewing the sleek sailboats and handsome yachts, such as the Left Bank, farther south on Victoria Avenue. Across the channel on Bluefin Circle off Harbor Boulevard are two other harbor-front restaurants, the Whale's Tail and Port Royal. Besides serving lunch and dinner, both feature Sunday brunch and have entertainment most nights.

Just south of Channel Islands Harbor beyond Silver Strand County Beach is a neighboring boat basin. Despite being the home of the only deep-water harbor between Los Angeles and San Francisco, Port Hueneme isn't on the tip of many travelers' tongues. Perhaps that's because the place has such a funny-sounding name: *WHY-nee-me*. It's a Chumash Indian word meaning "halfway" or "resting place," referring to the midpoint on the canoe trips the Indians made between their coastal villages at Ventura and Mugu. During World War II Hueneme became a major port for shipping supplies to U.S. forces in the Pacific. It carries on a military role today as home of four Naval Construction Battalions, better known as the Seabees.

To get to the port from Channel Islands Harbor you have to skirt the naval base on a roundabout route. Go east on Channel Islands Boulevard to Ventura Road, then head south to Hueneme Road, and turn back west to the Hueneme harbor. Prior to construction of a wharf in 1871, Ventura County's farmers shipped their crops by lightering them through the surf on small boats to seagoing vessels anchored offshore. Now huge cargo ships operate with ease from the deep-water harbor, handling bananas from Ecuador, cars from Japan, cattle from the Channel Islands, and supplies for the Southland's offshore oil rigs. Port Hueneme's busy docks are closed to the public, but you can reach several deep-sea fishing boats that take eager anglers out in the ocean to try their luck. All-day fishing excursions with Port

Hueneme Sportfishing depart from Dock 1; from Hueneme Road turn right at the 141 YARD sign just inside the port property.

A right turn from the port entrance brings you to Surfside Drive and attractive Port Hueneme Beach Park with a wide sandy beach and picnic areas. You can stroll out on the 1,200-foot wooden pier, a favorite of fishermen day and night. Nearby is Port Hueneme's nicest accommodation, the Country Inn.

On the way back to Oxnard and Channel Islands Harbor, stop by the impressive Seabee Museum inside the navy base. From Ventura Road, turn left at Sunkist Street to enter the U.S. Naval Construction Battalion Center. Get a base pass from the gate guard before proceeding to the museum parking area. You can't miss the big gun-toting bee, symbol of the Seabees, that marks the entrance to this military museum, one of the most notable in the nation. On display are artifacts and souvenirs from Southeast Asia, the South Pacific, Antarctica, and other duty areas of the navy's Civil Engineer Corps. Religious masks, ceremonial swords, and hunting implements are among the memorabilia collected abroad by the Seabees. Don't miss the gallery that displays the uniforms and weapons of U.S. and foreign forces. Dioramas of the Seabees' major construction feats also are featured.

If you want to glimpse a little more of inland Oxnard, continue north on Ventura Boulevard to 5th Street and turn right (east) to Plaza Park, in the heart of town. At the left-hand corner with C Street is an outstanding example of the Grecian style of architecture with Ionic and Corinthian columns, the former city library, now the Carnegie Arts Museum, a showcase for local painters, sculptors, potters, and other artists. Go across the street to Plaza Park for a close-up view of an Oxnard landmark, the 1910 bandstand that resembles a Japanese pagoda. Then walk a block down 5th Street to see the Bank of A. Levy, noted for its Italian Revival style of architecture. Look up at the high-relief classical heads above the arched windows. It was French-born grain merchant Achille Levy who bought beet seed for the area's pioneer farmers over a century ago. That was the beginning of Oxnard's prosperity, which in turn encouraged Levy to open his family-owned bank.

When your visit to Channel Islands Harbor and environs is over, journey back to Los Angeles by taking California 1 north through Oxnard to join the inland freeway U.S. 101.

Round trip is about 136 miles.

SIGHTSEEING　*Ventura County Maritime Museum,* 2731 South Victoria Avenue (in Fisherman's Wharf Village), Oxnard 93035, 984-6260. Maritime past, present, and future depicted with ship models and displays. Open 11 A.M. to 5 P.M. Thursday through

Monday. Adults $2, kids 5 to 12 years $1. • *Channel Islands Landing,* 3821 Victoria Avenue, Oxnard 93030, 985-6059. Sailboat rentals. Open daily. • *Harbor Hopper Ferry,* 3600 Harbor Boulevard, Suite 215B, Oxnard 93035, 985-4677. Water taxi around Channel Islands Harbor; call for pickup. Single ride $1, all-day pass $8; seniors half price, kids under 5 years free. • *CISCO, Channel Islands Sportfishing Center—Oxnard,* 4151 South Victoria Avenue, Oxnard 93035, 985-8511 or toll-free (800) 322-3474. Deep-sea fishing; all-day and ¾-day boats. Open 24 hours daily. • *Port Hueneme Sportfishing,* 301 West Hueneme Road, Port Hueneme 93041, 488-2212 or 488-4715. Deep-sea fishing. Open daily. • *Seabee Museum,* Naval Construction Battalion Center, via Ventura Gate off Ventura Road, Port Hueneme 93041, 982-5163. Open from 9 A.M. Saturdays, 12:30 P.M. Sundays, and 8 A.M. weekdays to 4:30 P.M. Free. • *Carnegie Art Museum,* 424 South C Street (at 5th Street), Oxnard 93030, 385-8157. Open 10 A.M. to 5 P.M. Thursday through Saturday, and Sundays from 1 P.M.; closed during exhibit changes. Free.

EVENTS *California Strawberry Festival,* a 2-day wingding on the third weekend in May at Channel Islands Harbor.

LODGING *Casa Sirena* (*Marina Resort*), 3605 Peninsula Road, Channel Islands Harbor, Oxnard 93035, 985-6311 or toll-free (800) 228-6026; $89. 273 rooms and suites; special weekend packages. Also popular restaurant (see below). • *Mandalay Beach Resort,* 2101 Mandalay Beach Road, Oxnard 93035, 984-2500 or toll-free (800) 582-3000; $144–$244. 250 suites along beachfront. Rates include full cooked-to-order breakfast and happy-hour cocktails; no charge for children 12 years and under. Also restaurant (see below). • *Country Inn at Port Hueneme,* 350 East Hueneme Road, Port Hueneme 93041, 986-5353; $89. 135 minisuites; complimentary breakfast and afternoon cocktails. • *Casa Via Mar Inn,* 337 West Channel Islands Boulevard, Port Hueneme 93041, 984-6222; $69. 1 mile east of the Channel Islands Harbor at Patterson Road. 74 units, some with kitchens. 6 tennis courts.

DINING *Lobster Trap,* at Casa Sirena (see above), 985-6361. Lunch and dinner daily; also breakfast and Sunday brunch. Musical entertainment at cocktail time and every evening. • *Opus One,* at Mandalay Beach Resort (see above). Continental cuisine in a garden setting. Lunch and dinner daily, plus an impressive champagne buffet on Sundays from 10:30 A.M. to 2:30 P.M. ● *Oxnard Fisherman's Wharf Seafood Company,* 3920 West Channel Islands Boulevard (in Fisherman's Wharf Village), 382-8171. Fresh-fish market, plus seafood restaurant with patio dining. ● *Reuben's,* 3910 West Channel Islands Boulevard (in Fisherman's Wharf Village), Oxnard, 985-3922. Three meals daily and Sunday brunch. ● *Whale's Tail,* 3950 Bluefin Circle, Oxnard, 985-2511. Lunch and dinner daily, champagne brunch on weekends. Fresh seafood and beef dishes. Upper deck area features shellfish bar, lounge, and entertainment. ● *Port Royal,* 3900 Bluefin Circle, Oxnard, 984-1919. Lunch and dinner daily except Mondays; Sunday champagne brunch. Fresh seafood, steaks, and flaming desserts. ● *Left Bank,* 4151 South Victoria Avenue, Oxnard, 985-5200. Cozy bar and restaurant featuring 30 entrées. Open daily for lunch and dinner; Sunday brunch.

FOR MORE INFORMATION   Contact the Oxnard Convention and Visitors Bureau, 400 Esplanade Drive, Suite 100, Oxnard 93030, 485-8833. Also Channel Islands Harbor Association, 3600 South Harbor Boulevard, Box 234, Oxnard 93035, 985-4852.

South Coastal
Outings

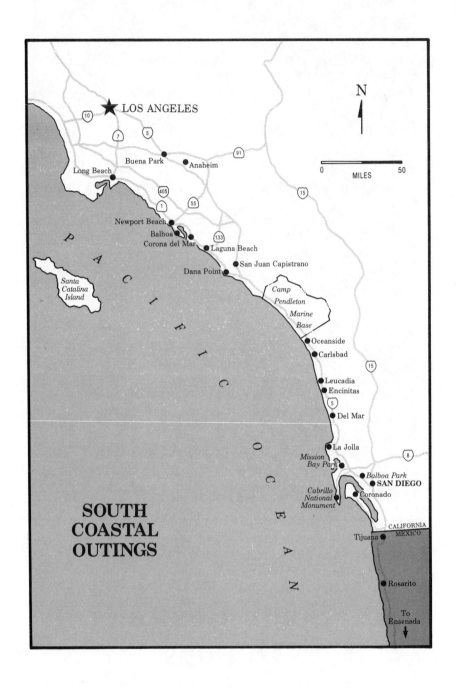

N

LOS ANGELES

⑩
⑦
⑤
91

Buena Park
Anaheim
Long Beach

0   MILES   50

405
⑮
① 55

Newport Beach
Balboa
133
Corona del Mar
Laguna Beach
San Juan Capistrano
Dana Point

P A C I F I C

Santa Catalina Island

Camp Pendleton Marine Base

Oceanside
Carlsbad

⑮

Leucadia
Encinitas

⑤

Del Mar

O

La Jolla

Mission Bay Park

⑧

Balboa Park
SAN DIEGO
Coronado

C

Cabrillo National Monument

E

A

SOUTH COASTAL OUTINGS

CALIFORNIA
MEXICO
Tijuana

N

Rosarito

To Ensenada

Catalina, the Island of Romance

Italy has its Isle of Capri, Greece its Mikonos, and Spain its Ibiza. California has Catalina. A weekend on Santa Catalina Island, as it's officially named, is a wonderful way to get off the mainland merry-go-round. Tensions of the big city fade away with the skyline as you cruise 22 miles across the ocean to tiny Avalon, the island's only town. As you ease into the pretty horseshoe-shaped harbor, Avalon almost seems to be a Hollywood set created for a 1940s movie. Many of the hotels, restaurants, and gift shops that line the bay and the hilly streets call to mind a resort town from an earlier era. Covering but one square mile and with only 3,000 year-round residents, Avalon is a small town in both size and flavor.

However, you won't be restless for something to do. Much of the action is along Crescent Avenue, a pedestrians-only street bordering the waterfront and Avalon's minuscule beach. Besides swimming and sunbathing, try your luck at fishing or go boating. Avalon also has tennis courts and a nine-hole golf course. Walking is the preferred way to explore this charming town, or you can rent a bicycle. And you can lope along some picturesque trails on horseback. There are myriad bus and boat tours of the island, which you can schedule at your own pace.

Settle in at one of the lodgings along the bay front, such as the remodeled Hotel Vista del Mar, where you can watch the colorful harbor scene from a balcony suite. Also on Crescent Avenue in the heart of things are the Pavilion Lodge, Hotel MacRae, and Villa Portofino. Catalina has three dozen other small hotels and B&Bs, including the Inn on Mt. Ada. Island dress is completely casual, so leave your elegant wear at home. Sometimes during your carefree weekend, have a drink or dine on delicious seafood at restaurants with breathtaking views of the bay, like Solomon's Landing, Armstrong's, Ristorante Villa Portofino, and Pirrone's.

One reason so many people escape to Catalina is its weather. Even when haze from autos or the atmosphere settles over Los Angeles, chances are the island is bathed by sunlight and ocean breezes. No wonder that Avalon's population often swells to 6,000 on summer days. On holiday weekends the invasion of visitors sometimes tops 10,000. Despite the seasonal crowds, Santa Catalina Island may be the most unspoiled part of Los Angeles County. Most of its 76 square miles have been privately owned and preserved, notably by the man who made chewing gum so popular, William

Wrigley, Jr. However, the Indians were here first (some Stone Age relics and more than 40 campsites have been discovered), and then European explorers claimed the island for the King of Spain in 1542. Pio Pico, the last Mexican governor of California, granted the land to its first American owner in 1846. Later, in the nineteenth century, brothers named Banning incorporated as the Santa Catalina Island Company and took possession. Wrigley's reign began in 1919, when he became the island company's major stockholder. The gum-making millionaire improved and promoted Avalon, but he kept most of the island off limits to the public, thus preserving its coastline and interior.

Fortunately, in 1975 a nonprofit foundation dedicated to continued protection of this land in its natural state gained title to 86 percent of the island. The Santa Catalina Island Conservancy shares use of the land with Los Angeles County for conservation and recreation. Cars are allowed in Avalon but not encouraged anywhere; auto access to the interior is controlled by electric gates, and a key to open these barriers costs residents $125 a year.

Nevertheless, visitors can see much of the island on a variety of guided tours. If you want to view land that's changed little since Spanish times, don't miss the Inland Motor Tour. You'll visit Wrigley's El Rancho Escondido, where handsome Arabian horses are still raised and trained, and the Old Eagle's Nest Stage Coach Stop, a resting place for early-day visitors. With luck you'll encounter some unexpected animals—wild boars and goats, mule deer, and even bison. About 400 buffalo roam around Catalina, a herd that originated in 1924, when the furry beasts were brought to the island by a movie crew. The half-day inland tour also takes you to isolated coves once frequented by pirates and smugglers and visits Catalina's mountaintop Airport-in-the-Sky.

Another way to enjoy Catalina is on a summer-season Coastal Cruise to Seal Rocks, which sails from Avalon to give visitors an offshore look at the island. Another summertime favorite is the Flying Fish Boat Tour offered in the evening. Powerful searchlights track schools of fish that skim across the water and sometimes even land in the excursion boat. You'll see some friendly seals as well.

Also in the summer, enjoy a Sunset Buffet Cruise aboard the *Phoenix*, a classic paddle wheeler built in Wilmington, California, half a century ago. With drinks from the deck bar and live musical entertainment, it's not surprising that passengers are happily engaged in a songfest when their cocktail-hour coast excursion boat returns to the dock in Avalon Bay. The *Phoenix* is a glass-bottomed boat, and during the day you can board her or other smaller vessels for an underwater look into Catalina's crystal-clear waters.

You have a choice of more tours on land too. The Avalon Scenic Tour takes you on a nine-mile excursion around the hills, valley, and beautiful bay of Avalon to view its major points of interest. On the Skyline Drive tour you'll head ten miles inland for a scenic look at the island's geography and native plant life. Some rare varieties you will see are Catalina ironwood, cherry and lilac trees, currant shrubs, and St. Catherine's Lace.

Visitors nostalgic for pre–World War II times should tour Catalina's landmark, the Casino, which Wrigley built for ballroom dancing, not gambling. The folks who attended dedication ceremonies in 1929 were thrilled by an immense motion picture theater, one of the first to be acoustically designed for the new "talkies." Samuel Goldwyn, Louis B. Mayer, Cecil B. DeMille, and other movie moguls used the casino's 1,200-seat theater to premier their latest sound films. And there was more. Above the theater is a dance floor unobstructed by support columns, which made it possible for as many as 3,000 dancers to swing to the sounds of the big bands. The Avalon Ballroom became well known when the music of Benny Goodman, Jan Garber, Kay Kyser, and other dance bands was broadcast across the nation from the Casino. After 50 years, the Casino continues to be Catalina's major entertainment center. Feature films are shown on weekends in winter, nightly in summer. And you can still hear some of the big bands, which are scheduled at various times throughout the year. From the balcony that surrounds the building you'll get picture-perfect views of Avalon and its bay. The Casino also houses the Catalina Island Museum, with a large collection of Indian relics. And take a look in the Casino's gallery at the work of local artists.

If you want to explore even more of the island, get aboard the Two Harbors excursion boat that leaves from Avalon. You'll cruise along the coast of Catalina to a favorite spot of filmmakers, where you can swim at the beach, hike the trails, enjoy a picnic, or eat and drink at Doug's Harbor Reef Restaurant.

Although you can fly by helicopter to Catalina, most visitors arrive by boat. Yachtsmen from everywhere tie up to buoys in Avalon's harbor, and daily cruise boats deposit passengers at the pier. The vessels of Catalina Cruises and Catalina Channel Express sail year round from the harbors at Long Beach and San Pedro. You also can cruise to Catalina from Newport Beach and San Diego. (Avalon also is a port of call for two cruise ships, the *Viking Serenade* and *Southward*, which make twice-weekly excursions from Los Angeles to Ensenada and Catalina.)

To reach the boat terminals at Long Beach, take the Long Beach Freeway (Interstate 710) south from Los Angeles to Long Beach. For Catalina Cruises, exit at Golden Shore (Downtown) and follow the Catalina signs to the harbor parking lot. For Catalina Channel Express, follow the freeway signs to the *Queen Mary*, and look for the Catalina signs. For departures from the Catalina boat terminal located under the Vincent Thomas Bridge in San Pedro, take the Harbor Freeway (Interstate 110) south from Los Angeles, exit at Harbor Boulevard, and follow the Catalina signs.

Round trip to the Catalina boat departure docks at San Pedro and Long Beach is about 48 miles. The cruise to the island takes from 1 to 1¾ hours.

Catalina Island Area Code: 310

PUBLIC TRANSPORTATION   Three companies offer boat service to Catalina Island from the Los Angeles area. Phone for departure times and reservations. • *Catalina Cruises,* 320 Golden Shore Boulevard, Long Beach 90802, toll-free (800) 888-5939. Year-round service on 700-passenger vessels to Avalon and/or Two Harbors from Catalina Landing, 320 Golden Shore Boulevard, in downtown Long Beach. 1¾-hour crossing. Minimum 2 trips daily; in summer, service increases to at least 5 trips every day. Round-trip tickets $28 adults, $18 children 2 to 11 years, $5 kids under age 2. • *Catalina Channel Express*, P.O. Box 1391, San Pedro 90733, 519-1212. Year-round daily service from Catalina Terminal in San Pedro and from near the bow of the *Queen Mary* in Long Beach to Avalon and Two Harbors. 55- to 350-passenger boats with airplane-type seats, cabin attendant service, and cocktails. 1-hour trip. Round-trip $34 for adults, $31 senior citizens, $25 children 2 to 11 years, $1.50 kids under age 2. • *Catalina Passenger Service*, 400 Main Street, Balboa 92661, (714) 673-5245. Service daily to Avalon from Balboa Pavilion in Newport Beach Harbor, except December 1–26 and Monday through Wednesday from December 27 until Easter week. Sleek 500-passenger catamaran makes crossing in 75 minutes, leaving Newport at 9 A.M. Round trip $28 for adults, $15 for children 12 years and under.

Also, helicopter service to Catalina is offered by two companies: *Helitrans*, 548-1314 or toll-free (800) 262-1472, and *Island Express*, 491-5550 or toll-free (800) 228-2566. Daily flights in jet helicopters from Long Beach and San Pedro to Avalon. Helitrans also has service from Los Angeles International and Orange Country airports.

SIGHTSEEING   Catalina Sightseeing Tours, Santa Catalina Island Company, P.O. Box 737, Avalon 90704, 510-2000, 510-2500, or toll-free (800) 428-2566, operates most of the island's guided tours. Tickets and schedules are available at the Visitors Information Center across from the Pleasure Pier on Crescent Avenue, Avalon. • *Inland Motor Tour* departs daily at 9 A.M., returns by 1 P.M. Adults $22, children 2 to 11 years $13. ● *Coastal Cruise to Seal Rocks*, a 1-hour boat tour, operates daily May through September. Adults $6, children $3.50. ● *Flying Fish Boat Tour* goes evenings only mid-May through September for 1 hour. Adults $6.50, children $4. ● *Sunset Buffet Cruise*, a 2-hour cocktail cruise aboard an authentic paddle wheeler, departs at 6 P.M. mid-May through September. Tickets $35, including buffet and open bar; kids 2 to 11 years $18. ● *Glass Bottom Boat* tours operate year round. 40-minute excursions. Adults $6, children $3.50. ● *Avalon Scenic Tour* lasts 50 minutes and covers the town's highlights. A good choice if your touring time is limited. Adults $6, children $3.50, all year. ● *Skyline Drive* is a 1¾-hour inland bus tour, by reservation only. Adults $11.50, children $8. ● *Casino Tour*, a 45-minute walking excursion. Adults $6.50, children $3.50. ● *Catalina Channel Express* (see Public Transportation above) also operates summertime boat service between Avalon and Two Harbors at the isthmus, where you can picnic, swim, and loll on the beach. Departs Avalon daily at 9:30 A.M. and 1:30 P.M. One-way fare is $12 for adults; children 2 to 11 years $9.25. ● *Catalina Island Museum* in the Casino on the bay front, Avalon, 510-2414. Open 10:30 A.M. to 4 P.M. daily, and also 7 to 9 P.M. May through October. Free. ● *Wrigley Memorial and Botanical Garden*, 1400 Avalon Canyon Road, Avalon, 510-2288. 38-acre garden with native plants. Open daily 8 A.M. to 5 P.M. Admission $1, under 12 years free. 2 miles from town; hourly tram service in summer. ● *Catalina Island Golf Club*, 100 Country Club Drive, Avalon, 510-0530. 9 holes, par 32, $10.

LODGING   2- or 3-night minimum stay required by some Avalon hotels on weekends and in summer season. Rates quoted below are for summer high season; subtract $5 to $30 in other seasons. ● *Hotel Vista Del Mar*, 417 Crescent Avenue (or P.O. Box 1979), Avalon 90704, 510-1452, $95–$165, balcony suites with double Jacuzzi $275. 15 rooms on bay front, most with fireplaces. Complimentary continental breakfast. ● *Hotel Metropole*, 205 Crescent Avenue (or P.O. Box 1900), Avalon 90704, 510-1884; $125. 47 modern rooms, some with gas fireplaces and whirlpool baths. ● *Villa Portofino Hotel*, 111 Crescent Avenue (or P.O. Box 127), Avalon 90704, 510-0555; $85. Overlooking the bay; 34 rooms. Also restaurant (see below). ● *Pavilion Lodge*, 513 Crescent Avenue (or P.O. Box 278), Avalon 90704, 599-1788; $99. 72 rooms across from bay-front beach. ● *The Inn on Mt. Ada*, Wrigley Terrace Drive (or P.O. Box 2560), Avalon 90704, 510-2030; $320–$590 year round. Former hillside home of William Wrigley, Jr., now operating as a deluxe country inn. 6 rooms with fireplaces; all meals included.

CAMPING   *Two Harbors Visitor Information and Reservation Center*, P.O. Box 5044, Two Harbors 90704, 510-2800. Handles reservations for Two Harbors and Parsons Landing campgrounds. For reservations at Avalon's Hermit Gulch and other island camp-grounds, contact Los Angeles Department of Parks and Recreation, P.O. Box 1133, Avalon 90704, 510-0688.

DINING   *El Galleon*, 411 Crescent Avenue, 510-1188. Seafood and steaks for lunch and dinner. • *Busy Bee*, 306 Crescent Avenue, Avalon, 510-1983. Year-round service on the bay. All meals. • *Ristorante Villa Portofino*, 111 Crescent Avenue, Avalon, 510-0508. Italian cuisine and seafood. Open all year for dinner only. • *Pirrone's*, 417 Crescent Avenue, Avalon, 510-0333. Italian dishes, seafood, steaks; Sunday brunch. • *Solomon's Landing*, in El Encanto Market Place, Marilla at Crescent Avenue, Avalon, 510-1474. Seafood and Mexican dishes. • *Armstrong's Fishmarket and Seafood Restaurant*, 306 Crescent Avenue, Avalon, 510-0113. Waterfront restaurant with seafood, charbroiled fish, and steaks. • *Doug's Harbor Reef and Saloon*, Two Harbors at the Isthmus, 510-0303. Breakfast, lunch and dinner; picnic boxes from the snack bar.

FOR MORE INFORMATION   Contact the Catalina Island Chamber of Commerce and Visitors Bureau, P.O. Box 217, Avalon 90704. Operates an easy-to-remember one-call-does-it-all number, 510-1520 (''five-ten-fifteen-twenty''), for lodging reservations and information about boat and air transportation and island tours. The office in Avalon is open daily on the green Pleasure Pier. Also contact the Visitor's Information Center on Crescent Avenue across from the Pleasure Pier, 510-2000, 510-2500, or toll-free (800) 428-2566.

Waterfront Treats in Long Beach

You don't have to go all the way to Venice, Italy, for a romantic ride in a gondola. A fleet of the man-powered boats plies the waterways of Naples, an attractive enclave on Alamitos Bay in Long Beach. With 5½ miles of sandy shoreline, the city is well named, and all along its wide waterfront visitors will discover a variety of aqua activities.

You can embark on tour boats to cruise busy San Pedro Bay amid pleasure craft, navy vessels, oil tankers, and container ships. Visitors can also make an excursion of the bay in a sea kayak, or see it all from the air on a thrilling two-passenger parasailing ride that lets you share the high-flying sights with a friend.

A harbor attraction you can't miss is the *Queen Mary*, once the world's longest ocean liner. On an opposite shore, it's fun to wander around Shoreline Village, a nautical-theme complex of shops and restaurants with a 1,700-boat marina. Inland, you'll be intrigued by two nineteenth-century Spanish ranchos that are open to visitors. Also go for a horse carriage ride in the beachfront neighborhoods of Belmont Shore, Naples, and the Alamitos Bay Peninsula. And walk around the downtown to view some of the restored historic edifices and brand-new buildings that have rejuvenated Long Beach and help make it such a pleasant city.

Long Beach offers a good choice of fine hotels, including the 542-room Hyatt Regency overlooking the waterfront. It's an ideal location for exploring the city, and easy to reach by driving south on Interstate 710, the Long Beach Freeway. Exit onto Shoreline Drive and follow it to Pine Avenue, then turn left. Nearby on a main downtown avenue, Ocean Boulevard, are other major hotels, including the Sheraton Long Beach, Ramada Renaissance, and World Trade Center Hilton.

The perfect introduction to the city's wonderful waterfront is to walk along the Promenade or ride a city shuttle to Shoreline Village, the Victorian-looking shopping and dining attraction that resembles a turn-of-the-century coastal village. It's neighbor to an aquatic park and a boat-filled marina, two other handsome additions to Long Beach's redeveloped bay front. From the landscaped walkways you'll have expansive views of the downtown skyline and picturesque harbor. The four tropical-looking islands you see are cleverly disguised oil wells that have been named in memory of astronauts Grissom, Chaffee, White, and Freeman, who lost their lives in America's space program. A special reason for visiting Shoreline Village is to ride its vintage carousel, a classic 1906 merry-go-round that takes you back to the days of oceanside amusement parks, like the former Long Beach Pike. Join the kids listening to the carousel's happy music while galloping along on its 62 hand-carved horses, camels, giraffes, and rams.

Shoreline Village is a departure point for a novel two-person parasail that offers bird's-eye views of the Long Beach coast. You and a companion can cruise 400 feet above the bay, tethered by a rope to a speeding boat. The parasailing apparatus allows passengers to fly away and return to the boat without touching the water or getting wet. A more sedate way to view the active harbor area is aboard one of the excursion boats that makes circle tours from Shoreline Village all around San Pedro Bay.

The cruises pass in the shadow of the *Queen Mary*, a luxury liner that was transformed into Long Beach's best-known tourist attraction after being permanently docked in the harbor in 1967. Unfortunately, at the time this book went to press, the fate of the grande dame of luxury ocean liners was in limbo because the management contract for its hotel, restaurants, and shipboard tours was ended in 1992 by the Walt Disney Company. In addition, an adjacent attraction was dismantled the same year and relocated in Oregon. It was the mammoth wooden *Spruce Goose*, the world's largest airplane, which was conceived, built, and flown only once by the eccentric billionaire Howard Hughes.

On a much smaller scale is the unusual enterprise of Michael O'Toole, who started offering gondola rides around the quiet canals in neighboring Naples in 1983. These days he operates a fleet of seven gondolas, all powered in the traditional manner by paddles and the muscle of gondoliers dressed in striped shirts and straw hats. Passengers may even be serenaded by an opera-singing boatman, but if the gondolier's voice isn't up to par, Pavarotti and other operatic stars provide the mood music from a cassette tape recorder. All cruises include cheese, salami, and bread, plus a silver wine bucket so you can bring your own champagne or other drinks for the romantic ride. It's no wonder more than 300 marriage proposals have been made during the gondola excursions.

Boat-minded visitors who would rather do their own paddling can rent a kayak to explore the Naples canals and Los Alamitos Bay. Novices can take an introductory class in kayaking, which ends with a paddling trip to a blue heron sanctuary in a protected estuary. For landlubbers who want a leisurely tour of the waterfront neighborhoods of Long Beach, hire an open-air horse-drawn carriage to clip-clop along the scenic streets.

The importance of horses in the area's early days comes to life when you head inland in your car to a pair of historic Spanish ranchos that have been restored and opened to the public. A few acres of two vast land grants, Rancho Los Alamitos and Rancho Los Cerritos, have been preserved with their adobe homes and gardens intact. They're sanctuaries from an earlier era when vast cattle herds grazed on the undeveloped land that's since become the L.A. megalopolis.

To reach them from Shoreline Village or downtown Long Beach, drive back north on the Long Beach Freeway (Interstate 710) and exit east on Del Amo Boulevard. Turn right on Long Beach Boulevard to San Antonio Drive, right again to Virginia Avenue, and another right to reach Rancho Los Cerritos. Surrounded by a private country club and golf course in a residential area, the rancho has been reduced to 5 of its original 27,000 acres and is now a national historic landmark. Tour the handsome two-story ranch house, made of adobe with redwood support beam shipped down the coast from Monterey. It was built in 1844 by Los Angeles merchant Jonathan Temple, who also developed one of California's first formal gardens. Look for some of the Italian cypress, black locust, and pomegranate trees he planted more than a century ago.

Head next to Rancho Los Alamitos. Go back to Long Beach Boulevard, turn right to the San Diego Freeway (Interstate 405), and follow it south about five miles to the Palo Verde Avenue exit. Continue south on Palo Verde to the guard gate, ask for a pass, then go up the hill to Bixby Hill Road and the rancho office. Volunteer guides take you back to yesteryear on a tour of the rambling ranch house, a complete blacksmith shop, and dairy and horse barns with equipment and displays. The adobe home was built in 1806 by the son of the Spanish land-grant holder, and eventually a series of owners renovated the house and expanded it to 19 rooms. Among the vintage furnishings is an extensive collection of American glassware. You'll also enjoy a walk in the extensive gardens. Some sections are formal, while others grow rather wild; be certain to see the area devoted to succulents and native California plants.

When your weekend shore excursions are over, return to Interstate 405 and go west to join the Harbor Freeway (Interstate 110) and head north to Los Angeles.

Round trip is 68 miles.

Long Beach Area Code: 310

SIGHTSEEING *Shoreline Village,* off Shoreline Drive, Long Beach 90802, 590-8427. 30 specialty shops open daily where you can buy everything from kites to yachts; also 8 dining spots and antique carousel ($.75 a ride). • *Shoreline Village Cruises*, 429 Shoreline Drive, Suite N, Long Beach 90802, 495-5884. 95-minute circle cruises of the Long Beach and San Pedro harbors offered daily in summer from dock by Parkers' Lighthouse restaurant in Shoreline Village. Adults $10, children $5, under 12 years free. Call for departure times. • *Express Bay Cruises*, depart from Shoreline Village and the dock near the bow of the *Queen Mary*, 519-1212. 30-minute excursions of Long beach waterfront Fridays and weekends at 1, 2, and 4 P.M. Adults $4.50, children 2 to 11 years $3. • *Skyrider Parasailing*, 407 Shoreline Drive, Long Beach 90802, 493-4979. 10-minute minimum parasail rides along the Long Beach waterfront, $38 per person. 2 riders per parasail ascension, with up to 6 riders in the boat; outing may last up to 1 hour. Departures from 1 P.M. until dusk from Shoreline Village, and from 9 A.M. until noon from Seaport Village, 150 Marina Drive. Reservations requested. • *Gondola Getaway*, 5437 East Ocean Boulevard, Long Beach 90803, 433-9595. 1-hour Italian-style gondola cruises through canals of Naples. Hors d'oeuvres provided; bring your own beverages. $50 first couple, $10 each additional person, up to 6 passengers. Open 10 A.M. to midnight year round. Make reservations and get directions to the departure dock. • *Long Beach Water Sports*, 730 East 4th Street, Long Beach 90802, 432-0187. Kayaks for rent in Alamitos Bay. Also half-day introductory kayak classes given Saturdays at 9 A.M. and 1 P.M.; $55 per person, including equipment. Call for more details and meeting place. • *Oceanside Carriages*, depart from corner of 2nd Street and Corona Road in Belmont Shore, 434-7665. One-horse Amish-built carriages leave every half hour Thursday through Sunday. 30-minute ride with 2 to 4 persons, $50; 5 to 6 persons $25. 1-hour ride $40 or $50, depending on the number of passengers. • *Rancho Los Cerritos*, 4600 Virginia Road, Long Beach 90807, 424-9423. Open Wednesday through Sunday 1 to 5 P.M., except holidays. Free. • *Rancho Los Alamitos*, 6400 Bixby Hill Road, Long Beach 90815, 431-3541. Open Wednesday through Sunday from 1 to 5 P.M., except holidays. Free. 60-minute guided tours of adobe ranch house, barns, and blacksmith shop.

EVENTS   *Toyota Grand Prix of Long Beach*, ticket hotline 436-9953. Annual April weekend of premier auto racing on downtown waterfront streets.

LODGING   *Hyatt Regency Long Beach*, Shoreline Drive at Pine Avenue, Long Beach 90802, 491-1234; $120. Grand 16-story hotel overlooking downtown bay front with its aquatic park, marina, and Shoreline Village. 522 rooms and 20 suites, plus gourmet dining room with view of waterfront. • *Ramada Renaissance Hotel*, 111 East Ocean Boulevard, Long Beach 90802, 437-5900; $135. Harborview high rise with 391 rooms and suites, 3 restaurants. • *Sheraton Long Beach*, 333 East Ocean Boulevard, Long Beach 90802, 436-3000; $140. 16-story convention hotel with bay views and 462 rooms and suites. • *World Trade Center Hilton Hotel*, Two World Trade Center, Long Beach 90831, 983-3400; $140. 15-story, 397-room lodging on Ocean Boulevard at Golden Shore Drive. Health club and restaurant. • *Travelodge Hotel Resort and Marina*, 700

Queensway Drive, Long Beach 90802, 435-7676; $78. Half mile from *Queen Mary* on causeway to Pier J. 192 rooms with bay and marina views. Also tennis, jogging path, and restaurant.

DINING *Beacon Restaurant*, in the Hyatt Regency Hotel (see above). Seafood, veal, pasta, and steaks are specialties in this formal dining room of the harbor-view hotel. Lunch weekdays, dinner nightly, and Sunday brunch. ● *Parkers' Lighthouse*, 435 Shoreline Village Drive, Long Beach, 432-6500. Best restaurant in Shoreline Village. Mesquite-broiled seafood. ● *Mardi Gras,* in Shoreline Village, Long Beach, 432-2900. Mexican grill specialties. Open for lunch and dinner daily. Harbor views. ● *Cannon's,* 600 Queensway Drive, Long Beach, 436-2247. Lunch and dinner overlooking Queensway Bay; also Sunday brunch. ● *The Reef*, 880 Harbor Scenic Drive, Long Beach, 435-7096. Also at the water's edge. Lunch, dinner, and Sunday brunch amid nautical decor. ● *555 East Restaurant*, 555 East Ocean Boulevard, Long Beach, 437-0626. New York–style bar and grill; local gathering spot for food and drink. ● *L'Opera Ristorante*, 101 Pine Avenue, Long Beach, 491-0066. Classic and modern Italian cuisine, fresh fish. Downtown location. Open weekdays for lunch, nightly for dinner. ● *Pine Avenue Fish House*, 100 West Broadway at Pine Avenue, Long Beach, 432-7463. Traditional seafood house with many varieties of fish; also oyster bar. Downtown. Open weekdays for lunch, nightly for dinner, plus breakfast on weekends. ● *Mum's Restaurant and Grille*, 144 Pine Avenue at Broadway, Long Beach, 437-7700. Specialty pizzas, pasta, northern Italian dishes, and American fare. Downtown. Open weekdays for lunch, nightly for dinner. ● *Belmont Brewing Company*, 25 39th Place, Belmont Shore, 433-3891. Bay-front restaurant featuring own beer. Breakfast, lunch, and dinner daily. ● *Legends*, 5236 East 2nd Street, Belmont Shore, 433-5743. This popular sports bar is well named; it has become one itself. Burgers, chili, buffalo wings from lunchtime to the wee hours. Breakfast on weekends. ● *Shenandoah Cafe*, 4722 East 2nd Street, Belmont Shore, 434-3469. Known for its Southern hospitality and home-cooked meals. You'll love the hot apple fritters. Open for dinner only.

FOR MORE INFORMATION Contact the Long Beach Area Convention and Visitors Council, One World Trade Center, Suite 300, Long Beach 90831, 436-3645 or toll-free (800) 452-7829. Open daily 9 A.M. to 5 P.M., except Sundays from 10 A.M. to 3 P.M.

Seaside Delights at Newport Beach and Balboa Island

One of the Southland's most attractive and affluent coastal communities, Newport Beach, has long been a glorious getaway. It began soon after the turn of the century when the Pacific Electric Railroad's big red cars began whisking pleasure seekers and potential land buyers from Los Angeles to a beautiful stretch of beach in the neighboring county that was better known for its oranges and other agriculture. Since then Newport Beach has become Orange County's seaside showplace, where residents and visitors alike are drawn by a plethora of popular pastimes that include sailing, shopping, and dining.

Water dominates Newport life, beginning with several miles of ocean surf that lap onto a broad sandy beach extending southwest along a finger of land known as the Newport and Balboa Peninsula. At its end an inlet from the Pacific leads to Newport's boat-filled harbor, where palatial homes and cozy cottages cover eight odd-sized islands, including well-known Balboa. Inland the ocean tides have created an estuary, Upper Newport Bay, that is both a wildlife preserve and a picturesque setting for handsome homes clustered around its bluff-top perimeter. And south beyond the harbor inlet is a popular beach park and peaceful residential community, Corona del Mar, also within the boundaries of Newport Beach.

While this water-oriented resort area has been spared high-rise hotels along its beach, you can still enjoy ocean vistas and spectacular sunsets by checking into luxurious hilltop accommodations at the Newport Beach Marriott Hotel and Tennis Club or its exclusive neighbor overlooking Newport Bay, the Hyatt Newporter. Either one can be reached easily from Los Angeles by driving south on Interstate 5 and California 55 toward Newport Beach and exiting onto the partially completed Corona del Mar Freeway, California 73. Then exit south (right) on Jamboree Road and head toward the ocean to the landmark Fashion Island and Newport Center shopping and business complexes. Turn left on Santa Barbara Drive to Newport Center Drive and the Marriott, or continue on Jamboree Boulevard and turn right to the Hyatt Newporter.

These hotels offer enough temptations to make weekend escapes in themselves. Each has fine restaurants, lounges with entertainment, guest privileges at championship golf courses, and tennis courts, and short shuttles to wonderful shopping in stores such as Neiman-Marcus. But to really experience Newport Beach, you must get to the water. Drive down Jamboree Boulevard to Pacific Coast High way, California 1, then turn right to reach Newport Boulevard going to the peninsula, which is flanked by the ocean and Newport Harbor.

Make your first stop Lido Marina Village, just beyond the overpass bridge that crosses the coast highway and a finger of Newport Bay. Turn left from Newport Boulevard on Via Lido to the attractive shopping village's parking structure, then stroll along red brick streets and pathways leading to high-fashion boutiques, art galleries, and specialty shops. Along the village's waterfront, where boats bob in their slips and cruise in the bay, relax with a snack on the boardwalk or have lunch in the Warehouse Restaurant.

From Lido Marina Village, walk or drive southeast along Via Lido and veer right on Lafayette Avenue to a district known as Cannery Village. When fishing was a major industry in Newport Beach, the canneries here operated around the clock. Although the fish-canning factories no longer exist, much of their original equipment can be seen in the Cannery Restaurant, a scenic place for drinks, a meal, or Sunday brunch. Another popular dining spot is Delaney's on the other side of the channel, where commercial fishing boats still tie up. Across the street on Lido Park Drive is the 30-room Little Inn on the Bay, an attractive alternative for weekend lodgings.

Between Lafayette Avenue and Newport Boulevard, explore the historic Cannery Village district from 22nd to 28th streets. Besides boat-related businesses, such as sail makers and marine-hardware dealers, you'll find a variety of gift shops, art galleries, and restaurants.

Not much farther south along Newport Boulevard are other casual places to drink and dine that also are favorites of Newport Beach people. Woody's Wharf is on the bay and has its own dock to lure hungry and thirsty boaters. And you can't miss The Crab Cooker, always crowded with seafarers and landlubbers.

For a look at the West Coast's only remaining dory fishing fleet, continue driving along the peninsula on Newport Boulevard—which becomes Balboa Boulevard—and turn right on 20th Street at the signs to Newport Pier and the business district. Park where you can, then walk to the north side of the pier to find colorful open wooden boats called dories.

Since 1891 Newport fishermen have been putting to sea in such boats every day before dawn. If you're early enough (about 7 A.M.), you can watch the returning fishermen haul their vessels onto the beach. Weighing scales and cutting boards have been set up in old dories, where the day's catch is offered for sale. Depending on the season, the dorymen bring in sea trout, red snapper, kingfish, flounder, crab, and lobster. Among the first customers at this unusual open-air fish market are the chefs from local restaurants. Across the street is a namesake B&B, the Doryman's Inn, as well as the classy 21 Oceanfront restaurant.

You can do your own fishing, without a license, from the adjacent Newport Pier, which juts into the Pacific. Rent a rod and reel from Baldy's tackle and bait shop at the foot of this 1940s wooden pier, which replaced one built in the previous century to offload supplies from coastal merchant vessels.

If you drive two miles farther along the peninsula and turn right at the signs to municipal parking lots on the beach, you'll spot the historic Balboa Pier, site of the first water-to-water aircraft flight in 1912. That's when Glenn Martin flew his seaplane from Balboa to Catalina Island, which was also the longest and fastest flight over water at the time. At the pier's end is Ruby's, a popular 1940s-style cafe. Walk back past the vintage but remodeled Balboa Inn, then cross Balboa Boulevard to the harbor and its 1906 Victorian-style landmark, the Balboa Pavilion. There you can board a harbor cruise boat, the *Pavilion Queen* or *Showboat*, for a narrated tour of Newport Bay. As home port for 10,000 pleasure boats of all descriptions, from rubber rafts to million-dollar yachts, the long and sheltered harbor is one of the busiest and most picturesque anywhere on the Pacific Coast. You'll also see some expensive waterfront homes, including those of the late John Wayne and "King" Gillette of safety-razor fame.

If you'd rather be at the helm when you cruise in the bay, small sailboats and skiffs with motors are moored near the Balboa Pavilion and can be rented by the hour or longer. Party sportfishing boats also sail from there for deep-sea fishing excursions that last half a day or longer. The same docks are the departure points for the Catalina Flyer, Newport's passenger service to Catalina Island, and winter whale-watching cruises.

View the bay from the seat of a four-story Ferris wheel or take a musical whirl on a merry-go-round, two carnival rides that have been part of the Balboa Fun Zone and a neighbor to the Balboa Pavilion since 1936. The modernized amusement center also boasts video arcades, souvenir stores, and food shops. Upstairs tables at a pair of adjacent restaurants, Parker's Seafood Grill and Newport Landing, offer views of the beautiful bay too.

A must for all visitors is to sail across the harbor on one of California's few remaining ferryboats. The three-car ferries make the trip to and from Balboa Island in minutes. The quick toll trips have been operating since 1919, when the island's residents (who numbered just 26 back then) petitioned for ferry service. Once you're on Balboa, sidewalks along the bay front offer a good look at the handsome boats and a peek into the harborview homes. Along Marine Avenue you'll find a number of gift stores and snack shops, including one that sells Balboa Island's own tasty invention, a frozen banana dipped in melted chocolate.

Of course, you should plan some time during the weekend to loll at the seashore. Join the sunbathers, swimmers, and surfers who fill up the four miles of white sand beaches stretching along the peninsula and also Corona del Mar State and City Beach just south across the harbor inlet. If it's midsummer, however, be warned that the population of Newport Beach multiplies into a traffic nightmare of 100,000 vacationers and residents; in the off-season months the scene is much more relaxing.

On Sunday, have breakfast at the Irvine Ranch Farmers Market, a novel grocery and food emporium in the Atrium Court at Newport Center Fashion Island. Then, if you prefer a peaceful alternative to Newport's seaside action, set your sights on a pair of delightful gardens nearby in Corona del Mar. From the Newport Beach Marriott or the Hyatt Newporter hotels, take Jamboree Boulevard north to San Joaquin Hills Road and go east to MacArthur Boulevard. Cross the highway, where you'll see "Roger's" spelled in flowers on the corner, and look for the entrance sign to Roger's Gardens. This flower-filled nursery unabashedly bills itself as America's most beautiful garden center, and few visitors dispute that claim after strolling amid the stunning displays of more than 50,000 plants. You'll also discover that this seven-acre attraction is more than a botanical haven. Weekend demonstrations give visitors step-by-step instructions for creating attractive hanging baskets, a Roger's Gardens specialty, and a professional "plant doctor" is on hand to offer advice for your ailing plants. You'll also find florists ready to make custom cut-flower arrangements, a library with all sorts of gardening books, patio furniture and accessories in outdoor settings, and even antiques and artwork for other home decorating ideas.

After visiting Roger's Gardens, return to MacArthur Boulevard and continue south toward the ocean to the Coast Highway. Turn left and go 1½ blocks to Corona del Mar's other botanical showplace, Sherman Library and Gardens. Hidden by the inconspicuous blue-gray slat fence and covering an entire city block is one of the Southland's most beautiful floral sanctuaries. Turn right on Dahlia or Fernleaf Avenue to reach the free parking lot behind the gardens.

Over 850 botanical species grow in the immaculate two-acre compound, ranging from tropical and seasonal flowering plants to rare cacti and succulents. Be sure to enter the temperature-controlled conservatory, where you're surrounded by a world of greenery and flowers that includes orchids, staghorn ferns, carnivorous plants, and anthuriums. Elsewhere in the garden you'll find an enticing shop with flower books, plants, pots, and gifts for sale.

If you get hungry before ending your weekend at Newport Beach, enjoy a meal in one of the charming Corona del Mar restaurants located along the Coast Highway, such as Rothchild's, Trees, or the Five Crowns. After dinner, go north on California 73 (MacArthur Boulevard), which becomes a freeway and intersects with California 55 to join Interstate 5 back to Los Angeles.

Round trip is about 110 miles.

Newport Beach Area Code: 714

SIGHTSEEING   *Pavilion Queen*, 400 Main Street at the Balboa Pavilion, Balboa 92661, 673-5245. Narrated cruises of Newport Bay on a double-deck excursion boat depart daily on the half hour from 10 A.M. through 7 P.M. in summer and 2 or 3 times daily in winter. 45-minute trips cost adults $6, children $1; 90-minute excursions are $8 adults, $1 children. Brunch cruises on weekends at 10:30 A.M. are $28, children 10 years and under $15. • *Newport Harbor Showboat Cruises*, operated by the Fun Zone Boat Company, 700 Edgewater Avenue, Balboa 92661, 673-0240. The *Showboat* departs from the foot of Washington Street, between the Balboa Pavilion and the peninsula ferryboat landing. 45-minute harbor excursions leave daily on the hour from noon to 6 P.M. in summer, and from 11 A.M. to 3 P.M. in winter. Adults $6, children 5 to 12 years $1. 90-minute bay cruises depart daily on the hour from 11 A.M. to 7 P.M. in summer, at 11 A.M. and 3 P.M. in winter. Adults $7, children $1. • *Davey's Locker*, 400 Main Street at the Balboa Pavilion, Balboa 92661, 673-1434. Half-day sportfishing trips depart daily at 6 A.M. and 12:30 P.M. year round, plus 6 P.M. twilight trips in summer. Adults $20, children 12 years and under $12. Also all-day and ¾-day deep-sea fishing excursions, including shark hunts. • *Newport Landing Sportfishing*, 503 E. Edgewater Avenue at the Balboa ferryboat landing, Balboa 92661, 675-0550. Half-day fishing trips depart at 6 A.M. and 12:30 P.M. Adults $20, children $12. Also all-day angling excursions to Catalina and San Clemente islands. • *Balboa Ferry*, cross Newport Bay from the end of Palm Street on the Balboa Peninsula to Agate Avenue on Balboa Island. Operates day and night during summer, early morning until midnight the rest of the year. Car and driver pay $.65, passengers and pedestrians $.25 each way. • *Corona del Mar State and City Beach*, off Ocean Boulevard, Corona del Mar 92625, 644-3044. Municipally operated beach park open daily from 8 A.M. to 10 P.M. Parking fee $5 in summer, $3 in winter. Volleyball, fire rings, and snack bar. • *Roger's Gardens*, 2301 San Joaquin Hills Road, Corona del Mar 92625, 640-5800. Open daily from 9 A.M. to 6 P.M. Free. Hanging-basket demonstrations year round on weekends at 1 and 3 P.M. •

Sherman Library and Gardens, 2647 East Coast Highway, Corona del Mar 92625, 673-2261. Open daily from 10:30 A.M. to 4 P.M. Adults $2, children 12 to 16 years $1; free admission on Mondays.

EVENTS *Festival of Lights Boat Parade*, a grand parade of yachts and sailboats festooned with holiday lights and decorations, cruises around Newport Harbor's main waterways every night from 6:30 P.M. for one week prior to Christmas Eve.

LODGING *The Hyatt Newporter*, 1107 Jamboree Road, Newport Beach 92660, 729-1234; $145. Over 400 rooms and suites in a popular 26-acre resort. Par-3, 9-hole golf course on the grounds. Also, guest privileges on 16 lighted courts at the adjacent John Wayne Tennis Club. ● *Newport Beach Marriott Hotel and Tennis Club*, 900 Newport Center Drive at Fashion Island, Newport Beach 92660, 640-4000; $165. Also tennis and weekend packages. Two towers with 600 rooms, many with ocean views. Lighted tennis courts with a resident pro. Golf privileges at nearby country clubs. ● *Four Seasons Hotel*, 690 Newport Center Drive, Newport Beach 92663, 759-0808; $235. Elegant 20-story hotel across from the shops at Fashion Island. Pleasant pool, lighted tennis courts. Also, exceptional (and expensive) French restaurant, The Pavilion. ● *The Little Inn on the Bay*, 617 Lido Park Drive, Newport Beach 92663, 673-8800; $98–$180. Only lodging on the water in Newport Harbor. 30 pleasant rooms, most with bay views. Guests are treated to cheese and wine welcome, evening milk and cookies, continental breakfast, and harbor cruise aboard inn's own boat. ● *Doryman's Inn*, 2102 West Ocean Front, Newport Beach 92663, 675-7300; $135–$275, breakfast included. Posh 10-room B&B that replaced a 2nd-floor rooming house by the beach at Newport Pier. ● *Portofino Beach Hotel*, 2306 West Ocean Front, Newport Beach 92663, 673-7030; $100–$235, continental breakfast included. 20-room restored 1920s hotel. *Renato*, good northern Italian restaurant, is next door.

CAMPING *Newport Dunes Travel Park*, 1131 Back Bay Drive, off Jamboree Road, Newport Beach 92660, 729-3863. 405 RV sites, $25–$50 per night with full hookup, depending on how close to the beach.

DINING *Warehouse Restaurant*, 3450 Via Oporto in Lido Marina Village, Newport Beach, 673-4700. International dishes and seafood served daily for lunch and dinner at the water's edge. Also weekend brunch, patio dining, and entertainment most evenings. ● *Cannery*

Restaurant, 3010 LaFayette Avenue in Cannery Village, Newport Beach, 675-5777. Seafood, steak, and fun along the water for lunch and dinner daily, plus Sunday brunch and brunch cruise on weekends. • *Delaney's*, 630 Lido Park Drive in Cannery Village, Newport Beach, 675-0100. A Newport favorite for Sunday brunch, plus fresh seafood for lunch and dinner daily. • *California Pizza Kitchen*, 1151 Newport Center Drive, Newport Beach, 759-5543. Big and busy "bistro" with pizzas of all descriptions; also pasta. Located in Fashion Island shopping complex. • *Woody's Wharf*, 2318 Newport Boulevard, Newport Beach, 675-0474. Informal local spot for food and drink at lunch and dinner with harbor views. Steak and seafood. • *The Crab Cooker*, 2200 Newport Boulevard, Newport Beach, 673-0100. Absolutely nothing fancy (the silverware is plastic!), but there's usually a line waiting for the broiled fresh fish, shellfish, and seafood chowder at this Newport institution. Lunch and dinner daily; no reservations. • *21 Oceanfront*, 2106 West Ocean Front, Newport Beach, 675-2566. Fancy candlelight spot for fresh seafood, pasta, and more. Dinner only. • *Parker's Seafood Grill*, 501 East Edgewater at Balboa ferry landing, Balboa, 673-3741. Dining with a view at lunch and dinner. Bouillabaisse is a house specialty. • *Newport Landing Restaurant*, 503 East Edgewater, Balboa, 675-2373. Have seafood for lunch or dinner at bay-view patio table on 2nd floor. • *Rothchild's*, 2407 East Coast Highway, Corona del Mar, 673-3750. Popular cheese-and-wine cafe serving salads, sandwiches, and pasta. • *Mezzaluna*, 2441 East Coast Highway, Corona del Mar, 675-2004. Informal trattoria with full range of fine Italian cuisine. Open for lunch and dinner. • *Five Crowns*, 3801 East Coast Highway, Corona del Mar, 760-0331. Pleasant Old English atmosphere, with prime ribs the specialty. Dinner nightly plus brunch on Sundays. Also a popular piano bar. • *Trees*, 440 Heliotrope, Corona del Mar, 673-0910. Informal, sidestreet restaurant with all-American food; complete dinner or separate entrees. Open daily for dinner.

FOR MORE INFORMATION Contact the Newport Beach Conference and Visitors Bureau, 366 San Miguel, Suite 200, Newport Beach 92660, 664-1190. Also the Newport Harbor Area Chamber of Commerce, 1470 Jamboree Road, Newport Beach 92660, 729-4400.

Festive Times in Laguna Beach

If you like art but aren't much for museums, you're going to love the summertime Pageant of the Masters in Laguna Beach, one of Southern California's prettiest coastal towns. Annually from mid-July through August, more than two dozen works of art are shown nightly to audiences comfortably seated in an outdoor amphitheater. You'll see works by Gauguin, Goya, Picasso, Monet, Delacroix, and many other famous artists. Instead of the original paintings, however, you'll be viewing remarkable reproductions—living pictures with real people posing as their canvas counterparts. Sculpture and decorative arts are re-created too. Even if you don't see the pageant, you'll have fun visiting Laguna Beach during the concurrent art festival, which originated in 1932, when several local artists displayed their paintings on a fence near a beach. Since then the festival has grown to three separate sites, with nearly 500 Southland artists and craftspeople displaying their work.

Also luring visitors to the art colony is a creation by Mother Nature, several miles of beautiful sandy beach enclosed by high bluffs that create intimate coves for sunbathing and beachcombing. Other joys for Laguna Beach vacationers are a wide choice of accommodations—from homey bed-and-breakfasts to oceanfront hotels—and a variety of restaurants for every taste and pocketbook.

To discover all its many year-round pleasures and enjoy the art festivals and pageants, drive south from Los Angeles on Interstate 5 or 405 and exit south on California 133. This short freeway merges into Laguna Canyon Road and winds through some scenic ranchland before becoming Broadway Avenue and ending at the town's main thoroughfare, Coast Highway (California 1), which parallels the Pacific.

For accommodations on the beach, it's difficult to top Laguna's Surf & Sand Hotel, where all 160 deluxe rooms and suites overlook the ocean. Whether you stay there or not, don't miss a sunset drink or the continental fare in its Towers Restaurant, decorated in art deco style with mirrored ceilings that reflect the mesmerizing Pacific nine stories below.

Another lodging, the Inn at Laguna, has a cliff-top location overlooking the ocean and is only a few steps down the hill to the Main Beach. In the heart of town and right on the beach is the historic Hotel Laguna, which keeps its 1930s character and features 68 remodeled rooms. A few steps from the ocean on Coast Highway is Laguna's first bed-and-breakfast, Eiler's Inn, a friendly 12-room hostelry where fellow travelers enjoy conversation by the soothing courtyard fountain during the late-afternoon wine-and-cheese hour. Laguna's B&B scene also includes the Carriage House, a colonial-style inn two blocks from Coast Highway toward the hills. Its six antique-decorated suites feature one or two bedrooms plus a sitting room and kitchen. Children and pets are welcome, too. Offering ocean views from a hillside above Coast Highway, the Casa Laguna B&B has 20 rooms and suites amid lush landscaping.

For a panorama of Laguna's stunning beach and cliff-rimmed coastline, head south a few blocks from the center of town to the bluff-top Laguna Village, a cluster of open-air shops with all kinds of art, crafts, and flowers, as well as an outdoor cafe.

An equally impressive view of the town that's built on gentle hills sloping down to the sea is from Heisler Park along Cliff Drive. Picnic on the grassy lawn while watching sailboats from Newport Beach and Dana Point race along the horizon. Or drink and dine with the same view at Las Brisas, a stylish Mexican seafood restaurant and cocktail spot.

Next door, see what's current in the world of art by visiting the Laguna Beach Art Museum, then stroll up and down the Coast Highway to find your favorite artworks in more than 70 art galleries. Gift shops also abound. You'll find Lalique, Baccarat, and other fine crystal creations at Lippe/Waren. For Chinese art and antiques, Warren Imports is internationally known. Laguna boasts at least two dozen antique shops, notably Richard Yeakel, which features French, English, American, and nautical pieces from the fourteenth to eighteenth centuries.

Visitors also are treated to a cornucopia of gift shops, ranging from the landmark Pottery Shack to offbeat Chicken Little's and the Sherwood Gallery. The Forest Avenue and Lumberyard malls are favorites among the town's cozy shopping plazas, which also include The Collection, The Art Center, The Pavilions, The Colonnade, and The Plaza.

Main Beach Park, Laguna's "Window on the Sea," draws not only sunbathers and swimmers but volleyball and basketball fans. Up in Heisler Park the older athletes prefer lawn bowling and shuffleboard. And you'll find scores of nature lovers strolling through the flower-filled grounds.

However, even Laguna's pretty parks are hard pressed to best the personal garden of Hortense Miller. On a hillside overlooking the sea, she's covered 2½ acres around her home with more than 1,200 species of native and subtropical plants. In keeping with the art community's enjoyment of beauty, Miss Miller invites everyone to visit her private garden. Call well in advance to reserve for one of the two weekly tours.

The Hortense Miller Garden is just one of the pleasant surprises for frequent or first-time visitors to this beach resort. Just north of the city limits, visitors enjoy the wide open spaces of Crystal Cove State Park, a pristine section of coast and canyons purchased in 1979 from the Irvine Ranch for public use. You can roam more than 3 miles of beach and 18 miles of inland hiking trails. For other activity, head to South Laguna for fishing off the pier at Aliso Beach Park or nine holes of golf on the Aliso Creek course in a scenic canyon. Adjacent is a quiet spot to spend the weekend, Aliso Creek Inn. Have Sunday brunch on the patio of its Ben Brown's Restaurant.

For good food and nighttime action, the place is the White House, Laguna's landmark roadhouse, opened in 1918. Adorned with Tiffany-type lamps, green plants, and photographs of Laguna Beach in its early days, the restaurant is popular for breakfast, lunch, and dinner. After 9:30 P.M. it's party time in the pub, with dancing to some of Orange County's best musical groups. Another spot for evening gatherings is Fahrenheit 451 Books and Coffee House.

The oyster bar is a treat at the Tavern by the Sea, and Southwest fare gets praise at Kachina. Other delightful dining spots are the lively Romeo Cucina, venerable Tortilla Flats, novel Five Feet, and cozy Partners Bistro. And for sunsets over the Pacific at cocktail time, the Terrace Cafe at the Hotel Laguna is a memorable treat. Linger longer to dine in style at Claes', also in the hotel and overlooking the ocean. In the Surf and Sand Hotel, there are sunset and coastal views from Splashes and The Towers.

During the summer art festival, be certain to make reservations for dinner as well as for weekend lodgings. And be advised that the Pageant of the Masters is so popular that all of its 2,500 seats are sold out for weeks in advance for every performance. However, there's always a chance for latecomers to see the show. Pageant tickets that have been returned are sold first come, first served on the day of performance between 10 A.M. and 4 P.M. at the Festival of the Arts ticket office, 650 Laguna Canyon Road.

The world-renowned pageant is worth the trouble for tickets, because you'll never see anything like it anywhere else. In costumes and makeup, volunteer townsfolk hold their breaths and positions in larger-than-life art re-creations that are surrounded by a huge picture frame. Clever lighting gives a painted look to the images on stage; viewers often bring binoculars to confirm that the people in the pictures are real. Orchestra music and descriptive narration about each artist and his or her work are part of this one-of-a-kind pageant, which has already celebrated its sixtieth season. The show always climaxes with a 13-man depiction of Leonardo da Vinci's *Last Supper*.

The pageant's showplace, the six-acre Irvine Bowl on Laguna Canyon Road, also is the site of the celebrated Festival of Arts. There you can view and buy all sorts of arts and crafts, including watercolors, hand-blown glass, photographs, jewelry, serigraphs, wood carvings, ceramics, and leathercraft.

Other artisans exhibit and even make some of their works on the spot at the Sawdust Festival, just down the canyon road from the main festival grounds. You can watch them fashioning jewelry, blowing glass, and shaping pottery. There's musical entertainment, too, amid the artists' fanciful booths, which are set in a grove of eucalyptus. Other artists and craftspeople show and sell their creations at a third festival site, the Art-A-Fair, also on Laguna Canyon Road.

As you'll quickly discover, parking is a problem in this favorite Southland beach resort, so take the Laguna Beach Transit trams to reach the pageant and art festival grounds in Laguna Canyon. Any time of the year, have plenty of coins for the city's ubiquitous parking meters, because meter maids patrol daily, including Sundays and holidays; the cost for an overtime parking ticket is a stiff fine and an unpleasant weekend memory.

Return to Los Angeles the way you came or take Coast Highway north.

Round trip is about 110 miles.

Laguna Beach Area Code: 714

SIGHTSEEING *Laguna Beach Art Museum*, 307 Cliff Drive, Laguna Beach 92651, 494-6531. Open 11 A.M. to 5 P.M. Tuesday through Sunday. Adults $3, students and senior citizens $1.50, children under 12 years free. ● *Hortense Miller Garden*, c/o Recreation Department, City Hall, 505 Forest Avenue, Laguna Beach 92651, 497-0716. Free 2-hour garden tour Wednesdays, Saturdays, and 2nd Tuesday and Thursday of every month. Call during last 2 weeks of preceding month to make a reservation. ● *Crystal Cove State Park*, flanking Coast Highway between Laguna Beach and Corona del Mar, 494-3539. Nearly 2,800 acres in one of the last undeveloped areas along the Southland coast. Open daily 6:30 A.M. until sunset. Parking fee $6 per vehicle. Beach use and backcountry trails; ranger walks and talks on some weekends. ● *Aliso Beach Park*, South Coast Highway, South Laguna 92677. Hours: 7 A.M. to midnight; meter parking. Free fishing from pier; also swimming and picnicking. ● *Aliso Creek Golf Course*, 9-hole, par-32 course; $18 weekends, $11 weekdays. Adjacent to Aliso Creek Inn and Ben Brown's Restaurant (see below).

EVENTS *Festival of Arts*, Irvine Bowl, 650 Laguna Canyon Road, Laguna Beach 92651, 494-1145. Open-air show of works by 160 artists and craftspeople, usually mid-July through August. Grounds open 10 A.M. to 11:30 P.M. daily. Adult admission $2. Special feature is *Pageant of the Masters*, a remarkable presentation of "living" artwork at 8:30 P.M. nightly. Tickets $9–$38; call 494-1145 or toll-free (800) 487-3378. Box office hours 10 A.M. to 4 P.M. ● *Sawdust Festival*, 935 Laguna Canyon Road (or P.O. Box 1234), Laguna Beach 92651, 494-3030. Over 200 artisans exhibit their works from 10 A.M. to 10 P.M. (to 11 P.M. Fridays and Saturdays), concurrent with the Festival of Arts. Adult admission $4. ● *Art-A-Fair Festival*, 777 Laguna Canyon Road, Laguna Beach 92651, 494-4514. Creations of 180 artists and craftspeople on display from 10 A.M. to 10 P.M. (to 11 P.M. Fridays and Saturdays), also concurrent with the Festival of Arts. Adult admission $3.50.

LODGING *Surf & Sand Hotel*, 1555 South Coast Highway, Laguna Beach 92651, 497-4477; $160. 9-story luxury hotel on beachfront; also two excellent restaurants (see below). ● *Inn at Laguna Beach*, 211 North Coast Highway, Laguna Beach 92651, 497-9722 or toll-free (800) 544-4479; $139. 70 rooms, many with ocean views from cliff-top location. Heated pool. Continental breakfast included. ● *Hotel Laguna*, 425 South Coast Highway, Laguna Beach 92651, 494-1151; $90. 5-story landmark hostelry with 70 rooms on the beach. Drinks and light meals served on oceanfront terrace; gourmet fare in adjoining restaurant (see below). ● *Aliso Creek Inn*, 31106 South Coast Highway (at Country Club Road), South Laguna 92677, 499-2271; $112. Secluded canyon location adjacent to golf course; also patio restaurant (see below). ● *Eiler's Inn*, 741 South Coast Highway, Laguna Beach 92651, 494-3004; $100, breakfast included. ● *Carriage House*, 1322 Catalina Street, Laguna Beach 92651, 494-8945; $95–$150, continental breakfast included. ● *Casa Laguna Inn*, 2510 South Coast Highway, Laguna Beach 92651, 494-2996; $79–$205. Garden setting with 20 rooms and suites in Spanish-style casitas. Breakfast buffet included.

DINING *The Towers*, atop Surf & Sand Hotel (see above). Continental cuisine with ocean view; jackets for men after 6 P.M. Breakfast, lunch, dinner, and Sunday brunch. Also, *Splashes*, overlooking the surf. Innovative menu for breakfast, lunch, and dinner. ● *Claes'*, in Hotel Laguna (see above). Fine continental fare with Pacific panorama. Also Sunday brunch. Adjacent *Terrace Cafe* has outdoor dining. ● *Las Brisas*, 361 Cliff Drive, Laguna Beach, 497-5434. Mexican-style seafood for lunch and dinner; also Sunday brunch. Bar and patio are Laguna's meeting place; delicious hors d'oeuvres at happy hour. ● *Ben Brown's*, at Aliso Creek Inn (see above), 499-

2663. Breakfast, lunch, dinner, and Sunday brunch. Music and dancing Wednesday and Saturday nights. Patio overlooks picturesque golf course. • *Kachina*, 222 Forest Avenue, Laguna Beach, 497-5546. Delicious Southwestern cuisine for dinner; also Sunday brunch. • *The White House*, 340 South Coast Highway, Laguna Beach, 494-8088. Diverse menu for all three meals. Nightly music and dancing (cover charge) in adjoining pub. • *Laguna Village Cafe*, 577 South Coast Highway, Laguna Beach, 494-6344. Bluff-top outdoor cafe. Go for the view, if not the limited breakfast and lunch menu. • *Romeo Cucina*, 249 Broadway, Laguna Beach, 497-6627. Varied Italian menu for lunch and dinner daily. • *Tavern by the Sea*, 2007 South Coast Highway, Laguna Beach, 497-6568. Popular bar and oyster bar. Seafood and pasta are dinner specialties. Open from 5 P.M. • *Cedar Creek Inn*, 384 Forest Avenue, Laguna Beach, 497-8696. Good food in pleasant surroundings. Lunch and dinner; oyster bar from 4 P.M. • *Five Feet*, 328 Glenneyre Street, Laguna Beach, 497-4955. Unconventional Chinese fare presented with style. Also unconventional decor. Dinner only; you'll need reservations. • *Renaissance Cafe*, 234 Forest Avenue, Laguna Beach, 497-5282. People-watching place with sidewalk tables. Varied menu. • *Tortilla Flats*, 1740 South Coast Highway, Laguna Beach, 494-6588. Large and lively spot for south-of-the-border specialties. Lunch and dinner daily. • *Partner's Bistro*, 448 South Coast Highway, Laguna Beach, 497-4441. Cozy place with tasteful decor and varied continental menu (check chalkboard specials). Nice saloon next door. • *Fahrenheit 451 Books and Coffee House*, 540 South Coast Highway, Laguna Beach, 494-5151. Favorite rendezvous for books, coffee, poetry readings, and music.

FOR MORE INFORMATION Contact the Laguna Beach Chamber of Commerce, 357 Glenneyre Street (or P.O. Box 396), Laguna Beach 92651, 494-1018.

Dana Point and San Juan Capistrano— for Boaters and History Buffs

When square-rigged ships plied the California coast, their sailors all knew Bahia Capistrano. It was the major port between San Diego and Santa Barbara—a quiet cove surrounded by steep cliffs where ships anchored to load cowhides from the nearby mission at San Juan Capistrano. Nowadays the harbor has a new name and is much busier than a century and a half ago.

In the past decade men and machines have shaped it into a $20-million marina complex that's home for nearly 2,500 pleasure boats. With sailing, fishing, swimming, and other recreational activities, as well as restaurants and shops, Dana Point Harbor draws boaters and other visitors year round. It's also a picturesque place to headquarter when you want to see a neighboring Orange County attraction, the historic mission at San Juan Capistrano.

To reach Dana Point Harbor from Los Angeles, drive south on Interstate 5 to the Pacific Coast Highway/California 1 off ramp. Follow California 1 north to Dana Point, then go left at the second stoplight onto Dana Point Harbor Drive, which leads to the harbor and the Marina Inn motel, overlooking the boat basin. For bluff-top accommodations in the grand 350-room Dana Point Resort, make the first right turn along Dana Point Harbor Drive onto the Street of the Park Lantern. Or take the first left turn from Dana Point Harbor Drive to enter Doheny State Beach and its popular ocean-view campground. If you opt for bed-and-breakfast at the Blue Lantern Inn overlooking the harbor, exit north onto Pacific Coast Highway through Dana Point to the Street of the Blue Lantern. For the most luxurious lodging, continue north to Ritz-Carlton Drive and the cliff-top Ritz-Carlton Laguna Niguel. You may never want to leave that opulent (and expensive) resort, which many consider the Southland's premier retreat at the seaside.

Have dinner at Cannons or the Chart House, two restaurants that offer a panorama of Dana Point Harbor from atop 400-foot cliffs. There you can imagine sailors of the past century hurling hides down to the beach so they could be loaded onto the square-riggers. Get to either dramatic dining spot by returning to Coast Highway and going up the hill through Dana Point to turn left on the Street of the Blue Lantern, just beyond the Lookout Point sign, then turning right to the Street of the Green Lantern.

From the cliff top you'll spot a replica of the *Pilgrim*, a two-masted brig that came to the harbor in 1835. One of its crewmen was Richard Henry Dana, who later wrote about his seagoing adventures in the now-classic *Two Years Before the Mast*. In his book Dana described the peaceful cove as the only romantic place along the California coast. Eventually it was named Dana Point in honor of the sailor-turned-author. Also in tribute, a handsome statue of Dana was erected at the harbor.

In the morning, get another view of the *Pilgrim* by following Dana Point Harbor Drive to the harbor's west end, where there's a county park with a small beach, swimming area, and picnic tables. Windsurfers skim around the harbor basin for a close look at the old-time sailing ship. From a short pier you can fish with drop lines and bait (sold in the pier shop). Also go into the adjacent Orange County Marine Institute to see a gray-whale skeleton and some other oceanographic exhibits. Beyond the road's end and breakwater is a marine preserve where you will be able to observe sea life in protected tide pools when the tide is out.

To watch all the sailboats parade by in the harbor's main channel, go back on Dana Point Harbor Drive and turn right on Island Way to the parking and picnic areas on Dana Drive. Along this scenic road paralleling the breakwater you'll also find Dana's bronze statue and a favorite seafood restaurant, Delaney's.

When you recross the jam-packed boat harbor on Island Way, turn right on Dana Point Harbor Drive to browse in some of the two dozen gift shops or have a drink in another of the waterfront restaurants located at Mariner's Village and Dana Wharf. Or go across from the harbor to the Pavilion, another attractive collection of shops and restaurants. If you'd rather not be a landlubber, go parasailing high above the ocean, rent a sailing sloop or a skiff with an outboard at Embarcadero Marina, or head out to sea on a ¾-day fishing excursion with Dana Wharf Sportfishing. That same company will take you on a whale-watching excursion in wintertime during the annual California gray-whale migration.

The following day, leave beautiful Dana Point Harbor and return to Interstate 5 going north toward Los Angeles. Exit at the second off ramp, Ortega Highway/California 74, and turn left over the freeway into Orange County's first settlement and home of the "Jewel of the Missions."

As everyone knows, a hit song in the 1940s about the annual return of swallows to San Juan Capistrano's old Spanish mission brought the small and sleepy town worldwide recognition and a steady stream of visitors. In recent years Capistrano has become one of the area's fastest-growing communities, and the fertile fields that used to serve a smorgasbord of insects to the swallows now host housing tracts and shopping centers. However, a few of the birds continue to build their mud nests in the archways of the old mission, which is just two blocks west of the freeway at the corner of the Ortega Highway and Camino Capistrano. Lucky visitors occasionally spot a swallow or two, but you'll find plenty of other feathered friends, especially the white pigeons that coo for food in the mission courtyard. Also look for doves, finches, hummingbirds, and warblers.

Of course, Mission San Juan Capistrano is much more than a bird sanctuary. It's one of the state's most important historical and archaeological treasures. The Spanish outpost that Father Junipero Serra began in 1776 eventually became a self-sufficient settlement for its resident priests, soldiers, and Indians. You'll see the padres' living quarters, soldiers' barracks, an iron smelter, tallow vats, kitchens, and even the punishment room for unruly Indians. Thanks to ongoing excavations and renovations at the impressive mission, visitors really get an idea of what life was like in early-day California.

A highlight is the narrow chapel, thought to be the oldest building in the state. Look for the original Indian decorations and religious relics that have been preserved since the eighteenth century. And don't miss the ruins of the Great Stone Church, a magnificent sandstone structure that was toppled by an earthquake in 1812. A $5-million replica has been constructed to serve as a place of worship for the mission's growing number of parishioners, who attend Sunday Services and send their children to the mission school.

You're welcome to visit Mission San Juan Capistrano any day of the week, and admission includes a self-guided-tour brochure with a map of the grounds.

On Sunday afternoon you can discover more about the intriguing town by joining a walking tour of its old adobes led by members of the San Juan Capistrano Historical Society. You'll hear folklore as well as facts, including stories of bandits, buried treasure, and even ghosts. Tours start from the courtyard of El Peon Plaza, a cluster of shops across from the mission. The historical society also offers a free map and leaflet for a self-guided tour of the adobes. Pick up a copy at El Peon Plaza or the society's headquarters nearby on Los Rios Street in the O'Neill Museum, a restored century-old home that displays local memorabilia.

Down that same street is the Rios Adobe, which takes you back another century. It was built by the local Juaneno Indians in 1794 for Feliciano Rios, a Spanish soldier stationed at the mission. His descendants still live in the house. Also along Los Rios Street are two other adobes constructed of mud and straw bricks soon after the mission was established. On the weekends, kids can enjoy pony rides at the Jones Mini-Farm. Older riders can saddle up for guided horseback trips along hillside trails that meander northwest of town from the Sycamore Trails stable. The undeveloped countryside recalls the landscape as it must have been in the days of the Spanish missionaries.

Just across the train tracks, look for the 1894 Santa Fe Railway station, built of handmade bricks and decorated with a cupola and red tile roof. Its interior has been attractively remodeled in railroad motif for a popular restaurant called the Rio Grande Bar and Grill at the Capistrano Depot. The bar and lounge are located within converted railroad cars and really jump on Sunday afternoons, when Dixieland and ragtime bands are the featured entertainment. Amtrak's sleek trains stop here several times daily on the Los Angeles–San Diego run. A block away on the town's main street, Camino Capistrano, you'll find more early buildings, including one that served as a stagecoach stop, courtroom, and jail. Today it's part of a well-known Mexican restaurant, El Adobe, another excellent choice for a meal. In between is the modern Franciscan Plaza, with shops, a movie theater, and two popular restaurants, a re-created 1940s diner called Ruby's, and B.J.'s Chicago Pizzeria. Across from the mission grounds is a favorite for French fare, L'Hirondelle.

When you're ready for the return trip to Los Angeles, retrace your route to Interstate 5 and head north.

Round trip is about 160 miles.

Dana Point/San Juan Capistrano Area Code: 714

SIGHTSEEING   *Orange County Marine Institute,* 24200 Dana Point Harbor Drive, Dana Point Harbor 92629, 496-2274 or 831-3850. Open daily from 10 A.M. to 3:30 P.M., with aquariums and other marine exhibits. Free. ● *Dana Wharf Sportfishing,* 34675 Golden Lantern, Dana Point Harbor 92629, 496-5794 or 831-1850. Daily ¾-day and longer open-party fishing trips. Adults $30, children 12 years and under $20. Also whale-watch cruises in winter and parasailing. ● *Embarcadero Marina*, Embarcadero Place, Dana Point Harbor 92629, 496-6177. Open daily for powerboat and sailboat rentals. ● *Mission San Juan Capistrano*, Ortega Highway at Camino Capistrano, San Juan Capistrano 92675, 493-1111 or 493-1424. Open daily from 8:30 A.M. to 5 P.M. Adults $3, children under 11 years $2. ● *O'Neill Museum*, 31831 Los Rios Street, San Juan Capistrano 92675, 493-8444. Open Sundays 12 to 3 P.M., Tuesday through Friday 9 A.M. to 12 P.M. and 1 to 4 P.M.; closed

Saturdays and Mondays. Donation appreciated. Restored 1880s home with local history exhibits. Headquarters of San Juan Historical Society. For society-led 1-hour walking tours of town, meet Sunday at 1 P.M. at El Peon Plaza, 26832 Ortega Highway, across from the mission. Adults $1, children $.50. • *Jones Family Mini-Farm*, 31791 Los Rios Street, San Juan Capistrano 92675, 831-6550. Pony rides weekends from 11 A.M. to 4 P.M. $1.75 per ride. • *Sycamore Trails*, 26282 Oso Road, San Juan Capistrano 92675, 661-1755. 1-hour guided horseback rides, $20 per hour. First ride 8:30 A.M., last ride 4:15 P.M. Make reservations.

EVENTS *Festival of the Whales*, at Dana Point Harbor, 496-2274. Annual 3-weekend fest in late February and early March celebrating the California gray whale with talks, movies, and exhibits on marine wildlife and ocean lore. Whale-watch cruises depart every hour. Also, other events and entertainment. • *Fiesta de las Golondrinas*, annual Swallows Day celebration in San Juan Capistrano. Week-long festival centering around March 19, traditionally the day when the swallows return from South America to the mission. Outstanding equestrian parade with bands and floats, pancake breakfast, barbecue, and contests.

LODGING *Ritz-Carlton Laguna Niguel*, 33533 Ritz-Carlton Drive, Laguna Niguel 92677, 240-2000; $195, on oceanfront $400. Classy cliff-top resort hotel overlooking the Pacific. 393 rooms and suites (Presidential Suite has antiques, grand piano, Jacuzzi, 2 bedrooms, and $2,500 tab). Health club and shuttle to beach. Well-dressed local folk also come for afternoon tea, gourmet dining, and the supper club (see below). • *Dana Point Resort*, 25135 Park Lantern, Dana Point 92629, 661-5000; $170–$280. Sprawling modern resort in Cape Cod–Victorian style on bluffs above Dana Point Harbor. 350 rooms with ocean views. 3 tennis courts, 2 swimming pools, health club. Children's program in summer. Locals like Sunday brunch in Watercolors restaurant. • *Marina Inn*, 24800 Dana Point Harbor Drive, Dana Point 92629, 496-1203; $70. Only accommodations within Dana Point Harbor. Heated pool and redwood sauna. Walk to restaurants, shops, and boat docks for sportfishing and whale watching. • *Blue Lantern Inn*, 34342 Street of the Blue Lantern, Dana Point 92629, 661-1304; $135–$250. Modern, romantic bed-and-breakfast overlooking harbor. 29 lovely rooms with fireplace and Jacuzzi tub, some with private sundecks. • *Edgewater Inn*, 34744 Pacific Coast Highway, Capistrano Beach

92624, 240-0150; $85, ocean view $120. 30 rooms with kitchenettes, across coast highway from state beach. ● Other lodgings in San Juan Capistrano, including *Capistrano Inn*, 493-5661.

CAMPING   *Doheny State Beach*, 25300 Dana Point Harbor Drive, Dana Point 92629, 496-6171. 120 sites (32 on oceanfront), $16–$21 per night; no hookups. Reserve through MISTIX well in advance; call toll-free (800) 444-7275. The park is very popular for swimming, fishing, surfing, and picnicking. Open for day use 6 A.M. to 10 P.M., $6 per vehicle.

DINING   *The Dining Room*, in the Ritz-Carlton Laguna Niguel (see above). Haute cuisine in elegant surroundings; the place to celebrate a special occasion. Fresh foie gras, lamb, veal, seafood, and all the fine touches. Dinner daily from 6 P.M. Jackets and ties for gentlemen. *The Cafe* is the resort's less formal dining spot, with an outdoor terrace. Breakfast, lunch, dinner, and Sunday brunch. *The Library* and *The Lounge* offer sophisticated afternoon tea and grand-piano music. For live music and dancing with dinner, try the Ritz-Carlton's supper club, *The Club Grill & Bar.* ● *Cannons,* 34334 Street of the Green Lantern, Dana Point, 496-6146. Open daily for lunch, dinner, and cocktails with spectacular harbor view. Seafood specialties. Also Sunday champagne brunch. ● *Chart House*, 34442 Street of the Green Lantern, Dana Point, 493-1183. Open daily from late afternoon for dinner only. Salad bar, seafood, and unbeatable harbor view. ● *Delaney's*, 25001 Dana Drive, Dana Point, 496-6195. Open daily for lunch and dinner at the harbor. Seafood and oyster bar. Also very popular for Sunday brunch. ● Other major restaurants in Dana Point Harbor are the *Jolly Roger*, with family fare for breakfast, lunch, and dinner; *Casa Maria*, with Mexican food for lunch and dinner; *Harpoon Henry's*, with prime ribs, seafood, and oyster bar for lunch and dinner; and *The Wind & Sea*, with steak and seafood, for dinner only. ● *Cafe Mozart*, 31952 Camino Capistrano (in Mercado Village), San Juan Capistrano, 496-0212. Delightful courtyard and indoor dining for lunch and dinner. German specialties. ● *Rio Grande Bar and Grill at Capistrano Depot*, 27601 Verdugo Street, San Juan Capistrano, 496-8181. Open daily for lunch and dinner; also Sunday brunch. Pleasant dining in a renovated railroad depot that's now an Amtrak station. Varied meat and seafood menu. Cocktails served in vintage train cars. Entertainment evenings and Sunday afternoons. Reservations advised. ● *El Adobe*, 31891 Camino Capistrano, San Juan Capistrano, 493-1163. Open Monday through Saturday for lunch and dinner, Sunday for brunch and dinner. Mexican and continental fare with mariachi music in historic surroundings.● *L'Hirondelle*, 31631 Camino Capistrano, San Juan Capistrano, 661-0425. Dinner only Tuesday through Sunday, plus Sunday brunch. Excellent French cuisine in an intimate restaurant across from the mission.

FOR MORE INFORMATION   Contact the Dana Point Chamber of Commerce, 24681 La Plaza, Suite 120 (or P.O. Box 12), Dana Point 92629, 496-1555. Also, the San Juan Capistrano Chamber of Commerce, 31682 Camino Real, San Juan Capistrano 92675, 493-4700, and the Mission Visitors Center, 31882 Camino Capistrano, Suite 218, San Juan Capistrano 92675, 493-1424.

Mickey Mouse and Many More Amusements in Anaheim and Buena Park

There's no debate that Orange County is a magnet for vacationers in Southern California, and most folks are drawn to a pair of neighboring cities that are host to a wonderful assortment of family amusements. Buena Park is home of the granddaddy of Southland theme parks, Knott's Berry Farm, already well known for its ghost town and family-style chicken dinners in the 1940s, a decade before Disneyland opened its gates six miles down the road in Anaheim.

Another ongoing favorite of Buena Park visitors is Movieland, a wax museum that brings more than 250 movie and TV stars almost to life in re-created Hollywood sets. At nearby Ripley's Believe It or Not! Museum, truth seems stranger than fiction when you see all the displays of bizarre, humorous, and very interesting real-life phenomena and curiosities. Not much of the Old West is left in modern Orange County, but you'll enjoy the antics of cowboys and Indians at a very different attraction, Wild Bill's Western Dinner Extravaganza. Guests are served a family-style dinner in a Western saloon and music hall, the setting for an evening of entertainment that includes rope tricks, Indian dances, a knife-throwing act, and foot-stomping country folk music. Another place in Buena Park, called Medieval Times, re-creates a spectacle of the Middle Ages with knights jousting on horseback and fighting with swords while you devour a four-course feast.

Before totaling up the number of attractions in Anaheim and Buena Park, add two more. Baseball and football fans flock to Anaheim Stadium, the 70,000-seat arena for home games of the California Angels and Los Angeles Rams. Also, the immense Anaheim Convention Center is host to all sorts of special events, from pop concerts to ice skating shows and the Ringling Brothers, Barnum and Bailey Circus.

With such an extensive menu of amusements, how do you see everything in a weekend? Obviously you can't, but some thoughtful planning will make the time you spend an enjoyable outing instead of an exhausting ordeal. Disneyland and Knott's Berry Farm *each* take a full day, perhaps even two, depending on the crowds, the weather, and how many are in your family group. Trying to tour both of these famed amusement parks in one weekend will tire your feet and exhaust your patience. For peace of mind, don't promise the kids Disneyland and Knott's on the same trip unless it's a three-day weekend or you're on a week's vacation. One good reason is that the berry farm alone offers 165 rides and other entertainment features. For another, on a holiday weekend or midsummer day, tens of thousands of visitors flock to Disneyland—and that means long waits in long lines.

Getting to Buena Park or Anaheim from Los Angeles is easy. Just drive south on Interstate 5, then take the Artesia Boulevard/Beach Boulevard (California 39) exit and follow the signs to Knott's Berry Farm or continue on Interstate 5 a few more miles to the Harbor Boulevard exit and follow the signs to Disneyland.

New freeway exits will be added for a planned three-billion-dollar expansion of the park, announced in 1992 as the 470-acre Disney-land Resort. It will include a second theme park, called WESTCOT Center, which is to be similar to EPCOT Center at Walt Disney World in Florida. A glittering golden sphere called Spacestation Earth, a reminder of the EPCOT's geosphere, has been designed as the new resort's landmark. Other additions are a six-acre lake bordered by dinner theaters, cafes, specialty shops, and open plazas, and a resort hotel district featuring three new themed lodgings. The Disneyland monorail will be extended and augmented by moving sidewalks and elevated people movers to transport guests throughout the enormous resort property.

Many things in the area will be changing during the several years it will take to complete the Disneyland Resort. One of the first changes was the closing of mom-and-pop motels that once lined the access streets to Disneyland, but the larger high-rise hotels offer hundreds of rooms convenient to the park.

While the 1,131-room Disneyland Hotel is considered ''the

official hotel of Disneyland'' and is the only one connected directly to the Magic Kingdom by the park's monorail, several other major hotels are on Disneyland's perimeter and have free shuttle service. These include the Anaheim Hilton and Towers, Pan Pacific Hotel, Inn at the Park, Anaheim Marriott, and Sheraton-Anaheim. There also is shuttle transportation between the hotels around Disneyland and Knott's Berry Farm. If you make your headquarters in Buena Park to be closer to Knott's Berry Farm and its surrounding attractions, try the Buena Park Hotel or the roomy Embassy Suites, and use the shuttle buses if you also plan to visit Disneyland.

True to Walt Disney's desire, Disneyland is one of the happiest places on earth, and one visit is never enough. Many Southland residents return year after year to fall happily under the spell of the Magic Kingdom. Mickey Mouse and all the other familiar Disney characters are on hand to extend a happy welcome to visitors of every age, and there are always new attractions to draw families back to the beautiful 80-acre park. A few years ago, for example, the world's largest flume ride was unveiled in Critter Country. That's one of seven theme areas that transport you to another place and time with rides and automated attractions created with incomparable Disney cleverness and care. The most recent addition is Mickey's Toontown, an animated downtown and suburban neighborhood where Disney cartoon characters live, work, and play in a three-dimensional cartoon environment.

Although Disneyland offers guided 3½-hour group tours to help you become acquainted with the park, it's not difficult to discover all the attractions on your own. Get a guide map at the entry gate, and agree with family members on a rendezvous spot in advance in case you get separated. Lost persons can be contacted at City Hall near the main entrance; lost children are cared for at the First Aid Center.

Entering Disneyland at the main ticket booths, a good idea for first-time visitors is to hop on the steam-powered train at the Town Square for a circle orientation tour of the park. Then disembark where you boarded and immerse yourself in the Magic Kingdom by strolling down Main Street, U.S.A., with its Penny Arcade and other delights of turn-of-the-century America. Not to be missed in the Opera House is the first of Disney's remarkable audio-animatronic displays, ''Great Moments with Mr. Lincoln.'' At the park's hub, Central Park, the kids are drawn to Disneyland's enchanting symbol, Sleeping Beauty's Castle. Beyond its drawbridge their imaginations wander on Pinocchio's Daring Journey, Snow White's Scary Adventures, Peter Pan's Flight, and Mr. Toad's Wild Ride. And even adults enjoy a trip on Dumbo's Flying Elephants. Or board a bobsled for a white-knuckle ride in and around another Disney landmark, the snowcapped Matterhorn.

In Tomorrowland, where some of the "future" technology has become reality since the park opened in 1955, Space Mountain offers other thrills on an interplanetary rocket ride. Star Tours also transports you into space, as does a 3-D musical motion picture called *Captain EO* that stars Michael Jackson. Equally spellbinding are the Circle-Vision cinema tours called "American Journeys" and "Wonders of China." Down-to-earth travel is on the opposite side of the park in Adventureland, where lifelike animals are seen on the exotic Jungle Cruise and birds serenade you with song in the Enchanted Tiki Room. Only a few steps away in Frontierland the perils of life in the Wild West come true on a runaway mine train at Big Thunder Mountain, and so do the old-time pleasures when you watch cancan dancing in the Golden Horseshoe saloon.

Nearby is lively New Orleans Square, added after the park opened, when land was so limited that this theme area's two most popular attractions are mostly underground. You'll disappear into the Haunted Mansion and also cruise in a darkened grotto with the Pirates of the Caribbean. Then head to the adjacent woods, Critter Country, to join the jamboree of the mechanical bears in a musical revue and the world's largest flume ride, Splash Mountain. Intermingled in all the theme areas are an assortment of shops with Mickey Mouse ears and other souvenirs and better-than-average gifts. And throughout the park you'll find two dozen restaurants and refreshment centers ready to provide nourishment and nonalcoholic drinks.

Adding to your enjoyment are the costumed Disney characters that cavort all over the Magic Kingdom, happily posing for pictures with young and old visitors alike. Musicians roam the grounds, band concerts and stage shows are featured daily, and there's always a colorful parade; summer evenings end with a grand fireworks display. A highlight is the nighttime show, called Fantasmic!, which mixes live performers and music with special effects that involve pyrotechnics, lasers, fog, fiber optics, and giant props.

Disneyland offers a variety of special services to keep guests happy. Lockers are available so you don't have to tote around the souvenirs you're bound to purchase in the park or sweaters or other clothes for the cooler evening hours. A baby-care center offers privacy for feeding and changing infants, while a kennel near the main gate provides day care for pets.

Disneyland's price of admission gives you unlimited use of all activities (except the shooting galleries). If you decide to leave the park and want to return the same day, be certain to have your hand stamped at the exit gate or Disneyland Hotel monorail station.

For the most enjoyment on holiday weekends or in the summer months, begin your visit as soon as the park opens, because there are fewer people and shorter waiting lines for the favorite attractions.

Then return to your hotel for a leisurely lunch and an afternoon nap, and go back to Disneyland later in the afternoon, when it's cooler, and stay for the special evening shows, Fantasmic!, the parade, and fireworks.

The same advice holds true for a visit to Knott's Berry Farm in Buena Park: Arrive when the gates open, take a break from the crowd for a restful lunch (perhaps in the adjoining Buena Park Hotel), and return later in the afternoon. Covering 150 acres, the park is twice the size of the original Disneyland and also well known for its fun-filled attractions, thrill rides, entertaining shows, and gift shops.

Knott's Berry Farm may seem like a funny name for the Southland's second most popular amusement park, but that's how it began. Cordelia and Walter Knott had a roadside berry stand in rural Buena Park in the 1920s, and later they began serving fried chicken dinners in the family living room to passersby. Word of their delicious home-style meals spread, and so did the line of hungry customers. To keep the guests occupied during a three- to four-hour wait for Cordelia's chicken, Walter began to re-create an Old West ghost town. Today it's one of the six theme areas in the expanded complex, which includes Indian Trails, Fiesta Village, the Roaring '20s Airfield, Camp Snoopy, and Wild Water Wilderness.

The Ghost Town's steam train and stagecoach rides still delight children, as does the Kingdom of the Dinosaurs. But you're likely to find most of the kids lined up for a breathtaking trip on the Corkscrew double-loop roller coaster, 20-story-high Parachute Sky Tower, or other daring rides like Montezooma's Revenge, Bigfoot Rapids, and Boomerang, a roller coaster that turns riders upside down six times in less than a minute. The trained dolphin and aquatic shows are also big draws, as are the musical variety shows and the top-name entertainers who appear on stages around the park and in Knott's 2,100-seat Good Time Theatre. Happily, all attractions at Knott's Berry Farm are included in the admission price. Of course, you'll have to pay extra for the old-fashioned chicken dinners that are still being served—and you'll still have to wait in line.

Unless you have time for an extended stay to enjoy the many other amusements listed in the "Sightseeing" section below, plan to come back for another weekend in Anaheim and Buena Park. Meanwhile, return to Los Angeles by joining Interstate 5 north.

Round trip is about 50 miles.

Anaheim/Buena Park Area Code: 714

SIGHTSEEING *Disneyland*, 1313 Harbor Boulevard, Anaheim 92803, 999-4565 or (213) 626-8605. Open daily year round. Open mid-June to mid-September from 8 A.M. to 1 A.M. Rest of the year open weekends from 9 A.M. to midnight, weekdays from 10 A.M. to 6 P.M. Unlimited-use Passport ticket $28.75, children 3 to 12 years $23. Parking $5. ● *Knott's Berry Farm*, 8039 Beach Boulevard, Buena Park 90620, 827-1776. Open daily from Memorial Day weekend through Labor Day from 10 A.M. to midnight, except Saturdays to 1 A.M. Rest of the year open from 10 A.M. to 6 P.M. weekdays, to 10 P.M. Saturdays, to 7 P.M. Sundays. Unlimited-use ticket adults $22.95, children 3 to 11 years $9.95, and senior citizens $15.95. Parking $4. ● *Knott's Berry Farm "Express,"* 978-8855. Shuttle buses operated by Pacific Coast Sightseeing Tours between 30 Anaheim hotels near Disneyland and Knott's Berry Farm in Buena Park. Contact hotel front desk or bellman for tickets; no reservations required. Round trip $6, children 4 to 11 years $4. ● *Movieland Wax Museum*, 7711 Beach Boulevard, Buena Park 90620, 522-1154. Open daily from June through Labor Day from 9 A.M. to 10:30 P.M. Rest of the year open daily from 10 A.M. to 9:30 P.M. Adults $12.95, children 4 to 11 years $6.95. ● *Ripley's Believe It or Not! Museum*, 7850 Beach Boulevard, Buena Park 90620, 522-7045. More than 200 oddities. Open daily 10 A.M. to 6 P.M., except Fridays and weekends to 8 P.M. Adults $8.95, seniors $6.95, children 4 to 12 years $5.25. ● *Wild Bill's Western Dinner Extravaganza*, 7600 Beach Boulevard, Buena Park 90622, 522-6414. Food and family shows nightly, plus Sunday matinee. Admission the same as at Medieval Times (see below). ● *Medieval Times*, 7662 Beach Boulevard, Buena Park 90622, 521-4740. Admission includes Middle Ages tournament and a meal with two rounds of drinks: Adults $31.95 Fridays and Saturdays, $28.95 other evenings, $26.95 Sunday matinees; children 12 years and under $20.95 Fridays and Saturdays, $19.95 other evenings, $18.95 Sunday matinees. ● *Anaheim Convention Center*, 800 West Katella Avenue, Anaheim 92803, 999-8950. Concerts, circus, and more; call for current events. ● *Anaheim Stadium*, 2000 South State College Boulevard, Anaheim 92803. Arena for California Angels home baseball games mid-April through September; call 634-2000 for schedule and ticket information. Also home stadium for Los Angeles Rams football games from August through December; call 937-6767 for schedule and ticket information.

LODGING   *Disneyland Hotel*, 1150 West Cerritos Avenue, Anaheim 92802, 778-6600 or toll-free (800) 642-5391; $155 summer, $130 winter. 60-acre resort with 1,131 rooms in three tower buildings surrounding a man-made marina and minibeach. Monorail transportation direct to the Magic Kingdom. Supervised youth program in summer. Also several restaurants (see below). • *Pan Pacific Hotel*, 1717 South West Street, Anaheim 92802, 999-0990 or toll-free (800) 321-8976; $125. 502-room deluxe hotel next to Disneyland Hotel and monorail station. 2 restaurants. • *Inn at the Park*, 1855 South Harbor Boulevard, Anaheim 92802, 750-1811; $115. Towering 500-room hotel near Anaheim Convention Center; free 2-block shuttle to Disneyland. Also novel family restaurant (see below). • *Anaheim Marriott Hotel*, 700 West Convention Way, Anaheim 92802, 750-8000; $180. Luxurious 1,050-room hotel near Anaheim Convention Center; free trolley to Disneyland. Indoor/outdoor swimming pool. Also elegant dining room (see below). • *Anaheim Hilton and Towers*, 777 Convention Way, Anaheim 92802, 750-4321; $160. Area's largest hotel with 1,600 rooms on 14 stories; adjacent to convention center. Free shuttle to Disneyland. Children's program in summer. 4 restaurants. • *Sheraton-Anaheim Hotel*, 1015 West Ball Road, Anaheim 92802, 778-1700; $95. English Tudor–style hotel with 500 rooms close by Disneyland, with free shuttle to the Magic Kingdom. • *Embassy Suites*, 7762 Beach Boulevard, Buena Park 90620, 739-5600; $149, with complimentary full breakfast and happy hour. Over 200 two-room suites with kitchen and bar opposite Knott's Berry Farm. Also, Le Bistro restaurant open for lunch and dinner. • *Courtyard by Marriott*, 7621 Beach Boulevard, Buena Park 90620, 670-6600; $90. 145 rooms, pool, exercise room, cafe. Close to Knott's Berry Farm.

DINING   *Granville's* in the Disneyland Hotel (see above). The resort hotel's premier restaurant, with candlelight dining, featuring regional American specialties. Dinner only, reservations advised. Jackets required for men. Also try the *Shipyard Inn* for fresh seafood, *Cafe Villa Verde* for Italian cuisine, and *Mazie's Pantry* for sandwich fare. • *JW's* in the Anaheim Marriott Hotel (see above). Acclaimed and expensive gourmet dining room featuring French cuisine, candlelight, and harp music. Dinner nightly except Sundays; make reservations and dress up. • *Mr. Stox*, 1105 East Katella Avenue, Anaheim, 634-2994. Award-winning restaurant featuring duck, veal, fish, prime rib, rack of lamb. Lunch and dinner daily. • *Thee White House*, 887 South Anaheim Boulevard, Anaheim, 772-1381. Continental fare for lunch weekdays, dinner nightly. In restored early-1900s home. • *Acapulco Mexican Restaurant*, 1410 South Harbor Boulevard, Anaheim, 956-7380. Mexican food and drink daily for breakfast, lunch, and dinner; also Sunday champagne brunch. • *Tony Roma's*, 1640 South Harbor Boulevard, Anaheim, 520-0220. Great baby-back barbecue ribs and onion rings. • *Overland Stage Restaurant*, in Inn at the Park (see above). Lunch weekdays and dinner daily, including roast buffalo if you dare, in Old West surroundings. • *Knott's Berry Farm Chicken Dinner Restaurant* at Knott's Berry Farm (see above). The place for home-style fried chicken dinners and the boysenberry pie that began the Knott family fame. Open daily for breakfast, lunch, and dinner. Also *Knott's Berry Farm Steak House*, serving non–chicken lovers prime beef and seafood for lunch and dinner every day.

FOR MORE INFORMATION Contact the Anaheim Area Visitor and Convention Bureau, 800 West Katella Avenue, Anaheim 92802, 999-8999. Also the Buena Park Convention and Visitor Office, 6280 Manchester Boulevard, Suite 103, Buena Park 92672, 994-1511 or toll-free (800) 541-3953.

Marina, Mission, and Marines at Oceanside

Oceanside is no secret to pleasure boaters. Midway between the marinas at Dana Point and San Diego, its attractive small-craft harbor is a popular refreshment stop for weekend sailors playing along the coast in their sleek motor yachts or sailboats. Other travelers tend to pass by Oceanside, racing through town on Interstate 5 or aboard Amtrak's San Diegan trains, and that's a mistake. Spend a couple of days at this unheralded beach town and you'll be pleased by its unhurried pace, value-priced accommodations, and wonderful variety of attractions. Not to be missed is a visit to the "King of the Missions," San Luis Rey, and history fans as well as military buffs will be intrigued by a tour of Camp Pendleton, the nation's largest Marine Corps base.

To reach Oceanside and its harbor from Los Angeles, drive south on Interstate 5 and take the Oceanside Harbor Drive exit west toward the ocean. Settle in marina-view lodgings at Oceanside's harbor, where the scene is more reminiscent of Cape Cod than Southern California. Especially recommended is the Villa Marina Resort, an apartment-style motel overlooking the ocean channel entrance.

The next day explore the peaceful harbor, where a lighthouse, sea gulls, attractive landscaping, and dock slips with 915 boats impart the charm of a small port in New England. At quayside you can browse in gift shops and snack on fish and chips or other seafood in one of the nautically decorated restaurants. Climb to the lighthouse lookout for a good view of the harbor. A small beach along the breakwater jetty also has thatched-roof ramadas where you can picnic in the shade and watch all the boat and bird activity.

Besides being a haven for sailboaters and yachtsmen, Oceanside harbor is home for commercial craft that will take you into the ocean for a half day of sportfishing. If you're an avid fisherman or just an amateur angler hoping to hook a deep-sea specimen, board one of the Helgren's Sportfishing vessels for some fishing fun on the Pacific. Feeding in kelp beds not far from the harbor entrance, rock cod, mackerel, bonito, and barracuda are waiting for your bait. Rental rods and the required state fishing license are available when you check in at Helgren's departure dock.

South of the harbor, across the San Luis Rey River, you can join the surf fishermen, swimmers, surfers, and suntanners who enjoy life along Oceanside's three-mile-long city beach. Families also flock to the picnic tables, barbecue grills, and playground equipment scattered across the sand. A waterfront landmark is the public pier, once the longest on the Pacific coast. Stroll out 1,942 feet for panoramic views and refreshments at the pier's end, where there's a two-story restaurant, the Fisherman. Also walk barefoot along the shore and promenade on the paved Strand bordering the sand. Facing the ocean is a long row of tourist cabins, simple lodgings from an earlier era that have been surpassed by Oceanside's newer accommodations. One overlooks The Strand and sand, the Southern California Beach Club, a time-share resort that also has rooms for rent for a night or longer. Inland you'll find the Oceanside Inn and Marty's Valley Inn, as well as the Franciscan Retreat Center, where former seminary rooms at Mission San Luis Rey are available to the public.

After enjoying a lazy day at the marina and beach, plan to have dinner at the harbor. Fresh seafood and other dishes are featured nightly at the Chart House, Jolly Roger, Monterey Bay Canners, and Mykonos.

Unless you opt for another leisurely day at the ocean's edge, make Sunday the time to tour the nearby mission and adjacent marine base. Oceanside was incorporated in 1888, but the area was settled 90 years earlier with the founding of Mission San Luis Rey de Francia. Named for Louis IX, king of France in the thirteenth century, it later earned another regal title, ''King of the Missions,'' by becoming the largest of all the missions in California. Get there from town by heading inland about four miles on Mission Avenue (California 76) and turning left at the entrance signs.

At one time Mission San Luis Rey's buildings covered six acres and served as home for as many as 3,000 Indians. Besides cultivating the countryside to grow grapes, olives, and oranges, the mission's Indians raised 27,000 head of cattle and almost an equal number of sheep. San Luis Rey was the eighteenth mission to be built, but geographically it is second in the famed California mission chain. It was founded in 1798 to fill the gap between the missions that were established earlier at San Diego and San Juan Capistrano. Some of the mission complex has been completely restored, and today it serves as a parish church and religious retreat center.

Start your self-guided tour in the mission museum, which features artifacts used by the early Franciscan fathers, including an impressive collection of old Spanish vestments. Visit the padres' restored bedroom and library, where there's a gray robe that's typical of the type worn by these missionaries until the past century. In the sewing and tallow rooms you'll see how the Indians wove cloth from wool, cotton, and flax and boiled animal fat to make candles and soap. The adjoining kitchen rooms have utensils like those used in the mission period. A highlight is the mission church, which is still the site for religious services on Sundays. Its original adobe walls are six feet thick, and the interior has lofty beamed ceilings with decorations done by the Indians.

You exit through the cemetery, where hundreds of Indians are buried, and then the tour continues outside the mission walls. Look past a gate into the monastery garden to see the state's oldest pepper tree, brought from Peru in 1830. Across the driveway are the ruins of barracks of Spanish soldiers who were stationed at the mission. Beyond, through an ornate arch and down a tiled stairway, is the partially excavated outdoor *lavanderia*, where the Indian women washed clothes. Archaeological work continues to uncover more of the mission's past. A picnic area in front of San Luis Rey Mission is a pleasant spot to relax before continuing to neighboring Camp Pendleton. Before you go, visit Heritage Park Village behind the mission. It re-creates an 1890s street of vintage Oceanside buildings that have been moved to the site to preserve their historical past.

If you really want to imagine what Southern California was like in the days of the Spanish missionaries, drive around Camp Joseph H. Pendleton to view the rugged coastal terrain, which has changed very little during the past two centuries. Most travelers speeding along the Interstate 5 freeway, which cuts through the base, catch only glimpses of the historic chaparral-covered land spreading from the ocean to the Santa Margarita Mountains. However, you're welcome to explore the 125,000-acre U.S. Marine training camp anytime during daylight hours. Despite modern facilities for a population of 45,000 marines and their families, much of the land appears as pristine as when Gaspar de Portola and his Spanish expedition camped there in 1796. You'll even see adobe structures built in the 1800s. Until the federal government bought the land for $4.25 million in 1942, it was the Rancho Santa Margarita, originally a huge Spanish land grant under custody of the Mission San Luis Rey padres. At one time the ranch was owned by Pio Pico, the last Mexican governor of California.

To reach Camp Pendleton from the mission, head back to town on Mission Avenue (California 76) and join Interstate 5 going north. Take the second exit, Harbor Drive/Camp Pendleton, to the Main Gate guard station. To enter as a visitor you need to show your driver's license, vehicle registration and proof of car insurance, and sign in. An auto tour is outlined in a free guide map; get a copy at the Main Gate entrance, and look for directional tour markers posted alongside the roads. These signs have an *O* and a *T* on top, representing the branding iron of Rancho Santa Margarita.

One points to the original adobe ranch house, now restored, that is the handsome private residence of the base commanding general. You'll also get exterior views of the two adjacent historic structures. In 1810, mission Indians built a winery that later became the ranch house chapel, and the 1835 bunkhouse is now a museum where ranch artifacts and photos are kept. The chapel and the bunkhouse are open by special request. Another stop to make is at the outdoor LVT (Landing Vehicle Track) Museum, where every type of amphibious vehicle used by the marines since World War II is on display.

You'll see considerable military activity as you drive through the vast training center, but also keep your eyes open for wildlife. Most likely you'll spot soaring hawks and, with luck, a golden eagle or white-tailed kite, both endangered species. In winter Canadian geese stop here to feed. Coyotes, bobcats, and mule deer are other inhabitants, and beavers have been spotted building dams in Las Pulgas Creek. Even a small herd of buffalo roams in the foothills. Near the tour's end, look for a windmill and barn that are part of a Boy Scout camp surrounding a historical landmark, the vine-covered Las Flores Adobe. It was built in 1867 from the ruins of Asistencia de San Pedro, a way station along El Camino Real, the old Spanish road that connected the missions up and down the California coast.

Leave Camp Pendleton by exiting at Las Pulgas Gate and rejoining Interstate 5 north to Los Angeles. There are no food facilities on the base for visitors except McDonald's and Burger King, so if you get hungry on the way home, exit inland on El Camino Real in San Clemente for outstanding Italian fare at Andreino's.

Round trip is about 183 miles.

Oceanside Area Code: 619

SIGHTSEEING *Helgren's Sportfishing*, 315 Harbor Drive, Oceanside 92054, 722-2133. Daily outings on well-equipped boats with helpful mates and full galley. Half-day $22; ¾-day $32. • *Mission San Luis Rey*, 4050 Mission Avenue, San Luis Rey 92068, 757-3651. Open daily from 10 A.M. to 4:30 P.M., except Sundays from noon. Adults $3, children 6 to 11 years $1, 5 years and under free. Also, lodging available in summer (see below). • *Heritage Park Village*, 500 Peyri Drive, Oceanside 92068, 966-4530. Historical park established on 4 acres behind Mission San Luis Rey. Open 9 A.M. to 4 P.M.; buildings open from 1 to 4 P.M. May to October. • *Camp Joseph H. Pendleton*, Joint Public Affairs Office, Marine Corps Base, Camp Pendleton 92055, 725-5566. Open daily during daylight hours for self-guided auto tours; get guide map at Main Gate. Free.

LODGING *Villa Marina Inn*, 2008 Harbor Drive North, Oceanside 92054, 722-1561 or toll-free (800) 252-2033; $75 in winter, $110 in summer. 1- and 2-bedroom suites with full kitchens, separate living rooms with fireplaces, and patios with harbor or ocean views. Also Jacuzzi and saunas. Guest boat slips by reservation. • *Southern California Beach Club*, 121 South Pacific Street, Oceanside 92054, 722-6666; $100–$150. 44 vacation condos with studio, 1- and 2-bedroom units. On the sand near municipal pier. • *Franciscan Retreat Center* at Mission San Luis Rey, P.O. Box 409, San Luis Rey 92068, 757-3659. 50 small but pleasant rooms in former seminary; bathrooms down the hall. Weekend lodgings $75 per person, including full breakfast and dinner. Also summer midweek programs. Facilities include swimming pool, basketball court, volleyball area. Unique experience. • *Best Western Oceanside Inn*, 1680 Oceanside Boulevard, Oceanside 92054, 722-1821; $65. • *Marty's Valley Inn*, 3240 East Mission Avenue, Oceanside 92054, 757-7700; $55 winter, $63 summer. On highway to Mission San Luis Rey.

DINING *Chart House*, 314 Harbor Drive South, Oceanside, 722-1345. Dinner only, featuring steaks, seafood, and salad bar, overlooking Oceanside Harbor. • *Jolly Roger*, 1900 Harbor Drive North, Oceanside, 722-1831. Harbor-view dining daily from 7 A.M. Fresh fish specialties. Also entertainment Wednesday through Saturday in summer. • *Monterey Bay Canners*, 1325 Harbor Drive,

Oceanside, 722-3474. Fresh seafood served daily for lunch and dinner with harbor view. • *Mykonos*, 258 Harbor Drive South, Oceanside, 757-8757. Greek specialties, including seafood. Patio dining overlooking harbor. Lunch and dinner daily. • *The Fisherman*, end of Oceanside Pier, Oceanside, 722-2314. Seafood specialties for lunch and dinner daily. Open for breakfast on Saturdays, brunch on Sundays. Park and ride tram to end of pier. • *Andreino's*, 1925 South El Camino Real, San Clemente, (714) 492-9955. Attractive and popular family-run restaurant with pasta, veal, chicken, and seafood specialties. Open Tuesday through Saturday for dinner; reservations advised.

FOR MORE INFORMATION   Contact the Oceanside Chamber of Commerce's Visitor Information Center, 928 North Hill Street, Oceanside 92051, 721-1101. Open every day from 8:30 A.M. to 4:30 P.M.

Seaside Frolics and Flowers in Carlsbad and Environs

Three neighboring coastal communities were rest stops for Los Angeles–San Diego drivers in prefreeway days, but now the traffic rushes past Carlsbad, Leucadia, and Encinitas on Interstate 5. However, by exploring along the old 101 coastal highway, you'll enjoy a relaxing weekend in this trio of beach towns. Although beginning to grow as fast as the rest of Southern California, they still retain the flavor and fun of earlier times. You'll also be treated to some of the most spectacular flower displays anywhere in the Southland.

As oceanfront cities go, Carlsbad is a sleeper. Called Agua Hedionda (Stinking Water) by early mission soldiers because of a foul-smelling lagoon, the site once was a Spanish rancho. Settlers arrived in 1881, when the railroad did. One was John Frazier, who dug a well and discovered its waters had properties similar to the mineral water in the famed Karlsbad health spa in Bohemia (now Czechoslovakia). A resort hotel was built, and health seekers came by train to take the waters and relax at the ocean's edge. Land development followed, and the new town was named Carlsbad. Mineral water no longer flows from Frazier's well, but vacationers keep coming because it's a wonderful place for sunbathing, swimming, surfing, and fishing. The beach is still a major Carlsbad attraction and now hosts two state parks. You'll find fire rings for ocean-view barbecues and more than 200 sites for overnight camping.

Since its incorporation in 1954, Carlsbad's original 7½-square-mile size has increased fivefold, and the 7,000 population has grown to 64,000. From its original coastal site, the city has annexed land east of the freeway and now includes the well-known La Costa resort, featuring a health spa, golf courses totaling 36 holes, and 23 tennis courts. The town also boasts Victorian homes, a wide range of antique shops, some excellent restaurants, and special events for visitors. On the first Sunday in May and in November, Carlsbad hosts the nation's largest street fairs, when eight blocks of the downtown area become an arts-and-crafts show with 800 exhibitors, plus food booths, street entertainment, and lots of fun. Carlsbad's pride and joy is its public library, and in mid-May the Friends of Carlsbad Library hold a big book fair and party in Holiday Park. And look for a multicolored blanket of ranunculus flowers blooming in full force from mid-March until late April on the flower farms that flank the Interstate 5 freeway.

To reach Carlsbad from Los Angeles, drive south on Interstate 5. The Carlsbad Village Drive exit just beyond Oceanside takes you to downtown Carlsbad and lodgings overlooking the ocean, the Tamarack Beach Resort, Carlsbad Inn, or Beach Terrace Inn. If you feel like splurging and staying at La Costa Resort and Spa, continue south on the freeway almost six miles more to the La Costa Avenue exit and head inland to El Camino Real and the entrance to that plush resort. There you have a grand choice of 482 accommodations, in hotel rooms, one- and two-bedroom suites, and even houses. Some guests come for the full-fledged spa program and never leave the resort. They're pampered with massages, herbal wraps, facials, manicures, body-toning exercises, whirlpools, saunas, and low-calorie gourmet meals. Even if you're not in the program, you can enjoy the spa facilities, as well as golf and tennis, for extra fees.

Reserve for Friday's dinner in one of La Costa's fine restaurants. If you feel like candlelight and European cuisine, put on your best bib and tucker for an evening in the Champagne Room. Otherwise, try Ristorante Figaro for Italian fare or Pisces for seafood. There will also be fine food at the Four Seasons Resort Avaria, due to open in Carlsbad in late 1993 with a health spa, sports club, and 18-hole golf course.

In the morning, explore the town by heading back north on the freeway to Carlsbad and exiting toward the ocean on Carlsbad Village Drive. Go six blocks to the railroad tracks, where you'll see Rotary Park and the old Santa Fe train station, which has been restored as offices for the Carlsbad Convention and Visitors Bureau. (The bureau folks advise everyone who wants to see the Carlsbad Caverns to go to New Mexico.) Beyond the tracks, turn right on Carlsbad Boulevard, the old coast highway, which is the main north-south street, and go past Grand Avenue to a town landmark, the Alt Karlsbad gift shop, a replica of a Hanseatic house built on the site of Frazier's well. Go inside and be guided to an underground gallery for a closer look at the well and the owners' minimuseum of Carlsbad history. Saltwater has invaded the well, so don't expect to sample the mineral water that put the town on the map. You'll enjoy the Alt Karlsbad's historical mementos and European handicrafts, however.

Cross the boulevard and go a block north to Beech Avenue and a city historical park, site of the restored Magee House, which was built more than a century ago by a pioneer family. It's now a minimuseum of the Carlsbad Historical Society and occasionally open to visitors. Also in the park, look for the Magees' barn and carriage house, and the early St. Patrick's church, which later served as the town's city hall, jail, and public library. Places to lunch and many of Carlsbad's gift and antique shops are nearby on Grand Avenue and State and Roosevelt streets. At the corner of Grand and Roosevelt is a complex of shops, the Old World Center, also home for a popular dinner house and Irish pub called Dooley McCluskey's. Another favorite is Henry's on Carlsbad Village Drive.

Back on Carlsbad Boulevard at Carlsbad Village Drive, you'll also enjoy dining at Neiman's. The century-old Victorian mansion was built by a Carlsbad land promoter and later became a boardinghouse. For 70 years before its recent renovation the old inn was famous as a restaurant serving all-you-can-eat chicken dinners. Now you can enjoy brunch on Sundays and lunch and dinner on other days. Across the boulevard in the Carlsbad Inn, Mexican fare is served at Fidel's Norte.

For some exercise after you eat, stroll along Carlsbad Village Drive to the beach or continue south on Carlsbad Boulevard until it turns to parallel the oceanfront and joins a bluff-top walkway overlooking the Pacific. A mile of the coastline below you is Carlsbad State Beach, a day-use park where the suntan set gather to swim, surf, and fish. For travelers with a tent or RV, three miles beyond is a longer stretch of sand, South Carlsbad State Beach, which has cliff-top campsites in sight of the ocean. On the way you'll pass the protected Aqua Hedionda Lagoon, where water skiing and windsurfing are favorite pastimes. Bird watchers should continue on to Batequitas Lagoon along La Costa Avenue at the city's southern limits or go back to the north end of town to Buena Vista Lagoon, a freshwater wildlife sanctuary that's home for 225 species of migrating waterfowl.

On Sunday continue south on Carlsbad Boulevard/S21 to Leucadia and neighboring Encinitas to visit several flower nurseries and gardens open to the public. As the growing center for potted and cut flowers that are shipped to florists all over the nation, those neighboring coastal communities have become Southern California's flower capital. If you're visiting in the springtime, look for a dazzling rainbow opposite South Carlsbad State Beach park where thousands of ranunculus grow in colorful rows in the Frazee flower fields. Continue south past La Costa Avenue to Leucadia and turn left on Leucadia Boulevard. Just before reaching the freeway, go right at the gas station onto Orpheus Avenue to Stubbs Fuchsia Nursery. You'll be awed by more than 30,000 flowering fuchsia plants, many in attractive hanging baskets. The owners of this wholesale nursery, Jill and Bob Meyer, invite visitors to view the spectacular display as well as to buy fuchsias. You'll see more than 300 fuchsia varieties in every size, shape, and color. Also popular and blossoming in summer are New Guinea impatiens.

Head back to Leucadia Boulevard, go right to cross over the freeway, then turn left immediately on Piraeus Street to Weidner's Begonia Gardens at Normandy Road. Under a shady tent of screen mesh that filters the sunlight is an acre of begonias—20,000 plants in gorgeous full bloom. Annually from July to September, you can wander among the orderly rows to pick out plants for your own patio or garden. Digging forks, instructions, and carrying cartons are supplied, or bring your own pots and replant the begonias on the spot. The price for each begonia you dig up is only a few dollars, regardless of its variety, color, or size. This novel begonia garden was established in 1973, when Evelyn and Bob Weidner "retired" from the nursery business. Other plants have been added since then, including the popular fuchsias and impatiens and the treasured royal purple brunfelsia. Wear old walking shoes, because the garden grounds may be muddy. While parents are searching for the perfect plant to take home, the kids will be entertained by watching the Weidners' chickens, ducks, pony, pig, sheep, goat, and other farm pets.

Return to the freeway and go south to the next exit, Encinitas Boulevard, then head inland a quarter mile to Quail Gardens Drive. It takes you to Quail Botanical Gardens, a county nature center with 30 acres of native, hybrid, and imported plants and trees. You're welcome to wander along five self-guided nature walks in this peaceful botanic preserve, which also serves as a bird and wildlife sanctuary. Rangers live on the grounds and will answer your questions, but most things are described in tour leaflets that are available near the outdoor guest registration book.

To glimpse what this area of Southern California coast was like before the twentieth century, take the Quail Gardens Nature Trail that starts on the unpaved walkway at the southwest corner of the parking lot. Numbered redwood stakes correspond to numbered descriptions in the tour leaflet. Besides a loop trail through the chaparral plant community, the area includes a pond where plants from other parts of California are displayed. Native birds and small animals rarely seen in other parts of the garden often come here, so walk quietly, because noise and other sudden movements scare them off. In addition to hummingbirds, doves, and the garden's namesake, California quail (seen late in the day), be on the lookout for cottontail rabbit, pocket gopher, long-tailed weasel, gray fox, and opossum. Along the trail you'll probably smell black sage, a pungent bush used as seasoning or medicinal tea by early Californians, and also yerba santa, a shrub with aromatic leaves that were brewed for tea.

On the far side of the pond is a Torrey pine, a handsome tree that is now one of the world's rarest pines and is native only to this coastal area of the county and Santa Rosa Island. You'll see many kinds of cactus, including one with seedy fruits that taste like watermelon. It is called mission cactus because the Spanish missionaries first brought it to California. The other self-guided tours also will introduce you to a surprising variety of plants and trees. Look for the camphor tree, which was important as the source of moth-repelling camphor until synthetic mothballs were made. The bunya-bunya tree is nicknamed a monkey-puzzle tree because its sharp-tipped leaves would puzzle a monkey as to how to climb it safely. At certain times you'll see green cones that are as big as pineapples at the very top of this tree. Take a picnic lunch and drinks to enjoy at shaded tables; no refreshments except soda pop are available in the botanic gardens.

You'll also enjoy a stroll through the gardens of the Self-Realization Fellowship, a religious retreat on a cliff overlooking the Pacific at the southern end of Encinitas. From Encinitas Boulevard, head south again on the coastal highway, S21. You can't miss the golden-domed towers, built by a sect from India in the 1930s. Members maintain a beautiful meditation garden inside the compound, and it's open to the public. If you decide to eat before the drive back to Los Angeles, you'll find a number of restaurants fronting the old coastal road. Two that are well known for Italian fare are Portofino's and When In Rome. Going north on S21 you'll also discover art galleries and clusters of gift shops in Encinitas and Leucadia. Look for the Lumberyard, Old Market, and Leucadia's shopping plazas. Then return to Los Angeles by rejoining Interstate 5 north.

Round trip is about 230 miles.

Carlsbad Area Code: 619

SIGHTSEEING   *Alt Karlsbad*, 2802 Carlsbad Boulevard, Carlsbad 92008, 729-6912. Gift shop with museum of local memorabilia, open Monday through Saturday from 10 A.M. to 5 P.M., Sundays from 1 to 4:30 P.M. • *Stubbs Fuchsia Nursery*, 737 Orpheus Avenue, Leucadia 92024, 753-1069. Open daily from 9 A.M. to 5 P.M., except Sundays from 11 A.M. to 4 P.M. • *Weidner's Begonia Gardens*, 695 Normandy Road, Leucadia 92024, 436-2194. Open 9:30 A.M. to 5 P.M. daily April to mid-September and November through December 22. • *Quail Botanical Gardens*, 230 Quail Gardens Drive, Encinitas 92024, 436-3036 or 436-9516 (ranger). Open daily 8 A.M. to 5 P.M.; guided tour every Saturday at 10 A.M. Free admission; parking $1. • *Self-Realization Fellowship*, 215 K Street, Encinitas 92024, 753-1811. Gardens open daily from 9 A.M. to 5 P.M. (from 11 A.M. Sundays). Free.

LODGING   *La Costa Resort & Spa*, Costa Del Mar Road, Carlsbad 92008, 438-9111 or toll-free (800) 854-5000; $250, suites from $470. Also spa, golf, and tennis packages. Several fine restaurants. • *Tamarack Beach Resort*, 3200 Carlsbad Boulevard, Carlsbad 92008, 729-3500 or toll-free (800) 334-2199; $120. Vacation condominium development with 23 rooms for overnight guests. On coast highway across from state beach. • *Beach View Lodge*, 3180 Carlsbad Boulevard, Carlsbad 92008, 729-1151; $88. Across from Carlsbad State Beach. Whirlpool and sauna. Some rooms with gas fireplaces and kitchens. • *Beach Terrace Inn*, 2775 Ocean Street, Carlsbad 92008, 729-5951; $95. On the beach. Rooms and suites with fireplaces and kitchens. • *Carlsbad Inn*, 3001 Carlsbad Boulevard, Carlsbad 92008, 434-7020; $115. Time-share vacation resort with 56 rooms for overnighters. Easy access to beach. Also restaurant (see below). • *Radisson Inn Encinitas*, 85 Encinitas Boulevard, Encinitas 92024, 942-7455; $79. 3-story inn with 96 rooms. Situated on hillside inland of coast highway; some ocean views.

CAMPING   *South Carlsbad State Beach*, off San Diego County S21/Carlsbad Boulevard, 3 miles south of Carlsbad, 438-3143. 224 sites, $16 per night; no hookups. Reserve through MISTIX, toll-free (800) 444-7275. Also, *San Elijo State Beach*, south of Encinitas at Cardiff-by-the-Sea, 753-5091. 171 sites, $16 per night; no hookups.

DINING   *Neiman's*, 2978 Carlsbad Boulevard, Carlsbad, 729-4131. Remodeled Victorian mansion with popular cafe; also large dining room. Lunch, dinner, and Sunday brunch. • *Dooley McCluskey's*, 640 Grand Avenue, Carlsbad, 434-3114. Seafood dinners daily from 5:30 P.M.; pub opens at 11 A.M. • *Henry's*, 264 Carlsbad

Village Drive, Carlsbad, 729-9244. Continental cuisine with an Italian accent. Lunch and dinner daily. • *Fidel's Norte*, in the Carlsbad Inn (see above). Mexican dishes for lunch and dinner. • *Dini's By the Sea*, 3290 Carlsbad Boulevard, Carlsbad, 434-6000. Sunday brunch, and fresh fish for lunch and dinner, with ocean views. • Also a restaurant row just south of Encinitas on old Highway 101 (now S21) in Cardiff-by-the-Sea, including *Charlie's*, the *Triton* and *Chart House* on the beach, and the *Fish House West* and *Bella Via* across the road.

FOR MORE INFORMATION   Contact the Carlsbad Convention and Visitors Bureau, Old Santa Fe Depot on Carlsbad Village Drive at the railroad tracks (or P.O. Box 1246), Carlsbad 92018, 434-6093. Open every day. Call toll-free (800) 227-5722 for Carlsbad lodging information and reservations. Also contact the Encinitas-Leucadia Chamber of Commerce, 345 1st Street, Encinitas 92024, 753-6041. Open weekdays.

La Jolla and Del Mar: A Pair of Coastal Charmers

As the most exclusive suburb of San Diego, La Jolla (*la hoy-ya*) is a residential community that displays an informal elegance. Known for a seven-mile coastline that's outstanding for surfing, swimming, and sunbathing, it's no wonder the attractive village also is a magnet for visitors. Ocean-view parks for picnics and tree-lined sidewalks for strolling—plus a wonderful variety of restaurants, art galleries, and shops—help make it a great getaway spot. Despite its upper-income status (just glance at the prices of homes pictured in real estate office windows), La Jolla isn't stuffy. In fact, the town has a very youthful and alive atmosphere, thanks in part to the students from the neighboring University of California San Diego campus.

During a weekend visit you'll find plenty more to enjoy on a side trip to Del Mar, another coastal charmer that's just ten miles north of La Jolla. On the way, see the aquarium at the famed Scripps Institution of Oceanography, watch hang gliders soar from cliff tops along the beach, stroll among rare Torrey pines, and then relax on the beach. Once just a summer place, Del Mar overflows with visitors from May through mid-September because of three major Southland events: a national horse show, then the Del Mar Fair (San Diego's county fair), and finally Del Mar's renowned thoroughbred racing season. But travelers have discovered that this mellow village makes a delightful diversion any time of the year.

Get to your weekend lodgings in La Jolla by driving south from Los Angeles on Interstate 5 to the La Jolla Village Drive exit. Head west along the edge of the UCSD campus, turn left on Torrey Pines Road, and then go right on Prospect Place to join La Jolla's main roadway, Prospect Street. This curving thoroughfare, lined with shops and restaurants, leads to a La Jolla landmark, the classic 1926 Hotel La Valencia, conspicuous because of its pink tower with gilded top. Check in there or next door at another delightful lodging, the Prospect Park Inn, a 23-room bed-and-breakfast.

As you'll discover while taking an evening stroll along Prospect Street, many shops and dining spots are clustered in pleasant complexes called McKellar Plaza, Coast Walk, Prospect Mall, Prospect Square, and La Jolla Cove Plaza. Local favorites if you're splurging for dinner are George's at the Cove and the Top O' the Cove, or dine in the Sky Room atop the Hotel Valencia. Or give up an ocean view to be part of the scene in the hotel's venerable Whaling Bar and Cafe La Rue. For musical entertainment with your meal or after-dinner drinks, join the jazz crowd at Chuck's Steak House. Another street with recommended restaurants is La Jolla Boulevard between the 5500 and 5800 blocks, where you'll find both informal and fancy dining and drinking spots. They're south of the town center in the Bird Rock area, less than a mile beyond Windansea Beach, La Jolla's celebrated surfing area and a spectacular spot to watch the sun set.

With its curving park-studded coast and enticing shopping streets in the heart of town, La Jolla invites visitors to give up their cars for leisurely strolls to enjoy the scenery and shops, with pauses for refreshments at shaded sidewalk cafes. In the morning, go walking along Coast Boulevard. It leads to the La Jolla Cave and Shell Shop, where you can descend 145 steps through a ten-story tunnel to reach one of the seven caves carved by the ocean into La Jolla's sandstone cliffs. Topside again, enjoy more of the town's rugged coastal beauty by following an unpaved trail called Coast Walk, where you'll get a bird's-eye view of La Jolla's caves and coves. Also along Coast Boulevard are public parks with grassy expanses on the bluff top that welcome you to rest or picnic.

Located between Coast Boulevard and Prospect Street is the Museum of Contemporary Art, San Diego, where the main attraction is an excellent collection of post-1950 American art augmented by traveling exhibits. A dozen galleries along Prospect and Girard Avenue will also get your attention with avant garde, traditional, and Western artworks, as well as photography, fine crafts, and ancient arts.

On Sunday, plan time to make a sightseeing drive to Del Mar. Turn left from Prospect Place onto Torrey Pines Road, then bear left on La Jolla Shores Drive to Exposition Drive and the Stephen Birch Aquarium-Museum, part of the renowned Scripps Institution of Oceanography, which is a graduate division of UCSD.

The $10-million aquarium opened in 1992 to replace a much smaller Scripps facility that had attracted visitors for more than 40 years. You can peer at hundreds of aquatic specimens living in realistic habitats created in 33 tanks of various sizes, including one of 70,000 gallons that is home to a kelp forest. As you peer at this marvelous array of Pacific Ocean marine life and view the other exhibits about ocean geology and pollution, you'll understand why the aquarium at Scripps is considered one of the best in the nation. And there's extra fun when visitors get to watch the fish being fed.

Continue north on La Jolla Shores Drive and turn left onto North Torrey Pines Road. Skirting the campus of the University of California San Diego, drive north to Torrey Pines Scenic Drive, just beyond the famed Salk Institute for Biological Studies, then turn left and go to the very end until the road dissolves into an open area on the coastal cliff top. This is Torrey Pines City Park, a popular launch area for hang gliders. Walk to the ocean overlooks to watch the human butterflies make their dramatic takeoffs over the Pacific. Radio-controlled model airplanes often fill the skies here, too.

Returning to North Torrey Pines Road and continuing north, you'll pass Torrey Pines Golf Course, a championship 36-hole course that's open to the public. It's overlooked by the impressive Sheraton Grande Torrey Pines Hotel. After the highway descends to the ocean, turn left to the entrance of Torrey Pines State Reserve. This is California's only state park where picnics aren't permitted, smoking is forbidden, and dogs are unwelcome even if they're kept in the car. There's good reason for such strict regulations—the reserve is home for one of the world's rarest trees, the Torrey pine. This relic of the Ice Age is found in its native habitat in only two places in the world: isolated Santa Rosa Island, off the coast of Santa Barbara, and this windswept state reserve between La Jolla and Del Mar. After paying the park entry fee, drive up the steep hill to the main parking area, where you'll find a visitors center with a small museum. (In summer, when parking areas fill up, the entrance road is temporarily closed until some of the visitors leave.) The 1,000-acre reserve is a microcosm of what California looked like centuries ago. Foot trails lead to a variety of vegetation, including bent and gnarled Torrey pine trees clinging to eroded sandstone cliffs overlooking the ocean.

Be sure to view the natural-history displays in the visitors center, a former restaurant. You also can watch a brief slide show that introduces the park. Two of the most popular trails are a marked nature path in Parry Grove and the almost-level Guy Fleming Trail. On either one you'll be surrounded by the *Pinus torreyana*, as the tree species is officially called. Named in 1850 for the American botanist Dr. John Torrey, the pine has flourished in the protected reserve and now numbers 10,000, including seedlings. Collecting pinecones is prohibited because their seeds are needed to assure survival of the species. Guided nature walks begin from the park museum on Saturdays and Sundays.

Drive back down to the park road and continue north on the highway, San Diego County S21, which becomes Camino Del Mar and brings you into the heart of the coastal village of Del Mar. The bluff-top town was founded in 1883, shortly before an impressive hotel, the Casa del Mar, was built to attract prospective land purchasers from Los Angeles and elsewhere. The hostelry burned down in 1890, about the time California's early land boom ended. Twenty years later Del Mar returned to prominence with the opening of the Stratford Inn, an expansive resort that was a favorite of movie stars and other celebrities attending horse races at the Del Mar Turf Club, a thoroughbred racecourse opened in 1937 by Bing Crosby and Pat O'Brien.

That grand hotel was replaced in 1989 by another deluxe lodging, L'Auberge Del Mar Resort and Spa, which welcomes the public to its Durante Pub and Tourlas restaurant. Other popular places to have refreshments or lunch and slip into the town's easygoing mood are found across from L'Auberge at the same Camino Del Mar and 15th Street intersection. You'll spot the patio umbrellas at Carlos & Annie's sidewalk cafe, while across the street, diners waiting for a table at Il Fornaio (The Baker) enjoy coastal vistas from the top deck of multilevel Del Mar Plaza, an intriguing complex with 35 shops and eateries.

You'll discover more shops and restaurants along both sides of the four-lane Camino Del Mar, including a favorite of local folks, Bully's North. If you prefer to picnic, walk down 15th Street to Seagrove Park, overlooking the ocean. Just north is Del Mar's sandy beach, popular for swimming, surfing, and sunbathing. Two restaurants nearby on Coast Boulevard overlook the sand—the Poseidon, which draws the barefoot beach crowd, and Jake's, where shirts and shoes definitely are required.

Most of Del Mar's restaurants are crowded during the thoroughbred racing season from late July through early September; be certain to make reservations. Post time is 2 P.M. for the nine races that are run daily (except Tuesdays) by many of the world's best horses and jockeys.

If pari-mutuel betting on the horses doesn't offer you enough excitement, why not fly above Del Mar in a hot-air balloon? Four local companies offer bird's-eye views of the scenic bluff-top town, including A Beautiful Morning Ballooning Company. You'll rise in the sky during the early morning or late afternoon for an hour's flight over the coast and countryside, then come back down to earth for the traditional toast with champagne.

If your visit to Del Mar is the finale of your weekend and it's time to return to Los Angeles, continue north on Camino Del Mar/S21 past the racetrack and county fairgrounds and turn inland on Via de la Valle to join Interstate 5 north.

Round trip is about 270 miles.

La Jolla/Del Mar Area Code: 619

SIGHTSEEING *La Jolla Cave and Shell Shop*, 1325 Coast Boulevard, La Jolla 92037, 454-6080. Open daily 10 A.M. (Sundays 11 A.M.) to 5 P.M., to 6 P.M. on summer weekends. Entry to staircase to reach Sunny Jim Cave is $1 for adults, $.50 for children 3 to 11 years. ● *Museum of Contemporary Art, San Diego*, 700 Prospect Street, La Jolla 92037, 454-3541. Open daily except Mondays from 10 A.M. to 5 P.M., Wednesday evenings to 9 P.M. Adults $4, students and senior citizens $2, children 5 to 12 years $.50. Free on Wednesdays from 5 to 9 P.M. ● *Stephen Birch Aquarium-Museum*, 2300 Exposition Drive, La Jolla 92037, 534-3474. Open daily 9 A.M. to 5 P.M. Educational and fun for every age. ● *Torrey Pines Municipal Golf Course*, 1480 North Torrey Pines Road, La Jolla 92037, 570-1234 for computerized reservation service. Two 18-hole, par-72 courses. Greens fee $38 weekdays, $44 weekends, each course. ● *Torrey Pines State Reserve*, off North Torrey Pines Road south of Del Mar (or 2680 Carlsbad Boulevard, Carlsbad 92008), 755-2063. Open 9 A.M. to sunset year round. Entry $4 per car; walkers and bicyclists free. Museum open daily 9 A.M. to 5 P.M. Guided nature walks on weekends at 11:30 A.M. and 1:30 P.M. Bicycles not allowed on trails. ● *A Beautiful Morning Balloon Company*, 1342 Camino Del Mar, Del Mar 92014, 481-6225. Hour-long hot-air balloon flights in late afternoon or very early morning. $140 per person. Other Del Mar hot-air balloon companies include *Skysurfer Balloon Company*, 481-6800, and *Del Mar Balloons*, 259-3115.

EVENTS *Del Mar National Horse Show*, one of the largest in the nation, is held at the Del Mar Fairgrounds annually in May. Admission $5. Phone 755-1161. ● *Del Mar Fair (Southern California*

Exposition), old-fashioned county fair held annually at the Del Mar Fairgrounds from the third week in June through the first week of July. Phone 755-1161. • *Del Mar Thoroughbred Club*, 43 days of horse racing at the Del Mar Fairgrounds track. Nine races daily except Tuesdays from late July through early September. Post time 2 P.M. Grandstand admission $2.50, Clubhouse $5. Phone 755-1141; ticket reservations 792-4242.

LODGING   *Hotel La Valencia*, 1132 Prospect Street, La Jolla 92037, 454-0771; $135, suites from $300. Classy landmark hotel that sets the tone for a La Jolla visit. Guests gather in elegant lobby for the ocean views and relaxation in the heart of town. Heated pool, whirlpool, sauna, and exercise room. Also see several impressive restaurants and the town's best-known bar (see below). • *Prospect Park Inn*, 1110 Prospect Place, La Jolla 92037, 454-0133; $79–$119, suites from $145, continental breakfast included. A 25-room hotel in the European tradition. Located in the heart of town half a block from the beach. Breakfast in your room. • *Bed & Breakfast Inn at La Jolla*, 7753 Draper Avenue, La Jolla 92037, 456-2066; $85–$275. City historical site, once home for bandmaster John Philip Sousa. 10 rooms in 1913 Cubist-style house, 6 more in annex. Quiet spot near art museum. • *Colonial Inn*, 910 Prospect Street, La Jolla 92037, 454-2181; $130. Attractively renovated 1913 hotel with 77 rooms. In village center a block from the beach. Also popular restaurant (see below). • *Sheraton Torrey Pines Hotel*, 10950 North Torrey Pines Road, La Jolla 92307, 558-1500; $145. 400-room luxury hotel overlooking golf course with ocean in the distance. Butler service, fitness center, and daily luncheon buffets and Sunday brunch in the Torreyana Grille. • *L'Auberge Del Mar Resort & Spa*, 1540 Camino Del Mar, Del Mar 92014, 259-1515; $165. First-class 123-room resort hotel in center of Del Mar. Complete European health spa, 2 lighted tennis courts, restaurant, and bar. • *Del Mar Inn*, 720 Camino Del Mar, Del Mar 92014, 755-9765; $85, including continental breakfast and afternoon tea. English Tudor–looking hotel with many ocean-view rooms. • *Stratford Inn*, 710 Camino Del Mar, Del Mar 92014, 755-1501; $85. Expanded hostelry with spacious rooms overlooking ocean. • *Rock Haus*, 410 15th Street, Del Mar 92014, 481-3764; $75–$150, breakfast included. 2-night minimum stay on weekends and holidays. 10-room bed-and-breakfast in historic Del Mar home, one block from the heart of town. 4 rooms with private bath, others share 3 baths. No children or smoking.

DINING *Top O' the Cove*, 1216 Prospect Street, La Jolla, 454-7779. Continental cuisine for lunch and dinner daily; also weekend brunch. Entertainment most nights. Reservations recommended, as are coats for men. ● *Hotel La Valencia* (see above) has 5 dining areas and a well-known watering hole: 10th-floor *Sky Room* serves continental fare nightly except Sundays and lunch weekdays—all with majestic shoreline and ocean views. Coats required for gentlemen. Reservations a must. *Whaling Bar* and *Cafe la Rue* offer same menu of prime ribs, steaks, and seafood with different decor. Lunch and dinner daily, with Sunday brunch in the Cafe. The Whaling Bar is a legendary rendezvous and drinking spot. *Mediterranean Room* and *Tropical Patio* also share menus and serve three meals daily. Lunch and Sunday brunch in the Mediterranean Room; outdoor dining when weather permits. ● *Putnam's*, in the Colonial Inn (see above). Popular restaurant and watering hole. Open for breakfast, lunch, and dinner. ● *Chuck's Steak House*, 1250 Prospect Street (in McKellar Plaza), La Jolla, 454-5325. Soup and salad bar, choice beef and seafood for lunch and dinner daily. Jazz after 9 P.M. ● *George's at the Cove*, 1250 Prospect Street, La Jolla, 454-4244. Ocean-view dining for lunch and dinner, Sunday brunch. Award-winning menu includes seafood, pasta, lamb, and beef. ● *Bully's*, 5755 La Jolla Boulevard, La Jolla, 459-2768. Prime ribs and seafood for dinner nightly, salads and sandwiches for lunch weekdays only. ● *Su Casa Restaurant,* 6738 La Jolla Boulevard, La Jolla, 454-0369. Sonora-style Mexican dishes for lunch and dinner served daily. Also fresh fish. ● *Carlos & Annie's*, 1454 Camino Del Mar (at Stratford Square), Del Mar, 755-4601. Open daily for breakfast, lunch, and dinner. Sidewalk dining. ● *Bully's North*, 1404 Camino Del Mar, Del Mar, 755-1660. Locals flock here for prime ribs and seafood nightly; lighter fare for lunch. ● *Poseidon*, 1670 Coast Boulevard, Del Mar, 755-9345. Very informal dining and drinks on the sand. A favorite for breakfast. ● *Jake's Restaurant*, 1660 Coast Boulevard, Del Mar, 755-2002. On the beach, serving seafood and continental dishes for lunch and dinner; also Sunday brunch. ● *Il Fornaio*, 1555 Camino Del Mar, Del Mar, 755-8876. Northern Italian menu, bakery, and more. Casual indoor/outdoor service for lunch and dinner. Always a crowd. ● *Pacifica Del Mar*, 1555 Camino Del Mar, Del Mar, 792-0476. The place for seafood at lunch and dinner. Patio dining and Sunday brunch.

FOR MORE INFORMATION Contact La Jolla Town Council, 1055 Wall Street, Suite 110 (or P.O. Box 1101), La Jolla 92038, 454-1444. Also, the Greater Del Mar Chamber of Commerce, 1401 Camino Del Mar, Suite 101, Del Mar 92014, 755-4844.

San Diego
Part 1: Introducing
California's Oldest City

Like a precious pendant at the end of a string of jewels, San Diego is the brilliant gem that seems to outshine all of the other sparkling cities along the Southland seacoast. Its attractions are so numerous and diverse—from historic to scenic to recreational—that you need several visits just to sample what San Diego has to offer.

We've planned four weekends to help you see the highlights. As the first landing point for European explorers along the West Coast and home for the state's first non-Indian settlement, San Diego makes early California history come alive. Return to the time of Spanish soldiers and Franciscan fathers by touring three well-preserved places—San Diego's mission, the presidio, and Old Town. These simple beginnings of what has become California's second largest city offer a delightful introduction to the 200-year-old town, along with the Victorian homes and business buildings that abounded at the turn of the century and have been saved for the pleasure of future generations.

Plan another weekend to discover San Diego's wonderful waterfront of vintage ships, enticing shops, seafood restaurants, and resort hotels—all surrounding a picturesque bay that's home for countless pleasure craft, fishing boats, and naval ships. You'll need another weekend to thoroughly enjoy one of the nation's most impressive playgrounds, Balboa Park, home of the world-renowned San Diego Zoo. And for family fun and recreation or just do-nothing relaxation, Mission Bay Park and its famed Sea World make one more perfect getaway weekend in San Diego.

Get to San Diego from Los Angeles by driving south on Interstate 5, and set the mood for a yesteryear's weekend in California's oldest city by reserving a room in the heart of the city at the beautifully renovated U.S. Grant Hotel, which dates to 1910, or bed down in the Horton Grand Hotel, a classic reborn hostelry in the historic Gaslamp Quarter. Another choice is to plant yourself nearby San Diego's original roots, the presidio and Old Town, with accommodations in an 1889 Victorian that's become the Heritage Park Bed and Breakfast Inn. Or settle into modern-style lodgings such as the Hacienda Hotel at Old Town. Many other motels are close by on Hotel Circle in Mission Valley.

In the morning, begin following the city's Spanish trail by heading to the Mother of the Missions, San Diego de Alcala, the first of California's 21 missions. As the military and religious leaders of Spain's Sacred Expedition to Alta (upper) California in 1769, Gaspar de Portola and Father Junipero Serra established a presidio (fort) and a mission on a barren hill overlooking San Diego Bay. However, within five years a more reliable source of fresh water was needed, and the mission was moved to its present site, a few miles inland in Mission Valley. Reach it from Interstate 5 by joining Interstate 8 east for about six miles to the Mission Gorge Road exit. Turn left under the freeway and continue north to Twain Street, then go left again and follow the signs to the mission and its parking area on the right.

Surrounded by trees and flowers, this peaceful religious sanctuary now serves as an active parish church. It has been rebuilt and restored several times during the past two centuries. Especially fascinating is the sparse room of Father Serra, a remnant of the original mission. Note the rope bed, crosses, and candlesticks, as well as the adobe bricks under the whitewashed walls. At the front of the church, also look for the small statue of Father Serra that was carved in his homeland, the Spanish island of Majorca. More statuary is in the foliage-filled garden, dominated by a campanario of bells. When hostile Indians destroyed the mission in 1775, they also killed Padre Luis Jayme, who became California's first Christian martyr and lies buried in the church sanctuary. Spend some time in the Luis Jayme Museum room, where artifacts from the early mission days are on display, including Father Serra's crucifix. Don't miss the photos of the mission before its restorations—in the mid-1800s the buildings were occupied by the U.S. Cavalry. Outdoors on the perimeter of a courtyard you'll see excavations by college archaeology students of the Indian workshops and the monastery. Hear all about the mission's remarkable history by renting a tape recorder in the gift shop to guide you on a narrated tour through the buildings and grounds.

Afterward, return to Interstate 8 and go west to the Taylor Street exit, then cross the freeway toward Old Town. Follow the signs up the hill to Presidio Park, crowned by the Junipero Serra Museum. This imposing building was dedicated in 1929 as a memorial to the famed padre and is often mistaken by passersby as the San Diego mission. Civic leader George Marston donated it to the city, along with the park's 40 unspoiled acres where the first Spanish fort and mission were built.

You can view excavations in the park that have been made in search of the presidio ruins and objects that belonged to San Diego's settlers. Some of the unearthed artifacts are displayed in the museum, along with Father Serra mementos and examples of vintage Spanish furniture. Climb to the top of the tower to compare the sprawling city today with photos of the town taken from the hill earlier in the century.

As San Diego slowly grew, people moved from the presidio to the bottom of the hill and settled into what is now called Old Town. Since 1969, six square blocks of old San Diego have been preserved as a state historic park. To see some of the restored adobe structures of the 1800s, drive back down through Presidio Park to Old Town's free parking areas and stroll along Old Town's spacious streets, which are off limits to automobiles.

Intermingled with shops and restaurants are a dozen vintage buildings that re-create the setting of California life during the Mexican and early American periods. After Old Town was devastated by fire in 1872, San Diego was reestablished nearer the harbor in the present downtown, so the original town site was never obliterated by modern buildings. Park rangers reveal much of Old Town's history during their informative free walking tours, which depart daily in the afternoon across from the tree-shaded plaza. If you explore on your own, pick up a free guide map from any of the Old Town merchants or buy a guidebook at the park's visitors center. And be sure to go inside the small Historical Museum of Old California to view a detailed scale model of the entire town as it was in 1872.

Visit the 1830s Machado-Stewart Adobe to see the early San Diegans' simple living conditions. If you want to experience daily life in those early times, be there on Saturday morning to participate in the park's living-history programs, a favorite of children. With guidance from the rangers, youngsters bake bread, prepare salsa, create candles, or make adobe bricks just as Old Town residents did 150 years ago.

Near the Machado-Stewart Adobe, peek into the town's first public schoolhouse, where replicas of the 16 flags that have flown over California are displayed. Pay a fee to enter the handsomely furnished Casa de Estudillo, a grand adobe built in 1827 by the commander of the presidio. The ticket also admits you to the nearby Seeley Stables, a restored 1869 stage depot that features Western memorabilia and an impressive collection of horse-drawn vehicles. Included is a stagecoach Albert Seeley used on the stage line he ran to Los Angeles, a two-day trip in those days. Also watch the narrated slide show that describes life in early San Diego.

Next door to the stables is Casa de Bandini, once Old Town's social center and now a Mexican restaurant with mariachi music. Have lunch there to enjoy more of the village's authentic flavor. You also can eat at the edge of the plaza in the homesite of Pio Pico, California's last Mexican governor, now occupied by Bazaar del Mundo, an attractive complex of shops and popular restaurants. At

Casa de Pico, join the line of Old Town visitors waiting for a patio table, where you can relax with a refreshing margarita and nachos or a full Mexican meal.

Just outside the park boundary you'll find many more dining spots, shops, and historical sites within walking distance, including the Whaley House, which is thought to be the oldest two-story brick building in Southern California. This fine old home also has been a courthouse, store, theater, and church since being built in 1857, and it's believed to be haunted by ghosts. Several more of San Diego's vintage buildings have been preserved nearby in Heritage Park, but save them for the following day, when you also should make auto and walking tours of some wonderful Victorian homes and business buildings in other parts of town. Meanwhile, spend the evening at the intimate Theatre in Old Town, where historical dramas and comedies promise plenty of original entertainment.

Continue your tour of historic San Diego in the morning, starting with Heritage Park, just across from Old Town at the corner of Juan and Harney streets. This eight-acre park near the base of historic Presidio Hill was established in 1971 as a haven for endangered buildings that once were the city's pride but stood in the way of new development. Eventually a dozen or more architectural gems from Victorian times will be moved there and restored, serving not only as handsome reminders of the past but as shops and offices where visitors are always welcome.

Inspiration for the county park was a group of citizens who formed the Save Our Heritage Organization (SOHO) to move the Sherman-Gilbert House, an ornate 1887 structure that was going to be flattened by the wrecker's ball and replaced by a parking lot. On top of the house is a widow's walk for observing ships at sea, very common in New England seaport towns but now the only authentic widow's walk remaining in San Diego. You'll also admire the 1893 Burton House and the Busheyhead House, built in 1887. Another restored home is the 1896 Senlis Cottage, which houses the SOHO office and restoration library. The 1889 Temple Beth Israel, the first wooden synagogue in Southern California, has been moved to the park too. Also built that same year is the Queene Anne–style Christian House, now converted to a nine-room B&B called Heritage Park Inn.

Afterward, drive to another old section of the city to visit one of the finest and most unusual Victorian mansions on the West Coast, Village Montezuma. From Heritage Park and the Old Town area, join Interstate 5 south past downtown to the Imperial Avenue exit. Turn left and go under the freeway to 20th Street, then turn left again and drive two blocks to the mansion, which dominates the corner at K and 20th streets.

Villa Montezuma was constructed in 1887 and has been colorfully painted to represent the original color of its redwood exterior. The home's decoration inside and out is as eclectic as the man who had it built, Jesse Shepard, a composer, writer, and spiritualist medium. You'll discover his portrait in one of the building's exquisite stained-glass windows. The mansion has become a fascinating museum run by the San Diego Historical Society, with the second floor featuring an art gallery of changing exhibits.

While at Villa Montezuma, pick up a free booklet that describes and directs you to two dozen other historical homes and churches in the Golden Hill–Sherman Heights sections of southeast San Diego. First go east on K Street to 25th Street, then turn left and drive north 12 blocks to the hilltop park that overlooks the city and harbor. This section of town, called Golden Hill, is where many of San Diego's richest and most influential citizens lived at the turn of the century. By driving up and down A through K streets between 21st and 25th streets you'll discover a variety of Victorian and other interesting homes. Some have been painstakingly restored, while others are in disrepair. All are private residences or have been converted to offices, and you can view them only from the outside.

You're welcome to visit other vintage buildings that are downtown in San Diego's original business district; drive due west on Market Street or Island Avenue to Gaslamp Quarter. It covers 16 square blocks of structures dating from the post–Civil War period to World War I that are now part of a National Historic District. Since 1974 there's been an ongoing transformation of buildings in the city's once notorious red-light district into attractive shops, art galleries, restaurants, and professional offices. Drive or stroll along Fourth, Fifth, and Sixth avenues from Broadway to Harbor Drive.

Get a guide map to Gaslamp Quarter at the 1850s William Heath Davis House, Fourth Avenue at Island Avenue, now a period museum and also departure point for guided walking tours on Saturdays. For extra fun you can tour the old district in a horse-drawn carriage; climb aboard at the carriage stand in nearby Seaport Village. If you haven't made the Horton Grand Hotel your weekend headquarters, be certain to drop in this wonderful reincarnation of two century-old hotels that were saved from the wrecker's ball. Go for afternoon tea in its Victorian bar or skylighted lounge, or enjoy a meal in the Victorian hostelry's Ida Bailey's Restaurant. When it's time for your return to Los Angeles, rejoin Interstate 5 and drive north.

Round trip is about 288 miles.

San Diego Area Code: 619

SIGHTSEEING   *Mission San Diego de Alcala*, 10818 San Diego Mission Road, San Diego, 92108, 281-8449. Open daily 9 A.M. to 5

P.M. Admission $1, under 12 years free. 30-minute tape tour, $1. • *Junipero Serra Museum*, in Presidio Park, at 2727 Presidio Drive, San Diego 92110, 297-3258. Open daily except Mondays from 10 A.M. to 4:30 P.M., Sundays from noon. $3, children under 12 years free. • *Old Town San Diego State Historic Park*, with the Visitors Center at 4002 Wallace Street, San Diego 92110, 237-6770. Buildings open daily from 10 A.M. to 5 P.M. Free parking and entry. Ranger-led walking tours at 2 P.M. Entry to Casa de Estudillo and Seeley Stables $2 for adults, $1 for senior citizens and children 6 to 17 years. Living History Programs for children at Machado-Stewart Adobe 1st through 3rd Saturdays of every month at 10 and 11 A.M. by advance reservation; call park office. Free. • *Whaley House*, 2482 San Diego Avenue, San Diego 92110, 298-2482. Open 10 A.M. to 4:30 P.M. Wednesday through Sunday. Adults $3, children 12 to 16 years $1.50, 5 to 11 years $1. • *Theatre in Old Town*, 4040 Twiggs Street, San Diego 92110, 298-0082. 200-seat horseshoe-shaped theater presenting historical dramas and comedies at 8 P.M.; matinees at 2 P.M. Adults $15–$20, children $5. Call the box office for the playbill and reservations. • *Heritage Park*, Juan and Harney streets, San Diego 92110, 565-5928. Open daily. Victorian buildings with shops. • *Villa Montezuma*, 1925 K Street, San Diego 92102, 239-2211. Ornate 1887 Victorian mansion open from 1 to 4:30 P.M. Wednesday through Sunday. Museum and headquarters of the San Diego Historical Society. Admission $3. • *William Heath Davis House*, in Gaslamp Quarter, at 410 Island Street, San Diego 92101, 233-5227. Museum of the Gaslamp Quarter Foundation. Open 11 A.M. to 2 P.M. Monday through Saturday. Also starting point for walking tours of the historic quarter Saturdays at 11 A.M.; $5 donation.

LODGING *Heritage Park Bed & Breakfast Inn*, 2470 Heritage Park Row, San Diego 92110, 299-6832; $80–$120. 1889 mansion with 9 rooms, some private baths. Decorated with antiques, which guests can buy. Catered dinners by reservation. • *U.S. Grant Hotel*, 326 Broadway, San Diego 92101, 232-3121; $155, less on weekends. Grand 1910 landmark hotel restored to its original elegance. 280 deluxe rooms. In heart of downtown at north end of Gaslamp Quarter. Also has regal restaurant (see below). • *Horton Grand Hotel*, 311 Island Avenue, San Diego 92101, 544-1886; $94. Two 1880s hotels restored brick by brick into one block-long Victorian hostelry. 132 rooms with fireplaces, antiques, canopied beds. Also afternoon tea, vintage Palace Bar, and restaurant (see below). • *Horton Park Plaza Hotel*, 901 Fifth Avenue, San Diego 92101,

232-9500 or toll-free (800) 443-8012; $119. 65 rooms in beautifully restored 1913 downtown building. Also, award-winning restaurant (see below). • *Best Western Hacienda Hotel—Old Town*, 4041 Harney Street, San Diego 92110, 298-4707; $107. 150 modern suites with coffeemakers, microwaves, and refrigerators in Old Town. Mexican restaurant on top floor.

DINING   *Casa de Bandini*, 2660 Calhoun Street in Old Town, San Diego, 297-8211. Open daily for lunch and dinner. Enjoy Mexican fare amid foliage and fountains in the patio of this handsome 1829 hacienda and former hotel. Mariachi music too. • *Casa de Pico*, 2754 Calhoun Street in Old Town's Bazaar del Mundo, San Diego, 296-3267. Open daily for all meals, Mexican style. Favorite for huge fruit margaritas and mariachis in the courtyard. Other restaurants in this international marketplace of 17 shops are *Lino's* with Italian dishes and *Hamburguesa* with you know what (and omelette brunch on weekends). • *Ida Bailey's Restaurant*, in the Horton Grand Hotel (see above), 544-6888. All-American favorites, from Yankee pot roast to apple pie, for lunch and dinner daily. Also breakfast and Sunday brunch. • *Grant Grill*, in the U.S. Grant Hotel (see above), 239-6806. Fine continental cuisine; rotisserie grill on view. Lunch weekdays, dinner nightly except Sundays (coats required for gentlemen). • *The Grill on the Park*, in the Horton Park Plaza Hotel (see above), 231-0055. Popular Gaslamp Quarter restaurant featuring mesquite-grilled ribs, chicken, and fish for lunch and dinner daily. Also, check out *Croce's Restaurant & Jazz Bar* and *Fio's* at Fifth Avenue and F Street, a hot corner for food and entertainment in the Gaslamp Quarter. • *Cafe Pacifica*, 2414 San Diego Avenue, in Old Town area, San Diego, 291-6666. Small, charming restaurant with seafood specialties. Lunch and dinner; reservations suggested. • *Pacifica Grill*, 1202 Kettner Boulevard (at B Street), San Diego, 696-9226. Varied menu, including fresh fish. Lunch weekdays and dinner nightly.

FOR MORE INFORMATION   Contact the Old Town Chamber of Commerce, 2461 San Diego Avenue, San Diego 92110, 291-4903. Also, the San Diego Convention and Visitors Bureau, 1200 Third Avenue, Suite 824, San Diego 92101, 236-1212.

San Diego
Part 2: The Southland's Most Enchanting Harbor

When Juan Rodriguez Cabrillo discovered California almost four and a half centuries ago, he couldn't have picked a prettier spot to drop anchor. Today's explorers will discover that beautiful San Diego Bay still holds all sorts of attractions for sailors and landlubbers alike. During a weekend there you'll enjoy cruising in the scenic harbor, touring historic ships that now are maritime museums, visiting aboard a naval vessel, shopping in a re-created waterfront village, and dining on fish that's fresh from the sea.

Spend a full day enjoying those nautical delights, which are conveniently clustered along picturesque Harbor Drive bordering downtown San Diego. Then reserve time the following day to follow part of San Diego's Scenic Drive around the bay to Cabrillo National Monument at the tip of Point Loma, the most southwesterly peninsula of the United States mainland.

Get to San Diego and its Embarcadero from Los Angeles by driving south on Interstate 5, exiting on Front Street (Civic Center) to Broadway, then turning right to Harbor Drive. Go left to the 39-story waterfront Hyatt Regency San Diego, or follow Harbor Drive to the twin-tower San Diego Marriott, which overlooks Embarcadero Marina Park at the water's edge. You also can headquarter around the bay in one of the hotels on Harbor or Shelter islands, man-made resort havens and home for hundreds of pleasure boats.

In the morning, the best way to become acquainted with San Diego's vast and enchanting bay is to admire it from the deck of a tour boat. Along the Embarcadero at Broadway Pier you'll find the veteran San Diego Harbor Excursion company, which has been conducting sightseeing cruises since 1916. An hour-long cruise is available, but take the more extensive two-hour excursion which covers 25 miles and sails as far as the channel entrance at Point Loma. (Another choice is to tour the harbor on the sleek schooner *Invader*.)

Look back at the city's sparkling skyline as you pull away from the dock. You'll be sailing among all kinds of vessels in this busy port, home to the nation's largest armada, a tuna fleet, and dozens of sportfishing boats. En route to Ballast Point, where Cabrillo is believed to have first landed in 1542, your excursion boat mingles with yachts and sailboats going to and from their marina slips at Harbor and Shelter islands. Along the west shoreline is the navy's submarine base, and in the center of the harbor you'll see North Island Naval Air Station. After reaching Ballast Point, your narrated cruise continues around North Island and underneath the graceful Coronado Bay Bridge for a glimpse of the old and elegant Hotel del Coronado. Circling back to the Broadway Pier, the boat passes warships and tuna canneries. Open sun decks offer the best views, but the harbor excursion boats also have glass-enclosed lounge areas. There are snack bars aboard, too.

At the pier before or after your cruise, you can inspect the *Glorietta*, a ferryboat that went out of service when the Coronado Bay Bridge opened in 1969. Today the boat is a gift shop, and the kids can play sea captain with the ship's controls in the wheelhouse. Ferryboats still cross the bay to Coronado, but they carry only pedestrians. On weekend afternoons at the Broadway Pier, you're also welcome to visit a military ship when the navy holds open house for the public on one or more of its impressive vessels. Visitors are usually not allowed aboard the big cruise ships that stop over in San Diego on their weekly Los Angeles–Ensenada runs or that embark passengers for the Mexican Riviera.

Nearby are other waterfront attractions, three historic ships that are floating museums. You can't miss the towering three-masted *Star of India*, a magnificent square-rigger that's the oldest merchant ship afloat. Launched from England in 1863, she eventually circumnavigated the globe 21 times with cargo and passengers. Another ship of the Maritime Museum Association that can be boarded at dockside is the *Medea*, a steam-powered luxury yacht originally built for a Scottish gentleman at the turn of the century. An equally elegant vessel, the *Berkeley*, served six decades as a passenger ferry between San Francisco and Oakland.

As San Diego is home port of the nation's largest tuna fleet, you'll probably find some of the expensive oceangoing tuna boats tied up along the seawall just north along the Embarcadero. Look for the deep-sea fishermen mending their huge nets. The tuna seiners are close by a San Diego landmark, Anthony's Fish Grotto, where local folks and visitors have been enjoying tasty seafood since 1946. You have a choice of takeout or table service, and you can eat on the patio overlooking the water.

For other seafood dining spots, walk south along the waterfront to the Harbor Seafood Mart at the foot of Market Street, just beyond the commerical wharf, where fishing boats unload their daily catches. You can sample more delicacies of the sea at restaurants in this modern harbor facility or buy fresh fish to take home.

Around the corner is a highlight of San Diego's wonderful waterfront, Seaport Village, an attractive assortment of shops and restaurants on the bay front. The complex opened in 1980 on the site of the former San Diego–Coronado ferryboat landing, now marked by a five-story replica of a vintage West Coast lighthouse. A boardwalk leads to it and more than 65 shops in a series of plazas, where the architecture takes you back to early Monterey, Victorian San Francisco, and old Mexico.

Some shop specialties are as distinctive as the store's name, such as Wee Willie Winkie (candles), Southpaw Shop (left-handed items), and The Mugger (coffee cups). You'll also find shops devoted to lollipops, soap items, wooden puzzles, magic, T-shirts, artwork, antiques, and much more.

If the kids get restless while you're browsing for gifts, head to the kite shop and then the lawn of breezy Embarcadero Marine Park, which extends from the village into the bay. For other family fun, take a musical spin on the Broadway Flying Horses Carrousel, an original Coney Island merry-go-round. The colorful wooden animals you'll ride were carved by hand nearly 90 years ago. It's also exciting to climb aboard a horse-drawn carriage for a clippity-clop ride along the Embarcadero.

With more than a dozen eating spots, you won't go hungry at Seaport Village, and it's an ideal place to end an enjoyable afternoon with a leisurely dinner. For excellent seafood and the best bay views, get a window table at the Harbor House. At Ristorante Luigi Al Mare the specialty is seafood with an Italian flair, while the Jolly Roger is a favorite for traditional American fare. The San Diego Pier Cafe, a rustic restaurant built over the water, features fresh fish broiled over mesquite.

Return the next day to the Embarcadero at the Broadway Pier and join San Diego's Scenic Drive heading north on Harbor Drive. All you have to do is follow the birds—white sea gulls painted on blue-and-gold signs that are posted every quarter mile with directional arrows. Follow the route as it curves around the bay from the downtown harbor area to land's end at Point Loma. Visitors to that rugged promontory, which is crowned by one of California's oldest lighthouses, are presented with sweeping vistas of the Pacific Ocean and San Diego Bay from Cabrillo National Monument.

As you go north on Harbor Drive, look for the Teledyne Ryan buildings, where Charles Lindbergh had his famed *Spirit of St. Louis* built for the first transatlantic solo flight from New York to Paris. Beyond on the right is San Diego International Airport, originally named Lindbergh Field. You'll also spot the high-rise resort hotels on Harbor Island, a peninsula created with material dredged from the bay when the channel was deepened for naval vessels.

Some of the navy's training facilities flank the Scenic Drive before it turns south on Scott Street, past the sportfishing boat docks, and turns onto Shelter Island, a submerged shoal that was earth-filled and is connected to the mainland by a causeway. You'll pass the island's attractive hotels, restaurants, and marinas before reaching the huge Friendship Bell, a gift from San Diego's sister city, Yokohama, Japan.

The sea gull signs leads you back across the causeway and onto Talbot and Canon streets to the high bluff road, California 209, that goes down the middle of the Point Loma peninsula to land's end. You'll pass through Fort Rosecrans military reservation and national cemetery before reaching one of the state's most visited parks, Cabrillo National Monument. It's named for the first European explorer to visit the West Coast, Juan Cabrillo, a Portuguese-born mariner who claimed the land for the king of Spain.

Start at the visitors center, where there are exhibits and different programs about Cabrillo and Pacific Coast explorations. Pick up a guide map before walking around the outside terrace for a panoramic view of the busy bay and San Diego from more than 400 feet above sea level. Illustrated signs help identify the navy ships and aircraft that pass by almost constantly.

Nearby, another viewpoint is dominated by a statue of Cabrillo. It was carved in Portugal for the 1939 international exposition held in San Francisco and placed at the monument later. On clear days you can see Tijuana and beyond to the mountains in Mexico from here.

Stroll up to the old 1854 lighthouse, which has been restored and authentically refurnished by the National Park Service. A tape recording describes what life was like for the keeper and his family who lived there nearly a century ago. Because this lighthouse is located on such a high point, its beacon was often shrouded by fog. A new one was built near water level in 1891, and the coast guard continues to use it. You can see the current Point Loma lighthouse from another overlook, which is crowded with sightseers during winter months when the gray whales pass by on their annual migration from the Arctic to Baja. A tape recording at this observation station describes the event.

For some exercise and a closer look at native vegetation, walk down the mile-long Bayside Trail. A nature-guide leaflet is available at the visitors center. Heed the rangers' advice and be careful on the sandstone cliffs. On the ocean side, marine life can be observed in protected tide pools, where the viewing is best during low winter tides. Watch your step on the slippery rocks.

When your weekend along San Diego's waterfront is over, return from Point Loma on California 209 and follow it north to join Interstate 5 back to Los Angeles.

Round trip is about 265 miles.

San Diego Area Code: 619

SIGHTSEEING *San Diego Harbor Excursion*, Broadway Pier at Harbor Drive (or P.O. Box 751), San Diego 92112, 234-1111. 2-hour cruises of San Diego Bay depart 3 times daily in summer, once daily in winter. Adults $15, senior citizens and children 3 to 12 years $7.50. 1-hour cruises depart 4 times daily with an extra sailing in summer. Adults $10, seniors and children $5. Also, dinner and Sunday brunch cruises; call for details. • *Invader Cruises*, 1066 North Harbor Drive between Broadway and B Street piers, San Diego 92101, 234-8687. Harbor cruises aboard 151-foot schooner. 2-hour tour once daily; adults $15, children $7.50. 1-hour tours more frequently; adults $10, children $5. Call for departure times. • *San Diego–Coronado Ferry*, North Harbor Drive at Broadway, San Diego 92101, 234-4111. Regular pedestrian ferry service from Embarcadero to Old Ferry Landing at Coronado. 15-minute ride, $2 each way. No cars carried, but bicycles accepted. 10 A.M. to 10 P.M. daily, to 11 P.M. on weekends. • *Naval Ship Open House*, Broadway Pier on North Harbor Drive, San Diego, 235-3534. Visitors are welcome aboard one or more military ships most weekends from 1 to 4 P.M. Free. • *San Diego Maritime Museum Association*, 1306 North Harbor Drive on the Embarcadero, San Diego, 92101, 234-9153. Three historic ships open daily 9 A.M. to 8 P.M. Combined admission costs adults $5, senior citizens and children 13 to 17 years $4, kids 6 to 12 years $1.25, and family groups $10. Self-guided 45-minute tour tape rental $1. • *Seaport Village*, 849 West Harbor Drive at end of Pacific Highway, San Diego 92101, 235-4013. Most shops are open from 10 A.M. to 10 P.M. daily in summer, to 9 P.M. in winter. Vintage Broadway Flying Horses Carousel rides cost $.50. Also theme cafes and four restaurants (see below). • *Cinderella Carriage Company*, carriage stand located at Seaport Village (see above), 239-8080. Handsome one-horse carriages carry up to 4 passengers on ½-hour tour ($30) rides. Prices based on walk-up basis; add $10 if reservations made in advance. • *Cabrillo National Monument*, at end of California 209 on Point Loma (or P.O. Box 6670), San Diego 92106, 557-5450. Visitors center and museum open daily from 9 A.M. to 5:15 P.M., to 7:45 P.M. in summer. $3 per vehicle: $1 per person if arriving by bicycle or city bus. Also films, slide shows, and ranger talks. Viewpoint for California gray whale migration in winter. Historic Old Point Loma Lighthouse is open to monument visitors too. (Also see "Events" below.) • *H&M Landing*, 2803 Emerson Street, San Diego 92106, 222-1144. Sport-fishing trips in local and Baja waters.

EVENTS   *Cabrillo Festival* is a week-long commemoration of Cabrillo's discovery of the West Coast, held annually to coincide with the date of his arrival, September 28. Highlight is the reenactment of Cabrillo's landing staged at Shelter Island. Most events are free. Call 557-5450 for schedule and more information.

LODGING   *San Diego Marriott*, 333 West Harbor Drive, San Diego 92101, 234-1500; $140. Two curved 25-story towers with 1,355 rooms and suites presenting city and bay panoramas. Adjacent to Seaport Village and San Diego Convention Center. Tennis, swimming pools, sauna, and marina with rental slips, ● *Hyatt Regency San Diego*, 820 West F Street, San Diego 92101, 232-1234; $169. 875 rooms in the city's tallest hotel on the waterfront. Health club. Near Seaport Village and San Diego Convention Center. ● *Sheraton Grand on Harbor Island*, 1590 Harbor Island Drive, San Diego 92101, 291-6400; $145. 350 deluxe rooms, including penthouse floor with presidential and other suites. Adjacent is *Sheraton Harbor Island Hotel*, 1380 Harbor Island Drive, San Diego 92101, 291-2900; $150. 700 rooms. Together the Sheratons create a full-service resort offering wonderful bay and marina views, lighted tennis courts, swimming pools, health club, and more. Also evening entertainment and Italian restaurant (see below). Ask about family vacation packages. ● *Bay Club Hotel and Marina*, 213 Shelter Island Drive, San Diego 92106, 224-8888; $120. 105 rooms with marina or harbor views. Buffet breakfast included. ● *Humphrey's Half Moon Inn*, 2303 Shelter Island Circle on Shelter Island, San Diego 92106, 224-3411; $89. Tropical-style lodgings overlooking bay and yacht harbor. Putting green, shuffleboard, and Jacuzzi. Also restaurant (see below).

DINING   *Anthony's Fish Grotto*, 1360 Harbor Drive on the Embarcadero, San Diego, 232-5103. Open daily from 11:30 A.M. to 8:30 P.M. Seafood only. Harbor views and outdoor dining. Also *Anthony's Star of the Sea Room* at the same location, 232-7408. Gourmet seafood dining room open nightly for dinner only. Fancy silver-cart service. Jacket and tie for men. Reservations a must. ● *Fish Market & Top of the Market*, 750 North Harbor Drive, San Diego, 232-3474. Mesquite-broiled fish, oyster bar, sushi too. Indoor/outdoor dining. Open daily for lunch and dinner. ● *People's Fish Company*, 565 Harbor Lane, San Diego, 239-8788. Fish and chips and other deep-fried and grilled fish specialties; also fresh seafood market. ● *Anthony's Seafood Mart*, 555 Harbor Lane, San

Diego, 232-2933. Open daily for seafood lunches and dinners at harbor-view tables or for takeout. Also retail fish market. • Seaport Village, on Harbor Drive at the end of Pacific Highway, has numerous cafes with international dishes, plus four restaurants. *Harbor House*, 831 West Harbor Drive, San Diego, 232-1411. Fish specialties for lunch and dinner with bay-front views. Upstairs lounge has luncheon menu except Sundays; music and dancing in the evening. Also Sunday brunch. • *Ristorante Luigi Al Mare*, 861 West Harbor Drive, San Diego, 232-7581. Seafood prepared Italian style for lunch and dinner. Wonderful water views. • *San Diego Pier Cafe*, West Harbor Drive, San Diego, 239-3968. Fresh fish dishes daily for lunch and dinner in an informal restaurant built over the water. Also breakfast. • *Jolly Roger*, 807 West Harbor Drive, San Diego, 233-4300. Open daily, breakfast, lunch, and dinner. Family restaurant with American fare. • *Merlano's* in Sheraton Harbor Island Hotel (see above), 692-2255. Italian menu offered nightly. • *Humphrey's* in the Half Moon Inn on Shelter Island (see above), 224-3577. Serves all three meals daily, plus Sunday brunch. Outdoor dining at lunch and dinner with harbor view. Fresh seafood specialties. Also a local favorite for the boating crowd at happy hour.

FOR MORE INFORMATION   Contact the San Diego Convention and Visitors Bureau, 1200 Third Avenue, Suite 824, San Diego 92101, 236-1212.

San Diego
Part 3: Balboa Park
and Its World-Famous Zoo

San Diego has a city park that puts most municipal playgrounds to shame. Not only is Balboa Park a 1,074-acre recreational and botanical haven, it's the city's art and culture center. You'll discover a cluster of 13 museums and art galleries displaying everything from dinosaur bones and spacecraft to Russian icons and Rembrandts. Concerts and plays delight visitors, too, and so does the world-famous San Diego Zoo, which blends into the park's verdant scenery.

San Diego's foresighted citizens established City Park in 1868, when the town had but 2,300 residents. Later renamed Balboa Park for the discoverer of the Pacific Ocean, it annually attracts three million local and out-of-town visitors. For the most relaxing weekend there, plan to spend your first day at the zoo and then come back the next day to enjoy the park's many other attractions.

Get to San Diego from Los Angeles by driving south on Interstate 5. Stay downtown in one of the city's outstanding hotels, such as the Westgate, or at any other of the numerous lodgings that are convenient to the centrally located park, which can be reached from the freeway by following the Zoo-Museum signs.

Head for Balboa Park early Saturday morning to be there at 9 A.M., when the gates open to the San Diego Zoo's collection of more than 3,800 mammals, reptiles, and birds. Not only is the wildlife more active and fun to watch, the zoo is less crowded earlier in the day. One thing that surprises first-time visitors is that the zoo is a paradise for plant lovers, too. In fact, its flowers, shrubs, and trees are worth more money than all the animals, and zoo officials say many of their botanical specimens are irreplaceable.

The lush landscape that helps make the 100-acre San Diego Zoo such an enjoyable place to visit includes everything from orchids to cacti to redwoods. You'll find a garden of bromeliads, a canyon filled with ferns, and even a banana grove. Over 6,500 species of plants grow throughout the zoo, beautifying the once scrub-covered terrain that existed when the zoo began in 1916. Some plants are practical as well as pretty—they're fed to the animals.

A comfortable way to admire both the flora and fauna is to take an orientation tour of the extensive, hilly zoo. Board one of the open-sided double-decker buses near the entrance gate and you'll be treated to a 40-minute trip with an entertaining guide who identifies and talks about the wildlife as you ride along. The tour briefly covers about 80 percent of the animal displays as the bus follows a few miles of winding roads down canyons and up to the mesas. Many of the zoo's inhabitants live in roomy enclosures that have no bars but are guarded by moats. Look for long-billed kiwis from New Zealand, pygmy hippos from Africa, wild Przewalski's horses from Mongolia, and cuddly koalas from Australia. Choose an outside seat on the top deck of the tour bus if you want to take pictures.

Afterward go on foot to watch the gorillas, lesser apes, and playful monkeys. In nearby cages is a colorful collection of parrots and other birds; be sure to go inside the two walk-through aviaries. Equally fascinating is the reptile house, where main attractions are the New Guinea tree monitor, a five-foot-long lizard, and the two-headed cornsnake.

A multilevel exhibit of Southeast Asian primates and birds involves visitors in the rain forest environment shared by playful orangutans and rare langur monkeys. In this Heart of the Zoo display you'll also see the acrobatic siamang apes and hundreds of beautiful feathered creatures, including red-billed blue magpies and hornbills.

Strolling around the lush property you'll notice that the trend-setting San Diego Zoo is engaged in a long-range renovation project to group mammals, birds, reptiles, and plants from the same climate zone into habitats that resemble those occurring in nature. Over the next decade or two, at a cost of $100 million or more, the zoo is being reorganized into ten major exhibit areas that represent various environments found around the globe, such as the spectacular Gorilla Tropics habitat. Another is a tropical rain forest called Tiger River, which lets visitors feel the humidity, smell the flowers, and hear the birds and tigers as you might on a walk in the wild. Following the winding pathway through palms and other foliage, you'll encounter everything from Burmese pythons to milky storks among 35 species of animals that include the rare and endangered Sumatran tiger.

For an exciting overview of the zoo, ride the Skyfari aerial tramway that cruises six stories above the ground. Its high-flying gondolas run from the reptile house near the Children's Zoo across the treetops to Horn and Hoof Plaza, where the buffalo roam.

The animal nursery is a highlight of the Children's Zoo, which is built to the scale of four-year-olds but enjoyed by all ages. Through the windows you'll see young apes that have been rejected by their mothers and are diapered and bottle-fed just like human babies. Kids also like the small farm animals they can pet and the live exhibit that shows chicken eggs being laid, incubated, and hatched.

Free animal shows are presented daily in outdoor amphitheaters. Sometimes sea lions are the stars, or the audience gets to meet a few of the zoo's more exotic feathered and furry residents, like an emu and a cheetah. A coatimundi, hawk, llama, and other wildlife of North and South America also are featured. Show times are given in the zoo guide and posted at the Wegeforth Bowl and Hunte Amphitheater, where the animals perform.

The Jungle Bazaar, one of the zoo's gift shops, is worth a stop because of its authentic artifacts imported from all over Africa. In addition, you'll also discover books, toys, and other gifts from around the world. Hungry visitors can snack at food stands throughout the zoo, or dine in the Peacock and Raven Deli or Albert's, a restaurant named for the zoo's famous lowland gorilla. Pizza and other Italian dishes are offered at the Lagoon Terrace, and picnickers will find shaded areas with tables.

Sunday is an ideal day to explore the rest of Balboa Park, which began to blossom earlier in this century when it was selected as the site for the 1915–16 Panama-California Exposition, an international fair celebrating the opening of the Panama Canal. After the exposition was over, townsfolk decided to preserve some of the exhibits and the temporary buildings that were constructed with Spanish Colonial and Mayan Indian motifs. Later they also kept buildings from the 1935–36 California-Pacific Exposition, another early world's fair staged at the park. Some of those original structures and subsequent ones have been lost to decay and fire, notably the Old Globe Theatre and the Aero-Space Museum, which burned in 1978. San Diegans, who are justly proud of their municipal park and maintain an ongoing restoration and building program, reopened the aerospace museum and the theater in new quarters just three years after the conflagrations.

The best way to enjoy Balboa Park's many attractions is by foot. Dress casually and wear comfortable shoes for strolling among the gardens, fountains, and lush landscaping and visiting the museums and art galleries. You'll find several of these along El Prado (the promenade), a narrow street with exhibit buildings from the 1915–16 exposition. Look for the fancy 200-foot California Tower, housing a carillon that chimes melodiously every quarter hour.

Midway on El Prado, at the southeast corner of Plaza de Panama, stop at the Balboa Park Information Center in the House of Hospitality for a map of the park to help plan your outing. Adjacent is the park's major restaurant, Cafe Del Rey Moro, serving full meals and takeout picnic lunches. The Sculpture Garden Cafe and snack bars also offer refreshments, or bring your own picnic.

As you'll discover, the peaceful park is especially active on weekends. Every Sunday afternoon visitors gather in front of the Spreckels Organ Pavilion for an outdoor concert on the 5,000-pipe organ, a gift of the wealthy sugar family. Ask at the House of Hospitality about any special events or shows in the park at the time of your visit.

One of Balboa Park's most popular attractions is the Reuben H. Fleet Space Theater and Science Center on El Prado. Visitors are awed by spectacular Omnimax audiovisual shows on a huge hemisphere-shaped screen. Kids also love the scientific exhibits they can touch and work.

Across the way there are dinosaurs, whales, birds, plants, reptiles, shells, and more to see in the Natural History Museum. Nearby you can explore the Spanish Village—small cottages, built for the 1935–36 exposition—which now houses nearly two dozen studios for artists and craftspeople. Visitors are welcome to watch and buy.

Returning to El Prado, visit the Timken Museum of Art to see the works of old masters and early American artists, as well as Russian icons. More of the old masters, along with Asian art and a sculpture gallery and cafe, are next door at the outstanding San Diego Museum of Art.

Balboa Park is a haven for horticulturists. Even visitors without a green thumb are attracted by the 500 species of tropical and subtropical plants inside the Botanical Building. This immense greenhouse is the iron framework of a turn-of-the-century railroad station that has been covered with redwood lath. In front is a reflecting pool, the Lily Pond, once used as a swimming pool by World War II sailors recovering at the nearby naval hospital.

On the opposite side of El Prado, in the rebuilt Casa de Balboa, visit the Hall of Champions, which is filled with sports memorabilia and honors San Diego–area heroes such as boxer Archie Moore and swimmer Florence Chadwick. Adjacent is the Museum of Photographic Arts, which features still photography, cinema, and video. You'll also find the San Diego Model Railroad Museum with N-, O-, and HO-scale trains running around. West on El Prado in a building called the House of Charm, the San Diego Art Institute displays and sells the work of local artists.

A few steps farther west, by the carillon tower, visit the Museum of Man, featuring Indian cultures of the Americans and an excellent exhibit about human birth, "The Wonder of Life." Behind the museum is the Simon Edison Centre for the Performing Arts, which includes the Old Globe Theatre, Cassius Carter Centre Stage, and the Lowell Davies Festival Theatre, an outdoor amphitheater. Check the playbills to see what's on during your visit.

Stroll past the organ pavilion to Pan-American Plaza, stopping along the way at the House of Pacific Relations, a complex of cottages with art and cultural exhibits from 27 nations. A different country hosts an open house every Sunday afternoon.

At the end of the plaza you'll see the Aerospace Historical Center, the refurbished 1935 Ford Building that's new quarters for the original fire-devastated Aero-Space Museum. All sorts of aircraft are on display, including a replica of Charles Lindbergh's *Spirit of St. Louis*, the plane that was built in San Diego for the first solo flight across the Atlantic. In addition, an international hall of fame honors heroes of aviation and space.

If you don't go to a play in Balboa Park, and you're staying downtown, spend one of your evenings exploring Horton Plaza. It's a whimsical, one-of-a-kind complex that anchors the redevelopment of San Diego's city center. A potpourri of architectural styles covers six blocks and unites four department stores, 120 specialty shops, good restaurants, a fast-food row, repertory theater stages, and a multiscreen movie house.

When your weekend is over, return to Los Angeles the way you arrived, via Interstate 5.

Round trip is about 254 miles.

San Diego Area Code: 619

SIGHTSEEING   *San Diego Zoo*, in Balboa Park via Park Boulevard and Zoo Drive, San Diego 92112, 234-3153. Open every day of the year from 9 A.M. to dusk. Adults $12, children 3 to 15 years $4. Tickets include Skyfari aerial tram ride and Children's Zoo. Deluxe Ticket Package also includes wonderful 40-minute guided bus tour; $15 adults, $6.50 children. • *Balboa Park*, via Park Boulevard to attractions along El Prado and near Pan-American Plaza. • *Balboa Park Information Center*, in the *House of Hospitality*, 239-0512. Open daily from 9:30 A.M. to 4 P.M. Buy the park map/guide. $9 park passport gives admission to 2 to 4 participating museums. • *Reuben H. Fleet Space Theater and Science Center*, 238-1168. Open daily from 9:30 A.M. until at least 9:30 P.M. (depending on evening programs). Adults $5.50, senior citizens $4, children 5 to 15 years $3. • *Natural History Museum*, 232-3821. Open 10 A.M. to 4:30 P.M. daily. Adults $6, children 6 to 14 years $2. No charge on Tuesdays. • *Spanish Village Art Center*, 233-9050. Most studios open daily from 11 A.M. to 4 P.M. Free. • *Timken Museum of Art*, 239-5548. Open daily from 10 A.M. to 4:30 P.M. except Sundays from 1:30 P.M. Closed during September. Free. • *San Diego Museum of Art*, 232-7931. Open daily except Mondays from 10 A.M. to 4:30 P.M. Adults $5, senior citizens $4, ages 6 to 18 years and students $2. Free on Tuesdays. • *Botanical Building* open daily except Fridays and holidays from 10 A.M. to 4:30 P.M. Free. • *Hall of Champions*, 234-2544. Open daily from 10 A.M. to 4:30 P.M. except Sundays from noon. Adults $3, children $1. • *Museum of Photographic Arts*, 239-5262. Open daily from 10 A.M. to 5 P.M., Thursdays to 9 P.M. $2.50. • *San Diego Model Railroad Museum*, 696-0199. Open first Tuesday of the month and every Wednesday through Friday from 11 A.M. to 4 P.M., weekends to 5 P.M. Adults $1.50, children under 14 years free. • *Museum of Man*, 239-2001. Open daily from 10 A.M. to 4:30 P.M. Adults $3, children 6 to 11 years $.25. Free on Wednesdays. • *Simon Edison Centre for Performing Arts*, 239-2255. Plays usually presented year round in the evenings on at least one of the center's three stages: Old Globe Theatre, Cassius Carter Centre Stage, and the Lowell Davies Festival Theatre. Also weekend matinees. Call for current playbill and ticket information. • *House of Pacific Relations*, 234-0739. Sunday afternoon open house March through October featuring cultural and art exhibits. Free. • *Aerospace Historical Center*, 234-8291. Open 10 A.M. to 4:30 P.M. daily. Adults $4, children 6 to 17 years $1. Free on Tuesdays. • *Horton Plaza*, between Broadway and G Street and First and Fourth avenues, San Diego, 239-8180. Store hours from 10 A.M. to 9 P.M. weekdays, to 6 P.M. on Saturdays, 11 A.M. to 6 P.M. Sundays; restaurants and some shops have longer hours.

EVENTS *Summer Festival*, features Shakespeare and other productions staged annually from mid-June to mid-September at the Simon Edison Centre for the Performing Arts in Balboa Park. Nightly performances except Mondays. Call 239-2255.

LODGING *The Westgate*, 1055 Second Avenue at C Street, San Diego 92101, 238-1818; $144. Live in eighteenth-century European elegance in this deluxe downtown hotel. View rooms on upper floors of this 20-story building. No swimming pool, but guests have privileges at private health club. Valet parking. Also intimate Plaza Bar and exquisite dining room (see below). ● *Doubletree Hotel*, 910 Broadway Circle, San Diego 92101, 239-2200; $109. High-rise hotel with 450 rooms and suites at Horton Plaza. Swimming pool and sun deck. ● *Embassy Suites San Diego Downtown*, 601 Pacific Highway (at Market Street), San Diego 92101, 239-2400 or toll-free (800) 362-2779; $129, with full breakfast. 337 suites with bay views. Family favorite in harbor area location. ● *Pan Pacific Hotel*, 400 West Broadway, San Diego 92101, 239-4500; $150. 436 rooms in downtown center. ● Also, see ''Lodging'' sections of other San Diego weekends.

DINING *Albert's* and *Treehouse Cafe* in the San Diego Zoo, Balboa Park. Fine-dining and cafeteria-style restaurants occupy the 4-story Treehouse on stilts adjacent to the Gorilla Tropics exhibit area. Food service also available at *Peacock and Raven Deli* and *Lagoon Terrace*. Open daily during zoo hours. ● *Cafe Del Rey Moro*, 1549 El Prado, in Balboa Park, San Diego 92101, 234-8511. Open daily for lunch and dinner except for lunch only on Mondays. Also Sunday champagne brunch. Reservations recommended. Fine food and cocktails indoors amid Spanish-Moorish decor or outdoors on the terraces. Also box lunches to take out for a picnic elsewhere in the park. ● *Sculpture Garden Cafe*, at San Diego Museum of Art in Balboa Park, 236-1725. Light lunches daily except Mondays, plus Sunday brunch. Also open before evening plays at the Simon Edison Centre for the Performing Arts. ● *Fontainebleau Room* in the Westgate hotel (see above). Lunch and dinner daily except dinner only on Saturdays. Fine French cuisine and white-glove service.

Expensive, but a refreshing change from a day of snack food at the zoo or Balboa Park. Reservations recommended. ● See "Dining" sections of other San Diego weekends for more restaurant suggestions.

FOR MORE INFORMATION   Contact the San Diego Convention and Visitors Bureau, 1200 Third Avenue, Suite 824, San Diego 92101, and visit the International Visitors Center, in Horton Plaza, with multilingual staff, 236-3101.

San Diego
Part 4: Aquatic Action
in Mission Bay Park

What's so attractive about hundreds of acres of marsh and mud flats? Nothing. But add some determined townfolk, nearly $60 million, 20 years for dredging and development—then you've got one of the West Coast's most beautiful aquatic parks and resort areas. San Diegans are rightly proud of their Mission Bay Park, less than ten minutes from the downtown area. The former eyesore and mosquito breeding ground has become a popular getaway spot for day outings and more extensive holidays.

Spreading from Mission Beach on the ocean inland to Interstate 5, the 4,600-acre aquatic playground is perfect for water sports activities. You can swim, sail, water ski, wind surf, fish, and more. All types of boats can be rented—pedal, paddle, power, or sail—or bring your own (public launch ramps are free). There's even a stern-wheeler that makes evening cruises along the park's scenic waterways.

Mission Bay Park has land activities, too. You'll find miniature and par-58 executive golf courses, paths for biking, jogging, or walking, and numerous places to picnic. The park also is the location of Sea World, an aquatic wonderland that features three dozen exciting marine life exhibits and shows, including the killer whale Shamu, the Shark Encounter, and the one-of-a-kind Penguin Encounter.

To reach Mission Bay Park from Los Angeles, drive south to San Diego on Interstate 5. Exit west on Clairemont Drive/Mission Bay Drive and stop at the visitors information center to get a map and more details about the park's features and facilities, including lodging if you haven't made advance reservations.

Make your weekend headquarters in one of Mission Bay's six resort hotels, like the San Diego Princess, Hyatt Islandia, or San Diego Hilton. Or settle down at a tent or RV site on the north shore at Campland on the Bay or the De Anza Harbor Resort. You'll enjoy a variety of restaurants and nightclubs at the park resorts, too. Since Mission Bay Park is San Diego's major recreation area, it's smart to reserve a room well in advance, especially in the summer months.

Plan to spend the first day of your weekend visiting Sea World, the 150-acre oceanarium that's considered one of the state's most popular tourist attractions. It's in the heart of Mission Bay Park, marked by a revolving sightseeing tower. The biggest and best known of its half dozen marine shows stars Shamu, a two-ton trained killer whale, but there are many other attractions that put the marine and animal kingdoms in the spotlight at Sea World. A multimillion-dollar expansion of exhibits and shows was made in 1992, after the theme park was purchased by Anheuser-Busch; you can even see the beer company's famous Clydesdale draft horses, which have taken up residence at Sea World.

A highlight is the Shark Encounter, which brings you face-to-face with more than 80 sharks of various species, including a 300-pound bull shark. After visitors watch a short film on the natural history of the shark, the movie screen rises to reveal a lagoon pool that you travel through on a moving walkway inside a transparent acrylic tunnel, while sharks, rays, and moray eels literally swim around you.

Another hit is the Penguin Encounter, a little polar region in sunny San Diego that makes 400 penguins feel at home—all behind a 100-foot-long window so you can observe their unusual life-style. As far as the emperor, king, Adelie, and other penguin species are concerned, it's paradise.

Behind the glass, where the bacteria-free air is kept below freezing and fresh layers of crushed ice are blown over the polarlike compound, you'll see the birds toddle to the edge of an artificial ice shelf and dive into a deep, clear-water pool for a swim. Then they pop back onto shore to dine on fresh fish, court each other with a wing-flapping love dance, or take turns sitting on eggs in the nesting season.

After riding the moving sidewalk to survey this Antarctic exhibit, you'll see another species on display outdoors, the temperate Humboldt penguin, an endangered species that lives along the coast of Chile and Peru. A third display area features Arctic birds of the alcid family—puffins, murres, and auklets—which are underwater swimmers like penguins but also can fly.

You'll see many other feathered friends in action at the humorous and educational Wings of the World show. It features such unusual birds as the ibis, ground hornbill, and African crown crane, as well as more familiar parrots, eagles, hawks, and crows.

Not to be missed, of course, is the killer whale show that stars Shamu, Namu, and Baby Shamu in Sea World's 3,500-seat Shamu Stadium. A 300-square-foot television screen helps you see the whales and the commands of their trainers in even greater detail, thanks to underwater cameras and instant replay. Don't sit in the front rows unless you want a bath from the whales as they splash on command and with precision in a series of jumps and water ballets. The Sea World shows last about 20 minutes and are staggered throughout the day, so you'll have plenty of time to see them all, including one featuring dolphins and whales, and another with some entertaining sea lions, an otter, and a walrus.

This lushly landscaped theme park also hosts a colorful collection of waterfowl, such as scarlet ibis, macaws, Caribbean flamingos, and harlequin ducks. Scattered around the grounds are all sorts of educational exhibits that are entertaining as well. Kids like to play with the anemones, sea stars, and other creatures in the shallow man-made tide pool. They can feed whiskered walruses and sleek sea lions and even pet some friendly dolphins. Also fascinating are numerous aquariums filled with hundreds of exotic fish from all over the world.

Pace yourself during the day so the family doesn't get too tired. You'll find snack bars throughout Sea World, as well as an Italian-themed cafeteria called Mama Stella's, and a sit-down dining pavilion with cocktail service. If the kids need to let off steam, head to Sea World's Cap'n Kids' World, a fun-filled playground for ages 4 to 14. They'll love jumping on air mattresses, punching foam-filled bags, and wading through a sea of plastic balls. Many of the park's exhibits and shows have corporate sponsors, but all meet Sea World's high standards for education and entertainment. For a peek at its behind-the-scenes activities, including marine research projects, join a 90-minute guided tour of the park.

On Sunday, plan to relax at your resort hotel or elsewhere in the park. For sunbathing, swimming, and shore fishing, select any spot along Mission Bay's 27 miles of beaches. Wind surfers and boaters have designated areas for their particular crafts, which means more fun and better water safety. A 1½-mile course is reserved for water skiers, with special pickup and landing areas. Powerboats can race over a marked three-mile course without fear of running into sailboats, which keep to the western areas of the bay. Boats of all types are available for rent at Mission Bay's resorts and Seaforth Boat Rental in Quivira Basin. Deep-sea sportfishing boats leave daily from Islandia Sportfishing and Seaforth Sportfishing, also in Quivira Basin.

On one of the previous nights you'll enjoy sailing aboard a replica of an old-time riverboat that plies Mission Bay on a musical party cruise. A band plays on the second deck of the *Bahia Belle*, where there's a dance floor and cocktail lounge. The paddle wheeler calls at the Bahia, Catamaran, and San Diego Princess hotels on its hour-long excursions Friday and Saturday evenings.

Exercise-minded visitors will appreciate the miles of scenic and level pathways in Mission Bay Park, which are ideal for jogging and bicycling. (Rental bikes are available at any of the resort hotels.) Golfers enjoy the 18-hole executive Mission Bay Golf Course at the north edge of the park, while fishermen find quiet bays and lure bass, perch, croaker, and flounder onto their hooks. The grassy areas along the bay shore are pleasant places to toss a Frisbee, fly a kite, or send a model airplane soaring into the sky.

When your relaxing weekend at San Diego's Mission Bay comes to an end, return to Los Angeles the way you came, via Interstate 5.

Round trip is about 240 miles.

San Diego Area Code: 619

SIGHTSEEING   *Sea World*, 1720 South Shores Road in Mission Bay off Sea World Drive, San Diego 92109, 226-3901. Open daily from 9 A.M. to dusk, to 10:30 P.M. in summer. Adults $23.95, senior citizens $18.95, and children 3 to 11 years $17.95, including all shows and exhibits. Also money-saving annual passes for frequent visitors. Guided tour, scenic skytower ride, and skyride are extra. Free parking. • *Mission Bay Golf Center*, 2702 North Mission Bay Drive, San Diego 92109, 490-3370. Weekend greens fee $14, weekdays $12. • *Bahia Belle* stern-wheeler cruise boat departs hourly from 7:30 P.M. to 12:30 A.M. from Bahia Hotel (see below), with calls at Catamaran Hotel and San Diego Princess. Adults and children $5. • *Seaforth Boat Rentals*, 1641 Quivira Road, San Diego 92109, 223-1681. Sailboats, ski boats, rowboats, and runabouts. • *Seaforth Sportfishing*, 1717 Quivira Road, San Diego 92109, 224-3383. Half-day deep-sea fishing departures daily at 6 A.M. and 12:30 P.M., plus twilight trips in summer at 6 P.M. Also whale-watching excursions in winter. • *Islandia Sportfishing*, 1551 West Mission Bay Drive, San Diego 92109, 222-1164. By the Hyatt Islandia (see below). Deep-sea fishing trips on same schedule as above. Also whale-watching cruises in winter.

LODGING   *San Diego Princess*, 1404 West Vacation Road, San Diego 92109, 274-4630 or California toll-free (800) 344-2626; $135. Popular Princess Cruises Resort on Vacation Isle in the heart of

Mission Bay with 450 cottage-style accommodations amid tropical landscaping. Tennis courts, 5 swimming pools, sandy beach, private marina with boat rentals, and 3 restaurants (see below). A unique resort that's a favorite of families. ● *Hyatt Islandia*, 1441 Quivira Road, San Diego 92109, 224-1234; $129. A towering 17-story hotel with 423 rooms and suites overlooking Mission Bay. Close to Sea World, Quivira Basin sportfishing docks, and Marina Village shops and restaurants. Also marina-view restaurants (see below). ● *San Diego Hilton Beach and Tennis Resort*, 1775 East Mission Bay Drive, San Diego 92109, 276-4010; $130. Beach and tennis resort at east edge of Mission Bay with beach, boat, and bike rentals, popular night spot, and restaurant (see below). ● Other resort hotels on Mission Bay are *Bahia Resort Hotel*, 998 West Mission Bay Drive, San Diego 92109, 488-0551; *Catamaran Resort Hotel*, Mission Boulevard, San Diego 92109, 488-1081; and *Dana Inn and Marina*, 1710 West Mission Bay Drive, San Diego 92109, 222-6440.

CAMPING   *Campland on the Bay*, 2211 Pacific Beach Drive, San Diego 92109, 581-4000 or toll-free (800) 422-7386. 42 acres on Mission Bay with 700 sites, most with hookups. Boat and bike rentals. $20–$50 for up to 4 persons June through September, $18.50–$36 rest of the year. ● *De Anza Harbor Report*, 2727 De Anza Road, San Diego 92109, 273-3211. 80 acres on Mission Bay adjacent to golf course. 275 full-hookup sites. $39 for up to 4 persons June through September, $27 rest of the year.

DINING   *Dockside Broiler* in the San Diego Princess (see above). Continental entrees, seafood, and steaks. Open nightly for dinner. Sunday brunch 10:30 A.M. to 2 P.M. Also, *Village Cafe* for all meals. Mission Bay views. ● *Tradewinds* in San Diego Hilton (see above). Dinner nightly amid nautical decor with windows on the bay. Seafood specialties. ● *Islandia Bar & Grill* in the Hyatt Islandia (see above), 221-4810. Pasta and seafood for lunch and dinner. Also Sunday brunch. *Baja Cafe* serves breakfast and other meals. ● *Salmon House*, 1970 Quivira Way in Marina Village, San Diego, 223-2234. Lunch and dinner daily featuring salmon and other seafood barbecued over a wood fire. Also prime ribs. Brunch on Sundays. ● *The Atoll* in the Catamaran Resort Hotel (see above). Excellent hotel restaurant, noted for its Sunday champagne brunch. Open for all meals.

FOR MORE INFORMATION   Contact the Mission Bay Park Visitor Information Center, 2688 East Mission Bay Drive, San

Diego 92109, 276-8200. Open daily 9 A.M. to dusk. Also, the San Diego Convention and Visitors Bureau, 1200 Third Avenue, Suite 824, San Diego 92101, 236-1212.

Escape to the Del and Coronado "Island"

More than a century ago, when Coronado was just a haven for small game, two wealthy visitors from the East Coast came to hunt rabbits. They left with the idea of building a splendid seaside resort that would attract investors to the undeveloped peninsula. Today the Hotel del Coronado is a remarkable reminder of the opulent hotels that once graced the West Coast and have since succumbed to fire and old age. And the peninsula is now a wealthy residential community and restful resort town that's perfect for a relaxing weekend.

Here you can escape the hustle and bustle of Los Angeles (or San Diego, for that matter). Although connected to the mainland by a graceful bridge, as well as a narrow neck of land called the Silver Strand, Coronado offers the quiet isolation of an island—and it's often called just that. With the blue Pacific on its front doorstep and handsome San Diego at the back, Coronado presents superscenic views from any place along its shoreline (although the northwest end is a U.S. Naval Air Station and off limits to civilians). Besides discovering beautiful beaches and some pleasant places to dine and shop, you can play golf on a waterfront course, sail in pretty Glorietta Bay, and take a historical tour to view Coronado's charming homes.

To get to Coronado from Los Angeles, drive south on Interstate 5 to San Diego and follow the Coronado exit road, which leads across a soaring boomerang-shaped toll bridge to the peninsula. The $48-million bridge replaced the car ferries that were the major route to Coronado until 1969. Continue from the blue San Diego–Coronado Bay Bridge to the main thoroughfare, Orange Avenue. Turn left and follow this attractive boulevard through the town shopping area to your weekend headquarters, the unmistakable Hotel del Coronado. You'll easily spot the red roof, turrets, cupolas, and Victorian gingerbread of this venerated hotel, which has been designated a city, state, and national landmark.

On Friday evening or Saturday morning, take time to explore the Hotel del Coronado, which is as much a museum as it is one of Southern California's best-known resorts. After all, not many hostelries in the state have been in business since 1888. And even fewer have retained a Victorian elegance while incorporating the modern amenities that today's travelers expect.

Two additions have been made to the hotel in recent years, but enter through the main entrance to the original building and you'll be taken back to the previous century. The busy lobby is of dark oak highlighted by a hand-cut Bavarian chandelier. In one corner you'll see the original Otis birdcage elevator, which still services the hotel's five stories. Look around the Crown Room, praised by architects for its unsupported ceiling of Oregon sugar pine that was assembled with wooden pegs instead of nails. On Sunday return to this vast dining room to enjoy the Del's popular buffet brunch.

Although still very fashionable with the so-called smart set, the huge hostelry also caters to convention groups. For the most romantic weekend, be certain to reserve one of the original hotel rooms—unless you prefer more modern accommodations in the newer towers or pool buildings.

As you stroll around the hotel's extensive grounds, don't miss the flower-filled courtyard, a favorite setting for weddings. Overhead are the room balconies, which extend for a third of a mile around each floor. Outside the entrance to the Prince of Wales Grille, the Del's premium restaurant and a sophisticated choice for your first-night dinner, you'll see the last of the old fire wagons that guarded the immense all-wood building until room sprinklers were installed in 1913.

If it's unoccupied, peek into the ballroom, site of banquets for the 11 U.S. presidents who have been guests at the hotel. In corridors on the basement level, walk along the History Gallery, where displays of photos and memorabilia relate more of the hotel's enchanting past. For the most comprehensive tour of the hotel, rent a recorder at the lobby gift shop and take an audio tape tour.

Many well-to-do Easterners built winter homes on Coronado early in this century, and you'll enjoy seeing their varied architecture on a self-guided tour that can occupy several hours. Get a copy of *The Crown Tour,* a guide to 74 homes and sites, from the Coronado Visitor Information Center. Or join the one-hour guided walking tour of historical homes organized by Coronado Touring. You also can rent a bicycle for a leisurely tour of the town.

One mansion not to miss was built in 1908 for sugar magnate John Spreckels and later occupied by newspaper syndicate owner Ira Copley. The home is now the attractive Glorietta Bay Inn, just opposite the Hotel del Coronado and overlooking Glorietta Bay. If you can't get into the Del or prefer more intimate surroundings, you should stay here. At least peek into the lobby of this 99-room lodging, where a marble staircase with solid brass railings leads to the mansion's second-floor view rooms and suites.

Nearby at Coronado Boat Rentals on Glorietta Bay, rent a boat to sightsee, sail, or fish in big, beautiful San Diego Bay. Or just cruise quietly around pretty little Glorietta Bay in a self-powered pedal boat. At sunset enjoy wonderful views over the water with drinks and dinner at the Chart House restaurant, a Victorian-style boathouse that belongs to the Hotel del Coronado. Or walk around the corner to dine on seafood at the Brigantine. Other recommended restaurants nearby are Chez Loma and Mandarin Cafe.

On Sunday follow Glorietta Boulevard from the bay for a drive along the Coronado Municipal Golf Course, a lush 18-hole, par-72 course with shoreline scenery that can be distracting to your game. Also, drive up Orange Avenue to its northern end and the Old Ferry Landing, a great spot for a panoramic view of San Diego's ever-growing skyline. You'll take the best photos on weekends, when all sorts of colorful pleasure craft are crisscrossing San Diego Bay. Among them are passenger ferryboats that bring visitors across the harbor from the downtown Embarcadero. (Cars are not carried on the ferries, but bicycles are welcome.)

The Old Ferry Landing was brand new in 1987 and has a collection of specialty shops and eateries. You can enjoy brunch or lunch at Peohe's at the water's edge, or at Bula's Pub and Eatery nearby on Orange Avenue. A few minutes away by foot is the bay-front Le Meridien hotel with two fine restaurants, as well as 300 deluxe rooms and suites. Awaiting all ferry arrivals are trolley-style buses that run along Orange Avenue to the Del on the opposite side of Coronado.

Midway on Orange Avenue in Spreckels Park, visit with area artists and craftspeople who display their work the first and third Sundays of every month, weather permitting. (Another delight at the park are Sunday band concerts, beginning at 6 P.M. June to September, which take you back to pleasant summertime evenings of yesteryear.) Spend the remainder of your lazy day at the beach, browse in the shops and galleries along Orange Avenue, relax at a sidewalk cafe, or play a few sets of tennis at the Del or on Coronado's public courts.

Return to Los Angeles via the bay bridge to rejoin Interstate 5 north. Or head south along the ocean on Silver Strand Boulevard, California 75, across a spit of land that was once laid with train tracks to bring building materials and then guests to the Del. It goes past the navy's amphibious base and a state beach park to Imperial Beach, where the road becomes Palm Avenue and meets Interstate 5.

Round trip is about 250 miles.

Coronado Area Code: 619

SIGHTSEEING *San Diego–Coronado Bay Bridge*, round-trip toll collected incoming direction only; $1 (free for 2 or more passengers who stay in the far-right-hand car pool lane). • *Hotel del Coronado*, 1500 Orange Avenue, 435-6611. Visitors as well as hotel guests are welcome to take their own tour of this Victorian landmark; see the History Gallery on basement level at any time, as well as photo gallery outside the Del Deli. Enjoy it more with an audio tape tour obtained at the Lobby Shop from 8 A.M. to dusk; adults $3, students under age 18 and seniors over 65 $2. • *Coronado Touring*, 1110 Isabella Avenue, 435-5993. A guided 1-hour 8-block stroll past oceanfront mansions, Victorian cottages, and quiet parks; $5 per person. Departs 11 A.M. Tuesdays, Thursdays, and Saturdays from Glorietta Bay Inn opposite Hotel del Coronado. • *San Diego–Coronado Ferry*, Star & Crescent Boat Company, P.O. Box 751, San Diego 92112, 234-4111. Passenger service across the bay to Coronado's Old Ferry Landing from Broadway Pier on North Harbor Drive at the Embarcadero. Boats depart San Diego on the hour, return from Coronado on the half-hour, from 9 A.M. to 10 P.M. weekdays, to 11 P.M. on weekends. Fare for 15-minute trip $2 each way. Get ferry tokens at San Diego Harbor Excursion office at Broadway Pier on the San Diego side, and at the Star & Crescent Gift Galley at the Old Ferry Landing on the Coronado side. • *Coronado Trolley Lines* has trolley-style buses that meet ferryboats at Old Ferry Landing and cross Coronado on Orange Avenue to Hotel del Coronado. $3 round trip, with unlimited boarding. • *Coronado Municipal Golf Course*, off Glorietta Boulevard, 435-3121. Greens fee $15; make reservations. • *Coronado Boat Rentals*, 1715 Strand Way on Glorietta Bay, 437-1514. Daily sailboat, outboard, and pedal boat rentals. • *Coronado Tennis Center*, 1501 Glorietta Boulevard, 435-1616. 10 municipal courts available from 9:30 A.M. to 6 P.M. daily. Free.

LODGING   Coronado ZIP code: 92118 • *Hotel Coronado*, 1500 Orange Avenue, 435–6611. A very special resort with a wide sandy beach, 6 tennis courts, heated swimming pools, excellent restaurants, shops. Rooms in original hotel are more interesting and less expensive than those in new complex: $149–$249 versus $189–$299; lanais and suites also available. 2-night minimum on weekends. • *Glorietta Bay Inn*, 1630 Glorietta Boulevard, 435-3101. Charming rooms and suites in 1908 Edwardian mansion, with most accommodations in newer guest wings; mansion rooms, $120, others $89. • *Le Meridien San Diego at Coronado*, 2000 2nd Street, 435-3000; $165–$250, higher for suites and villas. Impressive 300-room, low-profile resort on bay front, with view of San Diego skyline. 3 swimming pools, 6 lighted tennis courts, health club. One

of worldwide French-run hotels. Also 2 restaurants (see below). •
Loew's Coronado Bay Resort and Marina, 4000 Coronado Bay
Road, 424-4000; $200–$395, suites to $1,400. A grand resort a few
miles south of town along the Silver Strand. Located on its own
15-acre peninsula in the bay, next to the Coronado Cays. 440 rooms,
80-slip marina, health club, water sports, shops, and restaurants. A
quiet place to get away from it all. • *El Cordova Hotel*, 1351 Orange
Avenue, 435-4131. Remodeled mansion near the Del, bay, and
beach; $70–90.

DINING   *Crown Room*, Hotel del Coronado (see above). Magnificent main dining room of grand hotel. Eat here at least once. It's
worth standing in line for pricey Sunday brunch, served from 9 A.M.
to 2 P.M.; no reservations. *Prince of Wales Grille*, Hotel del
Coronado (see above). Veal, duckling, and other fine fare is served
with style in hotel's gourmet dining room; dinner only. Wake up
with a continental breakfast in the *Palm Court*. • *Marius*, Le
Meridien hotel (see above). Gourmet restaurant serves Provençal
cuisine for dinner, except Mondays. Also, brasserie *L'Escale* has
light French and California fare. Patio dining. • *Bula's Pub and
Eatery*, 170 Orange Avenue, 435-4466. Informal place with patio
for lunch, dinner, and excellent Sunday brunch. • *Bay Beach Cafe*,
at Old Ferry Landing, 435-4900. Burgers, fish, salad bar indoors or
outdoors. • *Peohe's*, 1201 1st Street, 437-4474. On bay near Old
Ferry Landing. Fresh fish specialties for lunch and dinner. Also
Sunday brunch. • *Chez Loma*, 1132 Loma Avenue, 435-0661.
When you want to splurge on fine French food for lunch or dinner
(except Mondays); in Victorian home. • *The Brigantine*, 1333
Orange Avenue, 435-4166. Casual spot for fresh swordfish and
other seafood; dinner nightly, lunch weekdays. • *Mandarin Cafe*,
1330 Orange Avenue, 435-2771. Excellent Mandarin fare for lunch
and dinner. • *Chart House*, 1701 Strand Way, 435-0155. Steak and
seafood with Glorietta Bay views; dinner only.

FOR MORE INFORMATION   Contact the Coronado Visitor
Information Center, 1111 Orange Avenue, Suite A (2nd floor),
Coronado 92118, 437-8788 or toll-free (800) 622-8300. Open 9 A.M.
to 5 P.M. weekdays, from 10 A.M. on weekends.

South of the Border
Part 1: Tijuana and
Rosarito

Margaritas and mariachis—for some people those are reason enough to spend a weekend in Mexico. But there's much more to savor south of the border than exotic cocktails and exciting music. Delicious food, bargain shopping, first-class accommodations, friendly people, and a different life-style are just a few of the other enticements. And for anyone in the Los Angeles area, a Mexican weekend doesn't take much effort or planning. Just drive south a couple of hours on the freeway to the Mexican state of Baja California, where you'll discover a trio of favorite tourist destinations: Tijuana, Rosarito, and Ensenada.

U.S. citizens don't need a passport or tourist card to enter northern Baja, just some identification such as a driver's license. Also, U.S. dollars can be spent legally in Baja without being exchanged for Mexican pesos. And don't worry about a language barrier, because many of the Mexicans you'll meet speak English.

Unless you're going on a three-day holiday, plan a weekend just for Tijuana, Baja's biggest city, and Rosarito, the popular Pacific beach town that's only a 25-minute drive beyond. Save Ensenada for another time (see "South of the Border, Part 2").

Drive south from Los Angeles on Interstate 5 past San Diego to the U.S.-Mexico border. Border officials won't stop you until the return trip, when you reenter the United States. Just before or beyond the border, pause at one of the special insurance offices to buy Mexican auto insurance for the length of your stay; U.S. policies aren't valid if you have an accident.

Follow the *Centro* signs from the border to downtown Tijuana (locals say *tee-wah-nah*) and drive down the main thoroughfare, Avenida Revolucion. At Calle 7 (7th Street), park in the guarded parking lot at the Frontón Palacio and join the enthusiastic spectators who gather there nightly except Wednesdays to watch and bet on the ancient Basque ball game jai alai (*hi-lie*). In the same building is TiaJuana Tilly's, a popular drinking and eating spot where you can enjoy an American-style dinner or choose from a full menu of Mexican dishes. For quieter dining, leave the jai alai palace and walk across Avenida Revolucion to Pedrin's, where the seafoods of Mexico are featured. Outstanding meals also are served at La Costa, located around the corner on Calle 7.

After spending the night in one of Tijuana's better lodgings, such as the luxury Fiesta Americana or the Hotel Lucerna, return downtown to Avenida Revolucion to browse or buy in the many shops that are filled with imported as well as Mexican goods.

The once raucous border town, now with a population exceeding 1½ million, has acquired some big-city refinements in recent years, and previous visitors especially will be surprised by the look of Tijuana's main street. After all utility wires were put underground, nine blocks of Avenida Revolucion were attractively repaved with bricks. Its sidewalks were doubled in width and planted with trees, and now sport open-air cafes. To make pedestrians feel even more welcome, parking is banned and local buses and taxis are prohibited.

Stroll along the beautified avenue between Calles 1 and 9 (1st and 9th streets) for Mexican handicrafts and foreign items at reasonable prices, and also seek out its alleylike shopping arcades. Be certain to bargain in the souvenir shops, but remember that in the boutiques and better stores—such as Sara's, Maxim's, and Sanborn's—prices are fixed. Don't be confused by dollar signs on price tags; if the amount is preceded by "M.N.$," the price is in Mexican pesos.

For quality Mexican-made handicrafts, visit the Tolan folk art shop across from the jai alai building. Other craft stores with jewelry, clothing, and leather goods also are along or near Avenida Revolucion. Among them are factory outlets for well-known brands of clothing, such as Calvin Klein, Benetton, Guess, Fila, and Ralph Lauren. The street hosts a number of restaurants, too, including one in the Hotel Caesar, where it is claimed the Caesar salad originated. You'll even find a Hard Rock Cafe.

Go a few blocks east from Avenida Revolucion to reach another main boulevard, Paseo de Los Heroes, and another shopping destination, Plaza Rio Tijuana, a huge, covered complex of over 100 stores in the city's reclaimed riverbed. You'll discover bargains in both the small shops and the major department stores like Dorian's and Comercial Mexicana. Also tempting in Plaza Rio Tijuana is the Suzett Bakery and Pastry Shop, where you can watch bakers create 300 varieties of breads, pies, cakes, and specialties like tasty filled *tortas*. If you're ready for lunch, enjoy some fine Mexican fare at the award-winning Restaurant Las Espuelas in the shopping center.

Or go along Paseo de Los Heroes to visit a city landmark, the Tijuana Cultural Center. You'll easily spot its immense eight-story sphere, which houses an Omnimax theater where a spectacular panoramic film presentation, *El Pueblo del Sol (City of the Sun)*, describes the history of Mexico and shows the nation's vast contrasts—from ancient temples to ultramodern cities. Time your visit for the 2 P.M. show, which is narrated in English. You'll also want to wander through the center's spacious museum to view masterpieces of Mexican arts and crafts that span 3,500 years; the creations of today's artisans are sold in government shops at the cultural center. With luck you may be there when a folkloric show is being presented on the open-air stage. Inquire at the center's ticket booth. Also ask about concerts and stage shows in the symphony hall.

Among Tijuana's longtime attractions are sporting events that take place at the Caliente Racetrack, three miles from downtown. Try your luck at betting at the Greyhound dog races, which are held most evenings and weekend afternoons.

When you're ready to leave Tijuana on Saturday, follow the Rosarita/Ensenada Toll Road (*Cuota*) signs through town to the four-lane highway that leads south to the beach at Rosarito. After passing through the first toll station, take the first Rosarito exit and enter the north end of town.

Don't expect a Puerto Vallarta or other fancy beach retreat like those on the Mexican mainland. Rosarito hugs a two-mile section of the old Tijuana-Ensenada highway, where roadside stands greet you with bamboo baskets, brightly painted pottery, and even saddle horses for hire.

Going south on Rosarito's main street, Benito Juarez Boulevard, you'll spot the Quinta del Mar, an extensive resort with hotel rooms and vacation time-share *casas*. Whether an overnight guest or not, you're welcome at the resort's La Masia Restaurant and the Beach-comber Bar. If you browse in the shops that flank the resort entrance, be sure to visit La Casa de Arte y La Madera (House of Gifts and Decor), which is jam-packed with handicrafts from all over Mexico. Opposite is the ever-busy Calimax supermarket, a good place to buy picnic and camping supplies, as well as Kahlua, tequila, and other Mexican liquor to bring home. (One quart per adult is allowed duty free by U.S. Customs.) Also check out the Comercial Mexicana department store at the rear of Plaza Quinta del Mar.

About a mile farther south you'll see the arched entrance to the town's landmark, the Rosarito Beach Hotel, built in the 1920s. Once a hideaway for Hollywood folk and international celebrities like Prince Aly Khan, the resort has been expanded to 281 rooms and is popular with families.

Wander through the lobby, hallways, and public rooms to view the immense murals and other artwork that contribute to the hotel's character. Look up for the hand-painted ceiling beams and go to the main dining room to see the framed images of six Aztec gods created with colorful wool yarn on a base of beeswax. In this Aztec Room, which overlooks the swimming pool, you can enjoy a Saturday evening dinner with such Baja specialties as quail and fresh fish, and watch the hotel's colorful weekend folkloric show of Mexican music and dances. A full-service health spa, Casa Playa, and a gourmet restaurant now occupy an elegant 1930s mansion on the resort property. Just in front of the hotel you'll be tempted by a colorful variety of gifts in the shopping arcade.

On Sunday, relax at your resort hotel or throw down a towel and sunbathe anywhere along Rosarito's beaches—all are public. At lunchtime, drive about 12 miles south of Rosarito on the old Ensenada highway to see more of the beautifully rugged Baja coast and to reach the fishing village of Puerto Nuevo (Newport) for a feast of fresh lobster. Enter through an archway to the village; look for it on the right about two miles beyond Las Gaviotas resort development.

Originally the fishermen's families served lobster to visitors in their homes at the kitchen table, but most have built restaurants and now live above them. You'll easily spot the two- and three-story structures of the enterprising Ortega family, which operates several restaurants in tiny Puerto Nuevo. Wherever you eat, it's hard to beat the enjoyment of a fresh lobster dinner (which includes rice, refried beans, and flour tortillas).

When you're ready to return to Los Angeles, continue a mile south to the Ensenada toll road entrance at Cantamar and head north to Tijuana. If you've always wanted to see a bullfight, arrive there by 4 P.M. for an exciting *corrida* in Tijuana's downtown building, El Toreo, or at the bullring-by-the-sea, Plaza Monumental, which you'll see from the toll road near the Playas de Tijuana beach area, on your way north from Rosarito. This traditional Sunday entertainment switches from one bullring to the other midway in the May-through-September season.

Afterward, follow the directional signs to San Diego, but prepare for a delay at the border for the customary check by U.S. immigration officials. Then continue north on Interstate 5 to Los Angeles. *Olé!*

Round trip is about 330 miles.

Tijuana/Rosarito Area Code: 011 526

SIGHTSEEING   *Tijuana Cultural Center* (Centro Cultural Tijuana), Paseo de Los Heroes, Tijuana, 684-1111 or 684-1132. Museum open 11 A.M. to 8 P.M. weekends, to 7 P.M. weekdays. Small admission. Omnimax theater with wraparound movie of Mexico shown in English at 2 P.M. daily. Spanish narration at other times. Admission $5, children $2.50. Restaurant open daily. • For quality handicrafts from all over Mexico, visit *Tolan Arte de Mexico*, Avenida Revolucion 1111. • In Rosarito, look for additional colorful Mexican crafts at *La Casa de Arte y La Madera* at the north end of the Quinta del Mar shopping arcade. • These are Tijuana's spectator sports: *Jai alai:* fast-paced action in the Basque ball court from 8 P.M. to 1 A.M. nightly except Wednesdays in the Frontón Palacio on Avenida Revolucion at Calle 7, with pari-mutuel betting. • *Dog racing:* greyhounds run at Caliente Racetrack off Boulevard Agua Caliente at 7:45 P.M. every night and at 2 P.M. Friday through Monday. • *Bullfights:* Mexico's top matadors perform Sunday afternoons at 4 P.M. in El Toreo bullring downtown from mid-May to mid-July, then in Plaza Monumental bullring-by-the-sea until October.

LODGING *Hotel Fiesta Americana Tijuana*, Boulevard Agua Caliente 4500, Tijuana, 681-7000 or toll free (800) 343-7825; $100 and up. 24-story hotel with 422 deluxe rooms and suites. Guests can play on adjacent Tijuana Country Club golf course. Also tennis courts, health club, shops, and restaurants (see below). • *Hotel Lucerna*, Paseo de los Heroes and Avenida Rodriguez, Tijuana, 684-0015; $60. Modern 6-story hotel, nearest to Rio Tijuana shopping center and downtown shopping area. Restaurant serves breakfast and French fare daily. • *Rosarito Beach Hotel*, Highway 1 (Boulevard Benito Juarez), Rosarito, 612-1106 or 612-1176, or toll-free (800) 343-8582; $55 and up. Rosarito's landmark lodging is the beach town's center of activity and entertainment. A favorite informal Baja resort; make weekend and holiday reservations well in advance. Also health spa, gym, and racquetball courts. • *Quinta del Mar Resort Hotel*, Highway 1 (Boulevard Benito Juarez), Rosarito, 612-1301 or toll-free (800) 228-7003; $45 and up. Rosarito's other major hostelry, where reservations also should be made well in advance.

DINING *Place de la Concorde* in the Hotel Fiesta Americana Tijuana (see above). Impressive gourmet dining room serving French cuisine nightly except Sundays. Also, hotel's skylighted *Plaza Cafe* features daylong champagne buffet on Sundays. • *TiaJuana Tilly's*, in Frontón Palacio on Avenida Revolucion, Tijuana, 685-6024. Happy hangout at the jai alai palace that's popular with the youthful drinking crowd. • *Pedrin's,* Avenida Revolucion 1115, Tijuana, 685-4052. Seafood is served for lunch and dinner in this attractive restaurant across from the jai alai palace. • *La Costa*, on Calle 7 around the corner from jai alai palace, Tijuana, 685-8494. Another good choice for seafood. • *Caesar's Bar and Grill*, in the Hotel Caesar at Avenida Revolucion and Calle 5, Tijuana, 685-2923. Home of the original Caesar's salad. •

Ortega's Beachside Restaurant, Puerto Nuevo, 614-1320. Tallest of 33 lobster restaurants in tiny fishing village off Highway 1 south of Rosarito. Menu features other dishes, including seafood pizza. Five *Ortega's Place* restaurants run by same family also serve lobster dinners. Another *Ortega's Place*, as well as *Ortega's Cafe*, are in Rosarito. • *El Nido Steak House*, Highway 1, Rosarito, 612-1430. It's hard to top the carne asada or regular steaks cooked over a mesquite wood fire; try the fried cheese for an appetizer. The same owner runs *Los Pelicanos* restaurant overlooking the beach.

FOR MORE INFORMATION   Contact the Tourism Department for Baja California headquarters in San Diego, (619) 298-4105 or toll-free (800) 522-1516 in California. They make hotel reservations, too. A Tourist Information Center is run by the Tijuana Chamber of Commerce at Avenida Revolucion and Calle Primera (1st Street), Tijuana, 685-8472. It's open daily from 9 A.M. to 7 P.M.

South of the Border
Part 2: Ensenada

You'll love spending a weekend in the relaxed fishing port of Ensenada, just 68 miles south of the U.S.-Mexico border on the photogenic west coast of Baja California. Visitors agree that it's much more "Mexican" in appearance and flavor than Tijuana, although Ensenada is far from being a sleepy little village. As the peninsula's main seaport, it's grown to be Baja's third largest city. Ensenada boasts Mexico's major Pacific Coast fish canneries, as well the nation's biggest winery—Bodegas de Santo Tomas.

In recent years, Ensenada has also become an increasingly popular resort town. One reason is that it's now a bona fide cruise port. Twice weekly Royal Caribbean Cruise Lines' *Viking Serenade* and Norwegian Cruise Lines' *Southward* sail with shiploads of holidaymakers into Bahia de Todos Santos (Bay of All Saints), Ensenada's enormous natural harbor. The cruise vessels make regular three-night and four-night party trips from Los Angeles to Ensenada, with a call at Catalina, plus San Diego on alternate voyages. Cruise passengers have enough time to explore Ensenada's myriad shops, savor just-caught seafood in the first-class restaurants or at street stands, and down a margarita in the town's most notorious cantina, Hussong's. (Ensenada's rowdiest place is now Papas and Beer, located across the street and up the stairs.)

But if you want to absorb more of the beauty and excitement of Baja, go by car and spend the weekend at one of Ensenada's resort hotels. The drive south along the sheer cliffs and sandy beaches of Baja's picturesque Pacific coast is worth the trip itself.

Get to Ensenada from Los Angeles by taking Interstate 5 to San Diego and continuing to the international border. Pause to purchase Mexican auto insurance at one of the special offices; U.S. policies aren't valid in case of an accident. Also, if you plan to stay longer than three days or to extend your trip beyond Ensenada, be sure to carry a Mexican tourist card. Get one at the border *migración* office (or later at the first road checkpoint, 12 miles south of Ensenada); you'll need proof of citizenship, such as a passport or birth certificate. Then follow the Rosarito/Ensenada Toll Road (*Cuota*) signs to bypass Tijuana and join the four-lane highway (No. 1-D) that takes you directly to Ensenada. Tolls are collected at three booths en route.

At the approach to Ensenada are a few ocean-view lodgings, such as the impressive Las Rosas, and in the heart of town you'll find several attractive motels along Avenida Lopez Mateos, including Mision Santa Isabel. A few blocks beyond is the popular San Nicolas Resort Hotel, Ensenada's largest lodging. Another pleasant resort, Estero Beach Hotel, is on the bay front six miles south of downtown Ensenada. There are several campgrounds and trailer parks, too.

Mexicans like to eat late, so you'll probably arrive in time for dinner on Friday. Ensenada is known for seafood, but restaurants feature Mexican, American, and international dishes as well. Favorites of frequent visitors are the French cuisine and Mexican fare at El Rey Sol Restaurant, an Ensenada landmark on Avenida Lopez Mateos for more than four decades. Seafood aficionados also like Casamar, a restaurant located near the bay on Boulevard Lazaro Cardenas.

The fish market at the foot of Avenida Macheros bustles with activity every morning when Ensenada's housewives and restaurant chefs bargain for seafood fresh off the commerical fishing boats. Ensenada's immense bay has abundant fish, and you can try your luck aboard sportfishing boats that make daily excursions for bottom-fish varieties or deep-sea specimens. Sign up at Fritz's, Gordo's, or one of the other sportfishing offices along the waterfront.

Baja's big Santo Tomas winery has been in business for more than a century, and you can see how wine is made during a visit to its downtown facilities. Tasting of various Santo Tomas vintages is a highlight of the tour. Another tour is to take a horse-drawn carriage ride along the bay-front boulevard; board the open-air vehicles not far from the fish market.

Several blocks south, at the end of Boulevard Lazaro Cardenas, you'll find sandy public beaches for sunbathing or swimming in the bay. Horses also can be rented there for a saddle ride along the water's edge.

Be sure to make the 20-mile drive to the bay's western trip on Punta Banda peninsula to see La Bufadora. Mother Nature created this age-old blowhole that spouts roaring geysers of seawater with each ocean wave. Don't forget your camera.

Back in town you can admire man's handiwork inside the Hotel Riviera del Pacifico, a 1930s bay-front casino and resort that has been renovated as the city's cultural, arts, and convention center. The original hand-painted wooden ceilings and other adornments date from earlier times, when the elegant hotel was a haunt of Hollywood film stars and heavyweight boxing champ Jack Dempsey was its honorary manager. Go inside to see the ornate decor or for drinks at its quaint bar.

Ensenada is a super place for shopping, and one shop not to miss is Fonart, the government-run store that's behind the cultural center, just beyond the dip in the road across the Ensenada riverbed. The shop is filled with original arts and crafts from all over Mexico, and prices are reasonable. Many other stores also specialize in Mexican wares, including pottery, ceramics, jewelry, furniture, leather goods, and clothing. But you'll also find a surprising array of imported products—French perfumes, Swiss watches, European fashions, and more. The supermarkets offer good buys in Mexican-made liquors and liqueurs, like coffee-flavored Kahlua, as well as Santo Tomas wines. (For U.S. citizens, up to $400 of whatever you buy in Mexico, including a quart of liquor, can be brought back to the United States without paying customs duty.)

Stroll along the main shopping streets, Avenida Lopez Mateos and Avenida Ruiz. Prices are fixed in the shops, but you can bargain with street vendors and at a few small street stalls. U.S. currency is accepted everywhere, although prices usually are given in Mexican pesos. The peso amount is indicated with a dollar sign too, but should be preceded by the initials "M.N." to indicate Mexican currency.

Return to Los Angeles via the same toll road to the border at Tijuana and rejoin Interstate 5 going north.

Round trip is about 410 miles.

If you'd rather visit Ensenada aboard a comfortable cruise ship, book a cabin on the *Viking Serenade* or *Southward*, which sail south of the border from San Pedro. Take the Harbor Freeway (Interstate 110) south to Harbor Boulevard and the port area. The weekend cruises leave Los Angeles Friday evening and return Monday morning. (Allow up to three hours for disembarkation while all baggage is put ashore and as many as 1,500 passengers clear U.S. Immigration and Customs.)

At sea you'll enjoy stage shows, music and dancing, movies, a captain's cocktail party, gambling in the casino, many more cruise activities, and plenty to eat. Cruise costs depend on the location and size of your cabin. Fares include all meals aboard ship; guided shore excursions are optional. Contact a travel agent for current cruise rates and to book passage.

Ensenada Area Code: 011 526

SIGHTSEEING   *Hussong's Cantina*, 118 Avenida Ruiz. An Ensenada watering hole and Baja institution that's frequently jam-packed, noisy, and lots of fun—especially after a few margaritas or cervezas. At least drop in to say you've been there. • *Bodegas de Santo Tomas*, 666 Avenida Miramar, Ensenada, 678-2509 or 674-0836. Guided half-hour tours of the downtown Ensenada winery at 11 A.M. and 1 P.M. daily and 3 P.M. weekdays. $1.50 per person, including wine tasting.

LODGING   *San Nicolas Resort Hotel*, Avenida Lopez Mateos at Avenida Guadalupe, Ensenada, 676-1901 or 676-4070; $58–$78. Modern motor inn with coffee shop, dining room, and discotheque. • *Estero Beach Hotel Resort*, 6 miles south of Ensenada via Highway 1 to resort's side road, 676-6225; $48–$86. Waterfront complex with beach, tennis courts, restaurant; a favorite of families. • *Villa Fontana Hotel*, 1050 Avenida Lopez Mateos, Ensenada, 678-3434 or toll-free (800) 422-5204; $58. Remodeled motel in the heart of town. • *Mision Santa Isabel Hotel*, Avenida Lopez Mateos at Avenida Castillo, Ensenada, 678-3616; $55. Attractive renovated hotel in town center. • *Las Rosas*, on Highway 1, 2 miles north of Ensenada, 674-4310; $101, suites $139. Handsome modern hotel overlooking the ocean with 31 rooms and 4 suites. Also, unusual swimming pool and enjoyable restaurant. • *Villas By The Sea*, at Bajamar exit from toll road, 21 miles north of Ensenada, (619) 295-3374; $50, to $350 for 4-bedroom house. 10 villas in gated community on an ocean overlook and surrounding area's only public golf course. Can rent bedroom, suite with kitchen, or entire villa. Isolated, quiet spot with 3 swimming pools, 4 tennis courts. Public bathing beach nearby.

CAMPING   *Estero Beach Trailer Park*, adjacent to Estero Beach Hotel Resort (see above), 676-6225. 62 sites with hookups, $14 per night, including use of resort facilities.

DINING   *El Rey Sol Restaurant*, Avenida Lopez Mateos at Avenida Blancarte, 678-1733. Open 7:30 A.M. to 11 P.M. Famous for French cuisine, with fresh vegetables, fruit, and poultry from restaurant's ranches. Its own bakery makes mouthwatering French pastries. ● *Casamar*, Boulevard Lazaro Cardenas 987, 674-0417. Seafood specialties for lunch and dinner daily. ● *La Cueva de los Tigres*, off Highway 1 (via gravel road), 2 miles south of Ensenada, 678-2653. Beachfront restaurant serving seafood, steaks, and Mexican fare for lunch and dinner. ● *Enrique's*, Highway 1, 1½ miles north of town, 678-2461. Well-known roadside restaurant open 8 A.M. to 11:30 P.M. Seafood, lobster, and steak.

FOR MORE INFORMATION   Tourist Bureau, 1350 Avenida Lopez Mateos, 678-2411. (Office is next to Fonart store.) Also, look for visitor information booth (near fish market) at 540 Boulevard Costero just after entering town from the north. ● Also, for advance information, call the Tourism Department for Baja California headquarters in San Diego, (619) 298-4105 or toll-free (800) 522-1516 in California. They also make hotel reservations.

"Thar She Blows!"— Watching the Annual Whale Parade

If you want a glimpse of California's official state mammal, look to the Pacific Ocean. The annual parade of California gray whales along the Southland coast runs from mid-December to April. This remarkable voyage, the longest known migration of any mammal in the world, is monitored by a flotilla of whale-watching boats, and you're welcome to climb aboard. It's a wonderful treat to include in one of your weekend getaways to the coast in the wintertime.

During the boats' 2- to 3½-hour outings at sea, you're almost certain to spot some of the marathon travelers, which are estimated to number more than 21,000. And there's a good chance you'll see whales spouting, fluking, and, with luck, even breeching—when they propel their multiton bodies out of the water. In winter you'll find these immense yet graceful cetaceans swimming south from the Bering Sea to their breeding and calving grounds in Baja's quiet lagoons, and in early spring they're guiding their newborn offspring back north to the Alaskan waters.

Starting in late December, whale-watching vessels depart every weekend and some weekdays from Ventura, Oxnard, San Pedro, Long Beach, Redondo Beach, Newport Beach, Dana Point, Oceanside, and San Diego. Later in the season, when the grays are making their return trip, boats also leave from Santa Barbara to look for the baby whales and their mothers. The whale-watching trips end by early March, when most of the north-bound leviathans have passed the Southland's shores.

Be certain to dress warmly for the ocean excursions by bringing a heavy coat and hat or scarf. You'll get better views and pictures by taking along binoculars and a telephoto lens. Most vessels sell refreshments, or pack your own snacks.

For extra excitement, board one of the San Diego–based sportfishing boats or fancier expedition vessels that head south to the quiet lagoons of Baja, Mexico, and be the first on your block to pet a whale. Gray whales are surprisingly relaxed in the calving grounds, and some of them, nicknamed "friendlies," seem to enjoy it when human visitors reach out to pet their barnacled backs. Details of those week or longer natural-history voyages to Baja follow, but first is a port-by-port summary of the shorter morning and afternoon whale-watching excursions from Southern California harbors.

Boat capacities vary, so be sure to make reservations. Also call to confirm departure times and get directions to the dock; unless otherwise indicated, the area code is 310. Adult fares range from $12 to $20; children usually sail at reduced rates. Prices of more costly trips will be noted.

SAN PEDRO: Four companies offer whale-watch cruises from L.A.'s harbor at San Pedro. L.A. Harbor Sportfishing at Berth 79 has boats leaving once each morning and afternoon on weekdays and three times daily on weekends. Phone 547-9916.

Also, at Ports O'Call Village at Berth W33, a plane spots whales for two motor yachts cruising daily. A schooner called *Spirit* also heads to sea in search of gray whales on selected weekends. Phone 831-1073.

From the Village Boat House at Ports O'Call Village, Berth 78, the *Bonanza* of Los Angeles Harbor Cruises sets out to see the whales twice daily at 11:30 A.M. and 2 P.M. Phone 831-0996.

Not far away, Skipper's 22nd Street Landing at 141 West 22nd Street operates whale trips every weekday morning and three times daily on Saturdays and Sundays with 150-passenger boats. Phone 832-8304.

LONG BEACH: From Catalina Landing, some of the triple-deck ferryboats of Catalina Cruises abandon their regular runs to Catalina Island in order to take up to 700 passengers on gray whale excursions. The spacious boats are more comfortable than the smaller sportfishing vessels that are used for most of the whale-watch cruises, and their 25-foot-high top decks offer excellent vantage points for spotting whales.

A representative from L.A.'s Cabrillo Marine Museum is aboard to give a commentary about the gray whale. The boats go out January through March every Wednesday, Friday, and Saturday at 10 A.M., with an extra trip on Saturdays at 1:30 P.M. Call 253-9800 for exact sailing dates and departure times.

Also operating from Long Beach Harbor, Long Beach Sportfishing at Queens Wharf has a morning and an afternoon departure every day. Phone 432-8993.

East of downtown Long Beach at Belmont Shore, a Belmont Pier Sportfishing boat goes in search of cetaceans twice daily on weekends and once every weekday from the pier off Ocean Boulevard. Phone 434-6781.

REDONDO BEACH: Every weekday and weekend in both morning and afternoon, the 144-passenger *Voyager* leaves Redondo Sportfishing's pier at 233 North Harbor Drive in Kings Harbor to seek the oceangoing gray whales. Phone 372-2111.

NEWPORT BEACH: Whale watchers also can embark from the Balboa Pavilion in Newport Harbor. You can board the 100-passenger *Western Pride*, operated by Davey's Locker, for morning or afternoon trips. Phone (714) 673-1434. Or set sail on the daily Monday-through-Wednesday outing with Catalina Passenger Service's 500-passenger *Catalina Flyer*. Phone (714) 673-5245.

DANA POINT: From the Dana Wharf Sportfishing pier in Dana Point Harbor, whale-viewing vessels head to sea three times every day. On weekends in February during Dana Point's annual Festival of Whales, the boats depart hourly from 8 A.M. to 4 P.M. Phone (714) 496-5794.

OCEANSIDE: Helgren's Sportfishing at 315 South Harbor Drive in Oceanside Harbor boards whale watchers on its 15- to 140-passenger boats every day in the morning and afternoon, with an extra trip on weekends. Senior citizens and teenagers get reduced adult rates. Phone (619) 722-2133.

SAN DIEGO: You'll find five embarkation points in San Diego for gray-whale excursions. H&M Landing's boats depart from Municipal Pier at Emerson and Scott streets, between Harbor and Shelter islands, every day in the morning and afternoon. Phone (619) 222-1144.

Fisherman's Landing sets sail from a neighboring dock with three trips on weekends and two trips on weekdays. Phone (619) 221-8500.

H&M Landing also runs longer day trips to the Coronado Islands to view whales and other sea life. Boats leave Municipal Pier Thursday through Sunday at 9 A.M. for the eight-hour outings. Tickets for H&M Landing's all-day excursion to the offshore islands are $32 for adults, $25 for juniors, and $20 for children 12 years and under. Bring a picnic or buy food on board. Call the number above for more details and reservations.

Also from Municipal Pier, Point Loma Sportfishing's boat searches for whales once every weekday and two times daily on weekends. Phone (619) 223-1627.

From San Diego's Mission Bay you can board Islandia Sportfishing vessels three times daily on weekends, twice daily on weekdays, at 1551 West Mission Bay Drive. Phone (619) 222-1164.

Also in Mission Bay, Seaforth Sportfishing at 1717 Quivira Road goes forth from Quivira Basin with whale watchers every afternoon and also twice in the morning on Saturday through Tuesday. For reservations to board the 188- to 150-passenger boats, call (619) 224-3383.

VENTURA: North of Los Angeles you can sail from Ventura Harbor aboard Island Packers' boats to look for whales in the Santa Barbara Channel. The three-hour trips depart twice daily from Island Packers' docks at the end of Spinnaker Drive. Fares are $21 for adults, $14 for children 12 years and under. Call (805) 642-1393 or (805) 642-3370.

For extra adventure, join an Island Packers' all-day excursion from Ventura to Anacapa Island with whale watching along the way. Depending on the demand, there are departures daily at 9 A.M. to explore Anacapa, one of the five islands that are part of Channel Islands National Park. Bring a picnic lunch to eat when you go ashore. Adult tickets cost $38, children $21.

OXNARD: Cisco Sportfishing also takes whale watchers from Oxnard's Channel Islands Harbor out to Anacapa but doesn't land on the island. Boats depart from 4151 South Victoria Avenue every day in the morning and afternoon. Phone (805) 985-8511 or toll-free (800) 322-3474.

SANTA BARBARA: Beginning in late February, Sea Landing's *Condor* sails from the Breakwater of Santa Barbara's boat harbor to seek out gray whales on their homebound journey. You can join one of three daily excursions, except Wednesdays. Fares are $20 for adults, $10 for kids 12 years and under. Phone (805) 963-3564.

In addition to the listed trips, L.A.'s Cabrillo Marine Museum in San Pedro can make reservations for you on boats that feature a naturalist or tour guide. Call (310) 832-4444 weekdays from 9 A.M. to 12. On most whale-watching trips the boat captain gives a brief background about the gray whales and their migration and announces to passengers where to look when whales have been spotted.

While whale watching anywhere along the Southern California coast makes an enjoyable wintertime outing, you can experience the added thrills of close-up encounters with the leviathans in the Baja lagoons where they go to give birth. You'll sail south from San Diego on a sportfishing boat to San Ignacio Lagoon to mingle with the gray whales that have completed their annual swim from the Bering Sea. Everywhere you look there seems to be activity. Saltwater shoots skyward with a roar when these warm-blooded mammals come to the surface to refill their lungs with air. Huge tail flukes flash above the water as the whales prepare to dive. And when they're playful, the blubbery beasts erupt from the water and then fall back with a resounding splash.

To encourage the "friendlies" to come close enough for you to pet them, small skiffs with only a few passengers are lowered from the main boat to slowly cruise the lagoon. With patience and luck, a whale or two will get curious and surface alongside. Watch out for the spray if one decides to take a breath!

At night you'll sleep in a cozy cabin or berth aboard the mother ship. The vessel's cooks dish up hearty meals, and there are plenty of snacks for hungry seafarers. After dinner the naturalists on board give illustrated talks and discuss the next day's events.

En route to the lagoon you'll stop at some of Baja's rarely visited islands and go ashore with the naturalists to explore the unspoiled wilderness. On Todos Santos, San Martin, San Benitos, and Cedros islands you see a rich array of animal and bird life, including elephant seals and blue-footed boobies. The naturalists will identify dozens of little-known plants and flowers, too.

These trips operate from late December through April, until most of the gray whales have headed back to their summer feeding grounds in the Arctic. Cost of a nine-day Baja whale adventure is about $1,650.

For more details to make reservations of these increasingly popular nature excursions, call Pacific Sea Fari Tours at H&M Landing, (619) 222-1144, or write to 2803 Emerson Street, San Diego 92106.

H&M Landing and a few other companies also operate longer trips to the Sea of Cortez on the eastern side of Baja. Most luxurious are Special Expeditions' adventures aboard its 70-passenger cruise vessels, the *Sea Lion* and the *Sea Bird*. You're pampered with fine meals and waiter service, and experience the excitement of going ashore in rubber landing craft with naturalists to discover the flora and fauna of uninhabited islands and remote places along the peninsula. The trips last from 8 to 12 days and give you a chance to see not only gray whales but several other species, including the big blue whales, sleek fin whales, and playful humpback whales. Get details and trip dates from Special Expeditions, 720 Fifth Avenue, New York, NY 10019, (212) 765-7740 or toll-free (800) 762-0003.

Backcountry
and Mountain
Adventures

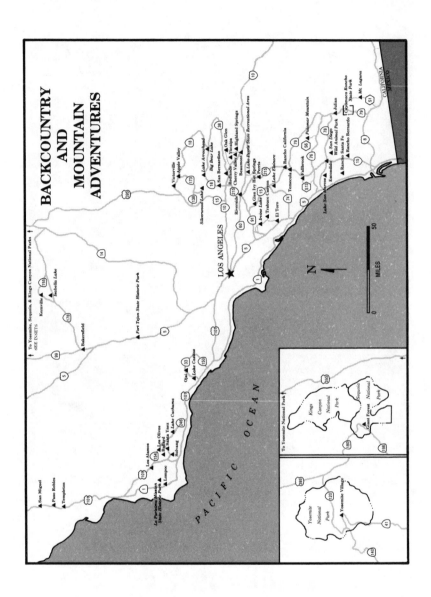

BACKCOUNTRY
AND
MOUNTAIN
ADVENTURES

Unsurpassed Yosemite—
A National Park
for All Seasons

Even the first visitors to the glacier-carved valley in the central section of the Sierra Nevada were awed by its uniqueness and beauty. The year was 1851, and a group of soldiers was in search of some troublesome Indians. The militiamen failed to capture the tribe, but they returned with glowing descriptions of the valley's natural wonders.

The search party also named the valley with the Indians' word for grizzly bear, *u-zu-ma-te,* which eventually evolved into *Yosemite* (*yo-sem-it-tee*). Yosemite Valley—with its unsurpassed scenery of massive granite monoliths, thundering waterfalls, alpine meadows, and handsome forests—was given protection by a special bill signed by President Abraham Lincoln in 1864.

Today the valley is the focal point of one of America's most scenic national treasures. Every year more than 3.5 million visitors enjoy nature's handiwork in the 1,200 square miles of Yosemite National Park. It's a wondrous place to visit in any season.

For the most enjoyment, plan a three-day weekend in the park and headquarter in Yosemite Valley at the renowned (and expensive) Ahwahnee, one of the West's grand hotels from a bygone era. Built in 1927, the Ahwahnee's stone-and-wood exterior matches the grandeur of its surroundings, all of which can be viewed through floor-to-ceiling windows in the imposing public rooms and from some of the guest-room balconies.

If the price of a room or suite in this historic hostelry is more than your budget can bear, at least make reservations for a meal in the Ahwahnee's Main Dining Room, where the tables are laid with fine linen, crystal, silver, and the hotel's exclusive china, and the food is excellent. Coats and ties are preferred at dinner.

The hotel is managed by a concessionaire, which also provides most visitor services and all accommodations in the park, including the two other places where you can stay in Yosemite Valley, the modern Yosemite Lodge and the more modest Curry Village. There are campgrounds, too, operated by the National Park Service.

To reach beautiful Yosemite from Los Angeles, go north on Interstate 5 to join California 99 and continue to Fresno. Then follow California 41 north to the park's southern entrance. A few miles beyond the entry station you'll be surprised by an expanse of green grass, the nine-hole golf course that's part of Yosemite's classic Victorian resort, the charming Wawona Hotel. This modernized lodge has hosted park visitors for over 100 years and is the perfect place to spend your first night in Yosemite after the long drive from Los Angeles. It's also an ideal alternative choice for accommodations for the entire weekend if you want to avoid the hustle and bustle of Yosemite Valley, 27 miles away. At least visit the hotel for dinner in its turn-of-the-century dining room.

In the morning, go back south from the Wawona on California 41 and take the nearby side road that leads to a parking lot for the Mariposa Grove of rare giant sequoias. Follow the footpaths or take a park tour tram to this group of 500 magnificent trees, some of them over 200 feet tall. Yosemite's oldest sequoia, nicknamed the Grizzly Giant, dates from about 800 B.C. You'll need 20 friends with outstretched arms to encircle its massive trunk. The much-photographed tunnel tree, with a hole large enough for cars to drive through, fell over from the weight of snow in 1969.

Also close by the Wawona Hotel, enjoy the summertime living history program offered in a minivillage of restored buildings called the Pioneer Yosemite History Center, then continue north through the park on California 41 to reach Yosemite Valley. Along the way, detour on the Glacier Point side road that leads to an outstanding panorama of the High Sierra and Yosemite Valley. Back on California 41, just after you emerge from the long Wawona tunnel, there's another excellent view of the picturesque valley.

As the road descends, it's easy to spot Yosemite's grand granite sentinel, El Capitan. To your right is famed Bridalveil Fall, created by melted Sierra snow that plunges 620 feet to reach the Merced River coursing through the valley. For a closer look, you can park and follow the footpath that leads to the base of this breathtaking waterfall. The road finally brings you to Yosemite Village, site of the Ahwahnee Hotel and other lodgings, as well as restaurants, stores, and park headquarters.

Summer, of course, is the peak time for vacationers, and most congregate in the valley's seven-square-mile area. To handle the crowds, and keep the scenic roads from resembling a freeway at rush hour, visitors with vehicles are encouraged to park and use Yosemite's free shuttle bus service instead. In fact, the roads to some points of interest in Yosemite Valley are off limits to all vehicles except the shuttle buses. You also can get around to see the sights by hiking, bicycling, and horseback riding.

Once you're settled in your lodgings or campground, stop at the visitor center to view exhibits that explain Yosemite's natural features. Subjects and times of walks and talks offered by park rangers also are posted. Among the publications at the center that will make your visit more worthwhile are the *Yosemite Guide*, with details of visitor activities, and the *Yosemite Road Guide,* which describes the sights to see.

Trails, and shuttle buses, will take you to Mirror Lake for excellent views of Yosemite's granite monoliths, including awesome Half Dome. And you can hike or ride a shuttle bus to Yosemite Falls, one of the world's highest waterfalls. The total 2,425-foot drop is divided into three sections, and there's a path to the base of the lower fall, which itself is twice the height of Niagara Falls. These and the park's other well-known falls—Bridalveil, Vernal, Ribbon, and Nevada—give their peak performances in May and June, although the water show continues into July and August.

A wonderful way to relax and get acquainted with Yosemite at the beginning of your visit is to take the narrated two-hour bus or open-air tram tour of Yosemite Valley. If there's a full moon, board one of the trams for a romantic evening tour of the valley too.

If you arrived by an alternate route or didn't stop to sightsee in the park on your way to Yosemite Valley, be sure to plan time during the weekend to take one of the half-day guided bus tours to Glacier Point or the Mariposa Grove or the all-day tour to both. Or leave early on the return trip to Los Angeles and visit both attractions in your own vehicle.

If you're in no rush to go home and want to see more of Yosemite, cross the Sierra Nevada Mountains on the Tioga Road, California 120, the only east-west highway through the park. (In winter this mountaintop highway is closed by snow.) You can stop for refreshments at Tuolumne Meadows before the scenic highway reaches 9,945-foot Tioga Pass, the highest automobile pass in the state. The road descends to Lee Vining and meets U.S. 395, which you follow south through the Owens Valley to join California 14 across the Mojave Desert. Then pick up Interstate 5 back to Los Angeles.

Round trip is about 710 miles.

If you want to enjoy this most popular park without the usual swarm of sightseers, plan your trip to Yosemite during the winter, spring, or fall. Each season has its own special appeal. In autumn the alpine weather is especially pleasant, and the trees are putting on a colorful show as Jack Frost turns the leaves to red, russet, and gold. Come springtime, the mountain meadows bloom with wildflowers and resemble pretty patchwork quilts that only Mother Nature can create.

Winter may be the best time of all for a trip to Yosemite. Snow makes this protected wilderness extra spectacular, and like the park's waterfalls, the number of park visitors slows to a trickle. Besides its pristine appearance and uncrowded conditions, Yosemite offers all sorts of activities in the winter season. You can go ice skating on an outdoor rink within sight of Half Dome and strap on snowshoes for nature walks with the park rangers at Badger Pass. Other options include scenic tours via bus, tractor-tread snowcat, or cross-country skis, as well as downhill skiing and snow camping.

For many visitors, the snow-covered scenery is enough enticement for a winter weekend in Yosemite. Snow plows keep the main park roads open, but carry tire chains because of changeable weather conditions. And be sure to have clothing that's appropriate for the season, including a warm hat, gloves, and boots.

You'll find the park's ski center at Badger Pass, 23 miles from the Yosemite Valley lodging area. The easiest way to reach it is by boarding the free ski buses. Rental skis, boots, and poles are available at the slopes, and there's a ski school if you want to improve your downhill or cross-country skills.

Badger Pass also is the place to view the High Sierra during an overland tour aboard a snowcat. It's exciting and inexpensive to take this unusual outing to the mountain ridge. Snowshoes can be rented if you decide to sightsee on foot.

A Nordic trail leads from Badger Pass all the way to Glacier Point for a dramatic view of Yosemite Valley. The park has more than 90 miles of marked trails for cross-country skiing.

Park rangers lead tours on snowshoes at Badger Pass; days and details are posted at the visitors center. Road and weather conditions permitting, bus tours will show you the best-known of the park's natural wonders in Yosemite Valley, including towering El Capitan and Bridalveil Fall.

In wintertime, reserve a cozy room in the Ahwahnee Hotel, Yosemite Lodge, or Curry Village, which are open year round; the Wawona Hotel is closed from after Thanksgiving weekend until Easter week, except for weekends and the Christmas holidays. At least one campground at Wawona and in Yosemite Valley is open for wintertime visitors. You can dine at the Ahwahnee or in two restaurants at Yosemite Lodge.

For the best route to the park in wintertime, head north from Los Angeles on Interstate 5 to join California 99 and continue through the San Joaquin Valley to Merced. Then follow California 140 northeast into Yosemite Valley.

Yosemite Area Code: 209

SIGHTSEEING   *Park Entry Permit,* $5 per vehicle. ● *Yosemite Valley Bus Tour,* 2 hours, at least twice daily year round, $13.75; also during periods of the full moon in summer. *Glacier Point Bus Tour,* 4 hours, twice daily June through November, $17.75. *Mari-*

posa Grove Bus Tour to the giant sequoias, 6 hours, once daily year round, $27.25. *Grand Tour* to Glacier Point and Mariposa Grove, all-day bus tour once daily spring through autumn, $37.75. All bus tours are operated by Yosemite Transportation System (YTS) from the Ahwahnee Hotel, Yosemite Lodge, and Curry Village in Yosemite Valley, 372-1241. ● Also tram tour of Mariposa Grove's giant sequoias with frequent departures during the day. Adults $5.25, children 4 to 12 years $2.50. ● *Saddle Horses,* daily guided 2-hour ($28), half-day ($38), and all-day ($55) trail rides except in winter, 372-1248. Stables are located in the Yosemite Valley, at Wawona and Tuolumne Meadows. ● Bicycles can be rented by the hour ($4.15) or day ($14.20) in Yosemite Valley at Yosemite Lodge and Curry Village. ● *Badger Pass Ski Area,* open daily Thanksgiving to mid-April for downhill skiing (adult all-day lift pass $25, children $11.75), snowcat tours ($6 per person), 372-1330. ● *Yosemite Ice Rink,* outdoor ice skating at Curry Village in Yosemite Valley. Open daily from Thanksgiving to mid-March; three 4-hour sessions, adults $4.50, children $3.75 per session. Skate rentals $1.75.

LODGING   All accommodations within the park are operated by a concessionaire, Yosemite Park and Curry Co., Yosemite National Park 95389, 252-4848. Make reservations well in advance, especially in summer and on holiday weekends. ● *The Ahwahnee,* a distinctive hotel with outstanding views in Yosemite Valley; $201.50 weekends, $182 midweek. Most elegant place to stay in the park. Some cottages adjoin main building. Nightly entertainment Tuesday through Saturday. ● *Yosemite Lodge,* more informal lodging in motel-type rooms or modest cabins; $47–$75 lodge, $47.50 cabin. Most lodge rooms have balcony or patio with Yosemite Valley views. ● *Curry Village,* large (600 units) and rustic accommodations in Yosemite Valley in hotel-type rooms ($56.75), cabins ($47.50), and tent cabins ($24.50). *Housekeeping Camp,* covered cabins in Yosemite Valley, $34. Almost like living outdoors; communal bath. Open mid-April through September. ● *Wawona Hotel,* attractive century-old hotel near southern entrance to park; $79.75 with private bath, $59.75 without. Golf course. Open Easter week through Thanksgiving weekend, plus Christmas holidays and weekends in winter.

CAMPING   All campgrounds operated by the National Park Service, Yosemite National Park 95389, 372-4845. Make reservations for Yosemite Valley campsites (except walk-in camps) through

MISTIX; call (800) 365-2267. Yosemite Valley has 5 drive-in RV and tent campgrounds, $12 per night, no hookups. One of those camping areas, *Lower River,* is open all year; no charge in winter. *Wawona,* near park's southern entrance, also open year round, $7 per night except in winter.

DINING   Meal service in the park is available at the hotels and lodges, all operated by concessionaires. Grocery stores in Yosemite Valley and at Wawona have picnic and camp supplies. • *Main Dining Room at the Ahwahnee* (see above) serves park's finest fare. Breakfast menu features eggs Benedict, while seafood salad is a nice choice for lunch. Entrees at dinner (reservations required) include roast duckling à l'orange. • *Mountain Room Broiler,* one of three dining spots at the Yosemite Lodge (see above). Steak place with mammoth murals of rock climbing and view of Yosemite Falls, open only for dinner from May through October. • *Four Seasons Restaurant,* also in Yosemite Lodge, breakfast and dinner daily with step-above-coffee-shop fare that includes filet mignon. • *Yosemite Lodge Cafeteria,* open for breakfast, lunch, and dinner. • *Cafeteria at Curry Village* (see above), good for moderate-priced breakfasts and dinners from April to mid-October. • *Dining Room at Wawona Hotel* (see above), buffet lunch is especially popular; reservations required for dinner. Open from Easter week through the Thanksgiving weekend, Christmas holidays and weekends in winter.

FOR MORE INFORMATION   Contact the Superintendent, Box 577, Yosemite National Park, CA 95389, 372-4461. For lodging information (except camping) and room reservations, contact Yosemite Park and Curry Co., 252-4848.

In Search of the Giants in Sequoia and Kings Canyon National Parks

What towers 275 feet, weighs about 1,385 tons, and is at least 2,500 years old? It's the largest living thing on earth, a giant sequoia. You can view this immense tree, nicknamed General Sherman, not far from Los Angeles in Sequoia National Park.

A weekend in Sequoia and neighboring Kings Canyon National Park makes a wonderful outing away from the noisy metropolis. While relaxing in the quiet woods, you'll also be treated to sparkling waterfalls, beautiful rivers and lakes, lush mountain meadows, dramatic granite-walled canyons, and caves with fascinating marble formations. You're certain to see fleet-footed deer and other wildlife.

Sequoia was established in 1890 as America's second national park in order to protect its rare trees, the few giant sequoias that survived the last ice age and are found only along the western slope of the Sierra Nevada range. It adjoins Kings Canyon National Park, where you'll see other towering beauties like one called General Grant, a huge sequoia that's the nation's official Christmas tree.

Together these parks cover 1,324 square miles of America's most magnificent wilderness, crowned by Mount Whitney, the highest point in the United States south of Alaska. Of course, the majestic giant sequoias—close relatives of the soaring coastal redwoods—are the big attractions. You'll find them in two major groves, Giant Forest and Grant Grove, which are 32 miles apart but connected by a scenic and twisting mountain road named the Generals Highway.

To reach Sequoia and Kings Canyon National Parks from Los Angeles, take Interstate 5 north and join California 99 through Bakersfield to the California 198 exit. Follow that road past Visalia to Sequoia's Ash Mountain entrance and the final zigzag section to Giant Forest.

If you don't enjoy mountain driving or are traveling in an RV, the longer but easier alternative route is to continue on California 99 to Fresno (or exit near Tulare onto California 63 going north), then turn east on California 180 to reach Kings Canyon's Big Stump entrance and Grant Grove.

Except for the park-service–operated campgrounds, all facilities for visitors—accommodations, dining rooms and cocktail lounges, grocery markets, gift shops, gas stations, and bus services—are provided under government contract by Guest Services. Lodgings range from very rustic cabins with wood-burning stoves and communal bath facilities to more modern motel rooms with private showers. Make your headquarters at Sequoia's Giant Forest Lodge, which has the greatest choice of accommodations in either park. Camping is on a first-come, first-serve basis except at the most popular campground, Lodgepole near Giant Forest, which you reserve through MISTIX.

You won't go hungry in the parks, but the food is far from gourmet fare. Most meals are served cafeteria style, and there's limited menu service at a couple of coffee shops and snack bars. The nicest place to eat is the dining room of Giant Forest Lodge, where you'll also find a cocktail lounge. To savor more of the fresh air and mountain scenery during your visit, shop for groceries at the village markets and picnic under the trees.

Ask at the park entry stations or visitors centers for maps and trail guides to help plan your weekend. The *Sequoia Bark,* a free park newspaper, lists daily activities. You can join guided bus excursions, follow rangers on nature hikes, walk the self-guided nature trails, and go sight-seeing on saddle horses, too. Also attend the illustrated talks presented by park rangers in the evening.

On Saturday, head first to Giant Forest to see the General Sherman Tree, which measures 103 feet around its massive trunk. Also look for the Auto Log, a fallen tree wide enough to drive your car on. You can drive through another fallen giant, the Tunnel Log. A trail leads to Tharps Log, named for a cattleman who lived in the tree's burned-out trunk.

After seeing the sequoias, follow an old mountain road from Giant Forest to Crystal Cave. This marble cavern of marvelous stalactites and stalagmites is the only one of 79 caves in the parks open to the public. There are guided tours daily in summer only.

On Sunday, drive along the Generals Highway to Grant Grove, where you'll discover more memorable sequoias like the Fallen Monarch, a hollow log once used as a tavern, living quarters, and even a stable. Nearby is the world's second largest sequoia, General Grant, which stretches 267 feet into the sky and has a trunk 40 feet thick.

If it's summer, continue north on California 180 to Kings Canyon and the rugged Cedar Grove area bordering the south fork of the Kings River. There's terrific backcountry scenery along the hiking and horse trails, as well as a four-mile unpaved nature route for motor vehicles.

If you'd rather not drive in the park, bus tours of the sequoia groves and other nature sights leave daily in the summer from Giant Forest Lodge. There are short early-morning and late-afternoon tours in Giant Forest, and an all-day outing to Grant Grove, Kings River Canyon, and Cedar Grove. Make reservations at the lodge or with Guest Services.

The parks are open in winter, too, but be sure to carry tire chains. Some roads are subject to closure by snow, including the Generals Highway from Lodgepole in Giant Forest north to Grant Grove. Your best bet is to settle in at the lodge in Sequoia's Giant Forest, the parks' center of activity in wintertime and the most convenient to Los Angeles. Be sure to book well in advance for accommodations during the Christmas holidays, when both of these alpine parks are a winter wonderland and a big hit with families.

The snow-covered sequoias resemble huge candelabra and are a remarkable sight. Rangers will lead you to the big trees on snowshoes or cross-country skis, or follow the trails on your own.

For more wintertime fun, there are snow play areas where the kids can frolic on sleds, saucers, and inner tubes.

When your weekend is over, leave the park via California 198 or 180 to rejoin California 99 and Interstate 5 for the drive south to Los Angeles.

Round trip is about 480 miles.

Sequoia/Kings Canyon Area Code: 209

SIGHTSEEING Park entry permit $5 per vehicle; valid for multiple entries and exits in both parks. • *Guided bus tours* of the parks daily from mid-May to mid-September. 2-hour tour of Giant Forest area departs 9 A.M., and 1 and 5 P.M. from Giant Forest lodge; $9 adults, $4.50 children under 13 years. All-day tour of Kings Canyon departs 9:30 A.M. from Giant Forest Lodge; $21 adults, $10.50 children. • *Crystal Cave,* 1-hour tours, Friday through Monday from mid-May to mid-June, daily until early September, then Friday through Monday until the end of September. Adults $3, children 6 to 12 years $1.50. (Crystal Cave will not be open during the summer of 1993.) • *Guided walks and campfire programs:* Times and places for ranger-led activities are listed at visitors centers at Lodgepole (Giant Forest) and Grant Grove and in free park newspaper, the *Sequoia Bark.* • *Saddle horses* can be rented for trail rides in summertime from corrals at Grant Grove, Cedar Grove, Mineral King, and Wolverton near Giant Forest. • *Cross-country skiing,* Sequoia Ski Touring Center, at Wolverton Ski Bowl north of Giant Forest, Sequoia National Park 93262, 565-3435. Open 8 A.M. to 5 P.M. daily, late November through April. Rentals, lessons, and tours.

LODGING Four lodgings are operated by the park's major concessionaire, Guest Services. For reservations, call 561-3314. • *Giant Forest Lodge,* Giant Forest Village, Sequoia National Park 93262. Largest park lodging, with 243 motel, cottage, and very rustic cabin units; $35 basic to $110 best. Open all year. • *Grant Grove Lodge,* Grant Grove Village, Kings Canyon National Park 93633. 52 rustic cottage and cabin rooms; $35 basic to $70 best. Open year round (except coffee shop). • *Cedar Grove Lodge,* on Kings River in Cedar Grove, Kings Canyon National Park 93262. 18 modern motel rooms, $75. Open Memorial Day to September. • *Stony Creek Lodge,* Generals Highway, midway between the parks. 11 motel units open Memorial Day to mid-September, $75. Other accommodations available just outside park boundaries in Three Rivers.

CAMPING   Parks have 14 campgrounds with three open year round, 565-3341. Most sites $8 per night, except $10 in Sequoia at *Lodgepole,* largest with 250 tent and RV sites; reserve through MISTIX, (800) 365-2267. In Kings Canyon, *Azalea* is largest, with 116 sites. Camping (except for Lodgepole) is on first-come, first-served basis.

DINING   *Dining room in Giant Forest Lodge* (see above) over-looks Round Meadow. Dinner and Sunday brunch; also cocktail lounge. Open May to October. • *Cafeteria in Giant Forest Village* offers breakfast, lunch, and dinner year round. • *Coffee shop in Grant Grove Village,* with cocktail lounge adjacent. 3 meals daily. • *Snack bar in Cedar Grove Village* serves 3 meals daily during summer. • *Stony Creek Lodge,* midway between Giant Grove and Grant Grove villages, offers coffee-shop fare from mid-May to mid-September.

FOR MORE INFORMATION   Contact Sequoia and Kings Canyon National Parks, Three Rivers, CA 93271, 565-3341. Also, Guest Services, P.O. Box 789, Three Rivers, CA 93271, 561-3314.

Alpine Retreat at Lake Arrowhead and Big Bear Lake

Los Angeles is blessed with a convenient alpine retreat, the San Bernardino Mountains. If you're eager for a complete change from the maddening megalopolis, pack some casual clothes and outdoor gear for the short drive to a pair of mountain lakes. Tucked away in the mile-high evergreen forests are two informal year-round resorts, Lake Arrowhead and Big Bear Lake.

Crisp air, mountain scenery, friendly local folks, and all sorts of activities promise a delightful weekend. The resort villages are especially attractive when dressed with snow, but the family will have a wonderful time even when there's not enough of the white stuff for kids to pack snowballs or sled down a hill. (In wintertime, be sure to contact the California Highway Patrol to see if tire chains are required.)

Part of the scenic sojourn to Lake Arrowhead and Big Bear Lake is a ride along the Rim of the World Drive, which zigzags up and along the mountainside. Reach it from Los Angeles by driving east on Interstate 10 (the San Bernardino Freeway), then exiting north toward San Bernardino/Barstow on Interstate 215. Follow the freeway direction for Highland Avenue/Mountain Resorts, California 30. Then take the Crestline/Lake Arrowhead exit, Waterman Avenue, which is California 18.

The roadside flora changes from palms to chaparral to pines as the highway ascends into the San Bernardino National Forest. The original road was constructed by Mormons hauling timber from the mountains to build a new settlement at San Bernardino in the mid-1800s. The improved route you're driving was carved from the mountainside in 1915, with some portions later widened to four lanes for a less harrowing trip.

Pause at the turnouts for some inspiring aerial views over the cloud tops, far above the smog that's frequently trapped in the basin below. Continue on Rim of the World Drive until you meet California 173 and turn left to Lake Arrowhead.

The original 1920s resort village was replaced in 1981 by a new and larger village that features 60 shops and several restaurants, and other facilities for mountain residents and visitors. Part of the two-level, 38-acre complex is the Arrowhead Hilton Lodge at the lake's edge, a pretty spot to spend the first night of your weekend getaway. Have dinner in the hotel's gourmet Beau Rivage Cafe, then enjoy the musical entertainment and go dancing at the Lakeview Terrace Lounge, also in the Hilton.

On Saturday you can board the *Arrowhead Queen,* a paddle wheeler that takes you on a 50-minute tour of the man-made lake (weather permitting) from a nearby dock at Lake Arrowhead Marina. You also can charter a ski boat with driver for waterskiing on the lake.

Look for the spire-topped pavilion, a village landmark for more than a half century. Glenn Miller, Tommy Dorsey, and other big bands played there when the pavilion was a dance hall. Today it's home for a variety of shops where you'll find leather goods, needlework, jewelry, kitchenware, artwork, and more.

When activity or the alpine air makes you thirsty or hungry, stop in one of the village restaurants that also dish up views of the lake, such as Paoli's Restaurant and Bar.

Afterward, drive on narrow roads around the lake to see the varied architecture of Arrowhead's many vacation homes and residences, including some of French Normandy and Norman English design.

Head east from the village on California 173; just after you cross the dam is a nice lookout over the lake. Continue on the state highway, then turn left to go west on North Bay Road, which winds among the trees and attractive homes. Eventually it joins California 189 at Blue Jay, another mountain community with a year-round Olympic-size ice skating rink where you can have some family fun.

From there go south on Daley Canyon Road to rejoin California 18, then head east again along Rim of the World Drive through Running Springs to Big Bear Lake, where you should have reserved accommodations for Saturday night. There's a wide choice of family-run lodges with kitchen units, as well as vacation cabins, modern condominium units, and B&Bs scattered among the fragrant pine trees that surround the seven-mile-long lake.

If it's late afternoon, turn north off California 18 on Alden Road and go to the Blue Whale at lakeside to enjoy the sunset view and cocktails. Then cross the road for a seafood or prime rib dinner in the Blue Whale's restaurant.

You'll find plenty to do in this mountain valley, which is best known as Southern California's ski center. From Thanksgiving to Easter, thousands of skiers flock to Big Bear when Mother Nature and snow-making equipment turn the steep slopes into a winter playground at the Snow Summit, Bear Mountain, and Snow Forest ski areas. In the other seasons you can enjoy boating, hiking, horseback riding, golfing, fishing, camping, and much more.

On Sunday, choose your favorites from a host of activities that are easily reached from California 18, the south-shore highway that runs through the village of Big Bear Lake and is its main street, Big Bear Boulevard. Side roads take you to several marinas where craft can be rented for fishing, sight-seeing, or water sports, including skimming across the blue water on Jet-skis or a windsurfer. Less adventurous visitors can cruise around the lake aboard the *Sierra,* an excursion boat that sails from Pine Knot Landing, or the *Big Bear Queen,* out of Big Bear Marina.

If you want to try your luck catching lake trout, bluegill, or bass, the marinas also have tackle, bait, and the necessary state fishing license. Or go to a private trout farm, Alpine Lake, where you pay only for what you hook and no license is required.

Also off Big Bear Boulevard is Magic Mountain Stables with rental horses that will take you on a scenic trail ride through the trees. Nearby you'll spot the Alpine Slide, a snowless bobsled thrill ride that twists down the mountainside.

A few miles east, at the Bear Mountain ski area, you can play on a nine-hole public golf course. The kids will be fascinated by a black bear, timber wolf, and other local mountain wildlife on display in the adjacent Moonridge Animal Park, a free county-run zoo. Families always enjoy a tour of Big Bear in a surrey with fringe on the top. Look for the horse-drawn vehicles at the corner of Big Bear Boulevard and Pine Knot Avenue.

Visit the U.S. Forest Service ranger station on the north shore of Big Bear Lake and ask for the Gold Fever Trail tour map of historic Holcomb Valley, where gold was discovered in 1860. If you decide to explore this old mining area, figure two to three hours to make the rugged trip over dirt roads. The rangers have hiking and camping information, too. Also on the north shore is a Cal Tech–operated solar observatory, where visitors are welcome to watch telescopic studies of the sun on television monitors.

When your weekend in the mountains is over, drive east on California 18 to join one of the state's designated scenic highways, California 38. The road twists and turns as it descends through the forest and Barton Flats to Redlands, where you pick up Interstate 10 heading west to Los Angeles.

Round trip is about 210 miles.

Lake Arrowhead/Big Bear Lake Area Code: 909

SIGHTSEEING *Lake Arrowhead Marina,* Lake Arrowhead Village, 336-6992. 60-passenger paddle wheeler *Arrowhead Queen* departs hourly on 50-minute cruises from 10 A.M. to 7 P.M. daily, weather permitting. Adults $9.50, seniors $8.50, children 5 to 12 years $6.50. • *McKenzie Water-Ski School,* lakeside at end of the peninsula, Lake Arrowhead Village, 337-3814. Open 9 A.M. to 5 P.M. daily in summer for waterskiing lessons ($25) and ski-boat charters with driver, skis, and wet suits ($90 per hour). Cash payments only. • *Ice Castle,* 27307 Highway 189, Blue Jay 92317, 336-2111. Public skating daily on a beautiful ice rink. 2-hour sessions $5.75 adults, $4.75 children. Skate rental $1.50. • *Snow Summit,* Big Bear Lake, 886-5841 or 886-5766. Open daily from 7:30 A.M. to 10 P.M. from mid-November to mid-April. 6 double chair lifts, 3 triple chairs, and 2 quad chairs; daily lift pass $35.50, children $19. Lighted for night skiing. • *Bear Mountain,* Big Bear Lake, 585-2519. Open daily from 8 A.M. to 4 P.M. from mid-November to mid-April. 5 double, 3 triple, and 1 high-speed quad chair lifts; daily lift pass $36 adults, children $19. • *Snow Forest,* Big Bear Lake, 886-8891. 1 triple chair, 1 Poma, 3 rope tows; all-day pass $33, children $13. • *Magic Mountain Stables,* on Big Bear Boulevard at western entrance to town of Big Bear Lake, 886-7715. Guided horseback rides in national forest, $20 per hour. Children 2 to 7 years can ride double with an adult. Open every day. • *Bear Mountain Golf Course,* Clubview Drive, Big Bear Lake, 585-8002.

9 holes, $14 weekends, $10 weekdays; open daily May through September. • *Moonridge Animal Park,* Moonridge Road, Big Bear Lake, 866-3652. Open 8:30 A.M. to 4 P.M. daily, closed in winter. Free. • *Pine Knot Landing,* end of Pine Knot Avenue, Big Bear Lake, 866-2628. One of 8 marinas on Big Bear Lake. Open April to mid-November from sunrise to sunset; canoe, rowboat, motorboat, powerboat, sailboat, pontoon boat rentals. Also, 40-passenger *Sierra* makes 80-minute cruises of Big Bear Lake from April to November. Adults $8.50, children 4 to 12 years $5. • *Big Bear Queen,* at Big Bear Marina, Big Bear Lake 866-3218. 60-passenger pseudo-paddle wheeler makes 90-minute narrated excursions around the lake from May through October, weather permitting. Adults $8.50, seniors and children 5 to 12 years $6.50. Call for schedule. • *Alpine Lake,* 440 Catalina Road, Big Bear Lake, 866-4532. Private trout farm open March to November. $3.50 entry per family, then pay for your catch at $4.75 per pound. • *Victoria Park Carriage Company,* Big Bear Boulevard at Pine Knot Avenue, Big Bear Lake, 866-7137. Sightseeing rides in horse-drawn surrey; two passengers $25 daytime, $30 evenings. • *Big Bear Solar Observatory,* 40386 North Shore Drive, Big Bear, 866-5791. Free tours from 4 to 6 P.M. Saturdays only from mid-June until Labor Day.

EVENTS Oktoberfest, from Labor Day weekend to late October. For nine autumn weekends, Big Bear Lake is the place to go for oompah bands, bratwurst, and beer. Everyone joins in sing-alongs, dancing, yodeling, and log-sawing contests. Call the Big Bear Chamber of Commerce, 866-4607. • *Old Miner's Days,* late July. Colorful week-long celebration of the Big Bear area's early days. Burro races highlight the summertime high jinks, which include pie-eating contests and "whiskerino" contests, dances, parades, and barbecues. Call 866-4607.

LODGING *Lake Arrowhead Hilton Resort,* P.O. Box 1699, Lake Arrowhead Village, 366-1511 or toll-free (800) 800-6792; 261-room lodge nestled at lakeside among the pines; guests welcome at private health club. • *Saddleback Inn—Arrowhead,* 300 South State Highway 173, Lake Arrowhead, 366-3571; $100, including breakfast. Nice inn with cottage rooms and suites across from the village. • *Chateau Du Lac,* 922 Hospital Road, Lake Arrowhead, 337-6488; $95–$250. Very attractive 6-room bed-and-breakfast overlooking the lake. • *Escape for All Seasons/Snow Summit,* 41935 Switzerland Drive, Big Bear Lake, 866-7504; from $120 during ski season, mid-November to mid-April; $100 in summer. 75 townhouses with kitchens, fireplaces, and patios at base of Snow Summit ski area. ● *Forest Shores Estates,* 40670 Lakeview Drive, Big Bear Lake, 866-6551; from $120 weekends in winter. Modern condo units at lakeside near town center. ● *Knickerbocker Mansion,* 869 South Knickerbocker, Big Bear Lake, 866-8221; $75–$95. 1920s vertical-log mansion and carriage house converted to 9-room B&B with country decor. Close to town center. ● *Gold Mountain Manor,* 1117 Anita Avenue, Big Bear City, 585-6997; $75–$180. More remote 1920s lodge that's become a B&B. 7 rooms with fireplace or Franklin stove. Gourmet breakfast an extra treat. ● *Cozy Hollow Lodge,* 40409 Big Bear Boulevard, Big Bear Lake, 866-8886; $75. Cabins with fireplaces. ● *Krausmeir Haus Bavarian Village,* 1351 Midway Boulevard, Big Bear City, 585-2886; $55. Lodge and cottages in alpine meadow 6 miles from Big Bear Lake.

CAMPING   Six U.S. Forest Service campgrounds are near Big Bear Lake; Grout Bay is the only one at lakeside. Most are $8 per night (no hookups) and closed in winter. Contact ranger station on North Shore, 866–3437.

DINING   *Beau Rivage Cafe,* gourmet dining room in Lake Arrowhead Hilton Resort (see above). Also Sunday brunch. ● *Paoli's,* Lake Arrowhead Village, 336-9300. Lakeside restaurant serving lunch and dinner; Italian specialties. Also located in Big Bear Lake at 40821 Pine Knot Avenue, 866-2020. ● *Tulips,* Lake Arrowhead Village, 336-4302. Fun for family dining. Open daily for all meals. ● *Sportsman Restaurant,* 2 miles from Lake Arrowhead Village on Hook Creek Road in Cedar Glen, 337-9036. Steak, seafood, etc., for lunch and dinner, plus children's plates; reservations advised. ● *The Royal Oak,* 2 miles from Lake Arrowhead Village on State Highway 189 in Blue Jay, 337-6018. English pub decor with prime ribs, veal dishes, seafood specialties for lunch and dinner; reservations advised. ● *Chef's Inn and Tavern,* 29020 Oak Terrace, Cedar Glen, 336-4487. Good food in a historic home at the forest's edge. Lunch and dinner daily, plus brunch on weekends. ● *Blue Whale,* lakeside end of Alden Road, Big Bear Lake, 866-5771. A local favorite serving dinner from 5 P.M., also Sunday brunch from 10 A.M. ● *Captain's Anchorage,* Big Bear Boulevard at Moonridge Road, Big Bear Lake, 866-3997. Rustic dinner house specializing in steak and seafood. ● Always popular for breakfast, lunch, and dinner is *Boo Bear's Den,* 572 Pine Knot Avenue, Big Bear Lake, 866-2932. Open daily 7 A.M. to 10 P.M., longer on weekends. Fresh fish daily.

FOR MORE INFORMATION Contact Lake Arrowhead Village, P.O. Box 640, Lake Arrowhead 92352, 337-2533; and Lake Arrowhead Communities Chamber of Commerce, Building F, Lake Arrowhead Village (or P.O. Box 219), Lake Arrowhead 92352, 337-3715 or 336-1547. For lodging information, call toll-free (800) 545-5784. ● Also, Big Bear Chamber of Commerce, 41647 Big Bear Boulevard (or P.O. Box 2860), Big Bear Lake 92315, 866-4607 or 866-7000. Open weekdays 9 A.M. to 5 P.M., Saturdays, 10 A.M. to 2 P.M. Also 24-hour telephone accommodations service, 878-3000.

Escape to Old-Time Julian and Heavenly Palomar Mountain

When you yearn for some peace and quiet and a breath of fresh air, head to San Diego County's mountainous backcountry. In the scenic area between the Pacific Coast and the Colorado Desert you'll find plenty to entice you, including a century-old mining town that makes a quaint headquarters for your weekend escape.

Tucked in the foothills at the edge of Cleveland National Forest, the six-square-block village of Julian has old-fashioned lodgings, good places to eat, all sorts of gift shops, and a museum of pioneer memorabilia. Another drawing card is an annual fall harvest festival, when friendly townsfolk bake up mouth-watering apple pies and put on a crafts show for visitors.

Any time of the year you'll also have fun touring Julian's only remaining gold mine, going to a country dinner theater, and viewing Mother Nature's handiwork nearby in Cuyamaca Rancho State Park, a restful area of pine forests and oak groves. On the way home you'll be delighted by the fabled Dudley's Bakery at Santa Ysabel, as well as a charming Indian mission. And a mile high in the sky at Palomar Observatory you're welcome to view America's largest telescope.

Start your excursion from Los Angeles by driving south on Interstate 5 and heading east just beyond Oceanside on California 78. You'll see a mixture of suburban housing developments and rural ranch life before the road leads to Julian, your weekend hideaway in the hills.

The town was created when miners rushed there to stake claims during a gold strike in 1870. Its oldest lodging is still taking guests, but reserve well in advance for a room in the Julian Hotel. Opened in 1897 as the Robinson Hotel by a freed slave from Georgia, Albert Robinson, the 18-room inn still retains its Victorian flavor. Guests relaxing on the front porch and playing the piano in the parlor are reminiscent of travelers in earlier times. You'll slumber in four-poster beds and find most facilities down the hall. Or treat yourself to the private honeymoon cottage, with its own bath and a fireplace.

Visitors can opt for other lodgings in the newer Julian Lodge, or in cabins and B&B inns in the area. If you arrive in time on Friday, go to the rustic Pine Hills Lodge for its barbecue dinner theater and enjoy a musical or comedy starring local performers. (The popular country-style meal and show also are offered on Saturday evenings at the lodge.)

Julian is a place to park your car and explore on foot. At Washington and Fourth streets is a former brewery building that's now the Julian Pioneer Museum, jammed with local nostalgic items of the past century. On the hill behind you'll spot Julian's unusual library, a one-room schoolhouse built in 1880 and moved to town from nearby Witch Creek. Go a block to Main Street and stroll down the row of false-front buildings. Drop into the Julian Drug Store, circa 1886, and settle down at the old marble-topped fountain for a sarsaparilla or old-fashioned ice cream soda.

Then drive up the hill at C Street to the Eagle Mine, where you'll learn about Julian's gold rush days. In the past century the mine has yielded $3.5 million in gold. During a tour that goes 1,000 feet into the cool, dark tunnels, you'll get an insight into the mining process and be entertained with tales of early-day prospecting.

More productive today are the orchards that surround the town and fill roadside stands with apples, as at Farmers' Mountain Vale Ranch in Wynola. You can order homemade apple pie there and many other places, including the Julian Cafe, successor to the town's oldest eatery. A number of restaurants have opened in recent years, all with quaint decor that complements the village's vintage look. Enjoy lunch at Romano's Dodge House, the Julian Grille, or the venerable roadside cafe west of town, Tom's Chicken Shack.

To experience bygone times, you can board a horse-drawn carriage or wagon for a ride along a country road and through the tiny town. The old-fashioned vehicles wait for passengers at the corner of Main and Washington streets. Julian's quaintness has caught on with refugees from the city who like this rural area's informal life-style, and some have opened shops for transient guests and local folks alike. A winery has been established by Michael and Toni Menghini, who invite you to taste their vintages. The Julian

Cider Mill on Main Street, which boasts 40 kinds of honey and other tasty treats, is a good place to refresh yourself with freshly pressed apple cider before embarking on an afternoon outing to Cuyamaca Rancho State Park.

To enter this attractive 26,000-acre park, drive about ten miles south of Julian on California 79. Look for signs and a side road that lead to Stonewall Mine and an excellent mining exhibit in an old prospector's cabin. Nearby the entrance to Paso Picacho campground, visit the Interpretive Center to learn about the animals, flowers, and geology that you'll see in this natural preserve.

For unsurpassed vistas on a clear day, hike the three-mile trail to Cuyamaca Peak, where you can see the ocean, the desert, and Mexico. A little farther along California 79, turn left to visit the interesting Indian Museum in an old stone ranch house near park headquarters.

Unless you decide to camp at Cuyamaca Rancho State Park or at William Heise County Park, close by Pine Hills, return to Julian to spend the night. On Sunday morning, head to the Pine Hills Lodge for the Bloody Mary and Champagne Brunch, an all-you-can-eat buffet. Or drive west on California 78/79 for fresh pastries and coffee at Dudley's Bakery in Santa Ysabel. Located at a crossroads that seems to be in the middle of nowhere, this two-decade-old baking institution sells 17 kinds of oven-fresh bread to a clientele that comes from all over San Diego County. Few people ever pass Dudley's without going in to smell the wonderful bakery aromas and buy a loaf or two to take home.

Afterward, head north on California 79 about two miles to lovely Mission Santa Ysabel, founded in 1818 as an *asistencia,* or branch, of the mother mission in San Diego. It continues to serve the Indians of ten reservations, and visitors are welcome in the reconstructed church and its museum. Look for the religious murals painted by the Indians, and learn about stories of the lost treasure of Santa Ysabel and the mystery of its stolen bells. Also visit the Indian burial grounds.

Continue north and turn west on California 76 toward Lake Henshaw. Just past that popular fishing spot, turn right on San Diego County Road S7, East Grade Road, and follow it up to the summit road junction on Palomar Mountain. (In winter the mountain can become a white wonderland, and tire chains may be required; check with the highway patrol or the county road department.) Then go right on S6, the Highway to the Stars, which leads through some spectacular forest scenery to the famed Palomar Observatory.

An immense white dome houses its 200-inch Hale telescope, the nation's largest optical apparatus for peeking into the heavens. You can view the 530-ton instrument from a glassed-in gallery, but actual observations are not possible. The telescope is restricted to scientific researchers, who use it at night to make photographs and electronic images of the stars in our solar system and beyond. Its huge mirror, about two feet thick, was cast of Pyrex glass in 1935, but grinding and polishing the mirror to perfection took 11 years. Since then scientists have been able to see as far as a sextillion (1,000,000,000,000,000,000,000) miles into space! For comparison, our moon is less than 240,000 miles away.

Owned and operated by Pasadena's California Institute of Technology since 1948, the observatory was built more than 12 stories high in order to house the 55-foot-long telescope. Astronomers take pictures as the telescope follows the stars, which may be nearly one billion light years away. Scientists at Palomar spent seven years making a photographic map of the entire sky as seen in the Northern Hemisphere. Pamphlets in the viewing gallery describe other feats of the telescope. Stop first at the adjacent astronomical museum for a description of the telescope, samples of pictures taken with it, and a look at a life-size replica of the enormous mirror.

Flanking the Palomar Mountain post office at the summit road junction are a store and a restaurant, where you can get picnic supplies, snacks, and vegetarian meals. Both are run by a half dozen members of the Spiritual World Society of the Costa Mesa–based Yoga Center of California. Mother's Kitchen features homemade soups and breads, Mexican dishes, salads, sandwiches, ice cream, and fresh-baked pies. Beer and wine are available, too.

West from the summit road junction at the end of S7 is the entrance to Palomar Mountain State Park, a peaceful retreat for campers, picnickers, and hikers. Another attraction is Doane Pond, which is stocked with trout and open to fishing all year.

Return to S6 and descend that steep, switchback route through the dense forest to California 76. Then go west past hillside orchards of oranges and avocados to join Interstate 15 and head north to pick up California 60 (Pomona Freeway) back to Los Angeles.

Round trip is about 360 miles.

Julian/Palomar Mountain Area Code: 619

SIGHTSEEING *Julian Pioneer Museum,* Washington Street at Fourth Street, Julian, 765-0227. Open 10 A.M. to 4 P.M. daily except Mondays from May through November, then weekends and holidays only. Admission free but donations appreciated. ● *Eagle Mine,* eastward at the top of C Street, Julian, 765-0036. Open daily 10 A.M. to 3 P.M.; 1-hour escorted tours that are informative and fun.

Adults $6, children 15 years and under $3. • *Country Carriages,* 765-1471. Elegant carriage and horse depart from Julian Drug Store; half-hour ride $15 per couple, $20 per family. Evening rides from your hotel to restaurant and return, $20. • *Menghini Winery,* 2 miles north of town via Farmers Road to 1150 Julian Orchards Drive, Julian, 765-2072. Informal tastings Friday through Monday. • *Cuyamaca Rancho State Park,* along California 79 about 10 miles south of Julian (12551 Highway 79, Descanso 92016), 765-0755. The state highway runs through this forested park; there's a $5 per vehicle day-use fee to visit the park's picnic areas. Also camping (see below). • *Mission Santa Ysabel,* on California 79 (P.O. Box 128), Santa Ysabel 92070, 765-0810. Open daily from 7 A.M. to dusk. Admission free. • *Palomar Observatory,* at northern end of San Diego County Road S6 atop Palomar Mountain, 742-3476. Viewing gallery in dome open daily 9 A.M. to 4 P.M. Admission free. • *Palomar Mountain State Park,* western end of San Diego County road S7/State Park Road, Palomar Mountain 92060, 742-3462. $3 per vehicle day-use fee. Also camping (see below).

EVENTS   *Fall Harvest and Apple Days Celebration* is held in the Julian Town Hall every weekend in October with craft show, melodrama, and sing-along. Craft shows continue on weekends throughout November.

LODGING   *Julian Hotel,* 2032 Main Street, Julian 92036, 765-0201 or toll-free (800) 734-5854. Cozy turn-of-the-century hotel with 18 rooms; $82 on Fridays and Saturdays, $64 other days; add $12 for private bath. Also honeymoon cottage for $110 or $145. Fancy full breakfast included. • *Julian Lodge,* 2720 C Street, Julian 92036, 765-1420; $69. Attractive 2-story inn with 24 rooms; continental breakfast included. • *Julian Farms Lodging,* 2818 Washington Street, Julian 92036, 765-0250; $60. 4 antique-decorated cabins. • *Pine Hills Lodge,* 2960 La Posada Way (3 miles southeast of town), Julian 92036, 765-1100. 12 very rustic cabins in woodsy setting with private baths and patios, some fireplaces; $50–$125 Fridays and Saturdays, $60–$75 other days. Continental breakfast included (except Sundays). Lodge is popular for a dinner theater, and Sunday brunch (see below). • Julian area has other modest accommodations, including numerous bed-and-breakfast rooms in area homes; contact the Julian Chamber of Commerce (see below) or the Julian Bed-and-Breakfast Guild, P.O. Box 1711, Julian 92036, 765-1555.

CAMPING   *Cuyamaca Rancho State Park* (see above). Paso Picacho Campground has 85 tent sites, Green Valley Falls 81 sites; $14 per night, no hookups. • *William Heise County Park,* 1 mile west of Julian on California 78/79 to Pine Hills Road, then 2 miles south to Frisius Road and 2 more miles east, 565-3600 (San Diego County Parks information). 61 all-year tent and RV sites in a forest of oaks and pines; $11 per night, no hookups. • *Palomar Mountain State Park* (see above). 27 tent and RV sites at Doane Valley Campground; $14 per night, no hookups.

DINING   *Pine Hills Lodge* (see above). Enjoyable barbecue dinner theater Friday and Saturday nights with buffet of BBQ ribs and chicken preceding musical or comedy show; $27.50 per person, $22.50 for children 12 years and under. Seating for 96; reservations suggested. Sunday Bloody Mary and Champagne Brunch from 9 A.M. to 2 P.M.; all you can eat and drink for $11.95; children $6. • *Julian Cafe,* 2112 Main Street, Julian, 765-9932. Local favorite for breakfast, lunch, and dinner, or just a piece of apple pie. Whole apple pies to go, $7.50. Open every day. Also try *Mom's Pie Shop, Mrs. Glad's Bakery,* and *The Julian Pie Company,* all on Main Street. • *Romano's Dodge House,* 2718 B Street, Julian, 765-1003. Italian fare for lunch and dinner; boasting Julian's only full bar. Open daily, except Tuesdays and Wednesdays, with guitar player on weekend nights. • *Julian Grille,* 2224 Main Street, Julian, 765-0173. Lunch and dinner in a historic cottage. Reservations recommended. • *Tom's Chicken Shack,* on California 78/79 at Wynola Road, 3 miles west of Julian, 765-0443. Well-known cafe serving its namesake and other American fare for lunch and dinner. Closed Mondays and Tuesdays. • *Dudley's Bakery,* at California 78 and 79 junction, Santa Ysabel 92070, 765-0488 or toll-free (800) 225-3348. More than a dozen types of freshly baked bread to take out, plus savory pastries and other bakery treats. Open daily except Mondays and Tuesdays. • *Mother's Kitchen,* at junction of San Diego County roads S6 and S7, Palomar Mountain 92060, 742-3496. Restaurant (and store) with vegetarian menu and snacks. Open weekends from 8:30 A.M. to 5:30 P.M., weekdays from 10 A.M. except Tuesdays and Wednesdays.

FOR MORE INFORMATION   Contact the Julian Chamber of Commerce, P.O. Box 413, Julian 92036, 765-1857. Ask for the town map and a list of lodgings. Also call the Julian Information Center, 765-0707, for interactive recorded information.

Rambling Around Paso Robles

Pity the travelers who rush along U.S. 101 between Los Angeles and San Francisco. They don't have time to discover the delights that often can be found just off the freeway. Exit at Paso Robles, for instance, and you'll find an array of pleasant surprises to fill a weekend.

Named by the Spanish missionaries for a pass through the thick oaks, this pastoral place is now adorned with almond trees that were planted on the rolling hills that surround the town. They bring not only a bountiful crop of tasty nuts but a stream of visitors in late February and early March, when the trees paint the hillsides with their beautiful pink and white blossoms.

Any month of the year is a fine time to ramble around Paso Robles, which planted its roots along the El Camino Real stagecoach route, then became a well-known hot springs resort, and now is the hub for this scenic agricultural area in northern San Luis Obispo County. In addition to all the almonds, you'll see walnut, pistachio, and apple orchards, grain fields, and grape vineyards.

Winery tours and tastings are among the activities you'll enjoy in the Paso Robles countryside. To keep out-of-towners happy and around for a while, the chamber of commerce has compiled a list of 44 things to do. Save most of them for another time, but be sure to visit Mission San Miguel, a rural sanctuary that hasn't changed very much during the past two centuries. A leisurely circle excursion also will take you to a delightful doll museum and some historical adobes. And don't miss the perfect Sunday drive, a bucolic back-road route through the Santa Lucia Mountains to the ocean.

You'll need an early start from Los Angeles to reach Paso Robles by nightfall. Take U.S. 101 north to the Spring Street/Business exit at the south end of town. Go under the freeway and continue north 11 blocks to a local rendezvous, the Paso Robles Inn, where you can check into one of its unpretentious 1940s-era rooms. For home-style accommodations, exit U.S. 101 sooner on Vineyard Drive at Templeton and stay at the Country House Inn, a five-room bed-and-breakfast inn that was built when the town was established in 1886. Another choice is Templeton Manor, a two-room B&B in a private neighborhood.

In the morning, begin a lazy day of touring by heading seven miles north of Paso Robles to Mission San Miguel Arcangel. Along the way, leave U.S. 101 at Wellsona Road to visit Helen Moe's

Antique Doll Museum. Her intriguing collection of nearly 700 dolls includes a wooden one that belonged to the son of Henry VIII and dates to 1540. Especially fascinating are the miniature furnishings of bygone days that decorate a large dollhouse.

Continuing on U.S. 101 to the San Miguel exit, you'll be greeted by a campanile of bells and a rural scene reminiscent of the days when Franciscan fathers from Spain founded the mission in 1797. San Miguel is one of only four missions in the famed chain that are still run as parish churches by the brown-robed padres.

Enter the mission through its courtyard, now a cactus garden, and pick up a self-guided-tour leaflet in the gift shop. In St. Michael's Room you'll see a sixteenth-century wood carving that depicts the mission's patron saint overpowering the devil. Other rooms—including the friars' sleeping quarters and dining room and a kitchen with its original beehive oven—are filled with artifacts and prestatehood history. A highlight is the long, narrow, and unusually adorned church sanctuary, with adobe walls almost six feet thick. Its remarkably well-preserved decorations were painted in the early 1800s by the Indian neophytes, directed by Spanish artist Esteban Munras. Unique to this mission is the all-seeing eye of God represented above the altar.

Alongside the church you can view the cemetery, burial site for hundreds of Indians as well as the William Reed family, who purchased San Miguel after all the California missions were secularized by Mexico in the mid-1800s. The family was murdered at the mission by bandits. One of Reed's partners was Petronillo Rios, who built a family home nearby on the north-south stagecoach road that later was paved and became the original Highway 101. Today Rios's hacienda has been restored and is open as a museum.

Backtrack to the San Miguel exit from U.S. 101 and follow the signs to reach the Rios-Caledonia Adobe and gift shop, which are just down the road from the mission. During its lifetime this rustic residence also served as a stagecoach stop, hotel and tavern, schoolhouse, mattress factory, tailor shop, and 1920s tourist attraction. Volunteers known as the Friends of the Adobe restored the structure in the past decade and usually are on hand to answer questions and show you around. They also have a craft guild and run a gift shop to sell their work—homemade quilts, embroidered and crocheted items, dolls, and more—to support continuing restoration.

After your visit, head back north on Mission Street past the mission grounds and go into the town of San Miguel, which boomed during World War II, when there were 45,000 soldiers at neighboring Camp Roberts.

Top off your easygoing day with a tour and wine tasting at the award-winning Meridian Vineyards, and savor some back-road scenery along the way. From San Miguel go east on 14th Street, which crosses the wide Salinas riverbed and turns south to become River Road. Turn left to head east on Estrella Road, then go right on Airport Road until you see the white fence that surrounds the 1878 Estrella Adobe Church. This state historic landmark is open only occasionally, for weddings, but you can park on the road shoulder and explore its old pioneer cemetery.

Continue south past the Paso Robles municipal airport to busy California 46 and turn left to go east about four miles to the roadside vineyards of the Meridian winery. Slow down for the left-hand entrance, marked by a stone gateway. Drive past rows of grapevines to the hilltop winery, where you get a good view of the impressive vineyards before taking a tour and tasting the wine.

Returning to California 46 and heading west toward Paso Robles, you also can turn off the state highway to taste wines at the Arciero and Eberle wineries. Back in town on one of Paso Robles's oldest avenues, Vine Street, you'll find the Call-Booth House that's now home to the Paso Robles Art Association. Built by Dr. Samuel Call at the turn of the century, the Queen Anne–style cottage was renovated as a gallery and features local and guest artists in shows that change every six weeks. History buffs will enjoy a visit to El Paso de Robles Area Pioneer Museum, filled with memorabilia from the region's early ranching and farming days, including the state's largest collection of barbed wire.

The following day, continue your unrushed auto touring by heading into the close-by coastal mountains to visit two small, family-run wineries, and then proceed to the Pacific Ocean on a former horse-and-buggy lane, picturesque Santa Rosa Creek Road. That meandering country road meets the coast highway at Cambria, just eight miles from the state's most-visited historical monument, Hearst Castle.

From Paso Robles, go south on U.S. 101 and exit west on Vineyard Drive at Templeton into the Santa Lucia foothills, one of the county's main wine-making regions. After about three miles you'll see the large white buildings of Pesenti Winery and some of its 100-acre vineyard, mostly planted with Zinfandel grapes. Pesenti's red wine was an early favorite with Basque shepherds from the San Joaquin Valley. Three generations of the Pesenti family have been making wine since their winery was established in 1934. You might meet some of them in the tasting room or while walking around on a self-guided tour. In October visitors are welcome to watch all the activity during the annual grape harvest.

Continue on Vineyard Drive to California 46 and momentarily follow that modern highway west to York Mountain Road. Turn right and drive along the narrow, twisting road under arches of moss-covered trees to the York Mountain Winery, founded by the York family over a century ago. New Yorker Max Goldman purchased the property in 1970, eventually replanted 100 acres of grapes, and now produces more than a dozen different kinds of wine. You can sample some of them in the restored, handmade-brick winery building.

Return to California 46 and continue west a couple of miles before turning right onto Santa Rosa Creek Road, a quiet, rural two-lane road. The narrow pavement curls along 2,232-foot Black Mountain before it slowly descends and follows the stream bed of Santa Rosa Creek. The road is flanked by trees and pretty meadows interspersed with barns, lazy cows, and occasional fleet-footed deer. You'll also see roadside stands with fruit, produce, and refreshments; homemade olallieberry pie at Linn's Fruit Bin is a treat. Santa Rosa Creek Road eventually leads you to Marquart Park, an idyllic spot for a picnic, and then continues through a wooded hollow to the main street of the growing coastal community of Cambria.

If you didn't pack a picnic, this attractive town is a good place to eat before beginning the return trip to Los Angeles, or make Cambria your base for an extended weekend; see the itinerary for visiting Hearst Castle and nearby coastal towns (see page 3).

For the journey back to Los Angeles, go south on California 1 to rejoin U.S. 101 at San Luis Obispo.

Round trip is about 490 miles.

Paso Robles Area Code: 805

SIGHTSEEING *Helen Moe's Antique Doll Museum,* U.S. 101 at Wellsona Road (or Route 2, Box 332), Paso Robles 93446, 238-2740. Open daily 10 A.M. to 5 P.M., except Sundays from noon. Adults $2, ages 5 to 12 $.50. Also gift shop. • *Mission San Miguel Arcangel,* 801 Mission Street, San Miguel 93451, 467-3256. Open daily 9:30 A.M. to 4:30 P.M. Admission donation: $.50 per person, $1 per family. • *Rios-Caledonia Adobe,* end of Mission Street at U.S. 101, San Miguel 93451, 467-3357. Open Wednesday through Sunday 10 A.M. to 4 P.M. Free. At other times you can walk around the signposted grounds. • *Call-Booth House,* 1315 Vine Street, Paso Robles 93446, 238-5473. Gallery of Paso Robles Art Association. Open 11 A.M. to 4 P.M. (Sundays to 3 P.M.); closed Mondays and Tuesdays. Free. • *El Paso de Robles Area Pioneer Museum,* 2010 Riverside Avenue, Paso Robles 93446. Open weekends 1 to 4 P.M., also Wednesdays (same hours) in summer. Free. • *Meridian Vineyards,* 7 miles east of Paso Robles off California 46 (or P.O. Box 3289), Paso Robles 93447, 237-6000. Open for tours and tasting every day from 10 A.M. to 5 P.M. Free. • *Pesenti Winery,* 2900 Vineyard Drive, Templeton 93465, 434-1030. Open daily for tours and tasting 8:30 A.M. to 5:30 P.M., except Sundays from 9 A.M. Free. • *York Mountain Winery,* 10 miles west of Templeton on York Mountain Road (or Route 2, Box 191), Templeton 93465, 238-3925. Open daily for tasting from 10 A.M. to 5 P.M. Free.

EVENTS *California Mid-State Fair,* billed as "The Biggest Little Fair Anywhere," Paso Robles Fairgrounds, off U.S. 101 at 24th Street, 239-0655. Annual mid-August wingding with rodeo, horse show, livestock exhibits, carnival, and country-and-western and pop entertainers. • *Paso Robles Wine Festival,* annual mid-May party with tastings of local vintages in City Park, 12th and Spring streets. • *Paso Robles Farmers' Market,* weekly harvest of local produce sold at curbside every Tuesday from 3 to 8 P.M. on 14th Street, east of Spring Street.

LODGING *Paso Robles Inn,* 1103 Spring Street, Paso Robles 93446, 238-2660; $48–$58. 68 unassuming rooms above covered parking spaces scattered around well-landscaped grounds. Main Spanish-style building has dining room, coffee shop, and Cattleman's Bar (see below). • *Best Western Black Oak Motor Lodge,* 1135 24th Street, Paso Robles 93446, 238-4740; $48 (higher during county fair). Area's biggest and best-known motel. Restaurant on premises but not recommended. • *County House Inn,* 91 Main Street, Templeton 93465, 434-1598; $70. Friendly, antique-filled B&B with 6 rooms and 2 baths down the hall. Full breakfast included. No small children, no smoking. • *Templeton Manor,* 1442 Ridge Road, Templeton 93465, 434-1529; $105. Private home with 2 accommodations: suite in main house, and a separate cottage. Located on 18 acres with duck pond and executive golf course. Breakfast included. 2-night minimum.

DINING *Paso Robles Inn* (see above). Dining room and coffee shop open every day, with all-you-can-eat lunch buffet on Sundays. • *Bernardi & Sons,* 1202 Pine Street, Paso Robles, 238-1330. Third-generation Italian eatery in historic brick building. Traditional Italian fare; no pizza. Open weekdays for lunch, every night for dinner. • *Touch of Paso,* 1414 Pine Street, Paso Robles, 238-4140. Locals like the home-cooked breakfasts and lunches in this former stagecoach way station. Open daily; no dinners. • *Annie's Dinner House & Saloon,* 1229 Ysabel, off U.S. 101 freeway at Highway 46

East, Paso Robles, 238-6330. All-day dining; entertainment on weekends. ● *Lolo's Mexican Food,* 305 Spring Street, Paso Robles, 239-5777. Informal and inexpensive early California Mexican meals. Lunch and dinner daily. ● Also, see "Dining" suggestions for Cambria, page 8.

FOR MORE INFORMATION   Contact the Paso Robles Chamber of Commerce, 548 Spring Street, Paso Robles 93446, 238-0506.

Flowers and Franciscans at Lompoc

Flower fanciers and mission aficionados will have a field day in Lompoc (*lom-poke*), a folksy place in scenic Santa Barbara County. Plan your weekend for early summer, as the fields around town become a dazzling rainbow when 200 varieties of flowers burst into bloom. During June and July more than 1,000 acres blossom like a colorful patchwork quilt, a sight that's unique to Lompoc—the flower-seed center of the nation. And at the edge of town, you'll step back in time with a visit to the most authentically restored of all California missions, La Purisima.

Also return to yesteryear by staying in the Union Hotel, a reborn 1880 hostelry with a popular family-style dining room that's just over the pastoral hills in tiny Los Alamos. Sixteen upstairs rooms have been refurbished for weekend guests—with most bathrooms down the hall, of course. Next door is the bizarre Victorian Mansion with six "fantasy" guest rooms featuring unconventional beds that include a 1950s Cadillac convertible.

Begin your bucolic escape from Los Angeles by heading north on U.S. 101. Drive past Santa Barbara and the town of Solvang to the Los Alamos exit. Go under the freeway and down Bell Street to the pair of very unusual lodgings, a rustic two-story hotel with a false front of weathered barn wood and an 1864 Victorian home. Since buying the Union Hotel more than two decades ago, owner Dick Langdon has restored the former stagecoach inn and filled it with hundreds of period pieces and antiques, ranging from a $15,000 Tiffany clock to a pair of burial urns from Egypt. Langdon considers his Union Hotel a working museum and has made it one of the most unique turn-of-the-century inns in America. He rents out the cozy rooms only on Friday, Saturday, and Sunday nights. Those same days Langdon opens the dining room to walk-in guests, who sometimes drive the 160 miles from Los Angeles just for the family-style food and fun.

After the dinner crowd goes home, join the other overnight guests in the hotel's saloon. You can play Ping-Pong and table shuffleboard, too. Or go to the old-fashioned upstairs lobby to read, listen to vintage radio programs, or play a little pool. Even more relaxing is to slip into the bubbling Jacuzzi outdoors in the starlit garden.

In-room spas are part of the remarkable amenities next door at the big yellow Victorian Mansion, which conceals a half-dozen guest rooms resembling Hollywood film sets. Each room has its own theme and novel sleeping accommodations, such as the Fifties Drive-In, where you bed down in a 1956 Cadillac convertible. In the Gypsy room, your queen-size bed is a hand-carved gypsy wagon, while in the Fall of the Roman Empire room, you'll sleep in a chariot. Other choices for slumber are the Captain's Cabin and the Parisian artist's loft.

Appropriate theme music and video films are waiting to be played in your room, and there are costumed robes provided as well. You reach this house of dreams from the Union Hotel through a garden maze, a labyrinth of hedges that eventually leads to your room and a welcoming bottle of champagne and other treats. In the morning, breakfast appears as if by magic through a slot in your door, assuring total privacy to guests.

After breakfast, stroll around the town, which has a population of less than 1,000. There are several antique stores to explore, of which the largest is Los Alamos Imports and Antiques, filled with treasures from the United States and abroad, especially furniture. Also be sure to visit the 1880 Los Alamos General Store, which has been designated a historical monument and renovated as an antique shop.

After spending a lazy day around Los Alamos and another night in the Union Hotel or Victorian Mansion, get up early for a pretty drive over the Purisima Hills to Lompoc. Go south on Drum Canyon Road, then turn right on California 246 to go west and follow the signs to picturesque Mission La Purisima. The setting for its handsome adobe and tile roof structures is still pastoral—rolling hills, grazing sheep and cattle, and gardens with flowers and fruit-bearing trees. The mission buildings and 980 acres that surround them are now preserved and protected as a state historic park.

La Purisima, midway between missions at Santa Barbara and San Luis Obispo, was founded in 1787 as the eleventh in the chain of California missions that stretched from San Diego to Monterey at intervals of a day's ride on horseback. The original mission buildings, located within the present city limits of Lompoc, were knocked to the ground by an earthquake in 1812. A new site was chosen, and Mission La Purisima was reconstructed four miles northeast in a sheltered valley.

Make a leisurely two-hour self-guided tour of this handsomely restored mission after picking up a descriptive brochure or tour tape recording from the park office. Start at the visitors center, which is a little museum with interesting photos and artifacts. A path leads from there across a leather-tied wooden footbridge to the mission compound. Along the way, where animals graze in the field, you'll cross a wide dirt track that's the original El Camino Real, the Spanish road that once connected all the missions.

Compared to all the other missions, La Purisima's architecture is especially striking, with a row of long, low buildings that feature distinctive colonnades. Hoping to avoid future damage by earthquakes, the padres built some of the adobe walls four feet thick. When you come to the walled cemetery, look for the tower, with two of the 180-year-old bells that were made in Peru especially for the mission. Go inside the narrow church, which could hold as many as 1,000 Chumash Indians at twice-daily services, to view an altar inlaid with abalone shells.

Another building you can visit served as soldiers' quarters and housed workshops. Exhibits show many of the Indian workers' activities, such as weaving woolen blankets. And nearby the priests' stark residence you'll find the pottery workshop, kitchen, and gristmill. Outside are vats where the Indians made soap and tallow. The mission had an extensive water system, using pipes of ceramic tile to carry spring water to pools for doing laundry and to the garden for irrigation. Go for a stroll in the garden to see hundreds of native California plants that were known to the mission padres and Indians. Docents dress in early-day costumes the first Saturday of the month from March through October.

You can picnic in a shaded grove near the park office, or head into Lompoc for lunch before driving around the outskirts of town to see its annual floral extravaganza. Taking Mission Gate Road and California 246 from the mission into town, you'll spot a few flower fields and the Pan-American/Denholm Seed Company, but the best show is west of Lompoc. Follow Ocean Avenue (California 246) to the other side of town and an observation point that offers an aerial view of the bright fields and Lompoc Valley. Turn left from Ocean Avenue on V Street to Olive Avenue, then go right to Bodger Road. The narrow road is opposite the Bodger Seeds company buildings and goes uphill to the panoramic lookout. (To the northwest is another big influence on Lompoc's economy, Vandenberg Air Force Base, the West Coast's aerospace center.)

To enjoy the beautiful crop close up, go back down the hill and drive slowly along the side roads that cut through the flower fields stretching from California 246 to the Santa Ynez River. You'll see marigolds, sweet peas, zinnias, asters, petunias, cornflowers, lark-spurs, poppies, nasturtiums, calendulas, columbine, lavender, alyssum, lobelia, ageratum, and more. A free flower field tour brochure from the chamber of commerce gives specific identities and locations of the flowers.

Sorry, you won't be able to buy any of the beautiful blooms to take home. But their seeds eventually will be for sale in your neighborhood and throughout the world; the Lompoc Valley produces more than half the flower seeds grown around the globe. Back in town at Civic Center Plaza, off Ocean Avenue, you can learn the names of the various flower varieties by visiting a display garden where the plants are labeled.

For extra fun, try to plan your trip for the last weekend in June, when the folks in Lompoc Valley hold their annual flower festival. Highlights are a floral parade, flower show, and tours of the flower fields. And you'll enjoy arts-and-crafts exhibits, outdoor entertainment, a carnival, and plenty to eat. An exhibit and film about the flower seed industry is on view in the Lompoc Museum. It's located in the historical Carnegie Library building, where you'll also see local Indian artifacts and other memorabilia of Lompoc's past.

Return to Los Angeles by driving south from Lompoc on California 1 to join U.S. 101.

Round trip-is about 330 miles.

Lompoc/Los Alamos Area Code: 805

SIGHTSEEING   *Mission La Purisima State Historic Park,* 2295 Purisima Road, Lompoc 93436, 733-3713. Open daily 9 A.M. to 5 P.M., to 6 P.M. in summer. Admission: $5 per car. ● *Lompoc Museum,* 200 South H Street, Lompoc 93436, 736-3888. Displays portray the history of Lompoc Valley since Indian times. Open from 1 to 5 P.M. Tuesday through Friday, 1 to 4 P.M. on weekends. Free.

EVENTS   *Lompoc Valley Flower Festival* during the last weekend in June, 735-8511. Festival's activity center is Ryon Park, Ocean Avenue and O Street. From noon until dusk, hour-long bus tours of flower fields depart hourly from park ($3). Saturday-morning parade of flower floats. Flower show in Veterans' Memorial Building, end of H Street; $2 donation, children under age 12 free. One of Southern California's best-known festivals. ● *Mission Fiesta,* Mission La Purisima State Historic Park (see above) on the third Sunday in May. Demonstrations of arts and crafts in the Spanish mission era, with free tortillas and beans served to visitors.

The mission's docents group, Prelado de los Tesoros, also organizes special activities and tours once or twice a month March through October; call 733-1303 for details and dates.

LODGING *Union Hotel,* 362 Bell Street (or P.O. Box 616), Los Alamos 93440, 344-2744. Open Fridays, Saturdays, Sundays only; no children. 16 rooms, $80 per night, including breakfast; three front rooms with private bath, $100. Reservations a must. Also, delicious dinners in dining room (see below). • *Victorian Mansion,* same address and telephone as Union Hotel, above; $200 per night, including welcoming champagne and a full breakfast. Dick Langdon's second historic restoration has 6 "fantasy" rooms, each with private bath. Open every day of the week. Book well in advance, especially weekends, for the theme room that appeals to you the most; many guests return in order to experience all six. • If the Victorian Mansion and Union Hotel are booked up or outside your budget, stay in one of Lompoc's hotels; be certain to reserve a room months in advance if you're planning to visit during the June flower festival. • Along H Street (California 1): *Quality Inn and Executive Suites,* 735-8555; $54; Lompoc's largest lodging with 225 rooms. *Embassy Suites,* 735-8311; $65; 155 rooms. *Days Inn,* 735-7744; $50; 90 rooms. *Best Western Flagwaver,* 736-5605; $45; 70 rooms. • Along Ocean Avenue (California 246): *Porto Finale Inn,* 735-7731; $35; 81 rooms.

CAMPING *River Park,* California 246 at Sweeney Road, Lompoc, 736-6565. 35 RV sites along Santa Ynez River, $12 per night with full hookup. Also, 5 tent sites at $8 per night.

DINING *Union Hotel,* Los Alamos (see above). Family-style dinner with choice of entrees is offered in the antique-decorated dining room to hotel guests and the public beginning at 5 P.M. on Fridays, Saturdays, and Sundays. • *The Jetty,* 304 West Ocean Avenue, Lompoc, 735-2400. Seafood specialties; lunch and dinner daily. • *Magellan's Fine Food & Spirits,* 1601 North H Street, Lompoc, 737-7171. Steaks, seafood, prime ribs, and pasta. Lunch and dinner daily except Sundays. • *Outpost Oakpit BBQ,* 124 East Ocean Avenue, Lompoc, 735-1130. Ribs, steaks, and seafood. All meals daily, except breakfast only on Sundays.

FOR MORE INFORMATION Contact the Lompoc Valley Chamber of Commerce, 511 North H Street, Suite J, Lompoc 93438, 736-4567. Open 9 A.M. to 5 P.M. weekdays.

History and Outdoor Adventure in Kern County and Isabella Lake

The Tehachapi mountain range north of Los Angeles hardly seems like camel country. Nonetheless, anyone traveling through Grapevine Canyon in California's early statehood days could count on seeing those strange beasts of burden. The dromedaries were stationed at Fort Tejon, a military, political, and social center in Southern California during the mid-1800s. The camels, and the U.S. Army's Camel Corps, are only memories today, but you can still visit the important fort. In fact, it's the first stop on a weekend excursion to inland Kern County for a bit of history in Bakersfield and some outdoor adventure at Isabella Lake. The menu of possible activities includes whitewater rafting down the mighty Kern River, as well as fishing, sailing, waterskiing, golfing, horseback riding, hunting, hiking, camping, and even downhill skiing in wintertime.

With so much to do and see, it's best to plan a long weekend. At least get an early start in order to visit Fort Tejon on the way to Bakersfield, where you should spend the first night at one of Kern County's most popular resorts, Rio Bravo. With its 19 tennis courts and 18-hole golf course, and river rafting nearby, you'll be tempted to stay awhile.

Begin your trip by driving north from Los Angeles on Interstate 5 and go six miles beyond the Tejon Pass summit to the Fort Tejon exit. Cross the freeway to the parking area and visitors center for this 200-acre state historic park. Established in 1854, the fort was regimental headquarters for the First U.S. Dragoons. During the decade they were stationed there, soldiers protected miners and Indians in the area, rounded up stolen horses and cattle, chased bandits, and gave band concerts. By happenstance, it also was a training ground for officers of the Civil War, including Grant and Sherman. In fact, 15 men from Fort Tejon served as generals during the War Between the States.

Today the interstate freeway runs through the old fort's boundaries, but a few of the original adobe brick buildings have been preserved or reconstructed. Interior furnishings and displays with life-size mannequins give you an idea of the frontier soldiers' dress and life-style more than a century ago. On the first Sunday of every month, designated as Living History Day at Fort Tejon park, docents dress in period clothes, cook food of earlier times, and perform army drills. On the third Sunday of every month from April through October, Civil War reenactments also are staged at the fort.

Continue north on Interstate 5 and join California 99 to reach Bakersfield, at the southern end of the San Joaquin Valley. Skirt the city by exiting east on California 58 and follow that freeway to the exit for California 184. Take it north to join California 178 going east toward Lake Isabella, then turn left a mile beyond that intersection and go north on the Alfred Harrell Highway to reach Lake Ming Road and the Rio Bravo Resort.

Check into the lodge, perhaps into one of the suites that features a fireplace and wet bar, then choose dinner from the varied menu offered in the resort's dining room. You'll soon discover why this year-round vacation center is a favorite of those who love the outdoor life. Guests of all ages love to go rafting on the Kern River, which runs nearby the resort. You also can play tennis on championship courts (15 are lighted for night play) and try to beat par on the 18-hole golf course. Nearby, you can view the state's plant and animal wildlife at the California Living Museum (CALM).

If there's another reason for a visit to Bakersfield, it's to tour Pioneer Village, a 14-acre re-created town of frontier buildings and artifacts gathered from all over the area. You'll see the houses and stores where some of the state's pioneers lived and worked, the clothes they wore, and the tools they used. Visitors can spend an entire day strolling around this rustic Williamsburg of the West.

To get to the Pioneer Village from the resort, continue on the Alfred Harrell Highway as it circles westward back toward town and becomes Panorama Drive. Merge into California 204 (Union Avenue) heading south, then turn right on 34th Street to Chester Avenue. Go right again to the large brick clock tower that marks the museum parking lot.

More than 60 structures and exhibits make up Pioneer Village, an outstanding outdoor museum that's been growing for more than three decades. At the village entrance, pick up a brochure or the illustrated guidebook that identifies the buildings and describes the displays you'll see on a clockwise tour of the town. To get a better idea of life in the Old West, peek in windows and doors as you walk around. Mannequins dressed in period clothes add a real-life look to the exhibits. It's easy to imagine you're in an actual nineteenth-century town, complete with blacksmith shop, general store, newspaper office, undertaking parlor, fraternal lodge hall, railroad station, dressmakers' shop, firehouse, one-room school, and bandstand. Don't be surprised to find a ball and chain in the old jail.

The open-air museum recalls Kern County's importance as an early agricultural center, too. You'll see an intriguing display of branding irons, a harness-making shop, and a quarter-million-dollar collection of vintage horse-drawn vehicles. Notice that even the sheepherder's cabin was built on skids, so it could be pulled from place to place by horses. A group of weathered structures recalls life on the county's early ranches. Look for a cider press and a hand-operated washing machine on the back porch of the Weller ranch house. Next to the barn are a wooden windmill, a hay derrick, and a cookwagon that fed the field hands.

After you've toured the village, be certain to visit the adjacent Kern County Museum, where other exhibits will bring back more memories of yesteryear. The collections of ladies' hats and dresses, fancy lacework, and hand fans will get your attention. Also look for vintage firearms and the exhibit about the local Yokut Indians.

After you've finished your historical tour, take Chester Avenue south to California 178 and go east to follow the twisting Kern River through Sequoia National Forest to Isabella Lake, a recreational retreat that resembles a mini Lake Powell. Boating and fishing are its biggest attractions, plus camping and hiking around the 38-mile shoreline.

Before the mid-1950s there wasn't a lake in sight there—only the Kern River, which often became a destructive torrent during the rainy season and when snow melted in the nearby Sierra Nevadas. Then the U.S. Army Corps of Engineers built a pair of earth-fill dams for flood control to protect valuable agriculture and oil fields downstream along the Kern River Valley. The L-shaped lake that resulted has become a favorite destination for folks who enjoy the outdoors. Summer is the busiest season, but wintertime draws a pretty good crowd as well, because snow often decorates the surrounding mountains without reaching the lake below. Most of the campgrounds around the lake are open year round, and there are a number of small and rustic lodgings where you can also spend the night.

Route 178 skirts the southern shore of the lake, but you should exit on California 155 toward Kernville and then take the turnoff to the Lake Isabella Visitors Center. From this hilltop location is a pretty panorama of the lake, and from the parking lot on the left you'll also get a bird's-eye look at the main dam.

In the center is a relief map that gives an overview of Isabella Lake and lights up to indicate the recreation areas. You'll be able to locate the lake's three marinas and five public boat ramps, campgrounds, an off-road motorcycle area, a wildlife preserve, and entrances to nature trails. Pick up the free maps and brochures, too.

Back on California 155, go north along the lake to Kernville. Boats can be rented and launched at Isabella Marina North Fork, and you'll also spot attractive campgrounds flanking the highway. About halfway to Kernville the state highway turns left at Wofford Heights and heads up to Alta Sierra and the scenic Shirley Meadows Ski Area atop Greenhorn Mountain. In winter, a chair lift and rope tows operate on three hills. Signs are posted when tire chains are required on the steep mountain road (chains can be rented in Lake Isabella).

As you continue on the lakeside Kernville Road to Kernville, look for the Kern Valley Golf and Country Club, which opens its nine-hole course to the public every day. The clubhouse serves refreshments, too. Spend the night in one of the family-run motels in Kernville or northward along the river. Campers can pitch a tent or park an RV in one of the numerous campgrounds by the river or lake.

Kernville itself is a small town with Western-style false-front stores around a little square. Nearby in Riverside Park you'll usually find plenty of people fishing for trout, and it's also a pretty spot to picnic. Upstream the rugged Kern River roars with white water and daredevil rafters in summer. There are some pleasant places to eat in town and up the river, too. Ewings on the Kern, a local favorite for dinner and Sunday brunch, offers a good view of the rafters floating down the river.

When it's time to head home, you can follow Sierra Way along the eastern edge of the lake and rejoin California 178 for the trip back toward Bakersfield. Then turn south at the junction with California 184 and meet Interstate 5 for the return trip to Los Angeles.

An alternate route back to Los Angeles is to turn east from the lake on California 178 and cross 5,250-foot Walker Pass to intersect California 14. Then turn south to go through the Mojave Desert and rejoin Interstate 5. Along the way you can visit Red Rock Canyon State Park.

Round trip is about 322 miles.

Bakersfield Area Code: 805
Lake Isabella/Kernville Area Code: 619

SIGHTSEEING *Fort Tejon State Historic Park,* off Interstate 5 north of Tejon Pass summit (P.O. Box 895, Lebec 93243), 248-6692. Grounds open daily 8 A.M. to 5 P.M. (buildings 10 A.M. to 4 P.M.) for self-guided tours. Adults $2, children and senior citizens $1. Members of the Civil War Association from Thousand Oaks stage mock battles in full-dress uniform every 3rd weekend of the month from April through October. • *California Living Museum* (*CALM*), 14000 Alfred Harrell Highway (or P.O. Box 6613), Bakersfield 92386, 872-2256. Open daily from 10 A.M. to sunset, except Mondays. Adults $3.50, senior citizens $2.50, children 4 to 17 years $2. Combination zoo, botanical garden, and natural history museum of California's wildlife. ● *Kern County Museum and Pioneer Village,* 3801 Chester Avenue, Bakersfield 93301, 861-2132. Open Saturdays from 10 A.M. to 5 P.M., weekdays from 8 A.M. Closed Sundays and holidays. Village admission: adults $5, senior citizens $4, and children 3 to 12 years $3; last tour tickets sold at 3 P.M. ● Activities at *Rio Bravo Resort* (see below): 1-day river rafting trip, $20 per person; 18-hole golf, $39 per person; tennis free to resort guests. ● *U.S. Forest Service Lake Isabella Visitors Center,* 4875 Ponderosa Drive, off California 155 at Isabella Lake (or P.O. Box 3810), Lake Isabella 93240, 379-5646. Open 8 A.M. to 5 P.M. daily from May through September; 8 A.M. to 4:30 P.M. weekdays during other months. Camping, boating, and touring information for Isabella Lake visitors. ● *Isabella Marina North Fork,* off California 155 at Wofford Heights (P.O. Box 808), Wofford Heights 93285, 376-3404. Boat rentals for fishing, waterskiing, and touring Isabella Lake. Open daily during daylight hours. ● *Shirley Meadows Ski Area,* off California 155 in Greenhorn Mountains near Alta Sierra (P.O. Box 509, Lake Isabella 93240), 376-4186. Open Fridays, weekends, and holidays Christmas Day through March. Rentals, 2 ski lifts, lessons; call for lift ticket prices. ● *Kern Valley Golf and Country Club,* off California 155 south of Kernville (P.O. Box 888), Kernville, 93238, 376-2828. 9-hole, par-36 course open daily from 7 A.M. to 7 P.M. Green fees $9 weekends, $7 weekdays. ● *Chuck Richards' Whitewater,* P.O. Box W.W. Whitewater, Lake Isabella, 93240, 379-4685 or toll-free (800) 624-5950. Oldest of several rafting companies that run exciting 1- and 2-day trips on the upper and lower Kern River. Call or write for current schedules and rates. ● *Kern River Tours,* P.O. Box 3444, Lake Isabella, 93240, 379-4616. Another well-known rafting company. Organizes 1-hour raft trips from near the Rio Bravo Resort that run four times daily from May to September; $20 per person. Call resort for details, 872-5000.

EVENTS *Whiskey Flat Days,* 4-day rip-roaring celebration of the gold-rush era, when Kernville was known as Whiskey Flat; held in February on Washington's Birthday weekend. Contact the Kernville Chamber of Commerce (see below) for details.

LODGING *Rio Bravo Resort,* 11200 Lake Ming Road, Bakersfield 93306, 872-5000 or toll-free (800) 282-5000; $78. Fine lodging and various activities (see ''Sightseeing,'' above). Also an excellent restaurant (see below). ● Bakersfield hosts a variety of other accommodations, and the Bakersfield Visitors and Convention Bureau or the Kern County Board of Trade (see below) will give you a list. • *Lazy River Lodge,* on Sierra Way, 2 miles north of Kernville (or Star Route 1, Box 60), Kernville 93238, 376-2242; $62. On 10 acres along Kern River; largest (31 units) and one of the nicest lodgings. • *Kernville Inn,* 11042 Kernville Road, Kernville 93238, 376-2222; $49. 26 units in town opposite pretty Riverside Park. • *Whispering Pines Lodge,* 13745 Sierra Way, Kernville 93238, 376-3733; $79. 11 units, including suite with Jacuzzi tub. Some fireplaces. • *Kern River Bed and Breakfast,* 119 Kern River Drive, Kernville 93238, 376-6750; $75–$85, breakfast included. 6 rooms, 3 with fireplace, 2 with whirlpool tub. Across from Riverside Park. • *Neill House,* 100 Tobias Road, Kernville 93238, 376-2771; $85–$125, with breakfast. Historic 5-room B&B.

CAMPING *Kern River County Park,* off California 178 on Alfred Harrell Highway near Lake Ming, 12 miles east of Bakersfield, 861-2345. 50 RV and tent sites, $10 per night. No reservations. For campers this is a convenient alternative to staying at the Rio Bravo Resort nearby. • *Isabella Lake* has 9 family campgrounds with 760 sites operated by the U.S. Forest Service. First come, first served; some site fees, others $5–$8 per night. • *Kern River* has 18 campgrounds operated along its banks in the Isabella Lake area by the U.S. Forest Service. $5–$8 overnight fee at some sites; no reservations. Call the Forest Service's supervisor's office in Kernville, 376-3781, for more information.

DINING *Rio Bravo Resort* (see above). Lodge dining room serves breakfast, lunch, and dinner daily. Also popular for Sunday brunch. • At Isabella Lake, many of the locally popular restaurants serve only dinner and are located at Kernville and northward along the Kern River. A few mom-and-pop cafes offer breakfast and lunch. *Ewings on the Kern,* Buena Vista Drive, Kernville, 376-2411. Dinner nightly, plus Sunday brunch. Musical entertainment and dancing. • *McNally's Fairview Lodge and Restaurant,* 15 miles north of Kernville on the river at Fairview, 376-2430. Great steaks and other dinner fare in cozy Western surroundings. Closed in winter. • *Paradise Cove Restaurant,* on California 178 overlooking lake, 379-2719. Dinner only, closed Mondays and Tuesdays. Steak, trout, and seafood, plus prime ribs on weekends. • *Peacock Inn,* 21 Sierra Drive, Kernville, 376-3937. Open daily except Tuesdays for lake area's best Chinese food.

FOR MORE INFORMATION   Contact the Bakersfield Convention and Visitors Bureau, P.O. Box 192, Bakersfield 93302, 325-5051. ● Kern County Board of Trade, Tourist Information Office, 2101 Oak Street (or P.O. Box 1312), Bakersfield 93302, 861-2367. Open weekdays 8 A.M. to 5 P.M. ● Kernville Chamber of Commerce, P.O. Box 397, Kernville 93238, 376-2629. ● Kern River Valley Visitors Council, P.O. Box O, Lake Isabella 93240, 379-2805. ● Kern Valley Information Line, 379-6323. 24-hour interactive recorded information.

Danes, Wines, and Old West in Santa Ynez Valley

When you're yearning for a no-pressure weekend in the countryside, head north to Solvang, the closest thing to a Danish village this side of the North Sea. Windmills dominate the skyline, good-luck storks decorate rooftops, and Carlsberg beer is drawn from cafe spigots. Many of the buildings, even the post office, embody Danish farm-style architecture of brick masonry walls crisscrossed with wooden beams. Danish national flags of red with a white cross fly everywhere, too.

An easy way to get to know the town is to climb aboard the *Honen,* a sight-seeing streetcar that's pulled by sturdy Belgian horses on a 20-minute narrated tour. The driver tells how Solvang was founded as the site for a Danish-type folk school in 1911. The school is gone now, but the 1928 Bethania Lutheran Church on Atterdag Road is worth a visit to see its fourteenth-century Danish style of architecture and the traditional miniature sailing ship suspended from the sanctuary ceiling.

It's easy to reach Southern California's little bit of Denmark. Just drive north from Los Angeles on U.S. 101 and exit east on California 246 to Solvang. Once there, the sight and smell of fresh-baked bread and Danish pastries will entice you into Solvang's many bakeries and cafes. Be sure to sample the aebleskiver, balls of pancake batter cooked until golden brown in a special skillet, turned with a knitting needle instead of a spatula, then served with powdered sugar or fresh jam. Order them any time of the day, with a cup of Danish coffee. Smorrebrod, Denmark's famous open-faced sandwiches, are another tempting treat. And restaurant smorgasbords feature old-country recipes for specialties that range from meatballs and red cabbage to marinated herring.

As you stroll the cobblestone sidewalks beneath old-fashioned gas lamps that once illuminated the streets of Copenhagen, you'll be tempted by gift shops that show off Royal Copenhagen china, crystal, woolen sweaters, and other goods imported from Denmark. Look for the *Little Mermaid,* a duplicate of the famous sculpture in Copenhagen's harbor. And there's a bust of Hans Christian Andersen in the park. Solvang is so Danish that you expect to see Victor Borge peeking around a corner.

About the only reminder that you're still in California is Solvang's Old Mission Santa Ines. It was constructed by Indians from the area as nineteenth in the chain of 21 missions established by the Spanish padres. The restored mission, which still serves as a church, is open daily for self-guided tours.

Solvang certainly is no secret, and visitors often jam its attractive streets. That's especially true during summer, when plays are performed in the outdoor Festival Theater, and in fall during the town's annual Danish Days Celebration, so be certain to have room reservations during those times.

You'll find a number of comfortable motels in Solvang and nearby in Buellton, but an extraspecial place to stay is the Alisal Guest Ranch, a deluxe and rather expensive resort on a 10,000-acre working cattle ranch six miles south of town. Horseback riding is a featured attraction at tree-studded Alisal, where trails wind for miles over the scenic ranchland. Wranglers will point out the hilltop hideaway of a neighboring rancher and horseman, Ronald Reagan.

This year-round resort is an especially good choice for a three-day weekend because you'll find plenty to do, like challenging the championship par-72 golf course that's set among clusters of oaks, pines, and sycamores. A PGA professional is on hand to help improve your game. Tennis buffs have seven courts for day play, with a resident pro ready to give lessons. Go swimming in a large pool near the bungalows that accommodate up to 200 guests, or enjoy the fresh air and peaceful surroundings while playing shuffleboard and croquet. When families flock to this ranch in summertime, Alisal's own lake is opened for boating and fishing.

To assure your escape from city life, telephones and television sets are purposely absent from all rooms at the guest ranch. Featured instead are blazing logs crackling in the bungalow fireplaces. Rates at the resort are Modified American Plan (breakfast and dinner included), and excellent meals are served in a dining room reserved for ranch guests only.

Besides enjoying the town and guest ranch, plan a scenic Sunday drive in the Santa Ynez Valley. You'll be charmed by three tiny nineteenth-century towns and some family-run and fancier wineries that produce prize-winning vintages.

With its verdant fields, rolling hills, and horses grazing in the pasture, the picturesque Santa Ynez Valley is the prettiest in all of Santa Barbara County. Savor the scenery as you drive east on California 246 to the valley's namesake, Santa Ynez, a town with false-front buildings that give it an Old West flavor. You'll have fun wandering among the memorabilia in the Santa Ynez Valley Historical Society Museum and Parks-Janeway Carriage House; turn north on Edison Street to Sagunto Street.

Then follow Edison Street north to Baseline Avenue and turn east to Ballard, the valley's oldest town. The wooden church you'll see at the junction with Alamo Pintado Road was built by volunteers in 1889 and cost only $320 for lumber. Today it's a privately owned chapel and a favorite place for weddings. Another landmark is a century-old little red schoolhouse at the north end of Cottonwood Street that's still attended by kindergartners through third-graders. If you don't stay at Alisal Guest Ranch, reserve one of the 15 antique-filled rooms in a quiet country hideaway, the Ballard Inn, on Baseline Avenue. Across the street is the well-known Ballard Store Restaurant on Baseline Avenue, where reservations are suggested if you want to dine on fine French cuisine in a country atmosphere. Another popular spot for dinner is Mattei's Tavern, a historic stagecoach inn that's just north of Ballard in Los Olivos; follow Alamo Pintado Road to Grand Avenue. Even if you're not hungry, drop into the fascinating saloon for a drink.

Established in 1886 by Swiss-born Felix Mattei, his inn was across the street from the terminus of the Pacific Coast Railway and also served as a hotel. Los Angeles–to–San Francisco passengers would arrive by stage, have a meal, and spend the night before continuing north by train. Mattei's Tavern is still a main attraction in Los Olivos, but also visit the town's other old buildings that have been restored and opened as antique and gift shops and art galleries.

In recent years the Santa Ynez Valley has become Southern California's Napa Valley and it now produces wines that please the wine makers and critics alike. Some have already won gold and silver medals. Make your own judgments and have a good time by visiting a few of the wineries as you tour the valley; pick up a wine tour guide map in Solvang.

Most wineries in the Santa Ynez Valley are small operations, so don't expect the fancy tasting rooms or tours offered at many Northern California wineries. Below we mention five of our favorites, which will introduce you to a variety of vintages and wine-making operations, as well as some friendly local folks.

On Alamo Pintado Road you'll find Carey Cellars, founded in 1978 by the Carey family of physicians and now owned by Kate and Brooks Firestone, the most well known winery family in the Santa Ynez Valley. Twenty-five acres of grapevines surround a red barn, where visitors can make a little tour and sample some of the fine wines.

A mile east of Santa Ynez on California 246 is the Gainey Vineyard, a modern winery surrounded by 65 acres of grapes. You can take an informative tour, then sample some of the five varietals produced at the winery. Tables are provided for visitors with picnic food.

On a hilltop along Zaca Station Road, you can't miss the immense modern building erected for the Firestone Vineyard, the largest winery in the valley. There you'll be treated to a comprehensive tour, beginning with the grapevines and ending in the handsome tasting room. The 325-acre vineyard is the chosen vocation for Brooks Firestone, who gave up his family's well-known tire business to produce an abundance of excellent wines.

Foxen Canyon Road leads to Zaca Mesa Winery, located in a big cedar barn where several wines are aged, bottled, and shipped nationwide. Visitors are offered free guided tours, and tasting is done in a handsome visitors center.

Several miles more along Foxen Canyon Road is the modest Rancho Sisquoc Winery, which began as a hobby of the former foreman of the 36,000-acre Sisquoc cattle ranch. He was one of the first to grow grapes in the area and finally built a small winery in 1977.

There are picnic tables at Rancho Sisquoc and a few of the other wineries, but the only thing you can buy is wine, so be sure to bring along some snacks from Solvang to enjoy with the various vintages.

When you're ready to return to Los Angeles, rejoin U.S. 101 by following California 154, a historic inland route that's now designated a state scenic highway. It's the old stagecoach route between Los Olivos and Santa Barbara, once part of a harrowing journey over 2,224-foot San Marcos Pass. As the highway begins to climb you'll pass a vast reservoir and county-run recreation area, Lake Cachuma, a favorite retreat for fishermen, boaters, and campers. Stop to view the man-made lake from an observation point above the dam.

After crossing the modern Cold Spring Arch Bridge, turn right on the old Stagecoach Road, which leads to Cold Spring Tavern, a cluster of rustic log cabins huddled in a tree-shaded glen. If you're hungry, have lunch or dinner at this aged stagecoach stop. A separate saloon, where water from the spring was once bottled, reverberates in the evening with bluegrass, country-western, and rock music. On summer weekend afternoons, the bands play outside.

As you continue on California 154 over the mountain pass and wind through Los Padres National Forest, pause at the roadside turnouts for vistas of the foothills and ocean. Just west of Santa

Barbara the road descends to rejoin U.S. 101 for the drive back to Los Angeles.

Round trip is about 334 miles.

Solvang/Santa Ynez Valley Area Code: 805

SIGHTSEEING   *Honen,* horse-drawn sight-seeing streetcar, departs frequently on Solvang tours from Mission Drive at Alisal Road. Adults $2.50, children under 12 years $1.50. • *Old Mission Santa Ines,* 1760 Mission Drive, Solvang, 688-4815. Open daily 9 A.M. to 5 P.M. in summer, 9:30 A.M. to 4:30 P.M. in winter (except Sundays from noon). Adults $2, children under 16 years free. Recorded tape tours available. • *Santa Ynez Valley Historical Society Museum and Parks-Janeway Carriage House,* Sagunto Street, Santa Ynez. Both open 1 to 4 P.M. Friday through Sunday; carriage house also open 10 A.M. to 4 P.M. Tuesday through Thursday. Donation. • *Carey Cellars,* 1711 Alamo Pintado Road, 688-8554. Open 10 A.M. to 4 P.M. daily. • *The Gainey Vineyard,* 3950 East Highway 246, 688-0558. Open 10 A.M. to 5 P.M. daily; last tour at 3:30 P.M. • *Firestone Vineyard,* Zaca Station Road, 688-3940. Open 10 A.M. to 4 P.M. daily. • *Zaca Mesa Winery,* Foxen Canyon Road, 688-3310. Open 10 A.M. to 4 P.M. daily. • *Rancho Sisquoc Winery,* Foxen Canyon Road, 937-3616. Open 10 A.M. to 4 P.M. daily.

EVENTS   *Danish Days,* third weekend in September. Colorful festival with local folks in costume, featuring a parade, folk dancing and singing, bands, stage plays, aebleskiver breakfasts, smorgasbord, and grand ball. • *Solvang Theaterfest,* summer-long repertory theater with mix of musicals, classic and modern dramas, and comedies performed evenings in open-air theater. Box office at 420 Second Street opens daily at 10 A.M.; tickets $12–$18. Theaterfest hotline 922-8313 or toll-free (800) 549-7272.

LODGING   Most accommodations listed are in Solvang; zip code 93463. *Alisal Guest Ranch,* 1054 Alisal Road, 688-6411; $240–$300 double, Modified American Plan (2 meals). A wonderful self-contained resort that can be a vacation in itself. 2-night minimum. Package plans also available. • *Royal Scandinavian,* 400 Alisal Road, 688-8000; $95. Solvang's largest with 135 rooms. • *Petersen Village Inn,* 1576 Mission Drive, 688-3121; $95. Modern hotel with Old World decor. • *Danish Country Inn,* 1455 Mission

Drive, 688-2018; $79. Luxury lodging at edge of town. • *Svendsgaard's Danish Lodge,* 1711 Mission Drive, 688-3277; $55. • *Dannebrog Inn,* 1450 Mission Drive, 688-3210; $70. • A few miles north of Solvang are two quiet retreats. *The Ballard Inn,* 2436 Baseline Avenue, Ballard, 93463, 688-7770; $145–$185. Delightful country bed and breakfast on rural road. 15 rooms, 7 with fireplaces. Ballard Store gourmet restaurant is across the street (see below). • *Los Olivos Grand Hotel,* 2860 Grand Avenue, Los Olivos 93441, 688-7788; $175–$300. Modern country inn in rural town. 21 rooms with gas fireplaces. Also heated pool. Home to classy Remington's Restaurant (see below).

CAMPING *Lake Cachuma County Park,* 12 miles east of Solvang on California 154, 688-4658. 457 sites, $12 per night, $16 with hookup.

DINING Danish Inn Restaurant, 1547 Mission Drive, 688-4813. A windmill marks one of Solvang's most popular restaurants, where chefs prepare Danish smorgasbord and American fare daily. • *Mollekroen Restaurant,* 435 Alisal Road, Solvang, 688-4555. Daily smorgasbord with 30 dishes, as well as Danish and American lunch and dinner menu. • *Massimi Ristorante,* 1588 Mission Drive, Solvang, 688-0027. Much-praised Italian restaurant in Petersen Village Square. Dinner nightly except Mondays. Indoor/outdoor dining. Reservations advised. • *Remington's Restaurant,* in the Los Olivos Grand Hotel (see above). Fine continental fare for lunch and dinner; also open for breakfast. • *Ballard Store Restaurant,* 2449 Baseline Avenue, Ballard, 688-5319. Unexpected gourmet dinners in renovated country store served Wednesday through Sunday. A special treat. Located across from the Ballard Inn (see above). • *Mattei's Tavern,* on California 154, Los Olivos, 688-4820. Delightfully restored stagecoach inn with dinner fare: steak, prime ribs, seafood, salad bar. Lunch weekends only from 12 to 3 P.M. Dinner nightly from 4:30 P.M. weekends, 5:30 P.M. weekdays. • *Cold Spring Tavern,* Stagecoach Road, beneath Cold Spring Arch Bridge off California 154, 967-0066. Very rustic roadhouse open daily for lunch (11 A.M. to 3 P.M.) and dinner (5 to 10 P.M.); breakfast on weekends. Reserve for dinner.

FOR MORE INFORMATION Contact the Solvang Conference and Visitors Bureau, 1511 Mission Drive (or P.O. Box 70), Solvang 93463, 688-6144 or toll-free (800) 468-6765. Open daily 9 A.M. to 5 P.M.

Idling Awhile in Idyllwild

Smoke curls from log cabin chimneys, majestic pines stretch into a brilliant blue sky, bushy-tailed squirrels scamper across the roads. It's a north woods picture postcard scene that some travelers are surprised to find in Southern California. You're bound to enjoy an outing to a tranquil village that's hidden in the San Jacinto Mountains. Aptly named Idyllwild, the mile-high community has a special charm in winter, especially after a snowfall. Best of all, its ruggedly beautiful scenery and invigorating mountain air are only a short drive from Los Angeles.

Head east on Interstate 10 beyond Redlands to Banning, then exit south on California 243, designated one of the state's scenic highways. You'll ascend quickly on this two-lane switchback road, the Banning-Idyllwild Highway, and pass through boulder-strewn terrain into the San Bernardino National Forest. Pause at the turnouts for bird's-eye views of the neighboring mountain ranges and valleys below.

Take a break at Lake Fulmor, stocked with trout and a focal point for fishermen. You'll find hiking trails at this minuscule recreation area, too, or stretch your legs just up the road at the Indian Mountain vista point. The early Cahuilla Indians, the area's first visitors, came here from the lowlands to hunt game and gather acorns and berries.

A few miles beyond, after passing through the hamlet of Pine Cove, stop at the Idyllwild County Park Visitors Center, where Indian relics and exhibits about lumbering and mining explain much of Idyllwild's history. The first route to this mountain valley was opened in 1875, a one-way toll road from Hemet that gave loggers access to thick stands of tall timber.

Once known as Strawberry Valley, Idyllwild became the site of a tuberculosis sanitarium at the turn of the century, and soon after, a resort was built that attracted families to the fresh mountain air. Visitors who loved the healthy climate and forest scenery built summer cabins, and some decided to stay; the year-round population has since grown to nearly 3,000.

Dioramas at the visitors center also introduce you to Idyllwild's birds and animals, and there is an unusual display of pine cones collected all over the Southland. Just outside the center, follow the half-mile self-guiding nature trail that reveals more of the forest's plant and animal life.

As you enter Idyllwild, look for the entrance to Mt. San Jacinto State Park and its year-round Idyllwild campground. Nearby is Idyllwild County Park campground with other sites; neither park has RV hookups.

Bear left on North Circle Drive to the heart of town, which is marked by a totem pole, free parking areas, and a crisscross of streets with shops and restaurants. Near the center you'll find the Idyllwild Inn, with both cottages and motel units, while a block away is the Silver Pines Lodge. Make a circular orientation tour of Idyllwild and adjacent Fern Valley to survey many of the area's other lodgings, as well as gift shops and restaurants.

Continue on North Circle Drive, then go right on South Circle Drive, and right again on Village Center Drive back to your starting point. Along the way you'll find a wide variety of accommodations at the Fireside Inn, Mile High Lodge, Fern Village Chalets, and Woodland Park Manor. Just south of town along California 243 are the Strawberry Creek Inn and Wilkum Inn, both bed-and-breakfast inns, and the Bluebird Motel with cabins.

An enjoyable option is renting a private cabin or home for your visit. Vacation residences are available with one to three bedrooms, and some have special features such as rock fireplaces and hot tubs. Set up house by bringing groceries, paper goods, sheets, and towels; everything else is furnished. Most rentals can be arranged through Mountain Greenery Realty or Idyllwild Property Management.

The main activity for visitors to this mountain community is just taking it easy. Go for a relaxing stroll through the pine-scented woods to look for chattering squirrels, squawking bluejays, and woodpeckers making their repetitive music on the tree trunks. Mountain birds and animals are carved on the 50-foot Tree Monument, the town's landmark totem pole created from a single pine tree by Jonathan La-Brenne, who is known as Idyllwild's chain-saw artist. A short drive to Humber Park at the end of Fern Valley Road gives you a close-up view of Lily Rock (some call it Tahquitz Rock), a towering granite monolith that's an Idyllwild landmark.

In summer the town is jam-packed with students and their families when the Idyllwild School of Music and the Arts (ISOMATA) is held on a 200-acre campus at the edge of town. Its highly praised programs in the visual and performing arts have been conducted there since 1950. More recently the woodsy campus also has become home to the high-school–level Residential Arts Academy, which emphasizes training in dance, music, theater, and the visual arts.

Around Idyllwild you'll discover the work of talented artists, as at the rather bizarre Horton & Fogg outdoor sculpture garden on lower Pine Crest Avenue. Shopkeepers give visitors a friendly welcome, and you'll enjoy browsing in places like the Feats of Clay Gallery, Village Crafts and Cook Shoppe, The Print Corner, and Maggie's

Attic. The Book Shop has best-sellers and used paperbacks to read in front of your cabin fireplace.

Most folks agree Idyllwild's best restaurant is the Gastrognome, serving continental fare as well as steak and seafood. It's in the village center and open daily for dinner, plus brunch on Sunday. Another favorite in the heart of town is O'Sullivan's Tavern in the Pines. The Chart House in Fern Valley also is popular for dinner and Sunday brunch. You can eat Italian (including pizza) at Michelli's and Mexican at Señor Ruben's or La Casita. Among the favorites for breakfast and lunch are the Bread Basket, Pastries By Kathi, and Jan's Red Kettle.

Before making an outing to Idyllwild in winter, call any of the businesses below for a weather report; tire chains may be required until the roads are cleared after snowfall.

You can come down from the mountain via an alternate route, California 74. Follow it west through Hemet to Interstate 215 and then go north to join California 60 back to Los Angeles.

Round trip is about 226 miles.

Idyllwild Area Code: 909

SIGHTSEEING   *Idyllwild County Park Visitors Center,* P.O. Box 341, Idyllwild 92549, 659-3850. Natural and local history museum 1 mile north of Idyllwild off California 243. Open Wednesday through Sunday. Summer hours 9 A.M. to 6 P.M. May through September; winter hours 10 A.M. to 5 P.M. weekends, to 4 P.M. weekdays. Excellent exhibits. Also area tourist information. Be sure to take ½-mile Yellow Pine Forest loop trail from center.

LODGING   *Associated Idyllwild Rentals (AIR),* P.O. Box 43, Idyllwild 92549, 659-5520, has a map to lodgings offered by its 21 members. Some feature cozy cabins with fireplaces and kitchens. AIR lodging brochure also available at Sugar Pine Shop, 54274 North Circle Drive. ● *Mountain Greenery Realty,* 54241 Ridgeview Drive (or P.O. Box 1010), Idyllwild 92549, 659-4628, and *Idyllwild Property Management,* 54085 South Circle Drive (or P.O. Box 222), Idyllwild 92549, 659-5015, can book you into a 1-, 2-, or 3-bedroom vacation cabin or home for 2 nights (minimum), a week, or longer. Reserve at least 3 days to 1 week in advance; you provide sheets, towels, paper goods, and firewood. ● *Idyllwild Inn,* 54300 Village Center Drive, Idyllwild 92549, 659-2552; $70–$81. Small cabins with kitchens and fireplaces. Also motel rooms, $67. ● *Silver Pines Lodge,* 25955 Cedar Street, Idyllwild 92549, 659-4335; $55.

Cabins with fireplaces and kitchens. Also motel rooms, $47. •
Fireside Inn, 54540 North Circle Drive, Idyllwild 92549, 659-2966;
$66–$75. Duplex units, some with fireplaces and kitchens. • *Mile
High Lodge,* 54605 North Circle Drive, Idyllwild 92549, 659-2931;
$45–$65. Remodeled cabins, some with fireplaces and kitchens. •
Fern Village Chalets and Motel, 65821 North Circle Drive, Idyllwild 92549, 659-2869; $60–$70. A-frame units, some overlooking
creek. Also motel rooms, $45. • *Woodland Park Manor,* 55350 South
Circle Drive, Idyllwild 92549, 659-2657; $65–$85. Large cottages
with private sundecks, fireplaces, and kitchens. • *Strawberry Creek
Inn,* 26370 Highway 243, Idyllwild 92549, 659-3202 or toll-free
(800) 262-8969; $80–$95. 9-room B&B at creekside. • *Wilkum Inn,*
26770 Highway 243, Idyllwild 92549, 659-4087; $55–$85. 5-room
B&B. • *Bluebird Hill Lodge,* 26905 Highway 243, Idyllwild 92549,
659-2696; $41. 26 rooms and cabins, some with fireplaces and
kitchens. • *Fern Valley Inn,* 25240 Fern Valley Road, Idyllwild
92549, 659-2205; $63–$90. 11 cottages, all with fireplaces.

CAMPING   *Mt. San Jacinto State Park,* 25905 Highway 243 (or
P.O. Box 308), Idyllwild 92549, 659-2607. Idyllwild Campground
has 30 sites among the pines at north end of town; $12–$14 per night
(no hookups). Book through MISTIX toll-free (800) 444-7275,
May through October; rest of year is first come, first served.
Day-use fee, $5 per car. • *Idyllwild County Park Campground,* P.O.
Box 341, Idyllwild 92549, 659-2656 (information), 684-0196 (res-
ervations). 90 sites (no hookups) at north end of town; $10 per
night. From California 243 in town, follow Riv Co Playground
Road. Day-use fee for picnicking and hiking, $3 per car.

DINING   *Restaurant Gastrognome,* 54381 Ridgeview Drive,
Idyllwild, 659-5055. Idyllwild's best dinner house, serving nightly
from 5 P.M. Also Sunday brunch. Continental fare as well as steaks
and seafood, plus lighter cafe-bistro menu. Patio dining in summer.
• *Chart House,* 54905 North Circle Drive, Fern Valley, 659-4645.
Open daily in summer, Thursday through Sunday in winter. Popular
dinner spot for prime ribs, steaks, and seafood. Also Sunday brunch.
Outdoor patio. • *Michelli's,* 26290 Highway 243, Idyllwild, 659-
3919. Italian favorites for lunch and dinner on weekends, dinner
only on weekdays. • *Señor Ruben's,* 25980 Highway 243, Idyllwild,
659-4960. Mexican specialties for lunch and dinner daily. • *Bread
Basket,* 54710 North Circle Drive, Idyllwild, 659-3506. Breakfast
and lunch daily, dinner on Fridays and weekends. Fresh pastries,

breads, and continental dishes. • *Pastries By Kathi,* 54360 North Circle Drive, Idyllwild, 659-4359. Popular bakery serving breakfast and lunch; closed Tuesdays and Wednesdays. • *Jan's Red Kettle,* 54220 North Circle Drive, Idyllwild, 659-4063. Open daily for breakfast and soup-and-sandwich lunches.

FOR MORE INFORMATION   Contact the Idyllwild Chamber of Commerce, P.O. Box 304, Idyllwild 92549, 659-3259 (recorded information). Lodging list and guide map and other brochures available at Sugar Pine Shop, 54274 North Circle Drive, Idyllwild, 659-2810.

Peaceful Pleasures of the Ojai Valley

The Ojai Valley works magic on all its visitors. First to fall under its spell were the Oak Grove Indians and then the Chumash Indians, who called the protected pocket of natural beauty the ''nest.'' Early settlers also were charmed by the secluded valley, 750 feet high in the mountains at the edge of Los Padres National Forest in Ventura County. In 1874 a village named Nordhoff was established, complete with a tourist hotel. Eastern vacationers soon discovered the valley's refreshing climate, and a grand summer hotel, the Foothill, was opened in 1905. One of its guests, millionaire Ohio glass manufacturer Edward Libbey, became mesmerized by the area and took a hand in its future. With Libbey's leadership and financing, Nordhoff's main street of ramshackle false-front buildings was transformed to handsome Spanish mission–style architecture, featuring arcades, a bell tower, and a tree-shaded park framed by arches and arbors. By 1917, even the town's name had been changed to what the Indians had called the valley—Ojai (*o-high*).

From the earliest days, townsfolk and visitors have enjoyed all sorts of outdoor activities, especially golf and tennis. You can play on the courts in downtown Libbey Park, site of the oldest annual tennis tournament in the United States, first held in 1899 and now played every April. Ojai's original golf course opened six years earlier, but today golfers challenge the 18-hole Ojai Valley Inn and Country Club course, which had its debut in 1920. Also popular is the city-run par-72 course at Soule Park.

Art and culture are other long-standing traditions in the valley.

Besides boasting an array of galleries and studios, Ojai's artists and craftspeople display and sell their creations every Sunday in the parking lot of the Bank of America. In springtime a fine-arts exhibition is staged in Libbey Park in conjunction with the annual Ojai Music Festival, a well-known event that draws hundreds of concertgoers to the valley. The musicians perform amid the oaks and other trees in the park's rustic Festival Bowl. Even when no special events are scheduled, Ojai offers all sorts of divertissements, including excellent restaurants, cycling and jogging trails, relaxing hot springs, and even a health spa.

Located near the coast but isolated from fog and offshore winds, the peaceful valley is also well known for its stunning scenery. When Hollywood needed a Shangri-La location for the movie *Lost Horizon,* they took their cameras straight to Ojai. To see that beauty for yourself and enjoy the valley's other pleasures during a weekend in Ojai, drive north from Los Angeles on U.S. 101 to Ventura, then continue north on California 33 to join California 150 leading east into the attractive town. On its outskirts you'll come to the area's best-known resort, Ojai Valley Inn and Country Club, a bucolic retreat that began in 1923 as a two-story lodge. Settle into one of the 218 new or remodeled rooms and suites that have offered luxury in the country since 1988, when the inn was renovated to the tune of $35 million. Guests enjoy room amenities such as terry cloth robes, a well-stocked minibar, and evening turn-down service. Dress is very casual for your Ojai weekend, but it is suggested that male guests at the inn wear coats in the Vista dining room after 7 P.M. Informal attire is welcome at the Oak Grill and Terrace.

In the morning, play a game of tennis or round of golf, then take one of the inn's bicycles to pedal along woodsy trails to Ojai. Or drive into town on California 150 and stroll along Ojai Avenue's arcaded sidewalk to browse in the art galleries and antique and gift shops. You'll find more stores behind in a courtyard shopping area, which also can be reached from Matilija Street. Be sure to go west on Matilija to Canada Street and an Ojai landmark, Bart's Books, an open-air bookstore shaded by an ancient oak tree. After business hours you can select books from shelves along the sidewalk and toss the money into a slot in the door.

On the opposite side of Ojai Avenue, wander in beautiful Libbey Park, home for the town's music festival and tennis tournament. Its eight courts are open to the public without charge, as are those in Soule Park, a few blocks west. Around the corner from Libbey Park on South Montgomery Street in the old firehouse, visit the Ojai Valley Museum, filled with Indian artifacts, pioneer mementos, and stuffed birds and animals of the area. Also go next door to view the work of local artists at the Ojai Art Center.

If you decide to lunch in town, try Cafe Emporium or the outdoor patio at L'Auberge. They are also good choices for dinner. Another outdoor dining treat awaits you in neighboring Meiners Oaks at the Ranch House, where tables overlook the chef's herb garden. Not far away in Mira Monte the Gaslight Restaurant also draws a crowd. For a refreshment break while poking around town, have coffee and fresh pastries at the Village Pastry or at Bill Baker's Bakery. Local folks also like to shop and eat at the Herb Garden Shop and Cafe.

Sometime in the afternoon, go west a few miles on California 150 to Lake Casitas, a man-made reservoir that's a favorite of fishermen. The biggest catches are bass and catfish. Rental boats are available at this municipally run recreation area, chosen as the site of canoeing and rowing events for the 1984 Olympics. Since Lake Casitas serves as a domestic water supply, swimming and wading are not allowed, but the park is the focal point in the Ojai Valley for picnickers and campers.

To view more of Ojai's backcountry scenery and enjoy refreshments made from local fruit, turn right from the park on Santa Ana Road and skirt the lake to Santa Ana Boulevard. Go a mile west to rejoin California 33 at the hamlet of Oak View, then head south for another mile and look left for the Rancho Arnaz roadside barn. There you can sample delicious homemade apple cider and bite into fresh apples, dried apple chips, and other snacks produced at the farm. Decorating the barn rafters are county fair award ribbons that go back to 1930.

If you prefer your fruit drinks fermented, head east on the adjacent Old Creek Road to the very end, where you'll see grapevines planted on the hillside and find the Old Creek Ranch Winery. Its 1981 vintage was the first for Carmel Maitland, who resumed the ranch's wine making tradition, which goes back to the turn of the century. She invites visitors to tour the tiny winery and taste or purchase the current vintages.

Also worth visiting is the Gallery of Historical Figures, a display of remarkable, one-quarter-life-size re-creations of famous personalities from important historical eras, ranging from America's founding fathers to the Romanovs of Russia. Ojaian George Stuart has handcrafted and clothed over 100 such figures, and you'll discover how he makes them seem so lifelike. Many of the figures are on permanent display in the county museum in Ventura. Here, George shows off a changing exhibit of a dozen or so in his gallery-workshop. It's east of town off California 150; bear left on Reeves Road to McNell Road.

Then continue beyond that turnoff about a mile along California 150 to visit Dennison Park, near the top of 1,280-foot Dennison Grade, where actor Ronald Colman looked off to Shangri-La in *Lost Horizon.* You'll have the same view of that idyllic paradise, the upper Ojai Valley, and also find tables to spread a picnic beneath the park's pine trees and giant oaks.

On Sunday, plan to explore more of the Ojai Valley area by going north on California 33 into Los Padres National Forest, where mineral hot springs that soothed the Chumash Indians in California's pre-Spanish era still flow. Nowadays the bubbling waters have been captured along Matilija Creek at a rustic health spa, where visitors are invited to soak away their aches and other troubles. En route to that sylvan hideaway, the scenic canyon road overlooks a curvy creek bed flanked by hillside orchards that produce succulent oranges and other fruit. Some of the best are sold at the roadside packinghouse of Friend's Ranch, where there's always fresh orange juice. Stock up on grapefruit, avocados, lemons, limes, and a variety of nuts.

Farther up the road is a renovated nineteenth-century spa, Wheeler Hot Springs. There you can luxuriate in redwood tubs located in private skylighted rooms that feature both hot and cold mineral baths. Swedish, Shiatsu, reflexology, and polarity massages can be arranged. An added attraction at this renovated rural spa is a pleasant dining room, and on some summer afternoons there are jazz concerts.

When your peaceful weekend in the Ojai Valley is over, return to Los Angeles by heading east on California 150 to Santa Paula, then take California 129 east to join Interstate 5 going south to the city.

Round trip is about 190 miles.

Ojai Area Code: 805

SIGHTSEEING   *Ojai Valley Museum,* 109 South Montgomery Street, Ojai 93023, 646-2290. Open daily except Tuesdays from 1 to 5 P.M. Free; donations accepted. ● *Ojai Art Center,* 113 South Montgomery Street, Ojai 93023, 646-0117. Gallery open Tuesday through Sunday from 12 to 4 P.M. Free. ● *Gallery of Historical Figures,* on McNell Road at Reeves Road (or P.O. Box 508), Ojai 93023, 646-6574. Open weekends only from 1 to 5 P.M.; other days by appointment. Adults $.75, children free. ● *Libbey Park Tennis Courts,* Libbey Park, Ojai. 8 courts, first come, first served. Free; lights for night play. ● *Soule Park Golf Course,* 1033 East Ojai Avenue, Ojai 93023, 646-5633. 18-hole municipal course with putting green and driving range. Pros available for lessons. Greens fee $16 weekends, $11 weekdays. Also 2 public tennis courts. ● *Lake Casitas Recreation Area,* off California 150 at 11311 Santa Ana Road, Ventura 93001, 649-2233. Day-use entry $3 per vehicle.

Boat rentals, fishing gear, and license at Boat, Bait, and Tackle Shop, 649-2043. Snack bar nearby. Also camping (see below). • *Rancho Arnaz,* California 33 at Old Creek Road, Oak View 93022, 649-2776. Fresh apple juice and fruit at roadside stand open daily from 8 A.M. to 6 P.M. • *Old Creek Ranch Winery,* 10024 Old Creek Road (or P.O. Box 173), Oak View 93022, 649-4132. Open 10 A.M. to 4 P.M. Saturday, 12 to 4 P.M. Sunday. Free. Also, seasonal U-Pick berries and other fruit. • *Friend's Ranch,* 15150 Maricopa Highway (California 33), Ojai 93023, 646-2871. Venerable roadside fruit stand open every day from 8 A.M. to 5 P.M. • *Wheeler Hot Springs,* 16825 Maricopa Highway (California 33), Ojai 93023, 646-8131 or toll-free (800) 227-9292. Open Thursday through Sunday from morning into evening; open daily in summer. Use of redwood tub baths, $10 per person per half-hour. Swedish and other massages, one hour $50. Reservations recommended. Also restaurant serving dinner and weekend brunch.

EVENTS *Ojai Music Festival,* an acclaimed weekend concert series held annually since 1947. A varied repertoire of music and song is performed outdoors in Libbey Park's Festival Bowl in late May or early June. Dress warmly for evening performances. Programs and tickets available from Ojai Festivals, Ltd., P.O. Box 185, Ojai 93023, 646-2094. • *Ojai Valley Tennis Tournament,* held annually in April with headquarters in Libbey Park. Since the 1960s the busy professional circuit has kept big-name players away, but 1,500 entrants compete in the men's and women's invitational, college, high school, and 12-years-and-under divisions. Contact the Ojai Valley Chamber of Commerce (see below).

LODGING *Ojai Valley Inn and Country Club,* Country Club Drive off California 33, Ojai 93023, 646-5511 or toll-free (800) 422-6524; $190 and up. Also golf packages that include greens fees. Country resort with golf, tennis, and swimming. Restaurants open to the public (see below). • *The Oaks at Ojai,* 122 East Ojai Avenue, Ojai 93023, 646-5573; from $125 per person, 2-night minimum. No children under 16 years. A veteran hotel in the heart of Ojai that was renovated and reopened in 1977 as a health spa. Price includes all low-calorie meals, a dozen daily fitness classes, and use of swimming pool, saunas, exercise equipment, and spas. Also evening workshops, lectures, and craft programs. Special services include massages, facials, and a hair salon. Spa program without lodging is $80 per person per day. • *Ojai Manor Hotel,* 210 East Matilija, Ojai

93023, 646-0961; $75. 1874 schoolhouse renovated as a 6-room, 3-bath bed and breakfast. ● *Theodore Woolsey House,* 1484 East Ojai Avenue, Ojai 93023, 646-9779; $50–$95. Country B&B on 7 acres a mile from town. 5 rooms, swimming pool. ● *Casa de la Luna,* 710 South La Luna Avenue; Ojai 93023, 646-4528; $95. Modern bed-and-breakfast inn with garden setting.

CAMPING *Lake Casitas Recreation Area* (see above). 453 sites, no hookups; $10 per night. First come, first served.

DINING *Ojai Valley Inn* (see above). The public is welcome to join inn guests in the Vista dining room and the Oak Grill and Terrace. Coats suggested for men in the dining room. Expensive but special Sunday buffet. Make reservations. ● *The Ranch House,* 102 Besant Road at South Lomita in Meiners Oaks, 646-2360 or 646-4384. Ojai's best-known restaurant, with delightful dining in a garden setting. Dinner served Wednesday through Sunday; also lunch Wednesday through Saturday and brunch on Sunday. Make reservations well in advance. Many choices from the continental menu. Also, the Ranch House's home-baked bread is sold by the loaf to take home. ● *L'Auberge,* 314 El Paseo Street, Ojai, 646-2288. French cuisine for dinner nightly except Tuesdays. Also weekend luncheons with crepes a specialty. ● *Ojai Cafe Emporium,* 108 South Montgomery Street, Ojai, 646-2723. Open daily for all meals except dinner on Sundays and Mondays. Vegetarian dishes a specialty. ● *The Gaslight,* 11432 North Ventura Avenue, in Mira Monte, 646-5990. Dinner nightly except Mondays. Varied menu; known for veal dishes. ● *Bill Baker's Bakery,* 457 East Ojai Avenue, Ojai, 646-1558. Open daily 5:30 A.M. to 3:30 P.M. A coffee-break spot where you can order fresh-baked pastries, muffins, Chinese eggrolls, and 15 varieties of bread. ● *Herb Garden Shop and Cafe,* 109 North Montgomery Street, Ojai, 646-7065. Light lunches served daily 11:30 A.M. to 3:30 P.M. Store has 300 types of herbs as well as gift items.

FOR MORE INFORMATION Contact the Ojai Valley Chamber of Commerce, 338 East Ojai Avenue, Ojai 93023, 646-8126. Open every day.

Old-Fashioned Fun in Oak Glen and Redlands

Fruit-filled orchards and stately Victorian homes are highlights of a weekend in the mountain foothills east of San Bernardino. Try to take your excursion in late spring or early summer during the cherry harvest or in the fall at apple-picking time. That's when orchard owners invite visitors to pick their own cherries and apples from the trees, or buy the ripe fruit at roadside stands. Add to that a mission outpost from Spanish days, as well as art and antiques— all part of a relaxing visit to some of the Southland's most scenic countryside.

Another treat is staying in the remarkable 20-room Victorian mansion known as the Morey Mansion, now a bed-and-breakfast inn in Redlands. Built in 1890 by a retired shipbuilder, the $20,000 dream house features impressive exterior detail work, including carvings of anchors, flowers, and fruit. The immense house has 96 windows; behind the rounded panes in the onion dome, look for a carved carousel horse.

Get there from Los Angeles by driving east on Interstate 10 to the Alabama Street exit for Redlands. Go south on Alabama Street to Barton Road, turn right to the next street, Terracina Boulevard, and turn left to number 190.

In the morning, dress casually for a circle excursion by car through a picturesque valley and mountain glen that abounds with cherry and apple orchards. Return to Interstate 10 and continue east about 17 miles to the Beaumont Avenue exit. Head north over the freeway through Beaumont to Cherry Valley, home for 35 or so orchards where ladders and buckets are available so you can pluck your own cherries from the trees. The rewards for such labor are fresh fruit at reasonable prices and plenty of fun. The cherry harvest begins in June, with various varieties ready for picking at different times. The sweet Tartarians usually are ripe first, followed by the much-favored Bings, then the Hardy Giants, Royal Ans, Windsors, and a dozen other kinds. By mid-July most of the cherries have been picked, ending with the luscious Lamperts.

As you drive along, look for U-Pick signs that will direct you to the orchards and indicate which varieties of cherries are ripe and ready for plucking from the trees. At the intersection of Beaumont Avenue and Cherry Valley Boulevard, you'll find a seasonal cherry-picking information booth on the northeast corner. Every June Beaumont celebrates the annual harvest with a Cherry Festival, which always draws a crowd for its parade, cherry-pie-eating contests, arts-and-crafts exhibits, and carnival games.

To follow the pretty back road that leads to the Southland's largest apple-growing region, continue north on Beaumont Avenue, which becomes Oak Glen Road. Just beyond Cherry Valley it brings you to Riverside County's art and cultural center, the Edward-Dean Museum of Decorative Arts, an unexpected treasure trove in a bucolic setting. After retirement, two world-traveling interior decorators deeded their 16-acre estate to the county, including a lifetime collection of art and antiques. The interior of the eight-room museum appears more like an eighteenth-century home filled with priceless furniture, paintings, tapestries, and porcelains from Europe and the Orient. Also featured is a gallery with changing art exhibits, as well as a gift shop.

Continue north on meandering Oak Glen Road and climb a mile high into the foothills of the San Bernardino Mountains to appleland. Every autumn since 1947 many orchard owners have opened roadside stands to sell their tasty fruit to passersby, and from September through December the Oak Glen area is a favorite destination for folks who savor fresh apples, apple cider, and apple pie. Drive cautiously on the curvy two-lane road as you look for entrances to the orchards that welcome visitors. They include, from south to north, Riley's Farm & Orchard, Los Rios Rancho Apple Orchard, Snow Line–Four Oaks Ranch, Law's Oak Glen Cider Mill, Hi Country Orchards, Parrish Pioneer Ranch, McFarland's Ranch, Johnny Appleseed, and Woods Acres.

More than half of their annual crop is the Rome Beauty variety, which is best for cooking. Others are great eating varieties: Red and Golden Delicious, as well as McIntosh, Spartan, Winesap, Arkansas Black, and Hoover. Some of the fruit is crushed in cider mills and served hot or cold by the cup and in jugs to take home. Most of the orchards have tree-shaded tables where you can picnic under an umbrella of multicolored leaves that change their hues in the crisp fall weather.

Buy an apple pie for your picnic at Apple Annie's Restaurant and Bakery, where hot slices of pie are also served. It's in Oak Tree Village, a center of craft and curio shops where you'll find more local fruit creations, such as apple butter, apple jam, apple jelly, apple syrup, and applesauce. Other popular places to stop for apple pie are Los Rios Bakery, Law's Oak Glen Coffee Shop, and the Apple Dumplings Restaurant and Bakery at Parrish Pioneer Ranch.

Spend another night in Redlands, which is dotted with palm trees and sometimes circled by snowcapped mountains. The city was founded more than a century ago and named for its iron-streaked soil. At that time the warm fertile valley was planted with citrus trees, and Redlands called itself the navel orange capital of the world. When the town became a popular winter resort for East Coast folks in the early 1900s, many of them built rather regal homes. Today you can still view a number of those showcase structures during a self-guided drive along the city's wide tree-lined avenues.

Nineteen historic houses, mostly Victorian, are described in the *Historic Redlands Driving Tour* booklet produced by the city's chamber of commerce. A map directs you to the homes, including two that are open for afternoon tours on Sundays. One is the Morey Mansion and the other is a French château–style home called Kimberly Crest, which also welcomes visitors on Thursdays, Fridays, and Saturdays. To get there from the Morey Mansion, continue on Terracina Boulevard to Cypress Avenue and follow it to Alvarado Street. Turn right to Highland Avenue, then cross that street and go up the narrow lane that's Prospect Drive. Soon you'll see Kimberly Crest, the three-story mansion built for a wealthy widow from New York State in 1897. When the J. A. Kimberlys of the Kimberly-Clark paper fortune purchased the home in 1905, they had Tiffany's of New York redecorate it. Formal gardens replaced the orange trees that once surrounded the palatial estate.

After viewing the home, go back down the hill as you came. Recross Highland Avenue back onto Alvarado Street and drive north to Olive Avenue. On the corner is the Holt House, a 13-room Mediterranean home built in 1903 for the developer of the Imperial Valley. There's a full-size bowling lane in the basement. Go right on Olive Avenue, then left on Eureka Street to Vine Street and park where you can to explore pretty Smiley Park, named for the city's founders. There you'll find Redlands' ornate Moorish-style library, which is now a state historic landmark, the octagonal Lincoln Shrine with its collection of Lincolniana, and the Redlands Bowl, an outdoor community amphitheater where free music and dance performances are presented every Tuesday and Friday evening in July and August.

As for the rest of the day's outing in Redlands, you can visit a mission *asistencia* built in 1830 to serve the area's Indians and browse in the modern San Bernardino County Museum. From Smiley Park and Eureka Street, turn left and go west on Brookside Avenue, which becomes Barton Road and leads to a bell tower that marks the San Bernardino Asistencia. Spanish padres from the San Gabriel mission had established Rancho San Bernardino in 1819 to teach the Indians about agriculture and livestock, and the *asistencia* was built there as a religious center for the natives. Falling into disrepair soon after California's missions were secularized in the 1830s, the *asistencia* was restored by the WPA 100 years later and is now an attractive museum, featuring artifacts and dioramas of the Indian mission and American pioneer periods. It's also a popular place for weddings.

Continue west on Barton Road to California Street and follow it north under the freeway to Orange Tree Lane. At the end is the impressive San Bernardino County Museum with its giant geodesic dome. Inside you'll find splendid displays of land and sea birds, with their varied eggs and recorded calls, as well as a mammal collection, Indian artifacts, and much more. Adjacent and almost hidden in a grove of orange trees is the Edwards Mansion, a restored 1890 residence that's now a popular place for weddings and private parties.

When you're ready for the return trip to Los Angeles, rejoin Interstate 10 going west.

Round trip is about 185 miles.

Oak Glen/Redlands Area Code: 909

SIGHTSEEING *Edward-Dean Museum of Decorative Arts,* 9401 Oak Glen Road, Cherry Valley 92223, 845-2626. Open weekends from 10 A.M. to 4:30 P.M., weekdays except Mondays from 1 to 4:30 P.M. Closed in August. Admission $1, children under 12 years free. ● *Historic Redlands Driving Tour,* self-guided-tour booklet, $5 from Redlands Chamber of Commerce (see below). ● *Morey Mansion,* 190 Terracina Boulevard, Redlands. Open for tours from noon to 3 P.M. every Sunday; $3.25, children under 12 years $2.50. Also a B&B (see below). ● *Kimberly Crest,* 1325 Prospect Drive, Redlands. Open for tours from 1 to 4 P.M. Thursday through Sunday; $3 donation. ● *San Bernardino Asistencia,* 26930 Barton Road, Redlands, 92373, 793-5402. Open daily except Mondays and Tuesdays from 10 A.M. to 5 P.M., Sundays from 1 P.M. Free admission; donations accepted. ● *San Bernardino County Museum,* 2024 Orange Tree Lane, Redlands 92373, 798-8570. Open daily except Mondays from 9 A.M. to 5 P.M., Sunday from 11 A.M. Free.

EVENTS *Cherry Festival,* annual mid-June celebration. Contact the Beaumont Chamber of Commerce (see below). ● *Oak Glen Harvest Festival,* held annually in September. Call 797-6833.

LODGING *Morey Mansion Bed & Breakfast Inn,* 190 Terracina Boulevard, Redlands 92373, 793-7970; $109–$225, depending on day of the week. An 1890s Victorian beauty that became a B&B in 1985. 5 rooms, plus private cottage. Also guided tours (see above). Full breakfast and afternoon tea. ● *St. Anley B&B,* 39796 Pine Bench Road, Oak Glen 92399, 797-7920; $125, including full breakfast. Modern 5-room B&B in apple country. Ask about picnic breakfast and romantic carriage ride. No smoking. Reservations required. • Redlands has several motels, including *Redlands Motor Lodge,* 798-2431; *Best Western Sandman Motel,* 793-2001; and *Redlands Inn,* 793-6648.

DINING   *Apple Annie's Restaurant and Bakery,* 38480 Oak Glen Road, Oak Glen, 797-7371. Open daily. Apple pie and meals to 6 P.M., Fridays and Saturdays to 8:30 P.M. • *Apple Dumplings Restaurant and Bakery,* at Parrish Ranch, 38578 Oak Glen Road, Oak Glen, 797-0037. Apple pie and meals from 9 A.M. to 6 P.M. daily. • *Law's Oak Glen Coffee Shop,* 38412 Oak Glen Road, Oak Glen, 797-1642. Open 8 A.M. to 7 P.M. daily except Mondays and Tuesdays. In apple season open every day, September until Thanksgiving. • *Griswold's Smorgasbord,* 1025 Parkford Drive, Redlands, 793-2158. Popular and inexpensive buffet open daily for all meals. • *Joe Greensleeves,* 222 North Orange Street, Redlands, 792-6969. Fine food in a historic 1890s building. Dinner served Tuesday through Saturday. • *Clara's,* 101 East Redlands Boulevard, Redlands, 335-1466. Italian dishes for lunch and dinner daily.

FOR MORE INFORMATION   Visit the Beaumont–Cherry Valley Cherry Growers Association info booth (in season) on corner of Cherry Valley Boulevard and Beaumont Avenue, Cherry Valley, 845-3628. • Oak Glen Apple Growers Association, Los Rios Ranch, 39610 Oak Glen Road, Yucaipa 92399, 797-6833 (recorded message), or 797-1005. • Beaumont Chamber of Commerce, 450 East 4th Street (or P.O. Box 637), Beaumont, 92223, 845-9541. • Redlands Chamber of Commerce, 1 East Redlands Boulevard, Redlands 92373, 793-2546. • San Bernardino Convention and Visitors Bureau, 440 West Court Street, Suite 108, San Bernardino 92401, 889-3980 or toll-free (800) 669-8336.

Orange County's Canyon Country

Burgeoning Orange County has many visitor attractions in its cities and by the sea, but you'll also be delighted by tranquil inland canyons that continue to forestall the bulldozers, housing developments, and high rises. A hundred years ago the people exploring the narrow, twisting canyons that lead into the rugged Santa Ana Mountains were looking for silver and other elusive ore. These days the quiet canyons are destinations for folks seeking a place to relax and savor nature.

During a weekend escape in the foliage-covered foothills only a few miles from the freeway, you'll discover a trio of parks for picnicking, boating, fishing, hiking, and horseback riding, as well as a wildlife sanctuary that's a favorite of bird watchers. Outdoor enthusiasts can settle down in their tents or RVs in a woodsy campground at O'Neill Regional Park or check in nearby at Coto de Caza, where a first-class tennis college is the main enticement.

Get to either retreat by driving south from Los Angeles on Interstate 5 beyond Santa Ana to Laguna Hills and then exiting east on El Toro Road/County Road S18. You'll wind past sprouting subdivisions on this once-rural road before reaching a roadhouse called Cook's Corner, where you should go right on Live Oak Canyon Road and follow it to the Orange County hideaways. First to be found is O'Neill Park, 1,700 acres extending along Live Oak and Trabuco canyons that are popular for overnight camping and daytime picnicking. There's even an equestrian camping area for visitors who bring their horses to explore the oblong park, originally part of a vast Mexican land grant. A posted warning about mountain lions and rattlesnakes indicates that the park continues to serve as a sanctuary for wildlife.

If you don't cook out on the evening of your arrival, turn right from the park entrance on Trabuco Canyon Road, continue to the next junction, and go left on Trabuco Oaks Drive to the area's best-known dinner spot, the rustic and very informal Trabuco Oaks Steak House. The featured fare is a steak for cowboys that weighs two pounds. For folks who feel like Mexican food, keep going on Trabuco Canyon Road to Rose Canyon Road and turn left to Señor Lico's.

In the morning, get to know more about the canyon's plants and wildlife by following Trabuco Creek Nature Trail in O'Neill Park, or join a ranger for the early-morning nature hikes on weekends. Across the road from the park at Live Oak Stables, guided horseback trail rides and pony rides are other available activities.

If you're not camping for the weekend at O'Neill Park, continue from Live Oak Canyon Road onto Trabuco Canyon Road and follow it and Via Plano Trabuco to Coto de Caza. This exclusive 5,000-acre residential community is home for the Vic Braden Tennis College, a world-class teaching facility and sports-research center. The impressive property also was chosen as the site of the 1984 Olympics' modern pentathlon—a five-event men's competition in horseback riding, fencing, pistol shooting, freestyle swimming, and cross-country foot racing.

You'll need a reservation for the tennis college in order to enter this pastoral property. Once you've checked into one of the college's condominium-style rooms, enjoy dinner in the clubhouse restaurant and get rested for activities on Saturday. In addition to tennis, you can play racquetball, go swimming, and even try your skill at trap shooting. This former ranchland also has miles of paths for jogging, hiking, and bike riding. And in the tree-shaded youth park, kids and their parents enjoy playing shuffleboard, horseshoes, and volleyball. After all this exercise, the saunas and whirlpool baths in the ladies' and men's locker rooms are a nice way to ease into the evening. Although the resort's master suites include complete kitchens, most guests have their meals in the clubhouse, or you can drive to the Trabuco Oaks Steak House.

On the final day of your getaway weekend, plan to explore more Orange County canyons. From Coto de Caza or O'Neill Regional Park, go back to Cook's Corner and turn right on Santiago Canyon Road. Go right again on the next paved road, Modjeska Grade Road, to Modjeska Canyon Road and bear right to reach the Tucker Wildlife Sanctuary. Modjeska Canyon was named for Madame Helena Modjeska, an acclaimed Polish actress who emigrated to the United States and later moved to a house in the canyon. A historical marker opposite the fire station describes her home, now hidden by trees. The property is an Orange County Park and will be open to the public once restoration of the Modjeska home is completed. At road's end, park for a visit to the wildlife sanctuary, best known for its abundance of birds. A viewing patio and porch overlook feeders that attract nearly 150 species during the year, especially the hummingbirds that you'll see darting here and there. Across the road in the visitor and nature center, look at the live local rodents and reptiles on display, then go for a walk on one of the nature trails in this unique preserve, operated by the Fullerton campus of California State University.

Follow Modjeska Canyon Road out of the canyon and head north (right) on Santiago Canyon Road. Turn right on Silverado Canyon Road, location of abandoned silver and other ore mines. A plaque in the parking lot of the modernistic Silverado Community Church marks the site of Carbondale, a boisterous boom town that developed with the discovery of coal in 1878 but has since disappeared. Now a quiet rural community has become established in rustic homes along peaceful Silverado Canyon. Locals like to gather at the unfancy Pali Cafe, open for breakfast, lunch, and early dinner. Try the homemade pie.

Return to Santiago Canyon Road and continue north to Irvine Lake, a haven for fishermen. Entry to the private park is a little pricey, but the sprawling Santiago Reservoir is stocked with trout, bass, and crappie, and boats can be rented if you'd like to try your luck. Otherwise, continue north on Santiago Canyon Road and turn right on Chapman Avenue to Irvine Regional Park, another county park on picturesque ranchland. Kids love riding ponies around a ring, petting small animals in the zoo, and boating in a lagoon. You can rent horses as well as bicycles, and there are hiking trails and plenty of picnic spots, too.

When it's time for your return to Los Angeles, go back on Chapman Avenue and follow it through the city of Orange to rejoin Interstate 5 heading north.

Round trip is about 120 miles.

Orange County Area Code: 714

SIGHTSEEING *O'Neill Regional Park,* 30892 Trabuco Canyon Road, Trabuco Canyon 92678, 858-9365. Open daily from 7 A.M. to sunset. Day-use fee $2 per vehicle. Guided nature hikes on weekends at 8 A.M. year round; additional ranger programs in summer. Also overnight camping (see below). ● *Live Oak Stables,* 31101 Live Oak Canyon Road across from O'Neill Regional Park, Trabuco Canyon 92678, 858-9922. Pony rides weekends only from 10 A.M. to 3 P.M. $2 for 10 rounds. Also guided trail rides, $20 per person. No reservations required on weekends. ● *Tucker Wildlife Sanctuary,* 29322 Modjeska Canyon Road, Orange 92676, 649-2760. Open daily from 9 A.M. to 4 P.M. Donation $1.50. Picnic tables. ● *Irvine Lake,* off Santiago Canyon Road, Orange 92676, 649-2991. Open from 6 A.M. to 4 P.M. Night fishing in summer on Fridays and Saturdays from 5 to 11 P.M. Adults $11, children under 12 years $9. Fishing for bass, catfish, trout, crappie, sturgeon, and bluegill. No license required. Rod and reel rental, plus rental motorboats and rowboats. ● *Irvine Regional Park,* 21501 East Chapman Avenue, Orange 92669, 633-8072. Open daily from 7 A.M. to 9 P.M. from April through October, to 6 P.M. the rest of the year. Day-use fee $2 per vehicle. Extra fees for pony rides, paddle boats, and bike rentals. Horses for rent daily except Mondays, $15 per hour; call Country Trails, 538-5860. Free petting zoo. No camping.

LODGING *Vic Braden Tennis College* at Coto de Caza, 23335 Avenida La Caza, Coto de Caza 92679, 581-2990 or toll-free (800) 225-5842; $79–$150. Lodging available only to persons (and their guests) enrolled in tennis college. 2- to 5-day tennis packages cost $130 per person per day and include use of 6 championship courts, geometric teaching lanes, classroom and on-court instruction, and instant video replay. Guests-only restaurant in the clubhouse on weekends (see below).

CAMPING   *O'Neill Regional Park* (see above). 80 sites, with water but no electrical hookups. $10 per night. First come, first served. Country store nearby for food and supplies.

DINING   *Trabuco Oaks Steak House,* 20782 Trabuco Oaks Drive, Trabuco Canyon 92678, 586-0722. Rustic dinner house open daily from 5 P.M., weekends from 4 P.M. Great beef and fun; don't wear a tie unless you want it cut off. Make reservations. ● *Señor Lico's,* 20722 Rose Canyon Road, Trabuco Canyon 92678, 858-0724. Open daily except Mondays at 5 P.M. (Sundays at noon) for dinner. Mexican plus limited American fare. ● *Coto de Caza Clubhouse Restaurant,* at Coto de Caza (see above). Open Friday evenings and weekends for Vic Braden Tennis College enrollees and guests only. Outdoor barbecue on Saturdays from noon to 8 P.M. Also cocktail lounge and occasional entertainment. ● *Pali Cafe,* 28272 Silverado Canyon Road, Silverado, 649-2622. Open Sunday through Thursday from 7 A.M. to 3 P.M., Fridays and Saturdays to 8 P.M. American favorites including homemade pie.

Boats, Trains, and Planes in Perris Valley

Paris was the focus of attention when Charles Lindbergh landed his *Spirit of St. Louis* after the first solo flight across the Atlantic little more than half a century ago. Nowadays aerial enthusiasts are still talking about Perris—in Riverside County. It's a major center for aerial activities in the Southland. At that rural community's airport you can watch or join in all kinds of airborne events—hot-air ballooning, parachuting, or even flying a micro-light aircraft. And for visitors who like to travel closer to terra firma, Perris is the home of the Orange Empire Railway Museum, where you can ride old-time trolleys that used to clang through the streets of Los Angeles and San Francisco.

This region also is outstanding for all kinds of outdoor activities, because of the Lake Perris State Recreation Area. It's an inland retreat for boaters, hikers, bicyclists, anglers, picnickers, swimmers,

hunters, water-skiers, bird watchers, and rock climbers. With 430
RV and tent sites for family camping, the park is the perfect base for
a weekend visit to Perris Valley. (Limited lodging also is available
at Perris's sole motel, and you'll find a greater choice of accommodations a few miles north in Moreno Valley.)

Get to Lake Perris by driving east on California 60 (Pomona
Freeway) past Riverside to the Moreno Beach Road exit. Turn south
to the park's 24-hour entrance, then head to the campground and
settle in for the evening. Plan to explore and enjoy this pleasure-
filled recreation area either Saturday or Sunday and spend the other
day of your weekend involved in the aerial and railway activities
around Perris.

Like Perrier, the water in Lake Perris is imported to Southern
California for your pleasure. No, it's not brought from overseas in
bottles. In fact, the journey of Lake Perris water is more fascinating.
Beginning as rainfall and melted snow in Northern California, it
courses down the state's rivers, tunnels, pipelines, and aqueducts to
a 2,000-acre reservoir that's the terminus for the 444-mile California
Aqueduct bringing water to the Southland from the Sacramento–San
Joaquin Delta. Lake Perris, along with 6,000 surrounding acres of
rocky hills and rangeland, has subsequently been developed for
public recreation. For a panoramic view of the lake and nearby hills,
drive or hike to the park's Interpretive Center, which offers an
excellent lookout and describes the land in earlier days.

Since it began forming in 1973, Lake Perris has expanded its
shoreline to a circumference of ten miles and is especially popular
with boaters. There are three ramps where visitors can launch their
own powerboats and sailboats, or you can rent a boat at the marina
for some fishing or sight-seeing. Jet-skis and water skis also can be
hired. Boaters can sail to the middle of the lake to swim and picnic
on Alessandro Island, named for the Indian hero of Helen Hunt
Jackson's well-known novel, *Ramona.* You'll also find sandy
beaches for swimming along the lakeshore, as well as numerous
picnic sites with tables and grills. Grocery and boat supplies are sold
in the small store up the hill from the boat slips, and a coffee shop
is adjacent.

Fishing usually is good, especially for channel catfish. Lake
Perris is stocked with Alabama spotted bass, bluegill, and rainbow
trout. You can get the required state fishing license at the boat rental
office.

For bicyclists and hikers there's a paved path around the lake. A
separate equestrian trail also circles the lake, but bring your own
horse or bike, because none can be rented in the park. At the south
end of the dam visit the Big Rock, a favorite attraction for rock
climbers as well as onlookers, who marvel at the human spiders
who scale the huge outcropping. Climbers must have a buddy but

no longer need a permit from rangers at the park entrance. Scuba divers must register with the rangers and be certified divers in order to use the special diving zone, where sections of huge concrete pipe have been placed on the lake bottom to attract fish. With the proper license, seasonal hunting is allowed in designated sections of the Lake Perris recreation area, too, but only shotguns can be used. Game includes rabbit, quail, dove, and some waterfowl.

Get up early on the day you want some high-flying fun, because the hot-air balloons are launched at sunrise. In the early dawn just south of the Perris Valley Airport, several of the colorful air carriers are inflated with heat from roaring propane burners and ascend into the sky, each with a gondola carrying a pilot and two to four passengers. These scenic flights, by reservation only, depart from a field at the corner of Goetz and Mapes roads. Get there from the Lake Perris State Recreation Area by taking the Perris Drive exit from the park to the Ramona Expressway. Go right to Perris Boulevard and follow it south through town, jogging left on 11th Street just past the railroad tracks and then turning right to join Goetz Road. Go beyond the airport entrance to Mapes Road to watch or help launch the big balloons. If you go aloft, the cost of the 30- to 90-minute flights includes the traditional champagne to celebrate the completion of your aerial excursion.

Afterward, go back on Goetz Road to the Perris Valley Airport, headquarters for one of the busiest jump centers in the world. In fact, it's popular with sport parachutists from all over the globe. Jumpers float down from the sky every day of the week, but most of the airborne action is on weekends. If you get the urge to parachute instead of just being an observer on the ground, the Perris Valley Skydiving Center offers a training course that takes just 4 to 6 hours and climaxes with your first jump.

Also in the sky around Perris Valley Airport are ultra-lights, one-person aircraft that resemble giant dragonflies. The latest rage in personal air transportation, these ultra-lights also are called micro-lights and often are erroneously referred to as motorized hang gliders. For a close-up look at the fabric-and-aluminum-frame flying machines, go to the white hangar, headquarters of the Valley Ultra-light Park. If you'd like to be a modern-day Orville Wright, arrange for introductory lessons and an individual flight.

A short distance from the airport you'll also enjoy the revival of earthbound transportation aboard an electric railcar. Clickety-clacking joy rides on refurbished trolleys are offered weekends and holidays at the Orange Empire Railway Museum. Get there by returning to Mapes Road and going east to A Street, then turning right to the museum parking area. Walk across the tracks to a world of bells clanging and wheels screeching on the steel rails. Hop aboard one of the vintage vehicles and join the other passengers swaying in their seats as the streetcar circles 2½ miles through the pastureland.

Two or three cars run different routes at varying times. They are selected from the museum's rolling stock, which includes a 1905 Huntington Standard, one of the Los Angeles Railway's Yellow Cars, and other Los Angeles streetcars from the 1920s and 1930s. Rides also are given aboard the newest streetcar, a streamlined version built for L.A.'s Metropolitan Transit Authority 30 years ago. It was retired from city service in 1963. Other cars that tour the museum grounds are Pacific Electrics that ran on the Los Angeles–Long Beach line until 1961. Along the way volunteer conductors and motormen describe the trolley's history and reminisce about city and interurban rail transportation.

Besides taking a nostalgic ride or experiencing a trip by trolley for the first time, you also can browse around the grounds to inspect nonoperating streetcars and train cars from a bygone era. Look for the *Descanso,* a special funeral trolley that transported coffins and mourners to Los Angeles area cemeteries from 1909 to 1939. Another streetcar, No. 913 from New Orleans, should remind you of playwright Tennessee Williams because of the destination on its headsign: Desire Street. Some trolleys are from overseas, including a double-decker that once ran in Dublin. A smaller car, with Japanese lettering, saw service in Kyoto until 1960. There are also open storage and restoration sheds, where volunteers are frequently working to return old and rusted cars to their original condition so visitors can sample electric rail transportation from earlier times. A gift shop sells mementos and books that describe some of the 150 train cars and trolleys at the outdoor museum. There's a tree-shaded picnic area, too, and refreshments are available.

Another item of interest for railroad buffs is back in town, the 1892 Perris train depot with its distinctive Queen Anne–style tower. The red brick building is now home for the Perris Valley Historical Society, with a small museum devoted to early-day artifacts from the area. Reach it by going north on A Street to 4th Street and turning right two blocks to the railroad tracks. Just beyond is D Street, the main street of Perris, which leads north to Interstate 215 to rejoin California 60 for the drive back to Los Angeles.

Round trip is about 170 miles.

Perris Area Code: 909

SIGHTSEEING   *Lake Perris State Recreation Area,* 17801 Lake Perris Drive, Perris 92370, 657-0676. Open daily. Day-use fee $6 per vehicle; fee for camping (see below) includes entry. Pick up $1 park map at entry gate. *Home of the Wind Indian Museum* open weekends from 10 A.M. to 4 P.M. and Wednesdays to 2 P.M. Lake Perris Marina open for boat and equipment rental from 6 A.M. to 8 P.M. in summer, to 5 P.M. in winter. Call 657-2179 for current rates. • *Scorpion Balloons,* 246 Lomita Drive (or P.O. Box 1147), Perris 92370, 657-6930, offers hot-air balloon rides any day by reservation. 1-hour flights $150 per person. • *Southern California Balloons,* 29740 Saw Grass Circle, Murietta 92563, 244-3511. Hot-air balloon flights $75 for half-hour, $110 for 1 hour (per person). • *Adventure Flights,* 19301 Jasmine Court, Lake Elsinore 92330, 678-4334. Hot-air balloon trips, $65 per person for half-hour. • *Perris Valley Skydiving Center,* 2091 South Goetz Road, Perris 92370, 657-9576, 657-1664, or toll-free (800) 832-8818. Same-day First Jump course costs $307, including equipment, instruction, and airplane flight. Tandem jump with 40 minutes of instruction, $160. • *Skylark Airsports Ultralites,* 2093 Goetz Road, Perris 92370, 943-8688. Introductory ultra-light flight lesson, $30 including half-hour of instruction and half-hour in the air. • *Orange Empire Railway Museum,* 2201 South A Street, Perris 92370, 657-2605. Open daily 9 A.M. to 5 P.M., but trolley rides offered only on weekends and holidays from 11 A.M. to 5 P.M. Museum entry free; all-day trolley passes cost $5, children 6 to 11 years $3. • *Perris Valley Historical Society Museum,* in old Perris railroad depot at 120 West 4th Street, Perris 92370, 657-5539. Open weekends 10 A.M. to 4 P.M. Free.

LODGING   *American Inn,* 1775 North Perris Boulevard, Perris 92370, 657-1002; $41. The only motel in Perris, 23 rooms; restaurant adjacent. Other accommodations in Moreno Valley.

CAMPING   *Lake Perris State Recreation Area* (see above). Open all year. Sites $8–$14, with hookup $12–$18. MISTIX reservations recommended Memorial Day weekend through Labor Day weekend; call toll-free (800) 444-7275.

DINING   Except for fast-food restaurants, Perris has few choices for dining out. *Amigos Tres,* 502 South D Street, Perris, 657-2636. Mexican fare for lunch and dinner daily. • *Richie's Real American Diner,* 1675 North Perris Boulevard, Perris, 657-3337. Open daily for hearty meals, including pot pie and barbecue. • *Taquito House,* 1019 South D Street, Perris, 657-3573. Mexican favorites for lunch and dinner daily. • *Carole's Feedbag,* 247 East 3rd Street, Perris, 657-6794. Hearty family fare for breakfast and lunch daily.

FOR MORE INFORMATION Perris Chamber of Commerce, 100 North D Street, Perris 92370, 657-3555. Open weekdays 8 A.M. to 5 P.M.

Lazy Days at Lake Elsinore and Glen Ivy Hot Springs

When you're eager for a casual outdoor weekend, escape inland to Riverside County and a popular state recreation area, Lake Elsinore, well known for its ups and downs. In the 1950s Lake Elsinore actually disappeared through evaporation and fissures in the lake bed. More than a decade passed before it was refilled with water from the Colorado River and underground springs. Then, in March 1980, the lake overflowed with melting snow and rainwater that poured down from the mountains encircling the Elsinore Valley. Most recently, there has been a project to stabilize the lake's water level, and recreational activities in and around the lake are going strong.

Since becoming a state recreation area in 1957, Lake Elsinore has been a favorite destination for boaters, water-skiers, and fishermen. Other sportsmen come to the valley to ride the thermal wind currents with a hang glider, soar in a glider plane, and sky-dive at the aviation center. Some settle for the weekend or longer in the state park campground at the lake's northwest end. In fact, many of Lake Elsinore's visitors are campers, because lodging in the area is limited to a few motels.

To reach the park and campground from Los Angeles, drive south on Interstate 5 to California 91, the Riverside Freeway, and follow it east just beyond Corona to the exit for Interstate 15 at the Lake Elsinore/San Diego sign. Go south to the California 74/Central Avenue exit and follow that state highway west to Lake Elsinore State Park Marina and Recreation Area.

Located at the base of the Elsinore Mountains in a valley that supports some agriculture and a growing number of housing developments, Lake Elsinore boasts a small town of the same name on its northern shore. Long ago the Indians knew the area as Etengvo Wumona, "hot springs by the little sea," and they came to soak away their aches and ills. Spanish explorers later named the lake Laguna Grande and it became part of the Rancho La Laguna land grant. A town was started in 1883 and called Laguna, but the state already had a community by that name, so Elsinore was chosen, in honor of the Danish town made famous by Shakespeare's Hamlet.

Thanks to its warm climate and hot springs, Lake Elsinore soon became a health resort. One of the original spa buildings still stands, the 1887 Crescent Bath House, now known as the Chimes and filled with antiques—as well as a resident ghost.

Drive there on Saturday from the state park by going back on California 74/Riverside Drive to Lakeshore Drive and following it east along the water. On the hillside overlooking the lake you'll see streetlights and impressive homes built by world-renowned evangelist Aimee Semple McPherson. When you reach the junior high school, bear left on Graham Avenue to the center of town, which has been spruced up with flower planters, trees, antique street lamps, and colorful awnings. Look left for a two-story colonial structure with fancy grillwork on the upper porch. The Chimes, a well-preserved redwood building, has been designated a national historic landmark. The large front rooms of this former bathhouse were the spa's recreation areas. Nowadays they're filled with vintage furniture, china, glassware, clocks, and other collectibles. Go down the long hall to see more antiques and the Roman-style bathtubs, as well as the former ladies' and gentlemen's massage rooms. One chamber is a minimuseum of Lake Elsinore memorabilia. Ask the Chimes's owners, Lory and Wilma Watts, about the poltergeist that occupies a room in their fascinating emporium of antiques.

To drive around the lake to see its sporting activities, follow Main Street past the town park to return to Lakeshore Drive. Go left and continue on Mission Trail, then turn right on Corydon Street toward the lake's southern end. A side road leads to an airfield which is headquarters for sky diving and soaring enthusiasts. Look to the sky to see the colorful parachutes and graceful glider planes in action.

To see hang gliders as they ride the currents along the top of the Elsinore Mountains, continue on Corydon Street to Grand Avenue. Then turn right to follow that road to California 74 at the Ortega Highway junction, which is just below the takeoff spot for these human butterflies.

Returning to Grand Avenue, continue circling the lake, and bear right on Riverside Drive to come back to the entrance of the state park. If it's summertime, when Elsinore Valley often heats up into the 90s, cool off with a dip in the lake. Or rent a rowboat, aquacycle, or pedal boat to cruise lazily on the water at twilight.

The next morning after breakfast, take Lakeshore Drive northwest from Riverside Drive and drive a mile to Terra Cotta Road and Torn Ranch, the valley's last walnut grove. Houses have replaced most of the walnut trees, but the ranch's rustic packing plant still stands, and has been converted to an old-time general store of gourmet food, wine, and gifts. Then continue north on Lake Street, which becomes Temescal Canyon Road and parallels the freeway before reaching the Glen Ivy Road, marked by a sign to Glen Ivy Recreational Vehicle Resort and Hot Springs Spa. Follow that country road a half mile past the RV camp to one of the Los Angeles area's oldest outdoor spas, Glen Ivy Hot Springs, a popular soaking spot since 1890 that's now dubbed "Club Mud."

Nestled in the foothills of the Santa Ana Mountains, this venerable health haven is a pleasant surprise for first-time visitors. With such a remote location, you'd hardly expect to find a full-size swimming pool of warm mineral water amid fruit orchards and restful palms. And there's much more: smaller therapy pools with bubbling 104-degree water straight from the hot springs, a shallow lounge pool where you can suntan on a raft, a warm wading area for the kids, individual whirlpool baths, an ocher-colored pool where bathers pat on red clay to tone up their skin, and private rooms for massages and wraps.

First to relax at the hot springs were the local Luiseno Indians, who named their valley Temescal after the sweathouses they built by the steaming water source. A hotel was erected to accommodate visitors during Glen Ivy's early days as a hot-springs resort. There is no longer any lodging, but spa bathing facilities have been expanded considerably. A single admission price lets you enjoy all the pools, including the Southland's only red clay bath, as well as aqua-exercise classes, a coed sauna, and sunning decks with plenty of lounge chairs. For additional fees you can get a shiatsu- or Swedish-style massage. Salt rubs and eucalyptus blanket wraps are also offered, along with facials and manicures.

With its elevation at 1,200 feet and in the path of ocean breezes, the spa boasts clear and invigorating air most of the year. Order a tasty salad or sandwich at Glen Ivy's snack bar and eat it poolside. Beer, wine, and other beverages are available too. Take towels, or rent them at the spa. Also, it's a good idea to have an old swimsuit for the red clay bath, because it may get stained. And don't forget suntan lotion. If you decide to spend another day at the spa, you'll find a lodging a few miles north in Corona; campers can bed down at the adjacent Glen Ivy RV Resort.

On your way home from Glen Ivy Hot Springs, continue north on Temescal Canyon Road, a rural highway that follows a route once used by Indians, pioneers, gold seekers, soldiers, and mail stages traveling between San Diego and Los Angeles. Along the way you can imagine those days of the Old West by renting a horse at El Cerrito Stables and riding on trails that crisscross the riverbed, hills, and fields in the Temescal Valley. Before reaching the stables, stop your car at Tom's Farms, an extensive roadside stand filled with fresh produce, dried fruit, nuts, and candies. You'll find plants, pottery, and baskets, too. Under a big tent is an antique mart with some originals as well as a variety of reproductions from other countries.

Before rejoining the freeway for the journey home, relax with refreshments from an adjacent self-service cafe that has outdoor tables overlooking a duck pond or continue on Temescal Canyon Road to a favorite local meal stop, the Live Oak Inn. Then head north on Interstate 15 to California 91 and go west to pick up Interstate 5 back to Los Angeles.

Round trip is about 180 miles.

Lake Elsinore Area Code: 909

SIGHTSEEING *Lake Elsinore State Park Marina and Recreation Area,* 32040 Riverside Drive (off California 74), Lake Elsinore, 674-3177. Day-use fee $4 per vehicle with 2 persons; extra persons $.50 each. Boat rentals and launching ramp. Also camping (see below). • *The Chimes,* 201 West Graham Avenue, Lake Elsinore, 674-3456. Open weekends only: 10 A.M. to 5 P.M. Saturdays, 11 A.M. to 4 P.M. Sundays. • *Torn Ranch,* 31307 Terra Cotta Road, Lake Elsinore, 674-2026. Open 10 A.M. to 5 P.M. except Tuesdays and Wednesdays. • *Glen Ivy Hot Springs,* 25000 Glen Ivy Road, south of Corona, 277-3529. Open 10 A.M. to 6 P.M. daily. Adults $16.75 weekends and holidays, $14.50 weekdays; $13.50 for senior citizens and children under age 13 on weekdays. • *El Cerrito Stables,* Temescal Canyon Road, south of Corona, 736-9075. Open daily from 8 A.M. to midnight. 150 rental horses for unguided rides over 1,000 acres of open range. One hour $15, second hour $10, third hour free. No reservations. • *Tom's Farms,* 23900 Temescal Canyon Road, south of Corona, 277-2857. Open from 8 A.M. to dusk daily. Cafe adjacent (see below).

LODGING *Lakeview Inn,* 31808 Casino Drive, Lake Elsinore 92330, 674-9694; $42. 55 rooms, 4 with whirlpool tubs ($60). • *Travelodge,* 31610 Casino Drive, Lake Elsinore 92330, 245-8998; $49. 60 rooms, 4 with whirlpool tubs ($68). • *Lake Park Resort,* 32000 Riverside Drive, Lake Elsinore 92330, 674-7911; motel room $36, cabin with kitchenette $44. Located on the lake with a marina and RV park ($16 per site with full hookup). • *Sahara Dunes Motel,* 20930 Malaga Road, Lake Elsinore 92330, 674-3101; $41. • *Executive Inn and Suites,* 1805 West 6th Street, Corona 91720, 371-7185; $42. 10 percent discount for Glen Ivy Hot Springs guests.

CAMPING *Lake Elsinore State Park Marina and Recreation Area,* 32040 Riverside Drive (off California 74), Lake Elsinore, 674-3177. 600 sites, $11.50 for 2 persons, extra persons $1 each; $3 additional for electrical hookup. • *Glen Ivy Recreational Vehicle Resort,* 24601 Glen Ivy Road, south of Corona, 227-4261. 350 sites, full hookup, $15–$18 per night. Swimming pool, tennis courts.

DINING Fast-food restaurants predominate in Lake Elsinore, but there are other choices. • *Manny's Grill,* 31706 Casino Drive, Lake Elsinore, 245-5040. Open daily with sandwiches, pizza, and steak. Breakfast also served. • *Golden Dragon Chinese Restaurant,* 31391 Riverside Drive, Lake Elsinore, 674-3080. Open daily. • *Park Plaza Family Restaurant,* 31731 Riverside Drive, Lake Elsinore, 674-5744. • *Ricco's Italian Restaurant,* 31361 Riverside Drive, Lake Elsinore, 245-9876. • *Knowlwood,* at Tom's Farms, 23900 Temescal Canyon Road, south of Corona, 277-2110. Boasts "the world's best hamburger." • *Live Oak Inn,* 21700 Temescal Road, Corona, 277-0605. Popular roadhouse with lunch weekdays and dinner daily except Mondays. Steaks, seafood, and Italian dishes.

FOR MORE INFORMATION Contact the Lake Elsinore Valley Chamber of Commerce, 132 West Graham Avenue (in the old train depot), Lake Elsinore 92330, 674-2577.

Historic Riverside, the "Inn" Place

The Mission Inn made Riverside the "in" spot for discriminating travelers more than half a century ago. In its heyday the imposing hotel welcomed six U.S. presidents, assorted royalty, stars of stage and screen, and business tycoons such as Henry Ford and John D. Rockefeller. Now designated both a state and national historic landmark, the inn is still a major attraction in Riverside, where the townsfolk are credited with saving this incomparable hostelry from the wrecker's ball. Covering an entire city block, the renovated hotel has been the keystone of Riverside's rejuvenated downtown. Unfortunately, financing problems have kept the Mission Inn from reopening as of the time this book went to press. Someday soon, however, you should be able to spend the night there, as did

Theodore Roosevelt, Grand Duke Alexander of Russia, Sarah Bernhardt, and other well-known visitors several decades ago.

Riverside's roots go back more than two centuries; explorer Juan Bautista de Anza camped there in 1774 on his first overland expedition in California. Founded as an agricultural colony, the town began to flourish at the side of the Santa Ana River and was incorporated in 1883. Riverside soon became one of the most prosperous places in the Southland, thanks to the navel orange from Bahia, Brazil, that was introduced a decade earlier.

Opulent Victorian homes and grand public buildings were erected amid acres of citrus groves, reflecting the city's status as the center of the Orange Empire. While many of those orchards have been lost to urban and industrial encroachment, much of historic Riverside remains and makes an enjoyable weekend. Get there from Los Angeles by driving east on California 60 to Riverside and exiting south on Market Street. Turn left at 7th Street and go a block to the Mission Inn, marked by a bell tower seven stories high.

Born as the Glenwood Cottage in 1876, the inn began as a two-story adobe boardinghouse run by the C. C. Miller family. Soon it was expanded to a 12-room hotel and managed by the eldest son, Frank. He devoted his life to the inn, eventually building the mission-style structure that Will Rogers once described as the most unique hotel in America. To decorate his inn, Frank traveled the world to gather antiques and other treasures, including a novel collection of bells and crosses. And he staged art exhibits, music recitals, and other cultural events that made the hotel a Southern California social center.

The Mission Inn's guest registers read like a *Who's Who* until the owner's death in 1935, and by the end of World War II the hotel had slipped from prominence and fell into disrepair. It was saved from demolition in 1976 by a determined citizens group and $2 million in city funds to purchase the property. After 80 guest rooms were refurbished and reopened, restoration work continued in order to bring all of the hotel back to its former glory. Then, in 1985, the entire Mission Inn complex was bought by an investment company and closed for a top-to-bottom renovation costing more than $40 million. At press time, it was still waiting to reopen as a 240-room world-class hotel. However, on Friday and Saturday mornings, you can take a free guided walking tour around the exterior of the inn led by volunteer docents of the Mission Inn Foundation. Meet at 10 A.M. at 6th and Main streets.

Once the inn reopens, there will be tours of the remarkable interior, including the St. Francis Chapel with its Tiffany stained-glass windows and eighteenth-century gold-leaf altar. The chapel was the marriage site for a number of Hollywood stars, including Bette Davis and Humphrey Bogart. In the chapel courtyard is the

Famous Flyers wall with plaques that honor and record the visits of prominent aviators, including Amelia Earhart and Orville Wright. The Mission Inn Foundation plans to open a museum in a former bank building at the corner of 7th and Main streets, which will feature much of Frank Miller's worldwide collection of bells and items that range from Oriental lacquer figures to Indian baskets. Memorabilia of the Miller family also will be on display, along with a model of the rambling inn.

Spend the afternoon browsing in the downtown shops and viewing more of the regal edifices that were erected earlier in this century with income from Riverside's orange groves. Much of the city's arresting architecture is concentrated in two blocks along 7th Street. Begin by looking across from the Mission Inn for wrought-iron balconies and a tile roof that mark the old Spanish-style city hall, now restored as an office building. On the opposite corner, across Orange Street, explore the marble-decorated Riverside Municipal Museum, built in 1912 as a post office. You'll find exhibits about area Indians, natural science, and local history, including the citrus industry. Across 7th Street you'll easily spot the Chinese Memorial Pavilion, an ornate shrine dedicated in 1897 to Riverside's Chinese pioneers.

A block away, at the corner with Lemon Street, two other eye-catching buildings along 7th Street are the First Unitarian Church, built of red sandstone brought from Arizona, and the mission-style Municipal Auditorium, crowned by a Moorish dome. Next door is the Riverside Art Museum, designed as a YWCA in 1929 by Julia Morgan, who gained fame as the architect of Hearst Castle at San Simeon. Drop in to view the permanent collection of artwork and buy some originals in the gallery shop. Lunch is served weekdays in the atrium.

Also be certain to stroll in another direction from the Mission Inn along the five-block Main Street pedestrian shopping mall. Capping one end is the city hall, designed with a modern version of the Spanish arch. On weekdays from its seventh-floor rooftop patio you can survey the thousands of ornamental trees that decorate this sprawling city. Walk another block to a beaux arts beauty, the Riverside County Courthouse, built in 1903 and modeled after the Grand Palace of Fine Arts in Paris. You can't miss its Ionic columns and classic statuary. At 3824 Main Street Mall, look for the 1930 Kress Building that's now the impressive California Museum of Photography, the largest space for photographic exhibitions on the West Coast. Since 1990 it's been the home of the University of California Riverside's multimillion-dollar collection of cameras and equipment, as well as photographic prints. A special feature is the Camera Obscura, where you can walk into the room-size apparatus and see images from outside projected onto the surrounding walls.

The next day you'll need your car to see more of historic and scenic Riverside. Head to a natural lookout in the heart of town, Mount Rubidoux, a city park on a bouldered mountain that rises to nearly 1,400 feet. Follow 7th Street several blocks northwest to Mount Rubidoux Drive, a narrow one-way road that spirals to a summit parking area near the World Peace Tower, dedicated to Frank Miller. In 1909 the Mission Inn owner initiated an Easter sunrise service on the mountaintop, now an annual Riverside event held at the huge concrete cross that was erected two years earlier as a monument to the founder of California's famed missions, Father Junipero Serra.

After enjoying a bird's-eye view of the Riverside area, especially worthwhile on a clear winter's day, descend carefully via the twisting road that joins Glenwood Drive and leads to 14th Street. Head east to the intersection of Market Street and Magnolia Avenue and turn right to go south on Magnolia. It leads to another busy intersection with Arlington Avenue, where you'll spot a tiny triangle of citrus trees behind a wrought-iron fence. Park where you can to have a close-up view of the Parent Navel Orange Tree, sole survivor of the original seedless orange stock planted in Riverside in 1873. This living historical landmark, which still bears fruit, is the ancestor of the thousands of trees that created the area's multimillion-dollar citrus industry. Also growing there is another honored fruit tree, the grapefruit, introduced to the Southland from Florida.

Continue south on Magnolia Avenue, which widens into a divided boulevard bordered by fan palms, eucalyptus, and pepper trees and brings you to the Heritage House, a restored Victorian mansion built in 1891. See its exquisite period decorations by taking a guided tour of that elegant home, now part of the Riverside Municipal Museum. Besides a beautiful staircase, tile-faced fireplaces, and gas-lamp fixtures, you'll like the Oriental rugs, oil paintings, clocks, and antique furniture.

A trio of schools line the left side of Magnolia Avenue as the boulevard continues southwest, beginning with the Spanish-style buildings of California Baptist College. After passing a public school, circle back at Jackson Street on the other side of the avenue to Sherman Indian High School, a federally run boarding school that opened in 1902 to educate young Native Americans from the area. One of the original buildings on this now-modernized campus is a museum of Indian artifacts. You'll see some wonderful beadwork, baskets, pottery, dolls, and other handicrafts, as well as dioramas that portray the California, Plains, Hopi, and Cherokee Indian cultures.

Heading southwest again on Magnolia Avenue, turn left on Van Buren Boulevard to join California 91 and then Interstate 5 back to Los Angeles.

Round trip is about 120 miles.

Riverside Area Code: 909

SIGHTSEEING *Mission Inn,* 3649 7th Street, Riverside 92501. 1-hour guided tours of the hotel's exterior are offered Fridays and Saturdays at 10 A.M. by volunteers of the Mission Inn Foundation, 781-8241. Ask if the foundation's Mission Inn Museum is open. ● *Riverside Municipal Museum,* 7th Street at Orange Street, Riverside 92501, 782-5273. Open weekends from 1 to 5 P.M., weekdays except Mondays from 9 A.M. to 5 P.M. Free. ● *Riverside Art Museum,* 3425 7th Street, Riverside 92501, 684-7111. Open Monday through Friday 10 A.M. to 5 P.M., Saturdays to 4 P.M.; closed Sundays. Also closed the last week of August and first week of September. Admission $1, under 12 years free. ● *California Museum of Photography,* 3824 Main Street Mall, Riverside 92501, 784-3686. Most significant collection of camera equipment and photo prints in the western United States. Open daily except Mondays from 10 A.M. to 5 P.M., Sundays from noon. Adults $2, students and seniors $1, after 13 years free. ● *Mount Rubidoux Memorial Park,* via Mount Rubidoux Drive from 7th Street, Riverside, 782-5301. Road open to cars only (no RVs or trailers) Sundays from 9 A.M. to 5 P.M. and Mondays, Tuesdays, and Wednesdays to 3 P.M. Closed to vehicles Thursday through Saturday; hikers and joggers welcome every day. Free. Pilgrimage to the summit for sunrise service on Easter Sunday. ● *Heritage House,* 8193 Magnolia Avenue, Riverside 92503, 689-1333. Guided tours on Sundays from 12 to 3:30 P.M., Tuesdays and Thursdays from 12 to 2:30 P.M. Donation $1 adults, $.50 children and senior citizens. ● *Sherman Indian Museum,* 9010 Magnolia Avenue at Sherman Indian High School, Riverside 92503, 276-6337. Open weekends by appointment, weekdays from 1 to 3 P.M. Closed July through Labor Day. Free; donations appreciated.

LODGING *Sheraton Riverside Hotel,* 3400 Market Street, Riverside 92501, 784-8000, $89. 12-story downtown hotel with 296 rooms across from city's convention center. Two restaurants and lounge with live music. ● Riverside has a "motel row" west of downtown along University Avenue. *Holiday Inn,* 1200 University Avenue, Riverside 92507, 682-8000; $68. ● *Hampton Inn,* 1590 University Avenue, Riverside 92507, 683-6000; $68, with continental breakfast buffet. ● *Days Inn,* 1510 University Avenue, Riverside 92507, 788-8989; $65. Coffee shop on premises.

DINING *The Atrium* in the Riverside Art Museum (see above), 369-9478. Light lunches served weekdays from 11 A.M. to 1:30 P.M.

• *Pedrito's Bar & Grill,* 3597 Main Street, Riverside, 686-1092. Mexican specialties. • *Carlos O'Brien,* 3667 Riverside Plaza, Riverside, 686-5860. Mexican fare. • Many chain restaurants along University Avenue. *Cask 'N Cleaver,* 1333 University Avenue, Riverside, 682-4580. Dinner from 5 P.M. nightly. Prime rib and more.

FOR MORE INFORMATION   Contact the Riverside Visitors and Convention Bureau, 3443 Orange Street (at Ben H. Lewis Hall, Riverside's Convention Center), Riverside 92501, 787-7950.

Fallbrook and Temecula for Antiques and a Taste of the Grape

You'll rekindle lots of childhood memories with a visit to Fallbrook, home for a number of antique shops brimming with memorabilia. And Fallbrook's fertile rolling countryside abounds with avocados, a prized taste treat that's featured in the town's restaurants and sold at roadside stands with all kinds of other homegrown fruit. Not far away is another old-time town, Temecula, that's also popular with antique seekers. It has become known for quality wines as well, and you'll have fun on a tasting tour of the area's wineries.

Embark on a relaxing rural weekend in northern San Diego County by driving south from Los Angeles on Interstate 5 to join California 91 (the Riverside Freeway) heading west, then turn south on Interstate 15. At Temecula, exit on California 79 south to go under the freeway, turn right on Pala Road at the first stop sign, then go right again on Rainbow Canyon Road to the Temecula Creek Inn. With its 27 holes of championship golf, the countryside retreat is a favorite of golfers and a pleasant place to headquarter for the weekend.

In the morning continue south on Interstate 15 to California 76 and exit west toward Oceanside to begin an antiquing escapade. Drive about eight miles, and just before crossing the San Luis Rey River, look right for the Bonsall Antique Mall. In the large historic building, once a dance hall and restaurant, you can browse through the Americana collections of 25 antique dealers. It's like being in a Grandmother's attic. Among the treasures are Depression glass, fine china, dolls and toys, solid oak furniture, and vintage kitchenware.

Go back on California 76 through Bonsall, then bear left on San Diego County Road S13/Mission Road to find more antique shops and reach Fallbrook's friendly downtown with its delightful restaurants. Along Mission Road, pull in at the Fallbrook Stage Stop, where four shops are filled with collectibles.

Once in town, don't miss Kirk's Antiques on North Orange Avenue, occupying one of Fallbrook's oldest homes. It's also the residence of the dealer, Kirk Kirkeeng, who will show you around. Weddings often take place in his lush garden beneath a 200-year-old pepper tree, where he also holds occasional luncheon fashion shows of vintage clothes. Other shops with mementos of the past include the Carved Lion and A Gaggle, both on South Main Street.

Besides antiquing, eating out is a treat in Fallbrook. At the top of the list is the Packing House, built in 1930 on South Main Street as a meat market. Meals are now served in a cozy book-lined dining room. Tucked upstairs in a building on North Main Street is Le Bistro, praised for its California cuisine.

If you'd rather picnic, take Stage Coach Lane from Mission Road to Reche Road and head east to Live Oak Park, a favorite spot for family outings in Fallbrook. After your lunch in the park, go back on Reche Road and bear right on Live Oak Park Road to The Collector, at number 912. Behind its unassuming facade is an elegant shop that's also a museum of gemstones from all over the globe. Tourmaline, opal, topaz, garnet, quartz, and other gems are displayed in rough and polished forms, and you'll be tempted by the exquisite handcrafted jewelry sparkling with the colored stones.

For the final day of your weekend, head north from Fallbrook on Interstate 15 to the Rancho California Road exit that leads under the freeway to Temecula. It's not quite St. Helena or Calistoga or one of the other quaint wine towns of the Napa Valley, but the once easygoing frontier town of Temecula has become the focal point of Riverside County's nouveau wine country. Test vineyards in Temecula Valley were planted in 1966, and now the area boasts 13 wineries. Visitors are welcome at most of them for tours and tastings, as well as other Temecula attractions that include a host of antique shops.

Temecula first flourished as a stop on the Butterfield Stage run and then was the trading center for the vast Vail cattle ranch that surrounded the town. In the mid-1960s the Kaiser Aluminum corporation acquired 90,000 acres of the ranchland to establish a sprawling planned community, Rancho California. Currently, 3,000 acres are covered with orderly rows of grapes watered by drip irrigation. The vineyards and wineries begin about four miles east of Temecula, and you can embark on a circular wine tour by going east on Rancho California Road. Start early if you'd like to see them all.

Make your first stop the Hart Winery, marked by a small sign on the left side of the highway. Drive up the dirt road to the hilltop building that houses the one-man operation of Joe Hart, a former junior high school teacher. He's usually around on weekends; look for his pickup truck. If the bearded wine maker isn't too busy, he'll show you the winery and let you sample his medal-winning cabernet sauvignon and other wines.

The adjacent winery along Rancho California Road is the Temecula area's biggest and best known, Callaway. Stop here first if you have time to visit only one or two wineries. Retired businessman Ely Callaway, who planted his first grapes nearly two decades ago, sold Callaway Vineyards and Winery in 1981 to Canadian liquor giant Hiram Walker in a multimillion-dollar deal. Praised for its chenin blanc and other whites, Callaway offers daily tours of the modern winery, where annual production has reached more than two million bottles. There's wine tasting (for a fee), and if you've brought a picnic lunch, buy a bottle to have with your alfresco meal at tables shaded by a grape arbor. Small signs near the picnic area identify the different varieties of grapevines, and you can climb a platform for a view of the vineyards and rolling countryside.

On the other side of Rancho California Road is the impressive John Culbertson Winery, which also features a restaurant that was established by John's wife, Martha. The couple began producing sparkling wine at their Fallbrook avocado ranch in 1981, but couldn't keep up with the demand for their champagne, which is produced by the traditional French *méthode Champenoise*. Seven years later they opened the larger winery and Cafe Champagne in Temecula Valley and quickly became a major attraction in the wine country. You can watch the chef and his staff in the open kitchen of this French-style cafe, which is a highlight of any Temecula tour. Enjoy a delicious lunch or dinner indoors or out on the lattice-shaded patio, and pay to taste five sparkling wines.

Just down the road you'll find the much smaller Piconi Winery, which was established by a Fallbrook doctor in 1981. Ribbons awarded John Piconi for his white, red, and rose vintages are displayed in the tasting room at the winery, which is now owned by Ben Drake.

Next door and hidden among the grapevines is the area's oldest winery, Mount Palomar. Look for the entrance marked by a wooden wine cask on Rancho California Road. John Poole, who once owned L.A.'s KBIG radio station, opened the winery in 1975 and now has nine varietals for sale, including a riesling that always wins a gold medal at the yearly Orange County Fair. Members of the Poole family take visitors on tours, and you're welcome to sample Mount Palomar wines in the tasting room. There also are delicious deli goods to buy for a picnic at shaded tables outside.

A hilltop tasting room of the Baily Winery offers samples of various vintages, which are made at their vineyards elsewhere in the valley.

If you have time to continue your wine tour, keep going east on Rancho California Road, turn right at the sign to the Cilurzo Winery, and go up the dirt Calle Contento Road. On weekends you're likely to meet Vince Cilurzo, lighting director for Hollywood TV shows. He started the family-run winery in 1978, ten years after planting the area's first commercial vineyard. Vince and his wife, Audrey, offer visitors informal tours and tasting. Cilurzo has several red wines for sale, some of them medal winners at the L.A. and Orange County fairs.

Go back down to Rancho California Road and cross over on Calle Contento to the hilltop winery of Clos du Muriel. The redwood and stained-glass building hosts tours and tastings. Visitors get a panoramic view of the vineyards from this modern winery, where a tasting counter is set up by the aging barrels and storage vats.

Going east again on Rancho California Road, you'll spot the Maurice Carrie Winery, a labor of love for Budd Van Roekel and his wife, Maurice. Besides tasting various vintages, you can picnic on the premises with food from the winery's deli.

To complete your circle winery tour, turn right from Rancho California Road onto Glenoaks Road before reaching Lake Skinner. When Glenoaks Road dead-ends, turn right on De Portola Road and follow it to the Filsinger Winery. Operated by Anaheim pediatrician Bill Filsinger and his wife, Kathy, the small winery has won medals at the L.A. County Fair. You can taste their award-winning wines on a weekend tour.

Farther along De Portola Road, look for the entrance to the Baily Vineyard on unpaved Pauba Road and go about a half mile to the family-run winery of Carol and Phil Baily. You can sample their vintages on weekends, or daily at the tasting room on Rancho California Road.

Return to Temecula by going right on De Portola Road past country ranch estates, then left on Anza Road and right on California 79. It goes north under the freeway, becomes Front Street, and leads you to the center of the older part of town. Turn left on Main Street to a historical building, the 1891 Temecula Mercantile, where 26 antique dealers display and sell their nostalgic collections. Across the street you'll see the two-story Temecula Hotel, rebuilt 90 years ago after a fire destroyed the original 1882 hostelry. Today the building is a private residence. The Emporium, also on Main Street, is another haven for antique hunters, and more vintage goods are for sale in Butterfield Square and other stores on Front Street.

On the corner at Front and Main streets you'll spot a brick

building that was built as a bank in 1912, with a second story that once saw duty as the community's dance hall. The Bank is now a Mexican restaurant, and the most private tables are in the vault.

An exciting way to view Temecula's wine country is aboard a hot-air balloon. Several ballooning companies take flight with early-morning winds over the rolling countryside. All celebrate the 45- to 90-minute flights with the traditional toast of champagne. In May you can join in the annual Temecula Valley Balloon and Wine Festival.

When it's time to return to Los Angeles, follow Interstate 15 and Interstate 215 north to join California 60 (Pomona Freeway) and head west.

Round trip is about 248 miles.

Fallbrook Area Code: 619
Temecula Area Code: 909

SIGHTSEEING   *Bonsall Antique Mall,* off California 76, Bonsall 92003, 758-0363. 25 shops open 10 A.M. to 5 P.M. daily. • Note: Fallbrook's antique shops usually open at 10 or 11 A.M. and close at 4 or 5 P.M.; most are closed on Mondays and Tuesdays. • *Kirk's Antiques,* 321 North Orange Avenue, Fallbrook 92028, 728-6333. • *Fallbrook Stage Stop,* 3137 South Mission Road, Fallbrook 92028, has 4 shops: Ivy House, Tin Barn, Millie's Antiquities, and Country Elegance. • *Carved Lion,* 128 South Main Street, Fallbrook 92028, 728-7323. • *A Gaggle,* 111 South Main Street, Fallbrook 92028, 723-0838. • *The Collector,* 912 South Live Oak Park Road, Fallbrook 92028, 728-9191. Precious gems, fine jewelry, minerals, shells, and fossils. Open daily from 10 A.M. to 5 P.M. • *Temecula Mercantile,* Main Street, Temecula 92590, 676-2722. Vintage furniture and other goods from 26 dealers. Open daily from 10 A.M. to 5 P.M. (some closed on Tuesdays). • *The Emporium,* Main Street, Temecula 92590, 676-2002. A trio of antique shops; look for the early-day slot machines. • *DAE Flights,* P.O. Box 1671, Temecula 92590, 676-3902. Hot-air balloon rides for 1 hour or longer, $125 per person ($100 for ages 13 and younger). • Also, *Southern California Balloons,* P.O. Box 1052, Lake Elsinore 92330, 244-3511. • *Hart Winery,* 32500 Rancho California Road, Temecula 92591, 676-6300. Open 9 A.M. to 5 P.M. weekends. • *Callaway Vineyard and Winery,* 32720 Rancho California Road, Temecula 92591, 676-4001. Open daily 10 A.M. to 5 P.M., with tours on the hour from 11 A.M. Free; optional tasting at end of the tour costs $2. Bring your own picnic. • *John Culbertson Winery,* 32575 Rancho California Road, Temecula 92592, 699-0099. Open daily from 10 A.M. to 6 P.M. (to 7 P.M. Fridays and Saturdays), but tours only on weekends. Tasting of 5 champagnes, $5. Also excellent restaurant, Cafe Champagne, open daily from 11 A.M. to 9 P.M. • *Mount Palomar Winery,* 33820 Rancho California Road, Temecula 92591, 676-5047. Open daily from 9 A.M. to 5 P.M., with tours at 1:30 and 3:30 P.M., plus 11:30 A.M. on weekends. • *Cilurzo Vineyards and Winery,* 41220 Calle Contento (off Rancho California Road), Temecula 92592, 676-5250. Open 9:30 A.M. to 4:45 P.M. daily. • *Maurice Carrie Winery,* 34225 Rancho California Road, Temecula 92592, 676-1711. Open 10 A.M. to 5 P.M. daily. • *Clos du Muriel,* 40620 Calle Contento, Temecula 92591, 699-3199. Open daily from 10 A.M. to 5 P.M. • *Filsinger Vineyards and Winery,* 39050 De Portola Road, Temecula 92592, 676-4594. Open 10 A.M. to 5 P.M. weekends, weekdays by appointment. • *Baily Winery,* 36150 Pauba Road (off De Portola Road), Temecula 92592, 676-9463. Open weekends 10 A.M. to 5 P.M. Tasting room at 33833 Rancho California Road is open 10 A.M. to 5 P.M. Wednesday through Sunday.

EVENTS *Temecula Valley Balloon and Wine Festival,* sponsored by the Temecula Valley Chamber of Commerce (see below), in May. Hot-air balloon races and rides, wine tasting, arts-and-crafts fair, and entertainment highlight the weekend fest.

LODGING *Temecula Creek Inn,* 44501 Rainbow Canyon Road (via Pala Road from California 79), Temecula 92592, 676-5631 or toll-free (800) 962-7335; $105. Rural resort with 84 rooms overlooking 27-hole golf course. Also 2 tennis courts and excellent restaurant (see below). • *Lome Vista Bed and Breakfast,* 33350 La Serena Way, Temecula 92591, 676-7047; $95–$125. Modern 6-room B&B amid the vineyards in the wine country. All private baths. Full breakfast. • *Doubletree Suites Hotel,* 29345 Rancho California Road, Temecula 92591, 676-5656 or toll-free (800) 528-0444; $89–$99. 136 well-furnished 2-room suites. Include refrigerator and microwave. • *Butterfield Inn,* 28718 Front Street, Temecula 92590, 676-4833; $45. Nice motel in historic part of town.

DINING *Temet Grill* in the Temecula Creek Inn (see above). Resort's fine restaurant overlooks golf course. Open daily for all meals (continental cuisine in evening), plus Sunday brunch. Entertainment in the lounge on weekends. • *The Packing House,* 125

South Main Street, Fallbrook, 728-5458. Seafood and beef dishes for lunch and dinner daily, plus champagne brunch on Sunday. • *Le Bistro,* 119 North Main Street, Fallbrook, 723-3559. Dinner daily except Mondays; reservations only. • *The Bank of Mexican Food,* 28645 Front Street, Temecula, 676-6160. Lunch and dinner daily. • Also, *Cafe Champagne* at the John Culbertson Winery (see above).

FOR MORE INFORMATION   Contact the Fallbrook Chamber of Commerce, 233-A East Mission Road, Fallbrook 92028, 728-5845. Also, the Temecula Valley Chamber of Commerce, 40945 County Center Drive, Suite C, Temecula 92591, 676-5090.

Wild Animals and Wunnerful Music Near Escondido

You don't have to leave the United States to find out what it's like to go on a safari. Just head to the Wild Animal Park, a vast preserve that's home for more than 2,500 mammals, reptiles, and birds. One of the most exciting ways to see and photograph the wildlife is to hop in the back of an open flatbed truck and be driven inside the 2,100-acre enclosure for a close-up view of its exotic residents.

That novel safari will be a highlight of a delightful weekend exploring along San Diego County back roads through the rocky countryside and fertile valleys that surround Escondido. Along with the wild animals, this wunnerful trip includes a museum honoring one of America's best-known bandleaders, Lawrence Welk. You also can tour three of the county's oldest and newest wineries and visit one of the early California missions that continues to serve the Indians.

Make your headquarters at the Rancho Bernardo Inn, a well-known golf and tennis resort. Overnight guests and day visitors are welcome to play the resort's 45 holes of golf and dine in the inn's excellent El Bizcocho restaurant. You'll need to dress for dinner, when some of the area's finest continental cuisine is served by candlelight. Casual attire is okay for other meals in the hotel's restaurants, including Sunday brunch, and you'll notice that some guests never change from their tennis togs or spa attire; the resort features a full-fledged tennis college and 16 courts, as well as a spa and fitness center.

Get to the Rancho Bernardo Inn by driving south from Los Angeles on Interstate 5 and turning inland beyond Oceanside on California 78. Just before reaching Escondido, join Interstate 15 going south and then exit east on Rancho Bernardo Road. Follow it through ever-growing suburbia to Bernardo Oaks Drive and turn left to the entrance of the impressive resort.

In the morning after breakfast at the inn, dress casually for a day at the wild-animal preserve. Head back north on Interstate 15 to the Via Rancho Parkway exit and go east to join San Pasqual Road, which leads to California 78 (San Pasqual Valley Road). Turn right and continue east one mile through the countryside to the San Diego Wild Animal Park.

The reserve was established in 1972 to help scientists learn about breeding in captivity in order to save many species of animals from extinction. Among the animals on the endangered list that have given birth in the park are the rare Indian one-horned rhinoceros, lowland gorillas, South African cheetahs, Arabian oryx, addax, slender-horned gazelles, and Przewalski's wild horses. A major objective of the nonprofit park, which is operated by the Zoological Society of San Diego, is to provide living conditions similar to the animals' native homelands while allowing visitors to observe the wild creatures.

The most popular way to view them is aboard the Wgasa Bush Line Monorail, which makes a five-mile circle tour through the animals' varied habitats in the vast parkland. Bring binoculars and a telephoto camera lens for even closer views. A guide on the silent tour train identifies the different species and describes their living habits as you glide along.

For closer encounters, reserve in advance for one of the special Photo Caravans that take you in the back of a truck to see the animals. Because food is brought to them in tan trucks like those used for these safari tours, you'll have some thrilling moments when the more fearless animals come right up to your vehicle in hopes of a handout. For views of species like lions, Sumatran tigers, and cheetahs, which are kept segregated in other natural enclosures, you can stroll along the Kilimanjaro Hiking Trail, a 1¼-mile path with observation points and places to picnic.

Visitors to the park also get to enjoy various wildlife exhibits, including an immense aviary that's home for more than 100 tropical African birds. You can walk through a climate-controlled green-house displaying delicate species that include butterflies and tropical hummingbirds. Another enclosed area re-creates a tropical Asian rain forest where more exotic birds can be observed easily. Through windows of the nursery you can watch newborn animals being cared for by park attendants acting as substitute mothers. And children like the kraal, where they can pet and feed gazelle, deer, and antelope.

It's also fun to observe the family of gorillas cavorting on the grassy terrace of their special grotto.

Be sure to attend the shows that reveal the natural behavior and intelligence of animals, including wolves, bears, coyotes, raccoons, and opossums. Trained birds also take the stage daily in the outdoor amphitheater. The Wild Animal Park is a botanical reserve, too, with nearly two million flowers, plants, trees, and shrubs. You'll enjoy them in the tropical Asian and Australian rain forests, along the Kilimanjaro Trail, and in Nairobi Village, the park's exhibit and entertainment area, where meals and snacks also are available.

If it's not too late when you leave the park, plan to stop at a winery or two on your way back to the Rancho Bernardo Inn. Return west on California 78 and turn left on San Pasqual Road at the sign to San Diego. Drive through the scenic San Pasqual Valley, an agricultural preserve, until you see rows of grapevines and the entrance to the Thomas Jaeger Winery. This modern hilltop winery opened in 1977 and visitors are welcome for informal touring and tasting. Several Thomas Jaeger wines already have won high praise from wine critics and medals at county fairs.

Continue on San Pasqual Road, then go left at Via Rancho Parkway to join Interstate 15. Head south and take the first exit, Pomerado Road, toward Rancho Bernardo. Turn left on Paseo Verano Norte and drive a mile through the housing developments to the Bernardo Winery, established in 1889. You're welcome to look around this old-fashioned winery and sample its products. Added attractions are several gift shops on the vineyard grounds, as well as a snack bar and picnic area. Return to the inn by going back to Pomerado Road, turning left to Rancho Bernardo Road, and then right to Bernardo Oaks Drive.

Enjoy the resort's evening entertainment and dance music, and in the morning lounge by the pool or have a game of tennis or round of golf topped off by Sunday brunch. Then check out and go north on Interstate 15 to the Deer Springs Road/Mountain Meadow Road exit and turn left immediately on Champagne Boulevard. It parallels the freeway north to Lawrence Welk Drive and the Lawrence Welk Resort, which the bandleader developed as part of an attractive mobile-home community.

Many visitors come to see the theater-museum that traces the accordion squeezer's life from North Dakota farm boy to headliner on the longest-running weekly musical show in television history, 27 consecutive years. Stand by a life-size cutout photo of the maestro and see yourself on television with Lawrence Welk.

The Lawrence Welk Resort Theater also presents live musical productions of favorite Broadway musicals, such as *A Chorus Line, Fiddler on the Roof, My Fair Lady,* and *Hello, Dolly!* There are daily matinees, or choose an evening show preceded by a buffet meal and cocktails served in the Resort Restaurant. Day-long Sunday brunch and other meals also are available in that dining room, where choice tables overlook the resort's verdant par-three golf course. (Adjacent is a 130-room inn that's a less expensive alternative to weekending at Rancho Bernardo.) Nearby at the Resort Center is a variety of shops.

If you like wine or classic cars, continue north on Champagne Boulevard to Deer Park, a roadside enterprise that combines a car museum, vineyards, wine-tasting rooms, deli, and gift shop. The museum features classic convertibles ranging from a 1953 Cadillac Eldorado to a tiny Nash Metropolitan. Also look for a 1956 Chevrolet Corvette, a 1957 Ford with a retractable hardtop, and an ill-starred Edsel. You'll get a kick out of the original factory list prices displayed with each auto; $550 would have bought you the 1928 Model A Ford. The wines are from Deer Park Winery, a Napa Valley vineyard owned by two San Diego couples who decided to open a wine-tasting outlet in Southern California. After looking over the vintage vehicles, buy a bottle of Deer Park sauvignon blanc, chardonnay, petite sirah, or zinfandel and order deli sandwiches for a picnic at the tables outside.

Before returning to Los Angeles, continue on Champagne Boulevard to rejoin Interstate 15 north, then exit east on California 76 and go about five miles past dairy farms and fields to San Diego County S16, Pala Mission Road. Turn left and continue a mile more to Mission San Antonio de Pala on the Pala Indian Reservation. It was built in 1816 as an *asistencia,* a branch of the San Luis Rey mission for Indians living inland. Of all the missions established by the Spanish padres, Pala is one of the few that continue to serve the Indians today, providing both a chapel and school for the people at Pala and other reservations in the area. Notice that the bell tower, modeled after one in Juarez, Mexico, is separate from the main building. Behind this companile you'll find the old cemetery where hundreds of Indians and pioneers are buried beneath a pair of ancient pepper trees. Walk into the long, dark chapel which was constructed and decorated by the Indians, where worship services are still conducted daily. The mission building's history and its unusual altar statues are described in a display case outside.

Also in the main building is a minimuseum with the original Indian-carved religious statues and other mission relics. There you also can buy silk-screened Christmas cards made from drawings by the mission schoolchildren. After your visit, return to Los Angeles by going back to Interstate 15 and driving north to join California 91 (Riverside Freeway) and then Interstate 5.

Round trip is about 250 miles.

Escondido Area Code: 619

SIGHTSEEING *San Diego Wild Animal Park,* 6 miles east of Escondido on California 78 (15500 San Pasqual Valley Road, Escondido 92027), 747-8702. Open daily 9 A.M. to 4 P.M. plus extended evening hours mid-June through Labor Day. Adults $15.95, children 3 to 15 years $8.95. Kids age 2 and under free. Wgasa Bush Line Monorail ride, animal shows, and other entertainment included in all entry tickets. Photo Caravans through the reserve in a truck operate May through September by reservation only, with departures weekends, Wednesdays, and Thursdays. 1¾-hour tours at 2:30 and 4:30 P.M. cost adults $60, children 12 to 15 years $45. 3½-hour tour at 2:30 P.M. costs adults $85, children $60. No children under age 12 allowed on Photo Caravans. Buy food and drink in the park, or bring a picnic. • *Thomas Jaeger Winery,* 13455 San Pasqual Road, Escondido 92025, 745-3553. Tasting room open daily from 10 A.M. to 6 P.M. Free. Tours daily at 11:30 A.M., 1:30, 3, and 4 P.M. • *Bernardo Winery,* 13330 Paseo del Verano Norte, Rancho Bernardo 92128, 487-1866. Open daily 9 A.M. to 5 P.M. Free. Gift shops open Wednesday through Sunday from 11 A.M. to 5 P.M. • *Lawrence Welk Resort Theater-Museum,* 8845 Lawrence Welk Drive, Escondido 92026, 749-3448. Free museum open daily from 10 A.M. to 1 P.M. (to 5 P.M. Mondays, Fridays, and Saturdays). Also, Broadway musicals staged daily except Mondays at 1:45 and 8 P.M. Tickets $26–$31; with preshow buffet lunch or dinner $29–$36. Call for show schedule and reservations. • *Deer Park,* 29013 Champagne Boulevard, Escondido 92026, 749-1666. Open daily from 10 A.M. to 5 P.M. Vintage car museum and wine tasting, plus deli and gift shop. • *Mission San Antonio de Pala,* Pala Mission Road (or P.O. Box 70), Pala 92059, 742-3317. Mission chapel open daily. Museum open daily except Mondays from 10:30 A.M. to 3 P.M. Admission $1, children under 12 years $.25.

LODGING *Rancho Bernardo Inn,* 17550 Bernardo Oaks Drive, Rancho Bernardo 92128, 487-1611 or California toll-free (800) 542-6096; $130–$185 seasonally, suites from $165. Golf, tennis, and spa packages available. Casual dining in the Veranda Room or outside on the terrace. Music and dancing evenings in the adjacent lounge. Gourmet meals and Sunday brunch served in El Bizcocho (see below). • *Lawrence Welk Resort,* 8860 Lawrence Welk Drive, Escondido 92026, 749-3000 or California toll-free (800) 932-9355; $100. Also theater package. A favorite of the senior set. Par-3 golf, tennis, and popular restaurant (see below). Adjacent Resort Center has gift shops and Lawrence Welk Resort Theater-Museum (see above).

DINING *El Bizcocho* in Rancho Bernardo Inn (see above). French cuisine for dinner in an award-winning restaurant. Wine list carries more than 700 vintages. Popular for Sunday brunch. Reservations required for all meals; jackets for men after 6 P.M. ● *Resort Restaurant* at Lawrence Welk Resort (see above). Hearty fare for breakfast, lunch, and dinner. A favorite is Lawrence's own chicken and dumplings. Sunday buffet served from noon to 4 P.M. ($13.95 adults, $7 children). Also, lunch and dinner buffets for theatergoers.

FOR MORE INFORMATION Contact the Escondido Visitors and Convention Bureau, 720 North Broadway, Escondido 92025, 745-4741. Open Monday through Friday from 8:30 A.M. to 5 P.M., Saturdays from 9 A.M. to 4 P.M. Also call toll-free (800) 848-3336 for 24-hour interactive recorded information.

Retreating to Rancho Santa Fe and Lake San Marcos

A blunder by the Atcheson, Topeka, and Santa Fe Railroad has become a benefit for the fortunate folks who live in one of Southern California's most exclusive enclaves, Rancho Santa Fe. The setting for that private community of elegant estates is a forest of eucalyptus trees that were planted for railroad ties. Spend a relaxing weekend there and in a newer residential retreat, Lake San Marcos, to sample their leisurely life-styles. Both are located in San Diego's bucolic north county area, only a few miles inland from the freeway and encroaching urbanization.

Drive south from Los Angeles on Interstate 5 and exit east on Lomas Santa Fe Drive at Solana Beach. This also is San Diego County road S8 and becomes Linea del Cielo as it winds past expansive ranch-style manors and leads to the tranquil village center of Rancho Santa Fe. The area originally was covered with scrub brush at the time a Mexican land grant gave the terrain to an early mayor of San Diego, Juan Maria Osuna. He named his 8,800 acres Rancho San Diequito and used it to graze cattle. After Osuna's heirs sold the land to the Santa Fe railway in 1906, more than three million eucalyptus seeds were imported from Australia and planted. Lumber was needed to make ties for the booming railroad, and it was reported that eucalyptus grew quickly in such an arid environment. Unfortunately, no one had checked to see if the wood would splinter when driven with spikes. The forest was a failure for the railroad, but a blessing for future homeowners.

Today the lofty eucalyptus offer dignity, shade, and fragrance to handsome country estates, which also are adorned with fruit orchards and riding horses. Residents of the Ranch, as they affectionately call their community, gather to gossip, shop, and dine in the minuscule business area that extends from the village's landmark hostelry, the Inn at Rancho Santa Fe. This rambling public showplace was the keystone of the planned community that the railroad's land-development subsidiary began in 1922. Nowadays the 20-acre resort allows visitors to slip into the easy yet swank life-style that is a main attraction for the Ranch's 5,000 residents. Check into one of the Inn's lodge rooms or garden cottages, then dress up for dinner in its Vintage Room restaurant. Have after-dinner drinks in the lounge, filled with the innkeeper's family heirlooms.

In the morning you can volley tennis balls on the resort's own trio of courts, play a quiet game of American six-wicket croquet on the front lawn, or swim and lounge at the heated pool. For a substantial greens fee, guests at the family-run Inn also have privileges at Rancho Santa Fe's 18-hole country club golf course in the afternoon.

Stroll through the village's 2½-block-long business district and you'll discover some lovely stores, such as the Country Friends Shop. Although appearing to be an antique store, it's actually Rancho Santa Fe's secondhand thrift shop, and all proceeds go to charity. You'll also enjoy browsing in the Two Goats, a fashionable clothing store.

The Ranch has some delightful places to eat, including the well-known and very expensive Mille Fleurs, where the menu features French cuisine. Much more casual is Quimby's.

After another night at the Inn, go west from Rancho Santa Fe on La Granada, which is county road S9 and becomes La Bajada and then Encinitas Boulevard. When you reach Rancho Santa Fe Road, which is county road S10, turn right and go north into Olivenhain, once a peaceful colony established by German families in the past century to raise olives.

Continue north on Rancho Santa Fe Road/S10 through farm country and home developments to a private community that has a country-resort flavor, Lake San Marcos. Go right on Lake San Marcos Drive, then left on San Marino Drive, and right at the shopping plaza to Quails Inn. Join the crowd for a Sunday brunch buffet in the inn's adjacent restaurant. It overlooks a quiet lake bordered by homes and dotted with waterfowl and occasional fishermen. An added attraction is a lakeside art show on the Quails Inn lawn the second and the last Sunday of every month. Overnight guests at this popular getaway spot can play golf at the private country club nearby and also rent boats for a cruise around the lake.

Afterward, drive north through agricultural land that's being transformed by light industry and housing developments. Just beyond Vista you'll find Guajome Regional Park, 600 pastoral acres of a Mexican land grant that are being preserved for future generations. Get there from Lake San Marcos by continuing on Rancho Santa Fe Road/S10 to join county road S14 and turn left to follow it north. The road becomes Santa Fe Avenue and leads to the Guajome (*guah-homey*) Adobe, a historic ranch house from California's early days. After passing a "Welcome to Vista" sign, go up the entry drive just beyond a roadside park information signboard at number 2210.

Built nearly 130 years ago, the old hacienda remained in the same family until it was acquired by San Diego County's park department in 1973. The rancho comes to life Saturday afternoons, when rangers escort visitors on guided tours of the 20-room adobe that Colonel Cave Couts constructed for his wife, Ysidora Bandini, after they were married in 1851. Ysidora received the ranchland as a wedding gift from her prominent brother-in-law, a wealthy Los Angeles merchant who had purchased the land grant for $550 from two Indians. On the informal tour you can see the painstaking work that's being done to restore the ranch house to its former grandeur. You'll start in the courtyard, where carriages with Rancho Guajome's frequent visitors were received. One guest was Ulysses S. Grant, who had known Couts earlier when the ranch owner served in the U.S. Army. During one visit the hard-drinking general is reported to have ridden his horse into the hacienda's parlor. You'll also hear from the rangers that Helen Hunt Jackson based the Indian heroine of her novel *Ramona* on a servant at the ranch.

Around the carriage courtyard visitors will see a blacksmith shop, the ranch's own jailroom, the majordomo's quarters, and a huge pepper tree planted as a seedling from nearby Mission San Luis Rey. A doorway leads to the garden courtyard, surrounded by rooms that include everything from a bakery and kitchen to a schoolroom for the family's children, servants' quarters, and a general store.

At the end of your rancho visit and weekend in the countryside, continue north on Santa Fe Avenue/S14 to join California 76 and drive west toward Oceanside to pick up Interstate 5 back to Los Angeles.

Round trip is about 250 miles.

Rancho Santa Fe/Lake San Marcos Area Code: 619

SIGHTSEEING   *Guajome Regional Park,* with Guajome Adobe at 2210 North Santa Fe Road, Vista 92083, 565-3600 (county park office phone weekdays only). 45-minute guided tours offered Saturdays and Sundays at 2 P.M.; meet by the adobe. Free; donations welcome. Parking fee for day use, $1. 17 lakeside campsites, $14 per night.

LODGING   *The Inn at Rancho Santa Fe,* Linea del Cielo at Paseo Delicias (or P.O. Box 869), Rancho Santa Fe 92067, 756-1131; $80–$185. Also suites with fireplaces. Classic country inn with 78 varied accommodations amid beautifully landscaped grounds. Ocean beach house nearby at Del Mar for guests' use in summertime. Also two dining rooms in the inn (see below). ● *Quails Inn,* 1025 La Bonita Drive, San Marcos 92069, 744-0120; $85, 2-night minimum on weekends. 142-room motel at the edge of Lake San Marcos. Also lakeview dinner house (see below). ● *Rancho Valencia Resort,* 5921 Valencia Circle (or P.O. Box 9126), Rancho Santa Fe 92067, 756-1123 or toll-free (800) 548-3664; $295–$600, with full breakfast. Exclusive country retreat featuring 43 spacious suites with fireplaces and private patios. 18 championship tennis courts, teaching pros, and clinics. Also, outstanding restaurant (see below). Ask about weekend and tennis packages.

DINING   *The Inn at Rancho Santa Fe* (see above). Garden Room serves American favorites daily for breakfast, lunch, and dinner; also Sunday brunch. Vintage Room offers lunch and dinner daily. Dinner reservations a must; jackets required for men after 6:30 P.M. ● *Mille Fleurs,* 6009 Paseo Delicias (in Country Square Courtyard), Rancho Santa Fe, 756-3085. Dinner nightly, lunch on weekdays. French haute cuisine served with European elegance in romantic surroundings; outdoor dining at lunch, weather permitting. Reservations and jackets for men required. ● *Quimby's,* La Granada at Paso Delicias, Rancho Santa Fe, 756-2855. Open daily for breakfast, lunch, and dinner, plus Saturday and Sunday brunch. Dine on California cuisine and seafood specialties amid country-kitchen decor or in flower-filled courtyard. ● *Quails Inn* (see above), 744-2445. 2-level lakeside restaurant and lounge open daily for lunch, dinner, and Sunday brunch. Salad bar and seafood specialties. ● *La Tapenade,* at Rancho Valencia Resort (see above). Fine French-accented California cuisine. Open for all meals from 7 A.M. to 10 P.M. daily. Indoor and patio dining. Make reservations.

High and Low
Desert Destinations

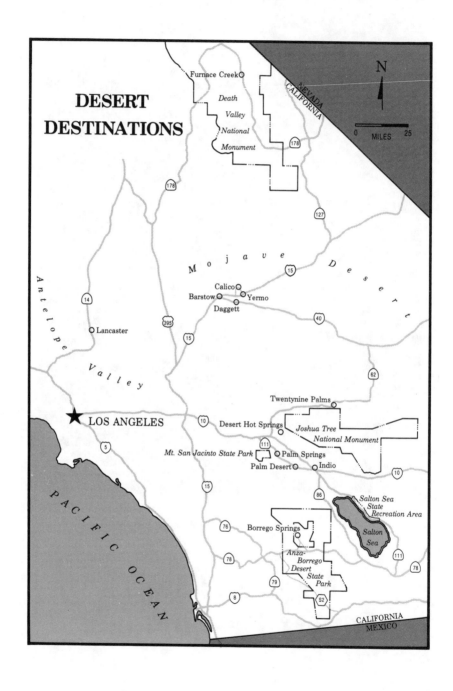

DESERT DESTINATIONS

The Delights of
Death Valley

Rushing to the California gold fields in 1849 seemed like a profitable idea to a group of Midwestern emigrants, but in their hurry to reach Mother Lode country, they made a mistake. The would-be miners decided to take a shortcut through a scorching, desolate valley. Suffering thirst and starvation, they gave the arid expanse an appropriate name—Death Valley.

With a name like that, you'd figure it's a good place to avoid. And there are places in the valley that sound equally foreboding: Hell's Gate, Devil's Hole, Dante's View, Furnace Creek, Badwater. Despite the names (or because of them), Death Valley is one of America's most popular national monuments. Ringed by a barrier of mountains, the vast valley of sand dunes and salt flats annually attracts thousands of fascinated visitors, who now drive on paved roads to the chief attractions.

Before the turn of the century, tales of gold and other precious metals drew prospectors year round to the Death Valley region, and towns like Rhyolite, Bullfrog, Panamint City, and Skidoo sprang up. Borax was discovered soon after, bringing 20-mule teams and more people to the valley.

A luxury-class hotel, the Furnace Creek Inn, was built for winter vacationers in 1927. Six years later the Death Valley area was declared a national monument by President Hoover. Today it covers two million acres in southeastern California and a bit of Nevada.

There are enough natural wonders in Death Valley National Monument to keep you sightseeing for several days; at least a weekend is needed for the highlights. Plan to come in the winter season from mid-October to mid-May, when daytime temperatures average 75 degrees. During the unmerciful summer months, the thermometer often rises to 120 degrees.

Make your headquarters at the elegant Furnace Creek Inn, its more rustic sister, Furnace Creek Ranch, or the motel complex at Stovepipe Wells. In addition, there are over 1,600 campsites in Death Valley. Reserve rooms well in advance of your visit to Death Valley, especially for holiday weekends. And try to avoid the Easter school vacation, when the park is especially crowded. (Campsites are on a first-come, first-served basis, except for the campgrounds at Furnace Creek.)

To reach this vast desert playground from Los Angeles, drive east and north on Interstates 10 and 15 to Baker in the Mojave Desert, then continue north on California 127. Just past Shoshone, go west on California 178 and follow it over the Black Mountains into Death Valley.

After the road descends below sea level, you'll pass the ruins of Ashford Mill, where ore from nearby mines was processed during the valley's gold rush days. At Badwater, look out to the lowest spot in the United States, 282 feet beneath sea level.

Just beyond, take the short side road to view the jagged pinnacles of rock salt spreading over an area called the Devil's Golf Course. Then continue north and make the loop trip on Artists Drive through some colorful badlands and canyons.

With this introduction to Death Valley's varied terrain, settle into the centrally located and surprisingly sophisticated Furnace Creek Inn. Pack something dressy for this extraordinary and rather expensive resort, where one of the treats for guests is nightly musical entertainment.

You'll enjoy suntanning at the palm-fringed swimming pool, a cool game of night tennis on lighted tennis courts, and golf privileges at the 18-hole course nearby at Furnace Creek Ranch. The Ranch is the central gathering spot for visitors in Death Valley because of its less expensive lodgings, several places to eat, grocery store, gas station, and trio of campgrounds. Another attraction at Furnace Creek Ranch is a stable where you can mount up for guided horseback rides.

Park visitors also overnight 28 miles north of Furnace Creek at Stovepipe Wells, the only other location in the park with lodging, cafe, store, and gas station. There's a big (but barren) campground, too.

Plan to make several excursions, starting with an orientation visit to Death Valley Museum at Furnace Creek. This is the visitors center, where you'll find out about all the things to see and do in the vast park. Also inquire about the enjoyable ranger talks and programs. Close by Furnace Creek, make another stop at the Harmony Borax Works ruins to take pictures of the family in front of the enormous 20-mule-team wagons that carried borax to the railhead at Mojave.

To view more of the park's unusual scenery, head south of Furnace Creek to Zabriskie Point, the best spot to photograph the valley's forlorn badlands. Farther along is Dante's View, a spectacular panorama that includes Death Valley's highest point, 11,049-foot Telescope Peak, as well as its lowest spot, Badwater.

Near Stovepipe Wells, go for a hike over the undulating sand dunes, especially picturesque in the late afternoon. Take off your shoes to make footprints that will soon be erased by the desert breeze, then sit for a while to watch the drama as the spectacular dunes change color with the setting sun.

Your weekend won't be complete without visiting Scotty's Castle, a 1920s vacation home that's a desert showplace. It was named for one of the real characters of the Old West, Death Valley Scotty.

Kentucky-born Walter Scott had been a trick rider with Buffalo Bill's Wild West Show prior to talking a wealthy Chicago insurance executive into giving him a grubstake to prospect for gold in California. Eventually Scott's benefactor, Albert Johnson, headed west to inspect the prospecting scene for himself, and he fell in love with the desert. Johnson brought his wife to Death Valley for yearly vacations, and they decided to build a retreat. With the help of Scott, who had become known as Death Valley Scotty, Johnson found a suitable location for his elaborate vacation home. Construction in the desert was a challenge, and workmen were busy for nine years.

As the consummate storyteller, Scotty spread the word that the project was financed by gold from his own secret mine. Johnson, who put more than $2 million into Death Valley Ranch, went along with the myth. As Johnson said later, Scotty repaid him with laughter and friendship.

With the stock market crash and subsequent Depression, Johnson didn't have the funds to complete the elaborate swimming pool, landscaping, and other finishing touches. But the handsomely furnished 18-room hacienda is just as it was in its heyday, when the Johnsons and Scotty lived there.

The National Park Service acquired the house and 15 acres of Johnson ranchland, and visitors are welcome. Besides making a self-guided tour of the grounds, pay the fee to follow a park ranger on a one-hour narrated tour of the home's Spanish-style interior. Redwood-beam ceilings, red tile floors, heavy wooden furniture, and wrought-iron chandeliers and decorations set the mood. You're certain to notice the handwoven carpets from Majorca and drapes made of sheepskin leather. The regally decorated music room houses a theater-size organ with 1,100 pipes. Guides play their own tunes or set an automatic player in motion to give an unexpected miniconcert in the desert.

If you have more time, plan a side trip to Death Valley Junction to enjoy the ballet and pantomime of Marta Becket in her famed Amargosa Opera House. She and assistant Tom Willett operate the former Death Valley Junction movie theater as a playhouse for her one-woman show.

Marta painted an audience of 260 on the walls so she'd never have to play to an empty theater, but now the intimate opera house is such an attraction that you need reservations for her performances October through May.

When it's time to return to Los Angeles, explore more of Death Valley National Monument by following California 190 south from

Stovepipe Wells through Emigrant Pass in the Panamint Mountains. Then pick up U.S. 395 beyond Trona and continue south to rejoin Interstates 15 and 10 back to Los Angeles.

Round trip is about 595 miles.

Death Valley Area Code: 619

SIGHTSEEING   *Monument Headquarters, Visitors Center, and Museum,* Furnace Creek, 786-2331. Open November through April 8 A.M. to 8 P.M. daily, other months 8 A.M. to 5 P.M. Free. Entry to the monument is $5 per vehicle, valid for 7 days. ● *Scotty's Castle,* 55 miles northeast of Furnace Creek. Grounds hours 8 A.M. to 6 P.M. daily. Free. Castle open 9 A.M. to 5 P.M. daily; by guided tour only. Adults $6, senior citizens and children 6 to 11 years $3. ● *Amargosa Opera House,* Death Valley Junction, 852-4316. Performances 8:15 P.M., Mondays, Fridays, and Saturdays in November and from January through April; Saturdays only in October, December, and May. Reservations required; tickets $8, children to 12 years $5.

EVENTS   *Death Valley 49ers Encampment* second weekend in November. Features fiddlers' contest, burro flapjack race, square dancing, special tours, Western art show, golf tournament. Contact park office for details, 786-2331.

LODGING   *Furnace Creek Ranch,* Furnace Creek, Death Valley 92328, 786-2345; $66–$94 year-round. Cottages and motel units. ● *Furnace Creek Inn,* Furnace Creek, Death Valley 92328, 786-2361 or 786-2345; from $245 double MAP (breakfast and dinner included). Luxurious desert resort open mid-October to mid-May. ● *Stove Pipe Wells Village,* Stovepipe Wells, Death Valley 92328, 786-2387; $65. Motel-type rooms.

CAMPING   Nine National Park Service campgrounds within the monument, 786-2331. At Furnace Creek, *Furnace Creek* (open all year), *Sunset,* and *Texas Spring* (open November to April), $4–$5 per night, $10 with hookup at *Furnace Creek* only. Near Scotty's Castle, *Mesquite Springs* (open all year), $5 per night. Also *Stovepipe Wells* (open November to April), $4 per night, $10 with hookup. No reservations; first come, first served, except at Furnace Creek. Call MISTIX toll-free (800) 365-2267.

DINING   *Furnace Creek Ranch* (see above), coffee shop, cafeteria, steak house. ● *Furnace Creek Inn* (see above), open mid-October to mid-May. Excellent dining room (men must wear jackets) and informal L'Ottimos restaurant (with dinner music nightly except Mondays); make reservations. • *Stove Pipe Wells Village* (see above), restaurant open at meal hours from mid-October to May.

FOR MORE INFORMATION Contact Superintendent, Death Valley National Monument, Death Valley 92328, 786-2331.

Beyond Barstow:
Fun for All Ages
Around Calico

You don't have to go north to the Mother Lode region to visit California's famed ghost towns. The Southland boasts one of its own, Calico, a century-old mining camp that boomed between 1881 and 1896. More than $86 million in silver was hauled from mines that honeycomb the colorful Calico Mountains behind the town, which grew from one prospector's shack to a bustling community of 3,500 residents. Besides homes, hotels, mine offices, and quarters for Chinese laborers, there were 22 saloons and a schoolhouse. But the ore played out before the turn of the century, and Calico quickly became a ghost town. Happily, it's now back in business, saved from obliteration by Walter Knott, founder of the famed berry farm in Buena Park.

Best of all, Calico is a "living" ghost town, a unique county park that's open to visitors year round. As in Calico's heyday, Lil's Saloon is packed with thirsty customers, the general store and other shops are open for business, and music and laughter spill from the melodrama theater. It's no wonder Calico Ghost Town has become a favorite family outing, despite its isolated location in the desert.

A visit to the Calico area in San Bernardino County is like opening a time capsule. Few places can match its range of historical sites—from the earliest man in North America to the latest in solar power.

For this enjoyable and educational weekend, make your tour base nearby in Barstow. Get there from Los Angeles by driving east on Interstate 10 toward San Bernardino and joining Interstate 15 north. Exit at East Main Street and check into one of the motels lining that highway, such as the Barstow Holiday Inn, the largest of the area's lodgings. Although it's the hub of the high desert, few travelers ever consider Barstow a getaway destination. Most folks rush through town en route to the high life in Las Vegas or some sun and fun on the Colorado River. However, as the central city of the Mojave Desert, Barstow has several nice overnight accommodations and good places to eat. For a hearty meal, have dinner at the Idle Spurs Steak House.

In the morning, head east again on Interstate 15 to the exit for Ghost Town Road. Follow it toward the mountains, where you'll see Calico nestled in a quiet canyon. Nowadays it's hard to imagine the town was in such ruin that it took 15 years of careful research and rebuilding to bring Calico back to life. Walter Knott began restoration in 1951 in memory of his uncle, John C. King, a San Bernardino County sheriff who grubstaked the prospectors whose silver discovery gave birth to Calico.

Take a short ride aboard the Calico & Odessa Railroad, a former mine train, while the engineer's recorded narration describes the town's boom days. Tour the tunnels in the Maggie Mine, and peer into the Glory Hole, which yielded silver worth $65,000. For other Old West action, join in the melodrama shows presented in the Calikage Playhouse. Musicians and actors also offer entertainment along the main street. Be on the lookout for Calico's sheriff, Lonesome George, and deputy marshal Doc Holliday.

Drop into Lil's Saloon to see paintings that depict the town in the good ol' days, when Wyatt Earp was a regular visitor. You'll find snacks and drink at Lil's, too. Cafeteria-style meals are served in the Calico House Restaurant. For dessert, head uptown to the Top of the Hill Cafe & Ice Cream Parlor.

As you stroll along the wooden sidewalks, be sure to go inside the rock shop, where a wall is constructed of translucent rocks. Another eye-catcher is the house made of bottles. Visitors always have fun poking around the general store, where ladies can even buy a calico bonnet. The Mystery Shack and its Western museum also are worth a peek. Be sure to watch the craftsman at work in the pottery shop.

After your visit to Calico, return to Barstow to explore that city and spend another night. Two diverse museums recall the area's early days and show off the natural attractions that make the region a popular place for outdoor recreation. Also, because it's the converging point for the Santa Fe and Union Pacific railways, Barstow is a special delight for train buffs.

As the desert junction for overland wagon trains in the 1860s, the Barstow area was first known as Fishpond. It became a railroad community called Waterman when the Southern Pacific laid tracks through the desolate terrain a century ago. When the Atchison, Topeka, and Santa Fe arrived in 1886, the growing desert crossroads was renamed in honor of William Barstow Strong, tenth president of that railroad.

You'll discover more historical lore by visiting the Mojave River Valley Museum, just north of Interstate 15 on Barstow Road at Virginia Way. Barstow's heritage is revealed through an assortment of exhibits that range from artifacts taken from the Calico Early Man site to models of space tracking devices at nearby Goldstone station. Also included are arrowheads, baskets, pottery, petroglyph replicas, and other reminders of the area's Indian days.

A little farther north on Barstow Road, look right for an adobelike building called the California Desert Information Center. It's the modern visitors facility of the Bureau of Land Management and features a number of displays about the natural history of the high desert. You can even sample native plants once used by the Indians for food and medicine. Be sure to walk in the cactus garden and look in the pond for endangered pupfish. Other exhibits emphasize desert ecology, recreation sites, and hazards for travelers. Visitors also are advised of desert road conditions and given free guide maps.

If you want to glimpse a bit of Barstow's role as a rail center for Southern California, continue north on Barstow Road, turn left on Main Street to H Street, then go right to reach a sprawling classification yard. From a visitors parking area you can view this impressive Santa Fe facility where hundreds of railroad cars are sorted out and switched to trains bound for destinations nationwide.

Go back east along Main Street to the interchange with Interstate 15 and a favorite travelers' stop called Barstow Station, a collection of railroad cars converted to souvenir stores and snack shops. The Bakery has tasty breakfast pastries, and you can stock up on refreshments for your day's outing to other attractions in the surrounding desert.

Join Interstate 15 and drive east beyond the Ghost Town Road exit to the Minneola exit, cross over the freeway, and follow signs to the Calico Early Man Site. This is the spot that famed anthropologist Dr. Louis Leakey and others believed to be the earliest trace of man in the Western Hemisphere, an ancient workshop for making stone tools. The site was excavated extensively from 1964 until Leakey's death in 1972. These days volunteers, including college students from as far away as Canada, continue the painstaking work that you'll see on a guided tour. Controversy surrounds the archaeological dig because previous evidence put the first humans in the Americas around 20,000 years ago, but the Calico site has been dated at about 200,000 years old. On certain weekends of every month, except in summer, you're welcome to attend lessons in archaelogical digging (by reservation only). Look for some of the early-man discoveries, or their replicas, in the site's visitor center.

Fossil remains of mastodons, camels, and even three-toed horses have been found north of Barstow in Rainbow Basin, now designated a Natural National Landmark. Visitors can drive along a loop road past colorful sedimentary rock formations that are textbook examples of folds, faults, and other geologic oddities that have occurred over millions of years. Return west on Interstate 15, exit on California 58 west to Irvin Road, turn north through a landscape of Joshua trees, then go left on Fossil Bed Road to the one-way circle route through remote Rainbow Basin (no RVs or trailers). A side road leads to a small campground in Owl Canyon.

Before heading home, many budget-minded Barstow visitors plan time to shop at the Factory Merchants Outlet Plaza, which features 50 name-brand outlet stores around an open-air courtyard. It's at the southwest entrance to Barstow off Interstate 15 at Lenwood Road.

When your visit to the high desert is over, return to the freeway for the drive back west to Los Angeles via Interstates 15 and 10.

Round trip is about 320 miles.

Special note: Be aware that temperatures in the Mojave Desert can soar in the summertime, often exceeding 100 degrees during the daytime. Take some drinking water in your car. The air is usually dry, but there are occasional breezes. Summer evening temperatures range in the 70s.

Barstow/Calico Area Code: 619

SIGHTSEEING   *Calico Ghost Town Regional Park,* Ghost Town Road or Calico Road exit from Interstate 15, 10 miles east of Barstow (or P.O. Box 638, Yermo 92398), 254-2122. Townsite open every day from 7 A.M. to dusk, shops from 9 A.M. to 5 P.M. Free admission; parking $5 per vehicle. Small extra fees for train ride, mine tour, and some other attractions. Also camping (see below). • *Mojave River Valley Museum,* 270 East Virginia Way, Barstow 92311, 256-5452. Open 11 A.M. to 4 P.M. daily. Donations appreciated. • *California Desert Information Center,* 831 Barstow Road, Barstow 92311, 256-8617. Open 9 A.M. to 5 P.M. daily. Free. Bureau of Land Management visitor information. • *Calico Early Man Site,* east of Barstow at Minneola Road exit from Interstate 15, no phone. Open 8 A.M. to 4 P.M. Thursday through Sunday. Guided tours at 9:30 and 11:30 A.M. and 1:30 and 3:30 P.M. Donation appreciated in lieu of tour fee. Archaeological dig on hillside site; wear comfortable walking shoes. To participate in digging lessons, except in summer, reserve by calling the county museum, (909) 825-8425. • *Rainbow Basin Natural Area,* 8 miles north of Barstow. Administered by BLM; office and tour brochure at California Desert Information Center (see above). Open daily dawn to dusk. Also campground (see below). ● *Factory Merchants Outlet Plaza*, Lenwood Road at Interstate 15, Barstow 92311, 253-7342. Manufacturer-owned discount stores open daily from 9 A.M. to 8 P.M.

EVENTS Calico Ghost Town Regional Park has 4 annual weekend festivities: *Calico Hulabaloo*, Palm Sunday weekend in March or April; *Calico Spring Festival*, Mother's Day weekend in May; *Calico Days* in October; and *Calico Fine Arts Festival* in November. Call park office, 254-2122, for dates and details.

LODGING Accommodations listed are in Barstow (zip code 92311). Catering to cross-desert travelers rather than weekend visitors, they are not resorts, but all have swimming pools and standard motel amenities. ● *Barstow Holiday Inn*, 1511 East Main Street (near Interstate 15 junction), 256-5673; $65. Barstow's largest lodging with 148 attractive rooms. ● *Desert Villa Motel*, 1980 East Main Street, 256-1781; $52. ● *Vagabond Inn*, 1234 East Main Street, 256-5601; $48. ● *Quality Inn*, 1520 East Main Street, 256-6891; $55. ● *Howard Johnson Lodge*, 1431 East Main Street, 256-0661; $47.

CAMPING *Calico Ghost Town Regional Park* (see above). County-run campground with 114 sites, $9 per night; with RV hookups, $15. ● *Owl Canyon Campground*, in Rainbow Basin Natural Area (see above). 31 sites (no hookups); $4 per night. First come, first served. ● *Barstow/Calico KOA Campground*, Interstate 15 at Ghost Town Road exit, Yermo 92398, 254-2311. 71 sites, $15 per night; with RV hookups, $20.

DINING Calico Ghost Town Regional Park (see above) offers *Calico House Restaurant*, *Lil's Saloon*, and *Top of the Hill Cafe & Ice Cream Parlor*. ● *Peggy Sue's Diner*, Ghost Town Road at Yermo Road, Yermo, 254-3370. 1950s atmosphere, great American food for breakfast, lunch, and dinner. Opens daily at 5:30 A.M. All other dining spots are in Barstow. ● *Idle Spurs Steak House*, north of town at 29557 West Highway 58, 256-8888. Very pleasant and popular spot for lunch and dinner daily (no lunch weekends). ● *Canton Restaurant*, 1300 West Main Street, 256-9565. Chinese/American fare. ● *La Scala*, 513 East Main Street, 256-3989, has Italian dishes.

FOR MORE INFORMATION   Contact the Barstow Area Chamber of Commerce, 408 East Fredericks, Barstow 92311, 256-8617. Open weekdays 9 A.M. to 5 P.M.

Desert on Display at Joshua Tree National Monument

Mormon pioneers would rather have avoided the desert when they came overland to settle in California a century ago. These days travelers deliberately set out to see the same terrain. Instead of a hot and hostile wasteland, the desert is now considered a unique natural attraction that should be preserved and enjoyed. An 870-square-mile area, noted for its rich and diverse vegetation, was given permanent protection as Joshua Tree National Monument in 1936.

Spanning both high and low deserts—the Mojave and the Colorado—the monument is host to hundreds of species of plants, birds, and animals. Best known is its namesake, the Joshua tree, a tall and grotesque plant that's actually a member of the agave family. It grows to heights of 40 feet and is believed to have been named by the Mormons, who imagined that its branches resembled the upraised arms of Joshua leading the Israelites into the promised land. Joshua trees, which are found mostly above 3,000 feet on the western side of the monument, often are confused with the Mojave yucca, which grows at lower elevations. You'll discover the difference and learn more of the desert's delights by getting away for a weekend in Joshua Tree National Monument.

To reach the park from Los Angeles, drive east on Interstate 10 and choose either the park's north or south entrance. Its southern gateway is just off the freeway 25 miles beyond Indio at the Cottonwood Springs exit. Or you can turn north earlier from Interstate 10 onto California 62, which goes through the Morongo Valley to Twentynine Palms and the monument's northern entry road, Utah Trail, where you'll find the main visitors center. (There's a western entrance 15 miles sooner at the town of Joshua Tree, but it's worthwhile to begin at the visitors center down the road.)

Within the monument you'll find quiet places to picnic and rustic campsites for spending a couple of peaceful nights under the stars. Camping in Joshua Tree is first come, first served, except at Black

Rock Canyon during the winter. You'll pay an overnight fee at only the two most developed campgrounds; seven other camping areas are free. Before entering the park, stock up on water or other beverages and any food you might like during your visit; no refreshment facilities are located within the national monument. There are major grocery stores in shopping centers along California 62 in Yucca Valley, where you'll also find a few restaurants. Other places to eat are in two neighboring high-desert towns, Twentynine Palms and Joshua Tree, where you'll also find inexpensive lodgings if camping doesn't suit your fancy. If you arrive or leave the park via its southern entrance, the nearest food stores, restaurants, and accommodations are 25 miles west off Interstate 10 in Indio or a few miles beyond in Palm Springs.

Start your exploration of the park at the Oasis Visitors Center, where displays will give you an idea of the varied flora, fauna, and geology in this rare desert sanctuary. The terrain ranges from mountains of twisted rock and granite monoliths, which are a favorite of rock climbers, to the flat Pinto Basin, where primitive man once roamed. Ask the rangers for a park map and the schedule of guided walks and campfire talks that are offered every weekend from late October through May. They also will advise you of the location of the wildflowers that pop up in profusion in the springtime.

On Saturday, you can make a leisurely loop by car to see most of Joshua Tree's points of interest. Also take the side road to the scenic lookout called Keys View for a panorama of Southern California mountain peaks, including 11,500-foot San Gorgonio and its slightly shorter brother, San Jacinto. In the central and western sections of the monument, growing at 3,000- to 5,000-foot elevations, you'll be surrounded by the wild-looking Joshua trees. Nicknamed the praying plant because of their upstretched arms, Joshua trees bloom with creamy white blossoms in March and April.

Some of the monument's most fascinating landscape can be seen on a winding dirt road that is an 18-mile motor nature route. The *Geology Tour Road* brochure describes its highlights. As you drive or walk among the massive boulders that give special character to this desert monument, look for dangling ropes and weekend climbers carefully making their way up and down the rocks. If you or the children decide to scramble over some of the boulders, beware of their slippery surfaces.

Very special attractions in the park are five oases of stately California fan palms. A self-guided nature trail from the Oasis Visitors Center leads to one of the shady palm clusters that were discovered by a government survey party in 1855. If you have time, also follow the southern park road to the Cholla Cactus Garden for a walk along the short nature trail. On the way the road passes through an ecological transition zone where the high and low deserts meet.

Cattlemen and miners were part of the desert scene before Joshua Tree was declared a national monument and protected wilderness area. You can see how they lived by joining a guided tour on weekends to the Desert Queen Ranch, also known as Keys Ranch. Almost like a mini–ghost town, the homestead of the William Keys family includes a derelict ranch house, guest cabins, a tiny school-house, and quarters for the teacher. An assortment of weathered machinery, including a stamp mill from the mine, decorates the landscape. Meet at the ranch gate near the Hidden Valley camp-ground, where the one- to two-hour guided ranch tours are given three times daily from late October until May.

By leaving the park early to return to Los Angeles via California 62, you can visit another high-desert attraction in Yucca Valley. On a hillside along Sunnyslope Drive you'll discover Antone Martin Desert (Christ) Park, with an unusual display of biblical statuary. Thirty-three larger-than-life statues are scattered in a desert land-scape that's reminiscent of the Holy Land. They're dedicated as a world peace shrine and are the work of one man, Antone Martin, a retired aircraft worker who devoted the final years of his life to creating the statuary in solid concrete molded around steel support rods. Each of the remarkable figures weighs from 4 to 16 tons. Near the parking area, a statue that was unfinished at the time of Martin's death in 1961 reveals his sculpting techniques. Don't miss the Sermon on the Mount scene, featuring 13 figures, or the massive Last Supper bas-relief, standing three stories high. There are tables where you can picnic in solitude in this one-of-a-kind public park, or eat in one of Yucca Valley's restaurants before continuing your trip back to Los Angeles on Interstate 10.

Round trip is about 295 miles.

Joshua Tree Area Code: 619

SIGHTSEEING *Joshua Tree National Monument,* 74485 National Monument Drive, Twentynine Palms 92277, 367-7511. Entry $5 per vehicle, valid for 7 days. Headquarters and main visitors center at northern entrance near Twentynine Palms open daily from 8 A.M. to 5 P.M. Visitors center at Cottonwood Springs southern entrance open same hours from mid-October through May. Desert Queen Ranch Tours, with guides from Joshua Tree Natural History Association, begin at 8:30 and 11 A.M. and 1:30 P.M. daily from late October until May. Adults $2, children 6 to 11 years and senior citizens $1. Each tour limited to 20 persons on a first-come basis. Nightly camping fee $10 per site at Black Rock Canyon (call MISTIX, toll-free (800) 365-2267, to make reservations in winter) and $8 at Cottonwood Springs campgrounds only. ● *Antone Martin Desert (Christ) Park,* north of Twentynine Palms Highway (California 62), Yucca Valley. Open 24 hours daily. Free.

EVENTS *Grubstake Days,* annual high-desert high jinks in Yucca Valley during Memorial Day weekend. Details from Yucca Valley Chamber of Commerce (see below). • *Pioneer Days,* annual weekend community celebration with cowboy rodeo on third weekend of October. Details from Twentynine Palms Chamber of Commerce (see below).

LODGING *Best Western Gardens Motel,* 71487 Twentynine Palms Highway, Twentynine Palms 92277, 367-9141; $58. One of the area's nicest accommodations. 71 rooms, including 8 suites with kitchens. • *Twentynine Palms Inn,* 73950 Inn Avenue, Twentynine Palms 92277, 367-3505; $59–$85. 12 vintage adobe bungalows with fireplaces amid palm tree oasis that's close to park entrance. Also restaurant (see below). • *Yucca Inn,* 7500 Camino del Cielo, Yucca Valley 92284, 365-3311; $45. 18-hole golf course nearby. • *Oasis of Eden Motel,* 56377 Twentynine Palms Highway, Yucca Valley 92284, 365-6321; $43. Some theme rooms.

DINING *Twentynine Palms Inn* (see above). Lunch and dinner daily. Also Sunday brunch. • *Reflections,* 56193 Twentynine Palms Highway, Yucca Valley, 365-8301. Prime rib, steaks, and seafood. Open daily for lunch and dinner. • Basic restaurants serving standard American fare for breakfast, lunch, and dinner are found in Twentynine Palms along Twentynine Palms Highway, including *Tom's Place* at No. 72317, *Erin's* at No. 72576, and *Rings* at No. 73669. Other eateries, especially fast-food and chain restaurants, are located along the highway in Yucca Valley.

FOR MORE INFORMATION Contact the Twentynine Palms Chamber of Commerce, 6136 Adobe Road, Twentynine Palms 92277, 367-3445. Also, the Yucca Valley Chamber of Commerce, 56020 Santa Fe Trail, Suite B, Yucca Valley 92284, 365-6323.

Sunning and Soaking at Desert Hot Springs

Southern California has its own Baden-Baden, but unlike that renowned German health resort in the lush Black Forest, the Southland's spa town sits smack-dab in the desert. At Desert Hot Springs you bask in Ol' Sol's rays as well as the mineral water that bubbles up from the earth. More than 60 hostelries welcome soakers and sunbathers to a spa-filled oasis only a dozen miles from Palm Springs. Get there from Los Angeles by heading east on Interstate 10 to the exit for Palm Drive. Follow it up the slope to Desert Hot Springs, at the base of the Little San Bernardino Mountains.

Spread along a gentle slope of the foothills at 1,070 feet, the unpretentious town presents wonderful panoramas of the desert valley and snow-topped Mount San Jacinto. At that elevation, winter sunshine lasts longer in the late afternoon, and summertime temperatures are often cooler too. About 12,400 soakers and sun seekers currently call Desert Hot Springs home, and hundreds of others escape there for a weekend or the winter.

Of course, Desert Hot Spring's main drawing card is its steaming mineral water, which has been touted as beneficial for arthritis, rheumatism, neuralgia, and gout. However, most visitors have no medical reason for soaking or swimming in the clear, odorless water—they just enjoy it. A half dozen of the town's motel resorts open their spas to the public for a daily fee, including the popular Desert Hot Springs Hotel and Spa, which has eight hot pools of varying temperatures and a cooler Olympic-size swimming pool. For more privacy while enjoying Desert Hot Springs's warm waters and sunshine, stay at a spa where the pools and other facilities are reserved exclusively for its overnight guests.

Topping the list of such resorts is Two Bunch Palms, named early in this century by a survey party of the U.S. Army Camel Corps. The pair of palm tree clusters noted on their maps still stand, thanks to the natural springs, which also nourish willowy tamarisk trees and other vegetation that create a secluded desert oasis. In the early 1930s it reportedly became the hideaway of Chicago mobster Al Capone. You can stay in his rockhewn bungalow, complete with a private rooftop sunning area that once served as a lookout for Big Al's bodyguards. That bygone era is re-created in Suite 14, with overstuffed velvet chairs, handcrafted stained-glass windows, an antique bar, and a bullet hole in the bedroom mirror. Two Bunch became a playground for Mafia bosses and movie stars, who enjoyed its hot-spring pools and private casino. More rooms were built for Capone's guests, and the 105-acre compound later became a public resort after the mobster went to the penitentiary.

The 44 bungalow and villa rooms have been redecorated with modern or antique furniture and art deco accessories, while the casino has become a gourmet dining room. Beneath the restaurant is a full-service spa offering a sauna, many types of massage, mineral water mud baths, salt and herbal steam baths, and hair treatments. Outside at this very friendly and informal resort you can relax in palm-shaded pools of steaming mineral water. Guests who want an allover tan are welcome to stretch out nude in secluded sun bins.

The town has several other private and pleasant spa accommodations, such as the 20-room Sunset Inn on Hacienda Drive. Get a complete list of lodgings from the Desert Hot Springs Chamber of Commerce.

Although Indians had long enjoyed its soothing natural springs, no one settled at Desert Hot Springs until Cabot Yerxa arrived as a homesteader in 1913. He left the town a landmark, Cabot's Old Indian Pueblo, a four-story adobe home hand-built in pseudo-Hopi style. Visitors can explore the uncompleted structure, which has 35 rooms and forgoes the traditional exterior Indian ladders for inside stairs.

Take a guided tour to learn about the colorful Yerxa, who was a miner during Alaska's 1898 gold rush before spending more than two decades constructing his remarkable pueblo. The rustic residence also is a museum of pioneer mementos, Indian relics, and artifacts of the Alaskan Eskimos that he collected. You'll find Cabot's Old Indian Pueblo about a mile east of Palm Drive on East Desert View Avenue. Look for a towering Indian head, a monument carved from redwood and cedar trees by Hungarian-born sculptor Peter Toth.

Happily, you'll also find a few good places to eat in the spa town. Very popular for dinner is Haydens Restaurant, with seafood specialties, and the Capri, serving Italian fare.

On Sunday golfers will enjoy playing the Robert Trent Jones, Jr.–designed Desert Dunes championship course, another 18-hole course at Mission Lakes Country Club, or the Desert Crest Country Club 9-hole course. For more outdoor enjoyment, leave Desert Hot Springs by midday on your way back to Los Angeles in order to detour from Interstate 10 at the Whitewater exit (just before the California 111 junction to Palm Springs). Drive five miles north on the winding Whitewater Canyon Road, which follows a river and heads into the hills to the Rainbow Rancho Whitewater Trout Company.

Even if you've never fished before, you'll be catching rainbows like a veteran angler at this picturesque trout farm, established in 1939. The frantic fish literally race to take the bait. Just squeeze the doughy fish food around the hook, drop in the line, wait for a tug, and then reel in your trout. It's not much sport, but a lot of fun. You'll find fisherpersons of all ages encircling the two freshwater pools that teem with trout. For a couple of bucks you get a rod and reel, bait, and a bucket for your catch. The kids or two friends can share your equipment without extra charge. No license is required. Fish are weighed and sold to you at a bargain price per pound, and the Whitewater trout farm staff will clean them if you ask. Adjacent to the fish ponds and hatchery is a 15-acre private picnic area, where you can cook your catch on an outdoor barbecue. Charcoal and sodas are available, but bring the other picnic supplies.

To continue your return trip to Los Angeles, go back on the same canyon road to Interstate 10 and head west.

Round trip is about 236 miles.

Desert Hot Springs Area Code: 619

SIGHTSEEING *Cabot's Old Indian Pueblo Museum,* 67616 East Desert View Avenue, Desert Hot Springs 92240, 329-7610. Open September through July from 10 A.M. to 4 P.M. daily except Mondays and Tuesdays; in June and August open weekends only. Other times by appointment. Adults $2.50, senior citizens $2, children 5 to 16 years $1. Includes 30-minute guided tour. ● *Rainbow Rancho Whitewater Trout Company,* at end of Whitewater Canyon Road (or Star Route 1, Box 549), Whitewater 92282, 325-5570. Open daily except Mondays from 9 A.M. to 5 P.M. General admission $.50. Fee for tackle, bait, bucket, and towel is $2.50, with up to 3 people permitted to use the same pole. Fish you catch are charged at $2.56 per pound; no limit or extra fee for cleaning and packing. Additional charge for use of picnic area. ● *Desert Dunes Golf Club,* 19300 Palm Drive, North Palm Springs 92240, 329-2941. Challenging desert 18-hole course; $70 in winter, $35 in summer. ● *Mission Lakes Country Club Golf Course,* 8484 Clubhouse Drive, Desert Hot Springs 92240, 329-8061. 18-hole par-71 championship course; $56 greens fee with cart in winter, $35 in summer. ● *Desert Crest Country Club Golf Course,* 69400 Country Club Drive, Desert Hot Springs 92240, 329-8711. 9 holes; $9 greens fee for 18 holes (go around twice).

LODGING *Two Bunch Palms Spa and Resort,* 67425 Two Bunch Palms Trail, Desert Hot Springs 92240, 329-8791; $175, continental breakfast included. Villa suites with living room and kitchen $272–$396, Capone Suite $380 with 2 bedrooms. Closed in August. Repeat guests often fill the resort's 44 units, so book weeks in advance; 2-night minimum. No one under age 18. Full spa services with expert staff; 1-hour massage, $68. Tasty gourmet dinners served nightly to resort guests in former casino; ever-changing menu with seafood specialties. ● *Sunset Inn,* 67585 Hacienda Drive, Desert Hot Springs 92240, 329-4488; $70 winter, $45 summer. Small, attractive spa with hot pools and sauna. Also restaurant. ● *Ponce de Leon Spa Hotel,* 11000 Palm Drive, Desert Hot Springs 92240, 329-6484; $60 winter, $37 summer. 107 rooms, a few with private hot mineral pool. Massages available; sauna. Also coffee shop. ● *Desert Hot Springs Hotel* *and Spa,* 10805 Palm Drive, Desert Hot Springs 92240, 329-6495; $79 winter, $49 summer. Large swimming pool, 8 hot pools, and sauna. Massages, body wraps, facials, and manicures available. • *Royal Fox Inn,* 14500 Palm Drive, Desert Hot Springs 92240, 329-4481; $61 winter, $41 summer. Modern 3-story hotel with 111 rooms; some suites with own whirlpool. Health spa facilities, including massage. Dining room. Also RV park, $20 with hookup.

DINING *Two Bunch Palms* (see above). Intimate dining room open for resort guests only. Chef changes menu frequently; usually a half dozen entrees. •*Hayden's Fishermen's Wharf Restaurant,* 66230 Pierson Boulevard, Desert Hot Springs, 329-5622. Dinner only; seafood a specialty. Closed Tuesday through Thursday in summer. • *Capri Restaurant,* 12260 Palm Drive, Desert Hot Springs, 329-6833. Dinner daily except Mondays; closed Sunday through Tuesday in summer. Local favorite for Italian fare. • *Budapest Inn,* 11349 Palm Drive, Desert Hot Springs, 329-8050. Hungarian dishes served daily from 5 to 9 P.M.

FOR MORE INFORMATION Contact the Desert Hot Springs Chamber of Commerce, 13560 Palm Drive (or P.O. Box 848), Desert Hot Springs 92240, 329-6403. Also, Palm Springs Desert Resorts Convention and Visitors Bureau, 69-930 Highway 111, Suite 201, Rancho Mirage 92270, 770-9000.

Palm Springs
Part 1: Touring the
Southland's Premier Resort

Where do you go for the best tour of celebrity and movie star homes? Not Beverly Hills, where the city fathers have outlawed tour buses from most residential streets. Make your destination Palm Springs, the affluent desert resort that's also home for many folks of television and film fame. While you probably won't see them in person, the stars are brought to mind as you drive around the area on streets such as Bob Hope Drive and Frank Sinatra Drive. Among many others with celebrity namesakes are (John) Wayne Road,

(Bette) Davis Way, (Spencer) Tracy Drive, and (Ginger) Rogers Road.

As you'll discover during a weekend escape to the Southland's premier desert destination, Palm Springs is unique in more ways than its street names. With about 1,200 palms lining the main thoroughfare, Palm Canyon Drive, the town's own name is well deserved. And there are springs, too, one still bubbling where the Cahuilla Indians first came to relax and find healing powers in its hot mineral waters. The Spa Hotel occupies that site now, but the land still belongs to the Indians. In fact, Palm Springs looks like a checkerboard in the real estate plat books, because every other square mile is owned by the Agua Caliente band of the Cahuilla Indians. They lease out their land in this prime recreational oasis and share in the revenue, making the tribe's 200 members the city's largest collective landowners and some of the wealthiest Indians in the nation. A pristine section of their 32,000-acre reservation known as the Indian Canyons is open to visitors. The rocky canyons with picturesque palm groves and bedrock mortar holes for grinding grain recall the simple life of the Agua Caliente's ancestors.

Since beginning as a winter haven for Hollywood's elite in the 1930s, Palm Springs is now a bona fide year-round playground for folks of all occupations and incomes. Although extensive development is evident in neighboring communities that sprouted later in the Coachella Valley, Palm Springs maintains a style that's unique to Southland vacation spots. Consider the city's strict ordinance that forbids flashing, rotating, neon, or garish signs, which means McDonald's may be in town but its golden arches aren't. Likewise, building codes prohibit new homes from casting a shadow on neighbors' houses. The tallest commercial structure in town, the Hyatt Regency Suites, rises only six stories.

Palm Springs has accommodations galore—more than 7,500 rooms—but don't look for a "motel." That word is banned, even for the nationwide Motel 6 chain, whose Palm Springs property is called *H*otel 6 Palms. Lodgings also can be named inns, resorts, lodges, and manors. Others are called villas, like La Mancha, where some of the posh accommodations feature your own private swimming pool. Certainly you'll have no problem taking a dip in Palm Springs; the last census of swimming pools tallied 7,300! And while recreational outlets are being counted, the city and adjacent Coachella Valley communities can boast more than 700 tennis courts and nearly 100 golf courses. No wonder golf carts have the right-of-way when crossing Palm Springs streets.

On some of the fairways or greens you might catch a glimpse of Gerald Ford and other well-known resident golfers; or come to town during the Bob Hope Chrysler Classic or the Nabisco Dinah Shore LPGA National Tournament to see an array of famous folk.

For those on a budget who like the hot and very dry desert air, summer is a good time to visit Palm Springs, because lower room rates are in effect at nearly all of the resort town's 120 lodgings. (A few hotels are open only during the winter season, which generally runs from October through May.) All lodgings, restaurants, and shops are air-conditioned, so you'll stay comfortable even when the midday summer temperatures top 100 degrees. A cooling alternative is to rise from the desert floor to the slopes of Mount San Jacinto aboard the Palm Springs Aerial Tramway, a dramatic cable car excursion that is another delight of this uncommon resort. An ice skating rink and a water park also help visitors keep cool in summertime.

With so much to see and do—including nothing but lounging at poolside while Ol' Sol gives you a tan—Palm Springs will fill up at least two weekends. To capture its flavor, plan to take an orientation tour of the town on your first trip, and also go aboard the tram for a ride up the mountain. Come back another time to discover more about the Indians and cowboys of Palm Spring's past and to become more familiar with the desert's amazing plant and animal life.

Get to this world-famous vacation retreat from Los Angeles by heading east on Interstate 10 and joining California 111 into the heart of Palm Springs. When checking into your hotel, name your favorite food and you'll be directed to the area's wonderful collection of dining spots; a number of them are along the desert valley's "restaurant row," a section of California 111 in Rancho Mirage. Supper shows, comedy clubs, and discotheques offer other evening diversions.

The following day join one of the guided tours that provide an extensive look at Palm Springs and adjoining resort communities, featuring the past or present homes of many Hollywood stars and other notables. Along the way you'll see elegant country clubs, designer boutiques, and impressive shopping centers, and also make a refreshment stop. Especially recommended are the trips offered daily by Celebrity Tours in 14-passenger vans.

Although many of the celebrity homes are hidden behind walls or landscaping to preserve the owners' privacy, from the tour vehicles you can peek at Frank Sinatra's estate and glimpse the train caboose next to his lighted tennis court that serves as a bar, barbershop, and sauna. The tours also cruise by Liberace's former abode, easily recognized by a huge candelabrum in his front yard, and you'll pass Elvis Presley's former desert home as well as the longtime residence of Red Skelton.

Your driver-guide will point out Bob Hope's multimillion-dollar mansion, which dominates a hillside like a mini-Superdome and has a dining room large enough to seat 300 guests. Along with Hope, the list of current or former celebrity homeowners in Palm Springs

includes Lucille Ball, Dustin Hoffman, Goldie Hawn, Paul New-
man, Kenny Rogers, Jack Benny, Kirk Douglas, George Burns,
Arnold Schwarzenegger, Barry Manilow, William Holden, Gene
Autry, George Hamilton, and Danny Kaye.

For a do-it-yourself tour of the town, go by bicycle. Palm Springs
has 35 miles of bike paths, marked by blue-and-white signs that
guide you to many of the city's sights. Hire any type of bike you
like, including a side-by-side three-wheeler or a tandem bicycle built
for two from several bike rental companies. Ask for a bikeway map,
too.

Whatever season you go to Palm Springs, be sure to pack a
sweater. That may sound like foolish advice for a trip to the desert,
but temperatures cool down considerably at night, even during the
summer. Besides, on Sunday you'll want to take the thrilling ride on
the aerial tramway, and thermometer readings at its mountain station
often are 40 degrees cooler than those on the desert floor. Get to the
cable car from downtown Palm Springs by driving north on
California 111 and turning left at the tramway sign. Follow the
four-mile access road up Chino Canyon to parking areas at the
desert valley station.

Initially the Palm Springs Aerial Tramway was conceived as just
a quick way for desert residents to escape to the cooler mountains
during the summer. The father of the tramway, Francis Crocker, had
that dream one scorching day in 1934, but nearly three decades
passed before it came true. Eventually men and material made
23,000 helicopter flights without mishap to create the longest
single-span passenger tramway in the world. The cost of construction exceeded $8 million. Since its inaugural run in 1963, the tram's
twin 80-passenger cable cars have carried several million people
from desert palms to towering pines at the 8,516-foot mountain
station.

As the enclosed gondola travels at 18 miles per hour on its
breathtaking journey, a taped commentary tells you about the unique
tramway and the sights you pass. Variations in temperatures,
geological formations, and vegetation during the trip are comparable
to what you'd encounter on a drive from Mexico to Alaska.
Awaiting you at the mountain station is a visitors facility with food
and drink and a 25-minute movie about building the tramway.
Observation decks and telescopes present inspiring views of Palm
Springs and the Coachella Valley, as well as the Colorado Desert
and the surrounding mountains.

After the easy 14-minute aerial ascent, energetic folks will also
like hiking on trails behind the tramway station in forested Long
Valley. It's part of Mount San Jacinto (*hah-sin-toe*) State Park,
where rangers often conduct nature walks and summer campfire
programs. And they issue wilderness permits in case you'd like to

explore more of the park's 54 miles of marked trails or spend a night at one of its primitive campgrounds.

If nature's sights aren't enough, plan your tramway trip for March for the annual sled-dog races held at the mountain station. Visitors can always enjoy a variety of activities on Mount San Jacinto, including Nordic cross-country skiing in wintertime. In summer you might wear a pair of jeans, because surefooted mules are waiting to take you on a short trail ride in the scenic mountain valley at the top of the tramway. Visitors can also enjoy a Western cookout at sunset while watching the desert change colors in the evening's afterglow.

A cool attraction, especially in summer, is the Ice Capades Chalet in the Coachella Valley's largest shopping complex, Palm Desert Town Center. Rent skates and go for a spin around the air-conditioned ice rink. Visitors also have fun keeping cool at the Oasis Waterpark, which has a wave pool, water slides, and thrill rides. The classy water park also features a health club and even valet parking.

A popular Palm Springs evening diversion is VillageFest, a downtown street bazaar held every Thursday night from 6 to 10 P.M. The long block of Palm Canyon Drive between Amado and Alejo streets is closed to vehicles and replaced by live entertainment, a farmers' market, food vendors, and booths with art, antiques, and gifts.

After becoming acquainted with Palm Springs and its enchanting surroundings, you'll be looking forward to another weekend at the enticing desert resort. Meanwhile, return to Los Angeles by heading north on California 111 to rejoin Interstate 10 west.

Round trip is about 210 miles.

Palm Springs Area Code: 619

SIGHTSEEING *Celebrity Tours,* 174 North Indian Avenue, Suite 10, Palm Springs 92262, 325-2682. 2-hour Palm Springs and Country Club Tour departs daily. Adults $14, senior citizens $13, children $7. Also 1-hour tours. Pickup at any hotel in Palm Springs; reservations required. ● *Burnett's Bicycle Barn,* 429 South Sunrise Way at Ramon Road, Palm Springs 92262, 325-7844. Open year round Thursday through Monday from 8 A.M. to 5 P.M.; also Tuesdays to noon. Bike rentals by the hour or day. ● Other bike rental companies are *Palm Springs Cyclery,* 325-9319, *Canyon Bicycle Rentals,* 327-7688, both in Palm Springs, and *Native Cycles,* 321-9444, in Rancho Mirage. ● *Palm Springs Aerial Tramway,* off California 111 via Chino Canyon Road (or P.O. Drawer FF), Palm Springs 92262, 325-1391. Open daily year round except for up to 2 weeks after first Monday in August for annual maintenance. First car up at 8 A.M. weekends, 10 A.M. weekdays; last car down at 9:15 P.M. in winter, 10:45 P.M. in summer. Adults $14.95 round trip, children 3 to 12 years $9.95. After 4 P.M. Ride 'n' Dine combination tickets include tram fare and buffet dinner or barbecue cookout at mountain station. Adults $18.95, children $12.95; no reservations required. • *Mount San Jacinto State Park,* Long Valley Ranger Station atop Palm Springs Aerial Tramway, Palm Springs (or P.O. Box 308, Idyllwild 92549), 327-0222. Free 45-minute guided nature walks in Long Valley offered weekends in summer by park rangers. Also daily 20-minute trail rides on mules in Long Valley available from 10:30 A.M. until dusk. Adults $7, children 12 years and under $4. In winter, Nordic Ski Center open for cross-country ski and snowshoe rentals, 327-6002. •*Ice Capades Chalet,* Palm Desert Town Center, Palm Desert 92260, 340-4412. Daytime or evening ice skating sessions $5, senior citizens $3, plus $2 for skate rental. • *Oasis Waterpark,* 1500 Gene Autry Trail, Palm Springs 92264, 325-7873. First-class water park with state's largest wave pool for board and body surfing, wet-and-wild water slides, kiddie splash pools, and an adult beach club with a physical fitness center. Open daily mid-March through Labor Day, then weekends only through October. Open from 11 A.M. to 8 P.M. in summer, to 6 P.M. in other seasons. Admission $15.95, senior citizens and children 4 to 11 years $10.95.

LODGING   *La Mancha Private Villas and Court Club,* 444 North Avenida Caballeros, Palm Springs 92262, 323-1773 or toll-free (800) 255-1773; $310 with private pools in winter season, $250 in summer. 54 Mediterranean-style accommodations, most with private swimming pool and/or whirlpool spa. A home away from home offering full kitchens, wide-screen television, and fireplaces, plus tennis and gourmet dining at the club's restaurant. • *Palm Springs Marquis Hotel and Villas,* 150 South Indian Canyon Drive, Palm Springs 92262, 322-2121 or toll-free (800) 458-6679; $160 in winter, $60 in summer. Nice resort in downtown. Lighted tennis, 2 pools, restaurant. • *Ingleside Inn,* 200 West Ramon Road, Palm Springs 92262, 325-0046 or toll-free (800) 826-4162; from $95 October through May, $65 in summer, including continental breakfast. Classic hacienda-style inn with 29 antique-decorated rooms. Some fireplaces and private patios. • *Hyatt Regency Suites,* 285 North Palm Canyon Drive, Palm Springs 92262, 322-9000 or toll-free (800) 233-1234; $195 winter, $99 summer. 194-suite hotel adjoining Desert Fashion Plaza in downtown Palm Springs. •

L'Horizon, 1050 East Palm Canyon Drive, Palm Springs 92262, 323-1858; $90; closed in summer. 22 secluded rooms in heart of town. Continental breakfast included. • *Ritz-Carlton, Rancho Mirage,* 68-900 Frank Sinatra Drive, Rancho Mirage 92270, 321-8282 or toll-free (800) 241-3333; $315 winter, $119 summer. Elegant 238-room full-service hotel on mountain hillside overlooking the valley; quiet spot adjacent to wildlife preserve. View pool and 10 tennis courts, plus fitness center. Gourmet dining room, all-day cafe, tennis club restaurant, and poolside bar. Traditional English afternoon tea served in lobby lounge.

DINING *Eveleen's,* 664 North Palm Canyon Drive, Palm Springs, 325-4766. Formal, intimate French restaurant with traditional cuisine and excellent service. Deserves its fine reputation. • *Las Casuelas Terraza,* 222 South Palm Canyon Drive, Palm Springs, 325-2794. Lunch and dinner daily. Favorite Mexican restaurant with patio dining in the heart of town. Try the chimichanga or tostada suprema. One of three Las Casuelas restaurants; others at 368 North Palm Canyon Drive, Palm Springs, and 70-050 Highway 111, Rancho Mirage. • *Tony Roma's,* 450 South Palm Canyon Drive, Palm Springs, 320-4297. Open from 11 A.M. to 1:30 A.M. daily. No reservations, but worth the wait for barbecued baby back ribs or chicken; split a loaf of onion rings. • *Bruzzi,* 117 North Palm Canyon Drive, Palm Springs, 327-0406. Contemporary Italian dining, with gourmet pizzas from wood-burning oven, fresh pasta, soups, salads, and deli. • *Louise's Pantry,* 124 South Palm Canyon Drive, Palm Springs, 325-5124. Tiny 1940s counter-and-booth diner with home-style cooking and delicious pies and pastry. A downtown landmark open daily for all meals. A newer, upscale Louise's Pantry (with patio dining) also serves home-style food at 44-491 Town Center Way in Palm Desert, 346-1315.

FOR MORE INFORMATION Contact Palm Springs Visitors Information Center, 2781 North Palm Canyon Drive, Palm Springs 92262, 778-8418 or toll-free (800) 347-7746. Open daily. Free hotel reservation service. • Also, contact the Palm Springs Desert Resorts Convention and Visitors Bureau, 69-930 Highway 111, Suite 201, Rancho Mirage 92270, 770-9000.

Palm Springs
Part 2: Cowboys, Indians, and Desert Lore

How did folks get around Palm Springs in the days before Cadillacs and golf carts? By horse, of course. A cadre of local equestrians still take to outlying trails on their trusty steeds, and visitors to this fashionable desert resort can do the same by mounting up at Palm Springs's first rental stable, Smoke Tree. It opened its corral gates to would-be cowboys and cowgirls in 1929, and later other stables did the same, but nowadays Smoke Tree is the only place in Palm Springs with horses for hire. Best of all, the horse trails take you to unspoiled canyons on the Agua Caliente Indian reservation, some of the most pristine places in this popular vacation spot. Although one of those hideaways, Palm Canyon, can be reached by car, making the trip on horseback takes you back to the era of the Old West.

During a wonderful weekend on the trail of history and nature in Palm Springs and environs, you'll become immersed in the area's early days with a visit to the Village Green Heritage Center, and discover all about the desert's animals, birds, and plants by touring Moorten's Botanical Garden and the Living Desert. In the hot summer months the desert reserve, heritage center, and Indian canyons are closed, so take this trip anytime from September through May.

Get to Palm Springs from Los Angeles by driving east on Interstate 10, then following California 111 along the base of the San Jacinto Mountains into town. Consider making your headquarters at one of the hotels in the heart of Palm Springs, then take a leisurely tour in a horse-drawn carriage along the city's pretty main thoroughfare, Palm Canyon Drive.

In the morning, continue on Palm Canyon Drive/California 111 as it goes through town and swings east. At the crossroad marked Sunrise Way, turn right and take La Verne Way to Toledo Avenue, then go left and continue to the Smoke Tree Stables entrance at the junction with Murray Canyon Drive. (Don't turn in at Smoke Tree Ranch.)

Over 100 miles of horse and hiking trails meander throughout the Palm Springs area, giving you close-up looks at desert plants and wildlife, as well as beautiful views. Many of the trails are located in the southeastern Palm Canyon section of the city, with convenient access from Smoke Tree Stables. Easy hour-long rides can be made along Palm Canyon Wash, a wide stretch of sand between a flood-control dike and Smoke Tree Mountain. Look for jackrabbits, quail, and roadrunners darting among the hardy desert willows and smoke trees.

A longer ride brings you to the Indian reservation, where an entry fee is paid before you proceed to the picturesque canyons. Popular for two-hour trail trips is Andreas Canyon. Besides Indian caves and grinding rocks, you'll ride past sycamores, willows, alders, and stately palms growing along the banks of an icy stream.

Another is Murray Canyon, a three-hour round trip on horseback. The trail winds back and forth by a creek that nourishes an oasis of palms and other trees in the canyon. By special arrangement, you can make a four-hour ride to see Palm Canyon and its most scenic section, where lofty palms have lined the stream bed for at least two centuries. Nearby you'll find an Indian trading post with welcome refreshments.

Before you mount up for a trail ride, be honest when the wranglers inquire about your experience in the saddle. The stable has dozens of horses, and they want riders and mounts to be matched for an enjoyable trail trip. You'll pick up some riding tips and learn more about the arid landscape from the wranglers who guide each of the trail trips from Smoke Tree Stables.

If you'd rather not see the Indian canyons from a saddle, you can drive into the reservation and then explore the canyons on foot. Get there from town by following Palm Canyon Drive south to the Agua Caliente reservation. (Don't turn onto East Palm Canyon Drive.) Visitors are welcome every day from September through June. Stop to pay the admission charge at the toll booth, then head three miles beyond to the Hermit's Bench parking area at the trading post that overlooks Palm Canyon; drive carefully on the narrow and winding road. A trail leads down to the lush grove of 5,000 Washingtonia palms.

A company called Desert Adventures also takes guided Jeep tours into the Indian Canyons, and other wilderness areas around Palm Springs. Another way to learn more about the desert is to explore part of the 13,000-acre Coachella Valley Preserve in a covered wagon pulled by a pair of mules. The comfortable outing is led by a naturalist and winds up with a steak cookout and country music sing-along.

Within the city limits of Palm Springs is another place that proves the desert is much more than sand and cactus, Moorten's Botanical Garden. Get there from the Indian Canyons by going back north on Palm Canyon Drive to number 1701, two blocks before the junction with California 111. The unique garden was begun in 1938 by Pat Moorten and her late husband, Cactus Slim, who collected more than 2,000 desert plants from all over the world. Most are identified by their popular and scientific names. As you wander through this plant showplace and nursery, you'll notice that it's also become a home for many species of birds and small desert wildlife.

Return to your hotel to relax and get ready for a night on the town at any of the Palm Springs area's excellent restaurants and entertainment spots. Don't sleep too late in the morning, because you'll want to visit the Living Desert, a botanical and wildlife sanctuary located at the base of the Santa Rosa Mountains in Palm Desert. Get there by following Palm Canyon Drive/California 111 southeast through Cathedral City and Rancho Mirage to Palm Desert, then turn right on Portola Avenue and drive up the hill to the reserve's parking lot. Established in 1970 as a branch of the Palm Springs Desert Museum, the Living Desert is a 1,200-acre area protected from development so that people will always have a place to observe the desert in its natural state.

Although most desert animals hide out during the day to escape the heat and conserve body moisture, you can view some of them at the visitors center. You'll see kangaroo rats, sidewinder snakes, fringe-toed lizards, desert hairy scorpions, tarantulas, and 20 other desert inhabitants. Some 200 species of birds make the area either their permanent or their winter home, and outdoor aviaries have been constructed so they can be observed more closely.

Also walk to a rocky hillside that's the fenced-in home for a family of desert bighorn sheep. They're under study by scientists who hope to learn the environmental needs of this rare breed and prevent its extinction. The sheep blend perfectly with the chalk-colored rock, so look carefully. You'll need a telephoto lens if you want to photograph these impressive animals, as well as some endangered species on display that include the Arabian oryx and gazelles native to Africa's Sahara Desert.

Stroll through the unusual exhibit gardens that re-create small portions of ten desert regions. The Mojave section has intriguing varieties of cactus—pancake, beavertail, barrel, calico, foxtail, and grizzly bear. Don't miss the ethnobotanical garden, a fascinating display of desert plants that the Indians of the Coachella Valley used for food, medicine, and building materials.

There are six miles of nature trails in the Living Desert, and a self-guided-tour booklet available at the entrance identifies plants and points of interest along the way. It also describes the destructive 1976 flood that roared through the reserve, and tells how the desert has made a slow but certain comeback.

You're bound to notice the contrast between the untouched desert and man's intrusion as you drive back to Palm Springs. It's another world entirely that you see along California 111, a busy highway bordered by stores, offices, residential enclaves, golf courses, restaurants, and resort hotels. There's no question that many of the lodgings in Palm Springs are pretty plush, a far cry from the desert resort's early days, when visitors slept in tents. Even the town's leading citizens had rustic living quarters, such as adobes and a house made of railroad ties.

To glimpse some of Palm Spring's pioneer era, visit the Village Green Heritage Center in the heart of town. It's just beyond the corner of South Palm Canyon Drive/California 111 and Arenas Road. On a bit of land amid downtown shops, you'll find a pair of restored desert homes from the previous century. One is considered the city's oldest building, an adobe built in 1884 by ''Judge'' John McCallum, Palm Spring's first permanent settler. It's now the main museum of the Palm Springs Historical Society. Among its exhibits are artifacts and photos of Cahuilla Indians, the area's earliest residents. Also look for the display of sun-tinted lavender glass.

Next door, with more memorabilia donated by local folks, you can tour the home of another Palm Springs pioneer, Cornelia White. She arrived in 1912 and bought the cottage from the town's first hotel proprietor, Dr. Welwood Murray. He had constructed the home 19 years earlier with railroad ties taken from a defunct spur line that real estate speculators ran to town from the Southern Pacific tracks.

Another Village Green building to visit is Ruddy's General Store, a museum of more than 6,000 items found in an old-time general store. The packaging and brand names are fascinating. Remember Rinso? Besides soap, you'll see everything from sewing notions to patent medicines, hardware, and clothing. Two other places to visit at the Village Green are the Agua Caliente Cultural Museum Center, featuring historical artifacts, photographs, and dioramas of the area's Cahuilla Indians, and a satellite shop of the Palm Springs Desert Museum, with art, toys, books, and other gift items.

Stroll a couple of blocks to tour the multimillion-dollar Palm Springs Desert Museum, the community's cultural center dedicated to art, natural science, and the performing arts. Visitors often spend several hours viewing the permanent art exhibits and traveling shows, as well as interpretive displays of the desert environment. There are Sunday afternoon concerts in the winter season, too. Also check the visitor booklets for events scheduled in the McCallum Theater for the Performing Arts at the Bob Hope Cultural Center in Palm Desert.

When your weekend with history and nature in Palm Springs is over, return to Los Angeles by retracing your route on California 111 and Interstate 10.

Round trip is about 230 miles.

Palm Springs Area Code: 619

SIGHTSEEING   *Smoke Tree Stables,* 2500 Toledo Avenue, Palm Springs 92262, 327-1372. Open daily; Labor Day weekend through mid-June from 8 A.M. to dusk, call for hours in summer. $20 per person per hour. 3-hour ride to Murray Canyon, $60 per person. • *Moorten's Botanical Garden,* 1701 South Canyon Drive, Palm Springs 92262, 327-6555. Open daily from 9 A.M. to 5 P.M. year round. Adults $1.50, children 5 to 16 years $.50. Self-guided tours. • *Indian Canyons,* end of South Palm Canyon Drive on the Agua Caliente Indian Reservation, Palm Springs, 325-5673. Open daily from 8:30 A.M. to 5 P.M. September through June; closed in summer. Adults $3.50, children 6 to 12 years $.75. Admission includes Palm, Andreas, and Murray canyons. Picturesque picnic spots. • *Desert Adventure Tours,* 68-733 Perez Road, Suite 16, Cathedral City 92234, 324-3378. Narrated visits to the Indian Canyons and other wilderness areas in open 7-passenger Jeeps. 2-hour tours $49, seniors and children $45; half-day tours $89, children and seniors $84. Call for itineraries and departure times. • *Covered Wagon Tours,* P.O. Box 1106, La Quinta 92253, 347-2161. Leisurely guided ride in mule-drawn, rubber-tired covered wagon through pristine nature area, the Coachella Valley Preserve. 2-hour tour $40, with steak cookout and entertainment $55; children 7 to 16 years half price. • *Living Desert,* 47-900 Portola Avenue, Palm Desert 92260, 346-5694. Open daily September through mid-June from 9 A.M. to 5 P.M.; closed in summer. Adults $6, children 6 to 15 years $3. Self-guided tours. • *Village Green Heritage Center,* 221 South Palm Canyon Drive, Palm Springs 92262, 323-8297. Open Sundays and Wednesdays from 12 to 3 P.M., Thursday through Saturday from 10 A.M. to 4 P.M. from mid-October through May; closed in summer. Adults $.50 per house, students and children free. Docents of the Palm Springs Historical Society will answer questions during your self-guided tour of 2 nineteenth-century homes. Also at Heritage Center, *Ruddy's General Store Museum,* 327-2156. Open Thursday through Sunday from 10 A.M. to 4 P.M. from October through June; other months open weekends only from 12 to 6 P.M. Admission $1, children under 12 years free. *Agua Caliente Cultural Museum Center,* at the Heritage Center, 323-0151. Cahuilla Indian exhibits. Open daily 8 A.M. to 4 P.M., Thursdays to 9 P.M., from September through May; closed in summer. Admission $.50. *Palm Springs Desert Museum,* satellite shop at the Heritage Center, 778-1152. Open weekends 9 A.M. to 5 P.M., weekdays except Mondays to 4 P.M., Thursdays to 9 P.M. Closed June through August. • *Palm Springs*

Desert Museum, 101 Museum Drive, Palm Springs 92262, 325-7186. Open mid-September through May from 10 A.M. to 5 P.M. on weekends, and 10 A.M. to 4 P.M. weekdays except Mondays. Adults $4, students and seniors $3, children 6 to 16 years $2.

LODGING   *Westin Mission Hills Resort,* 71-333 Dinah Shore Drive, Rancho Mirage 92270, 328-5955 or toll-free (800) 228-3000; $250 in winter, $135 in summer. Impressive resort with Moroccan motif spread over 360 acres, including two 18-hole golf courses. 512 rooms and suites, 7 tennis courts, 3 swimming pools, and health club. ● *Wyndham Palm Springs,* 888 East Tahquitz Way, Palm Springs 92262, 322-6000; $190 winter, $75 summer. 410 room-and-suite hotel adjacent to Palm Springs Convention Center. Courtyard swimming pool, 2 restaurants. 3 blocks to Palm Canyon Drive shops. ● *Autry Resort Hotel,* 4200 East Palm Canyon Drive, Palm Springs 92262, 328-1171 or toll-free (800) 443-6328; $135 winter, $95 summer. Gene Autry's namesake lodging. 185 rooms and bungalows on attractive grounds at edge of town. 3 swimming pools, 6 tennis courts, and pro. ● *Palm Springs Hilton Resort,* 400 East Tahquitz-McCallum Way, Palm Springs 92262, 320-6868 or toll-free (800) 522-6900; from $155 high season, $80 in summer. Convenient downtown hotel. Tennis, health and beauty center, 2 dining rooms. ● *Marriott's Rancho Las Palmas Resort,* 41-000 Bob Hope Drive, Rancho Mirage 92270, 568-2727 or toll-free (800) 458-8786; $240 winter, $99 summer. 456 rooms on 27-acre grounds with 25 tennis courts, 27 holes of golf. A relaxing hideaway with rooms in low-profile buildings scattered around lush grounds overlooking lake, golf links, duck ponds, and swimming pools. Outstanding service too. ● *Marriott's Desert Springs Resort & Spa,* 74-885 Country Club Drive, Palm Desert 92260, 341-2211 or toll-free (800) 228-9290; $240 winter, $125 summer. The Palm Springs area's largest lodging, a multiwing high-rise with 892 rooms. A very busy convention spot with 9 restaurants, lounges, and snack bars, plus 19 tennis courts, 36 holes of golf, and full health spa. ● *Doubletree Resort,* Vista Chino at Landau Boulevard, Cathedral City 92234, 322-7000 or toll-free (800) 528-0444; $95 winter, $49 summer. Northeast of airport just beyond Palm Springs city limits. 289 rooms, 18-hole golf course, 10 tennis and 2 racquetball courts.

DINING   Also see "Dining" suggestions in Palm Springs: Part 1. ● *Le Vallauris,* 385 West Tahquitz Way, Palm Springs, 325-5059.

Fine French food for lunch (except Saturdays), Sunday brunch, and dinner nightly. Also piano bar. Near Palm Springs Desert Museum in a former home, with delightful patio dining. • Ethnic choices include *Otani,* 266 North Avenida Caballeros, Palm Springs, 327-6700. Japanese display cooking at Teppan-yaki tables, plus sushi, tempura, and yakitori bars. • *Bangkok Five,* 69-930 Highway 111, Rancho Mirage, 770-9508. Desert version of popular Thai restaurants in Los Angeles and Orange counties. • *Señor Salsa,* 73-725 El Paseo, Palm Desert, 346-0245. Trendy, upscale Mexican restaurant with good food and great margaritas. • *Club 74,* 73-061 El Paseo, Palm Desert, 568-2782. This offspring of Eveleen's of Palm Springs has a 2nd-floor home on Palm Desert's renowned shopping street. Delightfully French. • *Cuistot,* 73-111 El Paseo, Palm Desert, 340-1000. More fine French fare along fashionable El Paseo. Closed Mondays. • *Doug Arango's,* 72-695 Highway 111, Palm Desert, 341-4120. Bistro atmosphere, pasta dishes, and varied menu which changes daily.

FOR MORE INFORMATION Contact Palm Springs Visitor Information Center, 2781 North Palm Canyon Drive, Palm Springs 92262, 778-8418 or toll-free (800) 347-7746. Open daily. Free hotel reservation service. Also, contact the Palm Springs Desert Resorts Convention and Visitors Bureau, 69-930 Highway 111, Rancho Mirage 92270, 770-9000.

A Date Down in the Coachella Valley

Although most folks say *Palm Springs* when they refer to Southern California's desert playground, many of the popular golf and tennis resorts are not within its city limits. You'll find them "down valley" in the neighboring communities of Cathedral City, Rancho Mirage, Indian Wells, Palm Desert, La Quinta, and Bermuda Dunes. They occupy an irrigated section of the Coachella Valley in the midst of the Colorado Desert.

Anchoring the valley's eastern end is its oldest city, Indio, the hub of a vast agricultural area that produces scores of crops, including 95 percent of all American-grown dates. Date palms from North Africa and the Middle East were planted in the Indio area early in this century, the beginning of an unusual crop that now yields 20,000 tons of fruit and $42 million annually. The Coachella Valley, nicknamed the Date Capital of the United States, is second only to Iraq in world date production.

If you've been indifferent about dates, don't judge them from the machine-processed dry type sold in supermarkets. The best dates are soft and rather delicate, picked and sorted by hand, and unpitted. These you'll discover in the roadside date garden shops clustered near Indio. Besides the naturally sweet fruit itself, look for all kinds of date products: the popular date shake, date nut bread, date butter, date cookies, and date candy. In addition, there's another date to remember—mid-February. That's when Indio hosts a lively exposition to celebrate the end of the date harvest.

Even if you can't time your weekend getaway for the colorful Riverside County Fair/National Date Festival, make a journey to the Coachella Valley to enjoy its abundant sunshine, golf courses, tennis courts, and swimming pools. Make your destination a deluxe resort, such as La Quinta Hotel at La Quinta, Stouffer Esmeralda, or Hyatt Grand Champions at Indian Wells. Get there from Los Angeles by driving east on Interstate 10 and exiting south on Washington Street just before Indio.

The road crosses California 111 and leads to Eisenhower Drive where stately Italian cypress trees flank the entrance to La Quinta (say *la keenta*), the venerable valley resort that opened its doors as a 20-room hostelry in 1926. An expansion project in 1988 increased the number of accommodations to 640 rooms and suites, all in Spanish-style casitas (cottages) spread throughout the beautiful 45-acre property. The resort is well known for its tennis club, where 30 grass, clay, and hard courts are set in groves of olive trees and date palms.

Also impressive are the 54 holes of championship golf available to guests, including 18 challenging holes designed by Pete Dye. Focal points for relaxation are La Quinta's two dozen swimming pools and more than an equal number of whirlpool spas located among the casitas. The resort also boasts several restaurants, including one that features a lavish champagne brunch that's long been a Sunday tradition at La Quinta Hotel.

West on California 111 from Washington Street is another relaxing headquarters for your "down valley" holiday, Hyatt Grand Champions Resort, a chain hotel in name only. Splurge by booking a Villa Suite, a secluded as well as splendid accommodation that includes your personal butler. Two challenging 18-hole courses designed by Ted Robinson surround the resort, and you also have a choice of a dozen grass, clay, and hard-surface courts. The resort's golf and tennis staffs will help improve your game; then enjoy the rejuvenation of steam, sauna, and massage in the health and fitness club.

Within sight of the Hyatt is another Indian Wells luxury resort, the Stouffer Esmeralda, with one of the prettiest swimming pools in the desert; it even has a sandy beach entrance. You'll be treated to a spacious room or suite, exceptional meals, and Stouffer's personal touches, including morning coffee and a newspaper delivered with your wake-up call. A pair of championship golf courses border the resort, which also offers guests seven tennis courts and a complete health spa and fitness center.

Many guests find little reason to leave their Coachella Valley resort, but you may be enticed by a hot-air balloon ride over the desert or the chance to watch horses and their riders compete in an exciting polo match played at the Empire and Eldorado polo clubs. And don't forget those dates—Deglet Noor, Medjool, Halaway, Khadrawy, Barhi, and Zahidi are among the different types.

When you're ready to embark on a sampler of date gardens, head east toward Indio on California 111 until you see Jensen's, one of the oldest and most interesting gardens. Stroll around this botanical showplace, which is planted with dozens of different trees, including one that has produced 14 varieties of fruit. Almost next door is another of the area's earliest date gardens, Shields. Established in 1924, it now suffers from being the biggest and most commercial shop. Shields does not offer date samples to visitors, having given up the tradition carried on at many other date garden shops.

You'll see more extensive date gardens and can visit a few other shops south of Indio. Along the way on California 111, you'll pass the Moorish-looking Desert Expo Centre between Arabia and Oasis streets. It's home for the Riverside Country Fair/National Date Festival, a ten-day event every February that includes comic camel and ostrich races in the afternoon. The unpredictable dromedaries and birds and their jouncing jockeys lead off the daily grandstand shows featuring musical and variety entertainment. Also staged nightly is the traditional *Arabian Nights Pageant,* a melodramatic musical fantasy with a cast of 75 singers, dancers, and actors from the community. The production is performed outdoors and is free to all fairgoers. Besides the shows, there are carnival rides, visitor contests, marionette performances, 4H and FFA livestock judging, and all sorts of exhibits, including a display of the festival's namesakes—119 varieties of dates grown in the Indio area.

To sample more fresh dates and see groves of the stately palm trees, continue on California 111 south to the city of Coachella. Bear right on California 86 to Lee Anderson's Covalda Date Company (at 6th Street) to watch the fancy fruit being graded and packed by hand. Seven miles farther south on California 86 is the Valerie Jean Date Shop, where you'll get a tasty date milk shake for a reasonable price. Or go left on Avenue 52 in Coachella to rejoin California 111, then turn right and continue south to the family-run Oasis Date

Gardens just beyond Thermal. Undoubtedly you're all dated up by now and ready for a relaxing evening at your resort hotel. Plan an early bedtime if you decide to rise with the sun in a hot-air balloon.

The most exhilarating way to sightsee in the desert is from a wicker basket, drifting along with the wind currents beneath a bag of hot air that billows seven stories high. Catching the prevailing breezes, you'll float like a bird over the golf courses, date palms, and resort complexes that dot the Coachella Valley between the San Jacinto and Little San Bernardino mountain ranges.

It's an exciting moment when you first rise from the ground, unrestricted by safety belts or Plexiglas windows. With such a unique view of the scenic Palm Springs area, be certain to take your camera and plenty of film. Early-morning flights depart from Thermal, while the afternoon excursions go aloft from Bermuda Dunes.

Several ballooning companies operate daily flights in the winter season, including Desert Balloon Charters run by John Zimmer. His handmade wicker baskets extend about waist high and are big enough for up to six passengers and a pilot, all standing. Also inside are three tanks of propane gas to supply the burner that fills an enormous nylon balloon with enough hot air to make it rise.

Your course is determined by wind direction and the pilot, who adds hot air with the burner or releases it by pulling a cord to a vent at the balloon's top. By raising and lowering the balloon he can catch different wind currents at different altitudes. After an hour or so you'll float back to earth and be met by a chase vehicle with a bottle of champagne for the traditional toast to a successful flight.

Champagne also flows at the Coachella Valley's neighboring Empire and Eldorado polo clubs, where visitors often enjoy picnics while watching teams of world-class polo players and their well-trained mounts race up and down the grassy fields. During the September-to-April season you can attend daily practice sessions, but most observers prefer the excitement of the weekend tournaments. Bring a blanket to relax at the field's edge, or sit at shaded tables or in the spectator bleachers.

With skill and daring the eight players swing their flexible mallets to whack a wooden ball between the goal posts. Exhausted polo ponies are frequently replaced during the game, which has six periods (called chukkers) of 7½ minutes each. Bring binoculars for a close-up look at the skillful horse handling by players who carry on this hard-riding sport that was made popular by British army officers in India more than a century ago.

Both polo clubs are south of Indio between Avenue 50 and Avenue 52, and which are intersected by Monroe Street. When it's time to return home, follow that street north to rejoin Interstate 10 back to Los Angeles.

Round trip is about 318 miles.

Coachella Valley Area Code: 619

SIGHTSEEING   *Jensen's Date and Citrus Gardens,* 80-653 Highway 111, Indio 92201, 347-3897. Open 9 A.M. to 5 P.M. daily. • *Shields Date Gardens,* 80-225 Highway 111, Indio 92201, 347-0996. Open 8 A.M. to 6 P.M. daily. • *Lee Anderson's Covalda Date Co.,* 51-392 Highway 86 (near Bagdad Avenue), Coachella 92236, 398-3551. Open daily from 9 A.M. to 5:30 P.M., except Sundays from noon. • *Valerie Jean Date Shop,* 66-021 Highway 86 at Avenue 66, Thermal 92274, 397-4159. Open 8 A.M. to 5 P.M. daily (to 6 P.M. in summer). • *Oasis Date Gardens,* 59-111 Highway 111, Thermal 92274, 399-5665. Open 8:30 A.M. to 5:30 P.M. weekdays. • *Desert Balloon Charters,* P. O. Box 2713, Palm Desert 92261, 346-8575. 1-hour hot-air balloon flights launch from the Balloon Ranch, 82-550 Airport Boulevard, southeast of La Quinta, at 7 A.M. and 3:30 P.M. daily from October through May; $125 per person, including champagne toast and flight certificate. Other ballooning companies flying over the Coachella Valley include *Fantasy Balloon Flights,* 568-0997; *Dream Flights,* 321-5154; and *American Balloon Charters,* 327-8544. • *Eldorado Polo Club,* 50-950 Madison Street, Indio 92201, 342-4133. Polo games take place weekends at 10 A.M., 12 and 2 P.M. November through mid-April. Admission for tournament games $6, children under 14 years free. You can watch daily practice sessions without charge. • *Empire Polo Club and Equestrain Park,* 81-500 Avenue 52, Indio 92201, 342-3321. From September through April polo games are held weekends in the morning and afternoon; call for game times and entrance fee, if any.

EVENTS   *Riverside County Fair/National Date Festival,* Desert Expo Centre, Highway 111 at 46-350 Arabia Street, Indio 92201, 863-8247. Annual Coachella Valley celebration beginning mid-February for 10 days. Hours 10 A.M. to 10 P.M. Admission $5, seniors $4, children 5 to 11 years $2, including all stage events. All-day parking $2, RVs $10. Home-town fun for everyone. • *Empire Balloon, Wine, and Polo Festival,* Empire Polo Club and Equestrain Park (see above), 775-1715. Mid-November hot-air balloon competition and other events.

LODGING   *La Quinta Hotel Golf and Tennis Resort,* 49-499 Eisenhower Drive, La Quinta 92253, 564-4111 or California toll-free (800) 472-4316; $185 winter, $80 summer. Opened in 1926. Classy resort with accommodations in Spanish-style adobe cottages spread among date groves and formal gardens. Lighted tennis courts and 3 golf courses. Also 5 restaurants (see below). • *Hyatt Grand Champions Resort,* 44-600 Indian Wells Lane, Indian Wells 92210, 341-1000; $199 winter, $119 summer. Impressive 336-room all-suite hotel surrounded by 2 golf courses and 12 tennis courts. Private Garden Villa Suites include your own butler; $525 winter, $350 summer. Health and fitness club, plus The Salon for personal beauty care. Excellent restaurants (see below). • *Stouffer Esmeralda Resort,* 44-400 Indian Wells Lane, Indian Wells 92210, 773-4444 or toll-free (800) 552-4386; $200. Posh 560-room resort with 36 holes of golf, 7 tennis courts, palm-fringed swimming pool, health spa, and outstanding service. Also, award-winning restaurant (see below). • *Hotel Indian Wells,* 76-661 Highway 111, Indian Wells 92210, 345-6466 or toll-free (800) 248-3220; $99 summer, $145 winter. 151 rooms with full concierge service. Adjacent to golf course and tennis club. Restaurant has American, Italian, and continental dishes. • *Best Western Date Tree Motor Hotel,* 81-909 Indio Boulevard, Indio 92201, 347-3421; $64 winter, $52 summer. Pleasant motel in landscaped setting. Restaurant adjacent.

DINING   *La Quinta Hotel* (see above). 5 restaurants, including *Montanas* with continental cuisine; reservations suggested. It's also the site for lavish Sunday champagne brunch with everything from fresh seafood, roast beef, and Oriental dishes to Belgium waffles and made-to-order omelets. Watch the chef at work in his display kitchen at *Morgans,* named for the hotel's founder and offering an all-day menu. *The Adobe Grill* has Mexican dishes for lunch and dinner. Dining rooms at tennis and golf clubs both serve breakfast and lunch. • *Hyatt Grand Champions Resort* (see above). Contemporary American fare is served with flair nightly at *Austin's,* the hotel's formal dining room. Exotic pizzas and Italian specialties are mainstays of *Trattoria California,* open daily for all meals; enjoy Sunday brunch on the terrace with a golf-course view. *Charlie's* is a favorite for fresh seafood in an informal atmosphere. • *Stouffer Esmeralda Resort* (see above). Specialties from France, Italy, and Spain are featured at *Sirocco,* the hotel's fine-dining restaurant, which also boasts an extensive wine list. Dress up to match the elegant decor. *Charisma* is the place for California cuisine and casual dining indoors or on the terrace. • *Vicki's of Santa Fe,* 45-100 Club Drive, Indian Wells, 345-9770. A popular rendezvous for drinks and American fare amid Southwest decor. • See "Dining" selections in Palm Springs, Parts 1 and 2 (pages 267 and 273–274), for other restaurant suggestions.

FOR MORE INFORMATION Contact the Indio Chamber of Commerce, 82-503 Highway 111 (or P.O. Box TTT), Indio 92201, 347-0676. Also, Palm Springs Desert Resorts Convention and Visitors Bureau, 69-930 Highway 111, Suite 201, Rancho Mirage 92270, 770-9000.

Adventures in Anza-Borrego Desert State Park

The folks in San Francisco were cheering in 1858 when the Butterfield Overland Mail stage rolled into town with its first passenger and pouch of letters. It heralded the beginning of regular overland transportation and mail service to and from the West Coast. Today's travelers might not be so enthusiastic. The bone-jarring journey from Missouri in a crowded stagecoach took 24 days and nights. Passengers paid $150 for a one-way ticket and were encouraged to bring blankets, a revolver or knife, and extra food for the desert crossing. Those who made it through the 2,600-mile trip lost an average of 23 pounds.

Reminders of those early days of travel can be glimpsed by driving along San Diego County Road S2 on the fringe of the Colorado Desert. It closely follows the first overland route to California, the Southern Emigrant Trail, which was used initially by trappers, then soldiers and gold seekers, and finally the stagecoach lines.

That quiet back road also cuts across the spectacular Anza-Borrego Desert State Park, the largest state park in all of the contiguous 48 states. One of California's first frontiers, the 600,000-acre preserve is now one of the state's last remaining undisturbed areas. For visitors from the city there's the promise of smog-free days and star-filled nights, wide-open spaces and wonderful serenity. And you'll see that despite its foreboding reputation, the desert has not been abandoned by Mother Nature. Plants and trees color the landscape, especially when a profusion of wildflowers bursts into bloom after the winter rains. Birds and animals, like the comical roadrunners and quick cottontails that scurry across your path, add other enjoyment.

With only a weekend and the family car, you'll just be able to glimpse the natural attractions in this vast, unspoiled land. While many desert devotees come with four-wheel-drive vehicles and plenty of time to explore along the hundreds of miles of paved and primitive roads, you'll become well acquainted with Anza-Borrego's wildlife, geology, and history by following a few of the park's self-guiding nature trails and auto tours. Park rangers and volunteer naturalists also lead special tours by car and foot on weekends in the winter season, which is the most popular time to enjoy the desert.

In the midst of this immense park is the hospitable little community of Borrego Springs and an outstanding hostelry, La Casa del Zorro, another of the desert's unexpected delights. A treat for campers is the freedom to select a site anywhere along the road; no other California state park permits such unrestricted camping.

Get to Anza-Borrego Desert State Park from Los Angeles by taking California 60 (Pomona Freeway) east past Riverside and joining Interstate 215 and then Interstate 15 south toward San Diego. Just beyond Temecula, exit east on California 79 to Warner Springs. En route, at Oak Grove, six miles past the Riverside–San Diego county line, a historical marker points out one of the original adobe stage stations on the Butterfield Overland Mail route. After only 30 months of service, the cross-country stages stopped running when the Civil War began in 1861. Continue on California 79 beyond Warner Springs and turn left on San Diego County Road S2. A half mile beyond is the Warner Ranch House, also a stage stop. U.S. troops fighting in the Mexican War of 1846–48 were billeted in this old adobe, which now shows the toll of time and is protected by a fence until it can be restored. Continue east about four miles to join S22, a road that winds down the mountainside to the vast Colorado Desert.

Appearing as an oasis is the resort and retirement community of Borrego Springs, your base for exploration of the desert park, which is two-thirds the size of Rhode Island. The flat arid land of Borrego Springs has been made green by irrigation, with majestic mountains for a backdrop. There you'll find warm sun, blue skies, pure air, and evidence of the good life—swimming pools, golf courses, tennis courts.

This is a friendly place, where the year-round townsfolk—numbering 2,700 at last count—gather weekdays at the post office to gossip and get their mail. Outside, a community bulletin board also keeps them abreast of the latest happenings. Many residents are retired, happy with the desert's peace and quiet, opportunities for outdoor recreation, and low property taxes.

Unless you camp in the park, bed down in Borrego Springs at La Casa del Zorro, the area's best-known lodging. It has grown around an adobe ranch house built in 1937 and has long been Anza-Borrego's favorite resort. Nestled in a grove of willowy tamarisk trees are a number of comfortable cottages and a trio of modern buildings with studio rooms and suites. Guests enjoy three

swimming pools and six lighted tennis courts, along with privileges on the 18-hole public golf course close by at the Rams Hill
Country Club. If this popular resort is filled, rent a home at Rams
Hill, a multimillion-dollar residential enclave. Borrego Springs
also has six motels and a number of condominium apartments for
rent.

You'll probably eat most of your meals at La Casa del Zorro,
which has the best food in town. Guests and drop-ins dine in the
Presidio and Butterfield rooms amid paintings of stagecoaches and
early California scenes. The surroundings may be Western, but
nobody shows up for dinner in blue jeans at this upscale desert
resort. You should also dress up for dinner at the clubhouse of the
Rams Hill Country Club. Among the choices for more informal
dining are the Whifferdil out by the Borrego Valley Airport, Panda
Chinese, a landmark eatery in old World War II Quonset huts near
the center of town, and the Las Palmas bar and grill at the Palm
Canyon Resort.

You'll quickly discover that enjoyment of the desert itself is a
significant part of the relaxed life-style in Borrego Springs. At the
western edge of town is the Anza-Borrego park headquarters and a
million-dollar visitors center. Like the shelters of desert animals, it's
built underground and topped with displays of native plants and
rocks. Exhibits inside explain more about the desert's history,
geology, wildlife, and weather. Be sure to watch the outstanding
slide show about desert life. For your weekend excursions in the
park, ask at the visitors center for a map, self-guided-tour leaflets,
and current road conditions. The rangers will tell you the subjects
and times of their weekend naturalist programs, too.

By hiking the nearby Borrego Palm Canyon nature trail, you'll
find out that the desert is more beautiful and alive than it sometimes
seems. Take your time ambling along this path, which offers a
close-up look at 15 desert plants once used by the Cahuilla
(*ka-WE-ya*) Indians for food, medicine, and shelter. You'll see
buckhorn cholla, creosote bush, honey mesquite, white sage, California fan palms, and more. Continue up the canyon to view a scenic
grove of those native palms, officially named *Washingtonia filifera*
in honor of the first U.S. president. The Cahuilla ate the palms' dried
fruit and used their fronds to make baskets, sandallike footwear, and
even houses.

Afterward, follow the park's auto-tour brochures and drive east
on S22 beyond Borrego Springs to witness more of the desert's
varied geography, including faults and fractures created by earthquakes.

An alternative to exploring the park on your own is to arrange an
outing with Big T's Desert Tours, a guide service run by naturalist
T. Curtain. He shares his intimate desert knowledge on itineraries
that are designed according to what you especially want to see and

experience. Book well in advance for this personalized outing, especially during the wildflower season.

There's not much in the way of evening entertainment in Borrego Springs, except for looking at the star-filled sky or attending a park campfire program at the Borrego Palm Canyon campground. During the winter season, La Casa del Zorro usually draws a crowd on Saturday night for its dinners, dance music, and live theater productions. Before turning in for a peaceful night's sleep, arrange at the hotel reception desk to have a picnic lunch ready for the next day's excursion to the southern part of the park.

You'll relive the travels of Old West pioneers by driving south from Borrego Springs on S3 and California 78 to rejoin S2, the county road that parallels the historic Southern Emigrant Trail. At Scissors Crossing, where the highways intersect, a marker recalls the location of the San Felipe Stage Station. Farther along S2, turn left at the sign to the Little Pass Campground and follow campground roads on the left side until you spot a canyonlike cleft in the hills. Walk to the marker that describes the Foot and Walker Pass, a place where stage passengers got out so the horses could climb the steep hill. Then stroll up to the high point, where you can look down on wagon-wheel tracks, traces of the original route that ran through the desert.

After driving south three more miles to Box Canyon, also take the walkway down to the spot where Lieutenant Colonel Cooke and his Mormon Battalion widened the trail through the gorge with picks and shovels in 1847, thus opening the first road into Southern California wide enough for wagons. As S2 descends to the western limits of the great Colorado Desert, you'll find the Vallecito Stage Station in a green oasis. Built in 1835 and first used as a stop on the San Antonio–San Diego "Jackass" Mail Line, the adobe was authentically reconstructed in 1934 and is now part of a San Diego county park. The Vallecito station was a welcome sight to westbound stage passengers, because it marked the end of their desert crossing. Read the plaques that tell about important events at the historic outpost.

Continue a few miles for a refreshing finish to your weekend in the Anza-Borrego desert, a relaxing dip in the therapeutic mineral pools at Agua Caliente Hot Springs, also a county park. Beyond are the sites of two more way stations on the Butterfield Stage route, at Palm Springs and Carrizo Marsh, but these can be reached only by vehicles with four-wheel drive.

Return to Los Angeles by following S2 northwest to join California 79 near Warner Springs and continue home the way you came. For an alternate route, you can make a longer circle trip back to Los Angeles by continuing southeast on S2 to join Interstate 8 at Ocotillo. Then go west toward San Diego and pick up Interstate 15 or 5 for the drive north.

Round trip is about 360 miles.

Borrego Springs Area Code: 619

SIGHTSEEING   *Anza-Borrego Desert State Park,* headquarters and visitors center located at west end of Palm Canyon Road (P.O. Box 428), Borrego Springs 92204, 767-5311. Visitors center open every day from 9 A.M. to 5 P.M., except June through September from 10 A.M. to 3 P.M. on weekends and major holidays. Free admission. Desert exhibits; also 20-minute slide show presented every hour. Naturalist programs offered weekends and holidays except in summer. • *Big T's Desert Tours,* 7572 Great Southern Overland Stage Route, Julian 92036, 765-1309. Personalized tours in an air-conditioned 4-wheel-drive vehicle. $60 per person all day; children under 13 years free. A rewarding experience. • *Rams Hill Country Club,* 1881 Rams Hill Road (near La Casa del Zorro Resort), Borrego Springs 92004, 767-5125. 18-hole public golf course; $50 per person for Rams Hill guests, $70 for the general public, including cart. • *Agua Caliente County Park,* 1 mile south of Agua Caliente Springs off S2, 565-3600. Day-use entry $2 per car. Popular since Indian days for therapeutic hot springs. Features mineral pools, bathhouses, recreation building, and general store, plus camping (see below) and picnicking.

LODGING   *La Casa del Zorro,* 3845 Yaqui Pass Road (or P.O. Box 127), Borrego Springs 92004, 767-5323 or toll-free (800) 824-1884; $98, casitas (cottages) from $180, mid-November through April. Rates considerably lower during hot summer months. Also excellent restaurants (see below). 2-night minimum stay on weekends. • *Rams Hill Country Club* (see above), 767-5028. Furnished 1- and 2-bedroom homes near the golf course; $145–$220, lower in summer. Meals served in the clubhouse (see below). • *Palm Canyon Resort,* 221 Palm Canyon Drive, Borrego Springs 92004, 767-5341 or toll-free (800) 242-0044; $72. 44-room motel resort complex with restaurant (see below) and 143 RV camping sites with hookups. • *Club Circle Resort,* 3134 Club Circle East (or P.O. Box 2130), Borrego Springs 92004, 767-5944; $80. Fully furnished condominium apartments surrounded by 9-hole, 3-par golf course. 2-night minimum. • *Villas Borrego Resort,* 533 Palm Canyon Drive (or P.O. Box 1077), Borrego Springs 92004, 767-5371; $100. Condominium apartments with kitchens. 2-night minimum.

CAMPING   Anza-Borrego Desert State Park (see above) has three main fee campgrounds, and visitors may also camp anywhere along park roads without charge. *Borrego Palm Canyon*, near park headquarters and Borrego Springs off S2, 52 RV sites with hookups ($18 per night) and 65 tent sites ($14). *Tamarisk Grove*, 12 miles south of Borrego Springs on S3, 27 sites, $14 nightly. *Bow Willow*, 12 miles south of Agua Caliente Springs off S2, 16 sites. $9 per night. Reservations through MISTIX advised in winter and spring wildflower season; call toll-free (800) 444-7275. • *Vallecito County Park*, 4 miles north of Agua Caliente Springs on S2, 565-3600. 44 sites, $8 per night. • *Agua Caliente County Park* (see above). 140 sites, $14 with hookups, $10 without. Bathing in natural hot springs.

DINING   *La Casa del Zorro* (see above). Breakfast, lunch, and dinner daily in the *Butterfield Room*; gourmet dinners in the *Presidio Room*, early-bird specials from 4 to 6 P.M. • *Le Pavilion*, at Rams Hill Country Club (see above), 767-5000 or 767-5006. Clubhouse has golf course–view restaurant serving lunch and dinner; closed Monday through Wednesday in summer. Snack bar is open for breakfast and lunch from 7 A.M. to 3 P.M. year round. • *Las Palmas Bar and Grill*, at Palm Canyon Resort (see above). Open daily in winter for all meals from 7 A.M. to 9 P.M. • *Whifferdil*, 1886 East Palm Canyon Drive, Borrego Springs, 767-4646. 3 miles east of town at Borrego Valley Airport. Lunch and dinner daily. • *Panda Chinese*, east of Christmas Circle at 818 Palm Canyon Drive, Borrego Springs, 586-0022. Chinese eatery in converted Quonset huts. Closed in summer.

FOR MORE INFORMATION   Contact the Borrego Springs Chamber of Commerce, 622 Palm Canyon Drive (or P.O. Box 66), Borrego Springs 92004, 767-5555. Hours 10 A.M. to 4 P.M. daily. Lists of lodgings and restaurants. • Also, Anza-Borrego Desert State Park (see above) for touring and camping information.

Springtime Spectacular: Viewing the Wildflowers

Springtime brings a profusion of color to the Southern California scene as wildflowers awake across the countryside. Winter rain, spring sunshine, and the altitude determine the extent of the annual floral extravaganza, but you're certain to find a good show somewhere in the Southland from mid-March through May.

Easter week traditionally is an excellent time to view the bright blossoms that are scattered like a patchwork quilt, first in the lower Colorado Desert regions and later in the higher Mojave Desert areas. Of course, Mother Nature can change her fickle mind and cancel the show. Too many overcast days or strong winds will fold up the flower petals and ruin the dazzling display.

With any luck, you'll see a colorful array on any weekend excursion during the wildflower season. The blossoms pop open in more shades than a rainbow, notably yellow, orange, pink, purple, and blue, as well as white. Easy to spot from your car is the brilliant golden California poppy, the official state flower. California lilac, lupine, and wild mustard also are obvious to passing motorists. However, many wildflowers are so small that you need to get on hands and knees to see their tiny petals. Some are so minute and close to the ground that veteran viewers have nicknamed them "belly flowers." For the most enjoyment, buy an illustrated wildflower book to take on your outing. Then be on the lookout for plants like fiddleneck, sand verbena, coreopsis, desert dandelion, blazing star, sand mat, woolly marigold, evening primrose, and dozens more.

To help you locate the best of the blooms, here are some suggestions for wildflower excursions in springtime. Before taking off, avoid disappointment by calling the flower folks at your destination for an up-to-the minute blossom report; phone numbers are given for those local contacts.

What follows is a county-by-county report on wildflower viewing around the Los Angeles area, starting to the south in the low Colorado Desert areas of San Diego County, where the flowers are on the road from March through May, so be sure to reserve accommodations before you take off for the weekend, especially in those desert areas where lodging is limited.

For specific places to shelter overnight and dine out, as well as driving instructions, refer to the weekend trips that include the wildflower areas described below.

If you'd rather not worry where to look for the flowers, hire a naturalist, T. Curtain, whose guide service goes by the name of Big T's Desert Tours. He'll take you in an air-conditioned 4-wheel-drive vehicle to see some of the best floral displays in Anza-Borrego Desert State Park. (See "Adventures in Anza-Borrego Desert State Park," page 280.) Big T charges $30 per person for a half-day tour, $60 for a full day; children under age 13 ride free. Call him at (619) 765-1309 or write 7572 Great Southern Overland Stage Route, Julian 92036.

Paul Johnson, a former park naturalist, guides groups of wild-flower seekers in their own cars for $30 per hour. Call Borrego Wildflower Tours at (619) 767-5179 or write P.O. Box 1555,

Borrego Springs 92004. Paul also leads photographic workshops in the desert park.

Park rangers will help you find the flowers too, including blooming ocotillo and cactus. Pick up the brochure, which is updated every two weeks with the sites currently in blossom. Also inquire which evening campfire programs feature talks about wildflowers and desert plants. Stop by the Anza-Borrego Desert State Park visitors center at the west end of Palm Canyon Road in Borrego Springs (P.O. Box 428, zip code 92004) or call (619) 767-5311.

You also can make your park wildflower excursion headquarters at the attractive town of Julian. (See ''Escape to Old-Time Julian and Heavenly Palomar Mountain,'' page 168.) It's a few miles southwest of Borrego Springs in San Diego's hilly backcountry. You might want to time your visit to Julian for its annual wildflower show in mid-May, when the flowers are blooming at higher elevations around that area. The local townsfolk collect several hundred varieties each day of the week-long show and display them in the town hall from 9 A.M. to 5 P.M.

The low Colorado Desert extends north into Riverside County, and so does a splendid assortment of wildflowers. In the Palm Springs area you'll see purple sand verbena, yellow-flowered desert gourd vines, wild daisies, buttercups, and many more types. (See Palm Springs Part 1, page 261, and Part 2, page 268.)

Visit Moorten's Botanical Garden at 1701 South Palm Canyon Drive to view 30 varieties of wildflowers that usually are in full bloom. They're part of a collection of nearly 2,000 desert plants that Pat Moorten and her husband began in 1937. She'll give you a free map to show you where to look for wildflowers in the Coachella Valley. Hours are 9 A.M. to 4:30 P.M. daily, except Sundays 10 A.M. to 4 P.M.; adult admission costs $2, children $.75. You also can phone for wildflower information, (619) 327-6555.

Continue on South Palm Canyon Drive to the peaceful canyons in the Agua Caliente Indian Reservation to view more flowering desert plants. Daily hours are 8:30 A.M. to 4:30 P.M., through May. Entry is $3 per adult, $.75 cents for children. Also explore for other bright blossoms in Chino Canyon along the road that leads to the desert station of Palm Springs Aerial Tramway.

Nearby in Palm Desert, head for the Living Desert, 47-900 Portola Avenue, where a sand dune is seeded annually with wildflowers and should be ablaze with color. The 1,200-acre wildlife preserve has many more desert plants and animals on display. It's open 9 A.M. to 4:30 P.M., through mid-June. Admission costs $6; children 3 to 15 years $3. The Living Desert also sponsors an annual all-day wildflower tour by air-conditioned bus in March. Phone (619) 346-5694 for details.

Northeast of Palm Springs is a very popular destination for folks in search of wildflowers, Joshua Tree National Monument. It spans the Riverside–San Bernardino county line, as well as high and low deserts, the Mojave and the Colorado. (See "Desert on Display at Joshua Tree National Monument," page 254.) Rangers at the visitors centers near Twentynine Palms and at the southern Cottonwood entrance will mark park maps directing you to the flowering areas. Buy the informative wild-flower brochure, *Pollen on Your Nose,* to identify what you see. Or join the rangers for escorted wildflower tours by foot during Easter week and April weekends. Phone (619) 367-7511 for meeting times and places. During April and May you also can count on the Joshua trees and other yuccas being in flower, although the abundance of their impressive creamy white blossoms is difficult to predict.

North of Joshua Tree National Monument in the Mojave Desert the staff at the California Desert Information Center will give you a high-desert map and can point out good viewing areas. Located at 831 Barstow Road in Barstow, the center is open weekdays from 9 A.M. to 5 P.M. daily. Phone (619) 256-8313.

Closer to Los Angeles, the Antelope Valley always draws a caravan of wildflower fans. Go north on Interstate 5 and California 14 to Lancaster, then head 15 miles west of town via Avenue I/Lancaster Road to see the floral fantasy at the Antelope Valley Poppy Reserve. Dedicated to preserving the Golden State flower, this 1,760-acre state park also features a hillside interpretive center with desert displays and paintings. During April, the poppy's top flowering time, it's usually open daily from 9 A.M. to 4 P.M. weekends and 10 A.M. to 3 P.M. weekdays. Entry is $5 per car. Phone (805) 942-0662 or (805) 724-1180.

If you decide to stay overnight in the area to spend more time in search of wildflowers, Lancaster has a number of lodgings, including the Best Western Antelope Valley Inn (948-4651), the Desert Inn (942-8401), and the Inn of Lancaster (945-8771)—all in area code 805. Contact the Lancaster Chamber of Commerce, 44943 North 10th Street West (zip code 93534), for a list of accommodations and restaurants. The phone is (805) 948-4518.

Wildflowers abound in Kern County as well, and its Board of Trade will help you find them. Bulletins noting the latest blooming areas are posted at the visitors information center, 2101 Oak Street in Bakersfield. On weekdays you can call (805) 861-2367. (See "History and Outdoor Adventure in Kern County and Isabella Lake," page 184.)

Travelers in the valley, mountain, and coastal areas of Santa Barbara, Ventura, and San Luis Obispo counties also are likely to see wildflowers during April and May. In fact, if you're enjoying a getaway weekend anywhere in Southern California from March through May, ask the local folks where the flowers might be blooming.

Finally, here's a plea from fellow nature lovers: Please leave the wildflowers for everyone to enjoy. If you're tempted to take some of their pretty blossoms home, take color pictures instead.

Index